HAROLD NICOLSON

A BIOGRAPHY

(Volume II, 1930–1968)

HAROLD NICOLSON

A BIOGRAPHY

1930–1968

By

James Lees-Milne

ARCHON BOOKS

1984

First published 1981 by Chatto & Windus.
Reprinted 1984 with permission
in an unabridged edition as an Archon Book,
an imprint of The Shoe String Press, Inc.
Hamden, Connecticut 06514

Printed in the United States of America

The paper in this book meets the guidelines for permanence
and durability of the Committee on Production Guidelines
for Book Longevity of the Council on Library Resources.

Library of Congress Cataloging in Publication Data
(Revised for volume 2)

Lees-Milne, James.
Harold Nicolson : a biography.

Includes bibliographies and indexes.
Contents: v. 1. 1886-1929 — v. 2. 1930-1968.
1. Nicolson, Harold George, Sir, 1886-1968—Biography.
2. Authors, English—20th century—Biography.
3. Diplomats—Great Britain—Biography. I. Title.
PR6027.I4   1984   828'.91209   82-135213
ISBN 0-208-02076-4 (set)

PR6027.I4   1984   828'.91209   82-135213

To his Grandchildren
Adam, Juliet, Rebecca
and Vanessa

CONTENTS

LIST OF ILLUSTRATIONS

ACKNOWLEDGEMENTS

I wish to record my gratitude to the following authors and their publishers from whose books I have quoted extracts in Volume II: the late Sir Cecil Beaton (*The Parting Years*); the late Roy Campbell (*Broken Record* and *Light on a Dark Horse*); Dame Felicitas Corrigan (*Siegfried Sassoon: Poet's Pilgrimage*); Mina Curtiss (*Other People's Letters*); Robert Rhodes James (*Chips: The Diaries of Sir Henry Channon*); Anne Morrow Lindbergh (*The Flower and the Nettle: Diaries and Letters, 1936–1939*); the late Sir Robert Bruce Lockhart (*Diaries and Papers*, ed. K. Young, Vol. I, and *Retreat from Glory*); Nigel Nicolson (*Portrait of a Marriage* and, with Dr. Joanne Trautmann, *The Letters of Virginia Woolf*, Vols. IV and V); Anne Scott-James (*Sissinghurst: The Making of a Garden*); Freya Stark (*The Coast of Incense*); and the late Denton Welch (*Journals*, ed. Jocelyn Brooke).

For permission to quote from letters written by Harold Nicolson to various correspondents from 1930 onwards I wish to thank most cordially Mr. Michael Colefax (to Lady Colefax); the late 2nd Viscount Maugham; Lady Alexandra Metcalfe; Monsieur Roland de Margerie; Miss Elvira Niggeman; Sir John Pope-Hennessy (to James Pope-Hennessy); and Mr. Anthony Powell. Also I am most grateful to Mrs. (Frances) Partridge for letting me use excerpts from letters to her from Clive Bell; to Mr. Derek Drinkwater for letting me read his brilliant thesis on Harold Nicolson's writings on diplomacy, and to Mr. Kenneth Rose for permission to quote from his private notes.

I am greatly indebted to many kind friends and strangers for various services – some for allowing me to talk to them about Harold Nicolson, and others for reading either parts or the whole of my typescript or proofs, making corrections and proffering invaluable advice. Amongst them are: Sir Alfred Beit, Mr. Michael Bloch, The Senior Assistant-Librarian, Dept. of Western MSS, Bodleian Library, Lord Boothby, Lord Clark, Miss Ursula Codrington, Mr. George Dix, Hon. Julian Fane, Mr. Colin Fenton, Sir Roger Fulford, Sir Rupert Hart-Davis, Mr. Eardley Knollys, Mr. Patrick Leigh Fermor, Prince Rupert Loewenstein, Monsieur and Madame Roland de Margerie, Rt. Hon.

Harold Macmillan, Mr. Stuart Preston, Lord Duncan-Sandys, Mr. John Sparrow, Mr. C. G. Tuthill, and my wife.

My gratitude to Mrs (Norah) Smallwood, the chairman of Chatto & Windus, for her encouragement, consistent help and patience knows no bounds. And finally, I must once again offer my profound thanks (which I know he would rather do without) to Mr. Nigel Nicolson for putting at my disposal the mass of papers without which this volume, like its predecessor, could not have been written, and for a hundred other benefactions.

J. L-M.
19 Lansdown Crescent,
Bath

JOURNALISM AND THE NEW PARTY, 1930–1932

THE break with his old settled profession of diplomacy and the launching upon perilous seas of journalism marked the great divide in Harold Nicolson's life. The decision which brought about this change had not been lightly come to. And when it was irreversible the future was still fraught with doubts. Meanwhile the present was for him disturbing. Naturally an ambitious man, he wondered whether the new career would bring him the fame which he craved. As though to assure to himself some central purpose and constant focus he began to keep a regular and full diary.[1] Hitherto he had not jotted down more than certain isolated events and desultory thoughts which struck him as worth noting. He had not recorded his day-to-day activities or systematically analysed his ideas, moods, perplexities and beliefs. Now he was to do so with the most commendable thoroughness until the year 1962 when the whole savour of life dissolved with Vita's death. He wrote in all more than three million words, which his son Nigel reduced with exemplary discretion and skill to one twentieth, publishing the cream of the whole in three volumes between 1966 and 1968.

Harold Nicolson explained on different occasions the motives which impelled him to keep a diary. When asked by his sons why he did it he replied that it was for their amusement in years to come. In a *Spectator* article[2] he postulated that a man should write a diary for his great-grandson; but should avoid the too private sort, which becomes self-centred and morbid. He boasted that not one word would be found in his diary to embarrass anyone, and that all sex gossip was eschewed. These claims were amply borne out. One should have a remote, he said, but not too remote an audience. Yet the diarist should write down candidly what he felt, for 'no diary that reveals a man's character can be dull, even if the character is not attractive in itself.'[3] What Harold Nicolson surely did not foresee was that his journals were to become the most acute commentary of twentieth-century history by one of the most astute commentators on that history in the making. In a sense his published diaries so compound his merits as an observer of and participant in the history of his own times that their very excellence has tended to obscure his importance as a writer of books. Harold Nicolson would not have wanted, nor should his reputation be allowed to rest upon them. There is more, far more to him than these jottings, attractive and invaluable though they be, of day-to-day events from his middle until his old age.

Parallel with the journals ran the continuous series of letters between himself and his wife. His to Vita, far from repeating what he communicated to the journals, which are often guarded, expand them, usually in a lighter and more humorous vein, as well as filling in the details of their shared domestic life. Furthermore his letters to her are enriched by the return of hers to him. If hers are not so cosmic or so humorous as his they are, in revealing her extraordinarily deep and interesting personality, just as intimate. Extracts from some of their letters were included in the three published volumes, but in the following pages I have made use, not only of many unpublished extracts of Harold's diary, but even more use of their mutual correspondence, hitherto mostly unpublished.

Harold Nicolson joined the staff of the *Evening Standard* on the 1st January 1930. His job was to compile, with his friend Robert Bruce Lockhart, some fifteen paragraphs a day of social, political and literary gossip for The Londoner's Diary. In the early months of the year Vita accompanied him to King's Bench Walk during the week. The two of them went down to Long Barn for the weekends.

From the first Harold disliked his new job. Within one month he was depressed. He did not feel he was any good as a journalist. He was not adept at extracting information from strangers and what he got from his friends was seldom fit for publication.[4] The assets he possessed, education and a facility for good writing, were not appreciated. He had no talent for producing sharp, snappy paragraphs. Towards the end of three months he pronounced his job degrading. He had what he called a 'nerve storm', even dreading lest he might get to like journalism, which would be worse than disliking it. 'The moment I cease to be unhappy about it will be the moment when my soul has finally been killed.' Lord Beaverbrook, proprietor of the *Daily Express* group of newspapers, his ear always close to the ground, his antennae quivering with sensitivity about his own concerns, was already aware of his new recruit's depression. By the middle of May Bruce Lockhart, who had got his friend the job, realised how fed up he was. Indeed Harold in a letter to Clive Bell wrote that he did not intend to spend a moment longer than necessary working at it. A month later he had the temerity to tell Beaverbrook that the Diary was becoming dull. Beaverbrook flatly denied it. By October Harold's depression was deeper still. 'I simply loathe writing for a newspaper, and have got an anti-vulgarisation complex.'[5] He felt he could not stand it for another two years, after which his contract was to expire. It gave him too little time for his own writing and was gradually sapping his reputation. 'I have got fame this year and lost renown. Damn!' Besides he was being overworked. He was miserable, and each morning brought him a fresh humiliation.

Harold's misgivings about his reputation as a journalist hack were grossly exaggerated. The Londoner's Diary was by no means his exclusive occupation. His fame, such as it was, came from other exploits. In the first place he wrote numerous additional articles in the *Express* and *Standard* on a wide variety of subjects. In April he succeeded St. John Ervine on the *Express* as reviewer of Books This Week in which some half a dozen at a time were touched upon. After paying handsome tribute to his predecessor Harold in his typically candid and engaging manner discussed in his first review how he ought to tackle the problem. He had consulted several authorities. They all gave different advice. Finally, a sleepy and irritable lawyer in a railway carriage told him to write about books as they struck him; and never to mention a book which bored him. He decided to take this man's advice. And in turn advised his readers not to be snobbish about books. They should read for pleasure long before they could hope to read for profit. It was better to read trash with enjoyment than masterpieces with an inward groaning of the soul.

Harold also found time to deliver a series of wireless talks from February 1930 to April 1931 under the title *People and Things,* extracts of which he was to publish in book form, at the request of his listeners.[6] His contract with the B.B.C. had been settled while he was still in Berlin. The talks were mostly about topical events. Some were trivia, like the lack of sagacity of dogs, and elephants being frightened by the red lion mascot of London University. Some were arch, and sentimental. Some were extremely funny, like the man who sat on his bowler hat; and others were historically interesting, like *The Treaty of Versailles* and *Reminiscences of Lord Balfour*. Typical too of Harold's candour was the last talk of the series, which explained why he was bringing it to a halt. The regular broadcaster, he maintained, ended by becoming insincere. One should leave before closing time, before weariness overcame the listener. A final reason was that he had allied himself with Sir Oswald Mosley's New Party and could no longer be an impartial commentator on events.

Harold feared too that he was becoming renowned as a radio comedian and would never be able to live down this impression. The truth was that he had suddenly leapt into the forefront of popularity with the middle-brow British listeners. He had developed a seemingly casual technique which enchanted them. An intimate, cosy, hesitant, but authoritative manner came quite naturally to him. St. John Ervine was among the first to appreciate it. 'I like the sleepy insolence of his style,' he wrote,[7] 'the slight thickness of his utterance, the reluctant way in which he begins his talk with "Er, good evening."' This er-ing, a vice in anyone else, became an inexplicable virtue in him. He would begin his talk with a high-pitched phrase, a sort of querulous tuning-fork note, almost effeminate, which vibrated and vanished when the voice descended to a lower sustained key. Thereafter the words would follow rapidly, if jerkily, for he would end a long sentence while he inhaled. His diction was remarkably clear. One critic referred to the 'pile' of his voice with unexpected sharp edges as of a diamond, cutting through. Only towards the end of his life did it become slurred and careless. Max Beerbohm once complained to Christopher Sykes that whereas he, when broadcasting, sometimes paused before a word in order to make emphasis, Harold paused as if he were searching for a word, which of course he was not doing, 'and is not playing the game, dear boy'. Ervine too liked the abrupt way in which he wound up his talks. The sentences began to dwindle and droop, to fade out as it were, and then in a little hailing shout came the 'Good Night!', lifting its tail and giving an intimate tone to the whole talk. It left the listener feeling he had just met Harold in the street and heard Harold talk to him alone, without however letting him get a word in edgeways. Already in March 1930 it was being said that Harold was becoming the most popular regular broadcaster from Savoy Hill. And on the 6th June he made history. The use of wireless telephony at sea was first demonstrated by an impromptu conversation between Harold and a passenger on the *Homeric* in mid-Atlantic.

These triumphs, which Harold dismissed as ephemeral and censured as meretricious, coincided in April with the publication and success of *Lord Carnock*. The book caused an instantaneous sensation. On publication day startled headlines appeared across the front page of the *Daily News* and the *Daily Herald* concerning the author's revelations about the declaration of war in 1914, and the imputation that France and Britain had seriously considered the violation of Belgian territory by landing troops there in 1913. Instantly the assumption by the left-wing press that the two nations had entertained the same aggressive intentions which Germany herself carried out a year later was strongly rebutted by the right-wing press. As for the Beaverbrook press, it made no mention of the book at all. It appeared that Arnold Bennett, asked by the *Daily Express* to review it, had declined on the ground that it was not his sort of book. In consequence Beaverbrook derived the impression that the book was not up to much and gave orders that it was not to be boosted in any way. When he woke up on the 3rd April to see it splashed across all the other newspapers he was furious, and cursed Percy Cudlipp, the editor of the *Express* over the telephone. Panic ensued in Shoe Lane, whereas Harold's curls remained unruffled. He was agreeably tickled.

The reviews in the leading papers were universally favourable. The *Times Literary Supplement* saw in it a departure from Harold's previous biographies, which had been composed in what it called the new intimate fashion introduced by Lytton Strachey. In *Lord Carnock* the author had steered a midway course between the new and the old narrative method. It was more than a biography. It was a history of the period leading up to the war. This was of course what Harold meant, but feared it had failed to be, for although he had put the whole of himself into the book he believed it to lack substance, because it lacked pomposity. Only the *Morning Post* was slightly repelled by the pro-German tinge which, it explained, was caused by the author's residence in Berlin while writing it. The German papers however seized upon the book as welcome proof that Germany was not the only country respon-sible for the war. In an otherwise laudatory review in the *New Statesman* Philip Guedalla criticised the son for brushing over his father's relations with his family. He hinted that some of Harold's descriptive scenes were imaginary unless they derived from Sir Arthur's diaries, as yet unpublished. He too blamed him for omitting Germany's war guilt in 1864, 1866 and 1870.[8]

A few months later Vita's *The Edwardians* was published by the Hogarth Press. Within four weeks 20,000 copies were sold. The story of a young heir to an ancient house (Knole) stifled by traditions and possessions, revolting against the false values of his mother (Lady Sackville's) world and conventions, had an immense appeal. The book rendered Vita a popular author and brought her renown and much needed money. As Harold wrote to her, 'We are both referred to now and quoted without explanatory comments as to who we are.'[9] Vita with renewed zest launched upon her next novel, which was to prove her best, and hardly less popular than *The Edwardians*, namely *All Passion Spent*; while Harold, during five days of a holiday in Portofino, wrote his only play *The Archduke*, a comedy about diplomatic life, which was never produced or published.

Harold's long absence in Persia and Germany had suspended his contact with the great. Now his prominence brought him into touch with a host of new as well as old acquaintances. There was Vernon Bartlett, 'a nice, shy man', whom he was to recognise years later as one of the most influential foreign correspondents there had ever been. Compared with him the average backbench M.P. was no more effective than a whimper in the wilderness. There was the young Evelyn Waugh, 'bright-eyed, pink-eyed, reddish haired, stocky jawed, coarse lipped', whom he grew to like in spite of his abominably quarrelsome nature. There was the equally young Stephen Spender, with wild blue eyes and a sense of sin. Harold was impressed by his immense seriousness about work and writing and his determination to be a great poet. He met again Bernard Shaw, amazingly young-looking. His shoulder blades at the back stick through his dinner jacket like those of a boy who has not finished growing . . . His eyes as simple and unmalicious as those of an animal. And yet behind their simplicity is a touch of reserve. He talks with a faintly effeminate voice and a soft brogue.'[10] He sat next to George Moore at one of Lady Colefax's dinner parties. George Moore told him that:

> One day Heinemann came bursting into my room at Ebury Street. 'My dear Moore,' he said, 'I have a terrible thing to tell you – Gosse has died suddenly.' I was very much distressed by this news. I did not realise till then how much I cared for him. I lay upon the *canapé*, turned my head to the wall and said, 'Dear Edmund! Dear Edmund!' I had never called Gosse by his Christian name before. I had always written, 'My dear Gosse'. Heinemann who was standing there in some embarrassment heard me. 'I didn't say Gosse,' he said, 'I said Ross.' Now I was fond of Robbie Ross but I could not go through the same emotion twice over. One never can. And that shows why Shakespeare was mistaken in making Juliet grieve for the death of her brother.

He met again Rowland Prothero, Lord Ernle, who told him how he once shot the Prince Consort in the bottom. Lord Ernle's father was Rector of Whippingham in the Isle of Wight. The Prince was interested in his church restorations, and came over to see how they were getting on. The Prince, the Rector and a local builder all climbed up the church tower. Lord Ernle had a grievance against the builder, and seeing him up the tower, took a shot at him with his catapult. He missed the builder but got the Prince Consort. The Prince was so angry that he prescribed to the Rector what punishment little Rowland should get. Lord Ernle also told how Lord Curzon snubbed him. They were great friends. One day the Marquis telephoned to say he was feeling dispirited and asked if Ernle would take him to a cricket match. They went to Lord's and sat in the pavilion, behaving like boys. At the end Curzon said to him, 'You can't think what good it does me to spend an afternoon with an ass like you.'[12]

Harold resumed his friendship with Ramsay MacDonald. Twice in 1930 the Nicolsons were invited to stay at Chequers. The second visit coincided with the announcement of the crash at Beauvais of the airship R.101. The Prime Minister was so upset that in introducing Canadian Prime Minister Bennett to Vita, he could not remember his name. 'My brain is going. My brain is going,' he kept repeating. Harold was impressed by the underlying simplicity of the man, his love of the country and his Turner paintings. Two subsequent meetings with Ramsay convinced Harold that the responsibility of office was proving too much for him. He was touched by the Prime Minister's evident fondness for him, while alarmed by his deteriorating condition owing to the pressure of forces against the Labour Party, rising unemployment and the worsening economic situation.

Indeed a group of brilliant younger M.P.s of all the parties were meeting from time to time in grave concern about the decay of democracy. At one such meeting at Oliver Stanley's[13] house they even discussed whether it would not be well to bring about a sort of Fascist coup. Perhaps the most brilliant and certainly the most active of the young dissidents was Sir Oswald Mosley, Chancellor of the Duchy of Lancaster in Ramsay MacDonald's Labour Government. Throughout 1930 Mosley grew more and more dissatisfied with the apathy which was bringing the country to economic disaster, and more and more contemptuous of what he called the old gang of politicians. The remedies he put before the Government for relieving unemployment were summarily turned down as impractical. In May, having meditated the step for several weeks, he resigned from the Government. He spoke against the Government at a special meeting of the Labour Party, whereupon he was expelled from the Party by the National Executive Committee for gross disloyalty. Loud publicity accompanied the event. Throughout the summer and autumn of 1930 Harold gravitated towards him, occasionally staying at his and his wife Lady Cynthia's country house, Savehay, near Denham, and greatly attracted by what he considered his bold and original schemes for putting the British economy to rights. On the 5th November he even confided in Beaverbrook his approval of Mosley's policies. The following day Harold lunched with Oswald and Cynthia Mosley. His host told him that he

7

was anxious to lead a new party of young Nationalists, and only lack of funds withheld him. He was seriously thinking of hitching his star to Beaverbrook's waggon. Harold warned him against so committing himself, for Beaverbrook was volatile and might easily turn against him.

> Tom [for that is what his friends called Sir Oswald], I think, agreed. I said I would be with him all the time. He begs me to do nothing till December. I shall hold my tongue, and hold my cards. I want to be in real things again, and not to feel that my batteries are wasted playing the spillikins of the Press.[14]

By the end of November Mosley told Harold that he was shortly launching a National Party, and was hoping to get Morris of Oxford, the motor manufacturer, to finance it; Maynard Keynes, Oliver Stanley and Harold Macmillan to join it; and Beaverbrook to promulgate it. This information decided Harold to decline an invitation extended to him to stand as Liberal candidate for Falmouth. On the 12th December he gave a broadcast on parliamentary government in which he hinted that in the national crisis with which the country was about to be faced, a junta of experts might be necessary to deal with it at the temporary expense of democracy; and that in any case a spirit of national sacrifice and determination must be called upon. On the 17th he stated categorically in an article in the *Listener*, entitled *The Mosley Memorandum*, that, while criticisms could be levelled against it, they were far outweighed by its merits. Before the year was out Harold was on the verge of committing himself to his friend's new doctrines.

What in brief did these doctrines amount to? They were in effect not original but virtually filched from the Liberal Party's 1929 Manifesto, *We Can Conquer Unemployment,* drawn up under the inspiration of Keynes, who was then a Liberal. For Keynes's conviction was that massive unemployment should and could be cured if there was will to cure it. And this will could only be implemented by a planned economy, the stimulation of effective demand by low interest rates and massive public investment in the promotion of public works, at least pending world recovery. But after the disastrous performance of the Liberals in the May General Election of 1929 Keynes and other bright young progressives deserted the Liberal Party, which never recovered. For a time Keynes belonged to no party. As we have seen, he was courted by Sir Oswald Mosley who adopted his economic theories with a vehemence from which their author eventually felt bound to dissent. For Sir Oswald advocated in addition some near-Fascist proposals, such as a Cabinet of five ministers without portfolio subject to the vaguest parliamentary control, a stringent Protection programme for industry, and proclaimed that for a new party to achieve power its ideology must be based on emotion.[15] This last was an extremely dangerous proposal which was to lead to uncontrolled hysteria and violence on the part of his youthful followers. It brought his movement the enduring fear and hostility of the majority of decent-minded British people.

A change in the Nicolsons' domestic circumstances of momentous importance to the family took place in 1930. In March intelligence reached them that a firm of poultry farmers were about to buy the land next door to Long Barn. Chicken huts would be in view from the terrace. The Nicolsons were appalled. They debated whether to bid for the land themselves, or clear out. The £23,000 required would, they decided, buy them some other place they liked as much. Besides, the environment of Long Barn was bound to deteriorate with the increase of commuters. Also, in spite of their great affection for Long Barn, the garden there had been completed and they were eager to create a new one. Vita, having finished *The Edwardians*, started house-hunting further south in the Weald on the Sussex border. On the 4th April she telephoned excitedly to Harold in London that she had come upon Sissinghurst Castle, a property one mile east of the village of that name, in wooded orchard country between Cranbrook and Biddenden. Her diary recorded succinctly, 'Fell flat in love with it.' It is easy to understand why. The place strongly appealed to her romantic nature. It was the remains of a castle which in Henry VIII's reign had belonged to the Baker family from whom she was descended. It was a ruin. It had distinct possibilities. As she was to write years later,[16] the place caught instantly at her heart and imagination. 'It was Sleeping Beauty's Castle; but a castle running away into sordidness and squalor; a garden crying out for rescue.' The following day Harold joined Vita and the two boys, and the four of them went down to Sissinghurst, guided down a narrow lane by a pair of conical Elizabethan turrets peering above the treetops. They walked all round it in the mud. Harold recorded: 'I am cold and calm but like it.' The next day Harold and Vita paid it another visit. Harold came upon a nut walk. That clinched the matter as far as he was concerned. All his practical reservations dissolved.

Sissinghurst was the cause of prolonged discussion. Philip Snowden's budget, which Harold listened to from the press gallery of the House of Commons, did not encourage a middle-aged couple living chiefly on their earnings to embark upon such an undertaking. It would be a gamble; but they were adventuresome, if not reckless. Much money would have to be spent, and the capital, such as it was, was all Vita's. Hence the decision whether or not to buy was basically hers, not his. And Harold knew that Vita wanted the place. He wrote to her: 'Through its veins pulses the blood of the Sackville dynasty . . . It is for you an ancestral mansion; that makes up for company's h. and c.' Exactly one month after their first hearing about Sissinghurst Harold listened to Vita speaking to the estate agent on the telephone. She put down the receiver and said, 'It is ours.' They embraced warmly.

They instantly embarked upon plans and improvements. Harold was determined to create a lake. Within weeks they had cleared away an appalling collection of rubbish from the castle remains, making first the Tower habitable for Vita, then the South Cottage for Harold, and lastly the Priest's Cottage for the boys. And they began planting the garden to designs made by Harold.

> Fortunately I had acquired through marriage [Vita wrote] the ideal collaborator. Harold Nicolson should have been a garden-architect in another life. He has a natural taste for symmetry, and an ingenuity for forcing focal points or long distance views where everything seemed against him, a capacity I totally lacked.[17]

It was true. In their collaboration over the layout of what is now recognised to be one of the most beautiful English gardens of the twentieth century, Harold was the designer and Vita the plantsman. The detailed story of their joint creation of the Sissinghurst garden has been told by Anne Scott-James.[18] Harold's satisfaction with what they both set out to do was expressed in a letter he wrote to Vita in 1937:

> We have got what I wanted to get – a perfect proportion between the classic and the romantic, between the element of expectation and the element of surprise. Thus the main axes are terminated in a way to satisfy expectation yet they are in themselves so tricky that they also cause surprise. But the point of the garden will not be apparent until the hedges have grown up, especially the holly hedge in the flower garden.[19]

Today the hedges are so well grown that the visitor's best means of appreciating the wonderful complexity and ingenuity of the design is by climbing to the top of the Tower and looking down upon this amazing creation, enisled within an ocean of hop gardens and woodlands stretching to the distant horizon of the Kentish Weald. Of all English gardens of this century Sissinghurst best exemplifies the fusion – the profusion one might say – of the formal with the natural.

While continuing to live at Long Barn the Nicolsons spent most weekends at Sissinghurst, scheming, plotting and digging with their own hands till nightfall, happy as larks. Not until mid-October were they able to sleep their first night in the top room of the Tower on two camp beds, reading by candlelight. Sheets of cardboard kept the rain and birds from sweeping through the windows. But as the winter advanced they would stay odd nights at the Bull Inn in Sissinghurst village.

Improvements to the house took years to complete, if indeed they ever were completed before their son inherited. Harold and Vita were content to work each in a separate establishment, and walk from one to the other and the communal dining-room whatever the season and weather. Their two bedrooms were both in the South Cottage. The habits of both were simple. Vita's were actually spartan. Her own bedroom walls were of bare brick, albeit of red and purple stretchers, but rough and bleak. Once on returning home she found builders plastering over the brick. She promptly ordered them to strip the plaster off. The Tower in which she wrote by day was perishingly cold in the winter. It was heated by a small inadequate radiator on which she would sometimes straddle her breeches-clad legs for the modicum of warmth it afforded. Only in July 1935 was the big room constructed. Even then it was used on rare occasions, serving as an additional store room for books and a display of Vita's surplus furniture.

Sissinghurst was for the Nicolsons a garden of Eden in embryo, and all the more beloved because it had yet to be perfected. But outside Eden there were vexations of a domestic as well as a cosmic kind. At half past one of a September morning Harold was woken by someone calling from outside No. 4 King's Bench Walk. It was Vita. Tearful and trembling she climbed the stairs. She had been dining with her mother, Lady Sackville, who now had a house in Streatham . They had had a row. Lady Sackville wished Vita to sign a deed renouncing all claims by her and the boys to her parents' marriage settlement money. This Vita was clearly unable to do, had she wished to; and so she told her mother. Lady Sackville began to rant and yell, 'I want my money, I want my money,' and then to abuse Harold. She told Vita that he had been dismissed from the Diplomatic Service and had not left of his own free will. Vita got up and walked out of the house to her car. The scene did not lead to more positive harm than worsening relations between mother and daughter, which had been bad enough before. A more serious trouble was the discovery that Lady Sackville had been giving certain tapestries and works of art to Sir Edwin Lutyens in payment for architectural services. When it was explained to Macned (as he was affectionately called by the family) that these objects were not B.M.'s absolute property to dispose of, being part of Vita's rightful settlement, he naturally understood, and gave Vita a signed paper stating that they were her property. Whereupon B.M. issued a writ against Sir Edwin claiming that he had stolen her possessions. After B.M.'s death Vita gave them to Macned.

When however Lady Sackville took it into her head to criticise Vita's friendship with Virginia Woolf and spread malicious gossip, Harold could contain himself no longer. He wrote her a sharp letter. There were no reasons whatsoever, he told her, why she should dislike Virginia, whom she had never met. He was not the very least jealous of Virginia, so what right had she to be? After all he was not jealous of B.M. who shared with Vita certain sectors of her love and memory which could never be his. Virginia's literary influence upon Vita was wholly admirable.

> My poor B.M. [he went on] – how I wish some fairy would descend from heaven and give you eyes to see things in more reasonable proportions. Has it ever occurred to you that you are one of the most difficult people on earth? Take Vita and myself. We never quarrel, either with ourselves, or with other people. Yet you have quarrelled at some time or another with every single human being with whom you have been brought into contact . . . Vita and I have done everything humanly possible to remove all cause of friction between you and us. Yet, having done so, you rush about trying to find causes of friction where none ought to exist . . . You go routing about for grievances. B.M. do please laugh at this.[20]

How B.M. received her son-in-law's reprimand is not recorded. But such was her quixotry and her readiness to see the humour of disagreeable situations, even when brought about by herself, that very probably she did laugh.

Far worse mischiefs from Lady Sackville were in store for Harold and Vita before the old lady's unhappy life came to an end.

If his mother-in-law was a thorn in Harold's flesh his elder son,

Benedict, was a cause of sadness and an object of compassion because he was so miserable at Eton. His letters to his parents wrung their hearts and provoked Harold to send him sweetly understanding replies. He did his utmost to reassure Ben, pointing out to him that he was an introvert, who would come into his own when all the extraverts among his contemporaries were as nought, and forgotten. He told him he would inspire love rather than good fellowship, and would have a small circle of very devoted friends. He made him promise to let him know if he got into any sex-scrapes at school. He would never be shocked, and would, on the contrary be amused and sympathetic. He also urged him to break down his shyness with his mother. When Ben complained that his form master, by name Whitfield, had a down on him, Harold wrote him a comical letter.

We all have our Whitfields . . . in life. Mine is called the *Evening Standard*. But now that I am old and grey I realise that one learns almost (though not quite) as much from the Whitfields as one does from the . . . John Sparrows. I feel that you thrive better in the greenhouse of encouragement and understanding, and that your leaves shiver in the winds of disapproval and injustice. So do mine.

And he went on to suggest that Whitfield's criticism of his Latin translations might possibly be justifiable. It was a mistake, for instance,

to say . . . 'damned heritage' for 'damnosa hereditas': to translate 'sunt lacrimae rerum' by 'there are tears of things': to translate 'debellare superbos' as 'fight out the superb': to translate 'sunt gemini somni portus' as 'the ports of sleep are geminal': and to translate 'vivos ducent te marmore vultus' as 'they will lead vivid vultures from the marble'.

And he exhorted his son to bear in mind that perhaps Mr. Whitfield was just as unhappy about Ben's not understanding him as he was about Mr. Whitfield's not understanding Ben. When Mr. Whitfield got back to his sad little room (with the picture of St. John's College Hockey Team of 1909) he probably wrote to his old aunt at St. Ives:

'My dear Auntie. I am not very happy at Eton. I try to make the boys understand, but I am shy of them, and that makes me impatient. There is a boy in my division called Nicholson – the son of the famous Horace Nicholson who wrote that book on Wordsworth – and his mother is Miss Violet Sackville West the poet. Surely a boy like that should see that I am not being merely tiresome when I tell him not to translate *Auctoritas* by *Authority*. I suppose I have a bad manner with boys . . . Sometimes I feel I am a dreadful failure. Thank you, my dearest Auntie, for the pen-wiper. I hope Uncle Gerald's cough is better,

> Your affectionate nephew,
> Alfred Whitfield.'

You see, my Benziedict, even the Whitfields of life (and there are many of them) have their human side . . . I KNOW that you will find yourself in the end. Only you have simply got to get up against the nettles of life and crush them.[21]

To which Vita appended the postscript, 'Darling Benzie, I do think you have got the very nicest and most intelligent and understanding father that ever was, don't you?'

In spite of the excitement of renovating the dilapidated ruins and creating out of nothing a garden at Sissinghurst, the year 1931 did not open cheerfully for Harold. True, his recent book *Lord Carnock* had proved a great success, but his play about the Archduke had been turned down. True, he was still only forty-four, but, owing as he supposed to his getting fat and middle-aged, the sexual adventures which all his life he had been in the habit of expecting and getting seemed to be diminishing.[22] Also he now felt his job on the *Evening Standard* to be equivocal. To his embarrassment Beaverbrook was playing him and Bruce Lockhart against each other, causing slight resentment in the latter. Harold with the kindest intentions had told Lord Beaverbrook that he was overworking Lockhart. The mischievous Beaver professed to be conscious-stricken, promoted Harold to sub-edit Lockhart's paragraphs and give them a Nicolson twist,[23] while telling everyone on the staff that Lockhart was ruining his health through sexual excesses. Lockhart not unnaturally felt humiliated. After all he was fully aware that Harold not only had little experience of journalism, which he positively disliked, but was not even giving satisfaction to the paper. Indeed the Editor confided in him that Harold's tastes were not those of the average Londoner's Diary reader. And when Harold reproduced a nude drawing of Gaudier-Brzeska by the model Nina Hamnett, whom Gaudier had been painting, the Presbyterian prude in Beaverbrook professed to be profoundly shocked. For the caption made the sculptor, who was depicted throwing off his clothes, say, 'Now you paint me.' Beaverbrook pronounced the drawing 'crude, rude and rather suggestive of a man on the cabinet or presenting his backside as an invitation.'

Harold was veering closer and closer to Mosley. Before the month of January 1931 was out Bruce Lockhart noted that he had abandoned all thoughts of becoming a Liberal and would soon present himself as a Mosley candidate, being convinced that Mosley would be Prime Minister one day. And when Cynthia Mosley lunching with Harold on the 4th February told him in some agitation, for she was a committed Socialist, that Tom was about to found a new party, he promised to join it. Tom was in fact already organising what for the first time he called his New Party, and wanted Harold to serve on its publicity committee. Harold felt bound to tell Beaverbrook who, while not approving, gave him his blessing provided he did not air his New Party views in the *Evening Standard*. Nevertheless on the 17th the *Daily Herald* announced that Harold had joined the New Party. The *Daily Worker* likewise followed the matter up, declaring the New Party to be Fascist and Harold an adherent of Fascism.

It is often argued that at this time Harold's sympathies were positively Fascist. But this is far from the case. He was from the first opposed to the Fascist and Nazi causes. In vindication of his disgust with Hitler's methods – and Hitler was still two years from power – he wrote an article in the *Evening Standard* on the 28th January about the Treaty of Locarno, by which, he insisted, this country was bound. It was essential that England made up her mind what in principle her attitude to Nazi objectives should be. There was only one mischievous thing in foreign policy, and that was to leave other countries and your own public under a misapprehension as to where you really stood. Harold was no more Fascist-inclined because he threw in his lot with Mosley in March 1931 than those young Conservative M.P.s like Oliver Stanley, David Margesson and Harold Macmillan who, believing the old party machinery to be worn out, were flirting with Sir Oswald but did not eventually join him. Macmillan told Harold two months later that his heart was entirely with the New Party whose cause he believed he could serve better by remaining within the Tory ranks.

And what, generally speaking, was Sir Oswald Mosley's policy in those early days after his break with the Labour Party? It was to combat Britain's lamentable financial plight and the terrible hardships of un-employment by a root-and-branch reform of the economy which would involve lavish spending of public money on things like road building, the clearance of slums, provision of decent houses and the improvement of social conditions. There is no question that Mosley was utterly sincere at this time in his desire to do good to the working-classes and the poor. But in setting his face resolutely against all forms of seditious dissension he was determined that implicit obedience to and support of the Police must be paramount among his supporters. As yet there was nothing ostensibly Fascist in the New Party policy.

Charles (later Air Marshal) Viscount Portal and Colonel John Moore-Brabazon (later Lord Brabazon), as representing the services, were likewise sympathetic to the New Party. Mosley even claimed that the Prince of Wales was a supporter.[24] J. M. Keynes told Harold that he would vote for the New Party because it stood to mobilise the country's productive power, and J. L. Garvin that he approved of its policy. Both men however soon opposed Sir Oswald's methods. Even Leonard Woolf, while bitterly regretting Mosley's defection from Labour, at first thought the New Party policy the best put forward. On the other hand Harold's old friend, Raymond Mortimer, strongly disapproved of his association with the New Party from the beginning.

Ramsay MacDonald's Labour administration dragged on until August. Before its demise Harold was asked to contest a by-election at Chiswick as New Party candidate, and felt he could not very well decline. In April he wrote asking Beaverbrook for his consent. Beaverbrook granted it while telling him he was mad and would make no appeal either to the working class or the aristocracy. But luckily for Harold he was spared this ordeal because the Conservative Member decided to retain the seat. Harold's action however earned, somewhat surprisingly, the commendation of Virginia Woolf, who wrote to Vita:

> I admire the way he takes his fences – that's what I should have done had I been Harold – been rash, foolish, perverse, incalculable – like a large bouncing cod in a pail of water. I think he'll get in: but a Member's wife isn't nearly so much of a wedding cake as an Ambassador's, I imagine. Now if I'd married Hilton Young . . .[25]

Instead, Harold felt obliged to help Mosley and his followers, like the Party's Secretary, Allan Young, who was contesting the Ashton-under-Lyne by-election. Harold was impressed, yet slightly disturbed by Mosley's emotional orations.

> He is certainly an impassioned revivalist speaker, striding up and down the rather frail platform with great panther steps and gesticulating with a pointing, and occasionally a stabbing, index . . .[26]

The seat was won by the Conservatives, the New Party candidate coming bottom of the poll.

Already by May there were signs that if Harold was not having slightly cold feet about the New Party venture, he was critical of its programme. He urged Mosley to concentrate at meetings upon an intellectual appeal to a new attitude of mind rather than upon economic problems which few of his audiences could understand. He also watched with misgiving the behaviour of the more hot-headed members of the Party, who were urging upon their leader dramatic actions. Harold interpreted this as a Fascist tendency, and warned Mosley not to listen to such imprudent counsels. In his remonstrances he was encouraged by Vita who all along maintained a sort of instinctive reservation, a mistrust of Mosley's motives. As it was she disliked him as a man, declaring that he gave her the creeps. In June Harold's misgivings about the direction in which the New Party was moving were still more pronounced. Allan Young was anxious for Harold to join the New Party Council and attend meetings regularly. Young was very uneasy lest the Party should swing too far to the right and become identified with Hitlerism. He was deeply opposed to Mosley's projected Youth Movement, and saw in Harold an ally to help him counter it.

Harold's partnership with Tom Mosley was from the first ambivalent. As characters the two men were miles apart. The one was gentle, hesitant and open to all reasonable opinion. The other was ruthless, determined and fanatical in the pursuit of a single objective. Although Harold professed friendship for Mosley he was never attached to him with bonds of deep affection. For his part Mosley regarded Harold with tolerant amusement, verging on contempt. He considered him too 'delicate'. In *My Life* he implied that Harold Nicolson was completely at home in academic circles and should never have left them. This was as much as to say he was not equipped for the battlefield. Indeed he went on to say that his field was diplomacy and the writing of belles lettres, 'to which he made charming and various contributions; in fact his erudition went further and entered some really interesting ranges of thought. . . He was one of the most civilised products of the London official and social world.' These words are tinged with sarcasm. And he continued:

> He was quite unsuited to politics, as he appears to have recognised in his later diaries . . . [and to] the rough and tumble of a new movement advancing novel ideas *contra mundum*. He was attracted by the thought, but repelled by the process; he loved the end, but could not bear the means.[27]

It cannot be denied that Harold was fascinated, almost to a masochistic degree, by Sir Oswald Mosley's compelling personality and autocratic manner. He too was ambitious to enter politics and excel. It was all very fine for him to protest to Vita, 'What a bore public life is. Yet I feel driven to it by some force I cannot account for.'[28] On the contrary he knew very well what the force was. It was a desire to be in the swim and to put to good use, at a time of great crisis to his country, the marked intelligence with which he had been endowed. He believed that if the New Party should get into power he might be offered the Foreign Secretaryship. As it was, on the 16th June Mosley invited him to edit his Party's new paper, *Action*. Without stopping to reflect Harold, wildly building castles in the air, accepted with alacrity. To do this he would have to get out of his contract with Beaverbrook which was not to expire till the end of 1932. And would he receive as large a salary from *Action* as from the *Evening Standard*? It was unlikely. Oddly enough, at this very moment Beaverbrook, whether seriously or in tease, made Harold a tentative offer of the editorship of the *Evening Standard*. One night Harold explained his quandary to Vita while they sat by the fire, and sought her advice. Vita, whom the very subjects of politics and journalism bored stiff, fell fast asleep. Matters were brought to a head by Beaverbrook writing Harold a letter begging him to drop the New Party altogether. Harold, feeling himself committed to Mosley, and realising that the *Evening Standard* would never now support him in advancing New Party opinions, asked Beaverbrook either to release him altogether from his contract, or allow him to continue reviewing books only. Beaverbrook wrote again, ignoring Harold's last proposal. Instead he deplored his hitching his wagon to Mosley's star, which was already on the wane. He also agreed that it would be foolish for Harold to remain in Fleet Street.

Lack of a collective policy led to dissent within the New Party and the resignation of two of its key members, John Strachey and Allan Young, who announced to the press that Sir Oswald was developing a Fascist tendency with which they could not associate themselves. Their resignation was followed by that of Professor C. E. M. Joad who considered the Party to be subordinating intelligence to muscular bands of irresponsible young men. The defections worried and alarmed Harold who in these unpropitious circumstances assumed the editorship of *Action*. On the 22nd August he left the *Evening Standard* office for good.

What I have so much disliked about [it] – he confided to his diary – is their lack of any moral or intellectual values. It is very soiling to live

among people so extremely empirical, quotidian, shallow and mean
. . . My fastidiousness has been increased and with it a loathing of the
uneducated.[29]

Indeed he had not always managed to confine these sentiments to his
diary, and sometimes ventilated them among his colleagues. In consequence he had not made himself popular in the *Evening Standard* office,
a fact of which he was fully aware.

Just two days later (on the 24th August) Ramsay MacDonald threw
in his hand. The Labour Government could no longer cope with the
mounting economic crisis without drastic retrenchments, involving
the essential reduction of social services and unemployment benefits.
And this was something which no Labour Government, and that a
minority one, could be expected to do on its own. After prolonged and
agonised discussion in Cabinet and at Buckingham Palace MacDonald,
in the face of violent opposition from the majority of his old colleagues,
courageously agreed to form the first (caretaker) National Government. Baldwin and Samuel, representing the Conservatives and Liberals, consented to serve under him. The immediate political crisis having
been surmounted and steps having been put in hand to grapple with the
economy a General Election was fixed for the 27th October. Had
Harold Nicolson been an unscrupulous man he might have thought
twice about his commitment to the editorship of *Action*. But he regarded himself as already pledged to Sir Oswald Mosley, and he would
not go back on his word. As it was, a Conservative-dominated Coalition was to implement, practically overnight, most of the economic
expedients advocated by the New Party, or rather those which had
been propounded by the Government's newly appointed economic
adviser, J. M. Keynes. The New Party's prospects were thus doomed.
Events had shown that there was no longer a need for it. Harold had
begun his parliamentary career on the wrong foot. Or, to put it more
brutally, he had missed the bus before it had even started.

Harold Nicolson's depression concerning the state of the country,
which owing to unemployment and grave threats to the whole British
economy was in his opinion on the verge of collapse, violence, civil
strife and communism, was not lessened by the forthcoming publication of Roy Campbell's vitriolic poem, *The Georgiad*. At the end of

July Osbert Sitwell warned him that Campbell was about to attack Bloomsbury and incidentally Vita and him in libellous terms, and offered all the assistance that he and his sister Edith could muster. In September Mary Campbell, with whom Vita had been lunching, confirmed that the satire painted the most horrible portraits of the two Nicolsons. Certainly *The Georgiad* did contain some lines very damaging to the Nicolsons' reputation. They were inspired ostensibly by disapproval of the 'Sevenoakians' solemn hypocrisy' and resentment of Vita's affair with Campbell's wife, but actually in jealousy of the Nicolsons' style of living. Having railed against the protracted adolescence of English Bohemianism and, as he explained, 'the dismalness of the English Lesbian, her grey, drowsy outlook, her grim, puritanical dress, and her atmosphere of a psychoanalysis case' Campbell turned to a personal gibe:

> it's hardly nice
> That envy should a happy pair unsplice
> Who lecture (both the wittol and his wife)
> Upon the radio about married life,
> As if their Life were one protracted kiss,
> And they the models of connubial bliss.

Harold and Vita were extremely hurt by the reference to themselves after all they had done to help 'that drunken tramp' and his maltreated wife, and were worried lest their sons might read the poem in years to come and be profoundly shocked. Their friends were incensed, and the gentle Desmond MacCarthy wished to reply to *The Georgiad*, even protesting that there were reserves of cruelty in himself which he had never suspected. However, the attack was wisely ignored by the Nicolsons and their friends, and the matter forgotten until Campbell raised it again by a repetition of the slanders in his autobiographical writings.[30]

While Harold was occupied with *Action*, constant meetings and correspondence with Mosley about New Party strategy, enlistment of candidates ('I think that Peter Howard is just the man to hold the right balance,' Mosley wrote to Harold. He 'must see that Mr. Kid Lewis [the professional boxer] is invariably accompanied on his tours by Mr. Sacheverell Sitwell. In a Siamese connection they might well form the symbol of our Youth Movement!'); while Harold attended a Party meeting in Trafalgar Square in drenching drizzle; and while Mosley was being attacked by Communists with razor-blades in Glasgow

('Tom says that this forces us to be Fascist and that we need no longer hesitate to create our trained and disciplined force. We discuss their uniforms. I suggest grey flannel trousers and shirts.') Vita was on a walking tour in Provence. Then Harold took a night off by going down to Magdalene College Cambridge as the guest of Sir Stephen Gaselee to meet A. E. Housman.

Having changed into his black tie Harold walked with Gaselee, who wore a smoking-jacket and top hat, to a small combination room for dinner. 'Why' he asked, 'a top hat?' 'Oh,' Gaselee replied, 'I always wear a hat when walking across the court from my room.' Then A. E. Housman arrived. He wore a neat little trilby and a tweed greatcoat. He was shy but not as old as Harold expected. He shook hands – a dry, boneless shake – the shake of a person who suffered from an inferiority complex. There was a touch about him of Alfred Gotch[31] and Edmund Gosse.

Old maidish he is, but not as much as I had expected. His whole manner is designed to escape observation. A moustache bulgy enough to be virile but not bulgy enough to bulge. Hair long enough to suggest scholastic but not long enough to suggest aestheticism or worse. Effeminacy indicated by the hands which . . . are boneless, small, flopping downwards, over the arms of chairs. Voice virile with a pernickety undertone. A sense generally, of something slightly brittle and febrile under a carefully conventional and self-protective exterior.[32]

At dinner they were given 1789 Madeira. Then tripe and oysters, then game pie, then mushrooms, all well cooked. Haut Brion accompanied these delicacies. Then some heavy Madeira of 1832.

The candles burnt steadily but slightly, and with a liability to flutter. So did the conversation. Housman made no remark of even passing interest. He talked a little about prosody. He said that Tennyson had misunderstood the galliambics of Catullus which in effect are 3,4, and then 2,4 time. He recited 'Super alta vectus Attis celeri rate maria.' It sounded exactly the same (except for a slight stammer) as when others recite it. Then he went away – again a limp, dry little hand. And I to bed. I enjoyed it. It was worth doing.[33]

While Vita was wandering among the huge quarries of Les Baux, like scenery by a super-Gordon Craig, writing poetry, lying in the sun and making bonfires with dried lavender and cypress-cones, Harold was delivering the first of ten broadcasts in *The New Spirit in Modern Literature* series. He found it an exhausting experience, like being a medium spinning things from ectoplasm. He was attempting to act as interpreter between the modern writers and the public who often find them difficult because they no longer address themselves to any particular audience. Harold's contract was in fact abruptly concluded after his tenth talk by Sir John Reith who, horrified by his recommendation of D. H. Lawrence's novels, forbade him to mention James Joyce's *Ulysses*. Harold found it impossible to reason with this self-centred and self-righteous Presbyterian, and refused to make the attempt.

The General Election was a disaster for the New Party. It was a straight fight by the Coalition against the Socialist Party. The result was overwhelming victory for the Coalition and the formation of the second National Government. Of the twenty-four candidates put up by the New Party none was elected. This was hardly surprising. The Party refused to support the National Government in any particular, and fought on the following principle which made little appeal to the electorate:

> We believe that within a measurable time this country will be exposed to the danger of a proletarian revolution. We believe that such a revolution will mean massacre, starvation and collapse. We believe that the one protection against such a disaster is the Corporate State. We shall not cease to proclaim that doctrine.[34]

Furthermore, the candidates were an extraordinarily ill-chosen and ineffective body of men. Only Sir Oswald and Lady Cynthia had parliamentary experience, and Lady Cynthia was not standing. Apart from Sir Oswald only Harold Nicolson and Christopher Hobhouse, then aged twenty-one and fresh from Oxford University, were even educated. Of the others some were barely literate, and some were frankly disreputable.

Since Harold contested the Combined English Universities seat (coming bottom of the poll) he had time to lend support to his colleagues in the constituencies by speaking. He travelled from platform to platform. At a meeting in Glasgow University on the eve of the poll he caused some confusion by confessing frankly that he did not suppose the New Party would do well in the Election. Nevertheless he begged those students who were on the roll to vote for Sir Oswald just to show the world they believed in him and his ideals.

The day following the Election results Harold Nicolson recorded that 'he felt more glad than ever that I should have courted disaster with the New Party than achieved success under this Tory ramp'.[35] What precisely did he mean by this? Was he being sincere? There can be little doubt that, from the point of view of his political career, his espousal of Mosley's New Party had already done him harm; and he very soon came to realise it. But when he so quixotically joined forces with Mosley, his motives were not simply expedient, dictated by a longing to rid himself of an uncongenial job with the Beaverbrook press and attach himself to a novel cause that might bring him fame. He was all his life an intensely honourable man, incapable of consulting his personal advantages at the expense of his principles. His honesty was transparent, and often naive. For instance, he could never in any circumstances tell a lie, not even a white lie (discounting matters of sex, which were his sole exception; and even there he withheld rather than gave false information to impertinent interlocutors). He often caused offence when asked direct questions by strangers whether, say, he admired their clothes or opinions. If Harold did not admire, he said so bluntly. Over politics he was never dishonest. He was sometimes unwise, and at other times muddle-headed. Conscious as he was of belonging to a privileged caste, he did not approve of privileged castes. He fervently believed that determined efforts should be made to give enhanced opportunities to intelligence and diminish the advantages of the incurious and idle rich. Uneasy with and unsympathetic towards the uneducated classes, he nevertheless wanted them to have the opportunities of becoming as educated as he was himself. In 1931 he was convinced, as was Sir Oswald Mosley, that the old gang of Tory politicians with their 'Safety First' slogans, and the incompetent and disunited Socialists, had brought about the catastrophe in which the nation was floundering. He was convinced that Sir Oswald's New Party, if it eventually came into office, would, by the reform of Parliament, a scientific protection of the home market, a national plan to revive trade, a cementing of links with the Dominions, and a General Powers Bill to set up a Government reduced to five all-powerful, all-wise individuals, be capable of taking immediate action in by-passing parliamentary red tape; he was convinced that these measures would be in the best interests of the country – he was fervently patriotic – by averting the very real threat of communism and benefiting the lot of the British people. After all, intelligent economists like Keynes and Salter had felt the same, until they saw, a little before Harold did, the way Mosley was going.

Until the end of the year 1931 Harold remained editor of *Action*. He watched its sales fall sharply week by week. In fact they fell from 160,000 to 16,000 within ten weeks. He soon became aware that *Action* was doomed, and with it the New Party. In spite of many distinguished contributors of articles – Christopher Isherwood, L. A. G. Strong, Osbert Sitwell, Francis Birrell, Peter Quennell – and reviewers – Gerald Heard and even Vita Sackville-West and himself – it was a pitiable little paper. Raymond Mortimer summed it up in a letter to Edward Sackville-West.

> *Action* seems to me about the limit. It's not only squalid but ineffective. As Aldous [Huxley] says, it seems to be made up of articles rejected by *John o' London*. Altogether the New Party has been grotesque, choosing boxers and such people and deserves its fate . . .
> It is depressing to see a person [HN] one is fond of making an incredible fool of himself.

And again he wrote: 'When I walk in the streets and see posters – *Action*, edited by Harold Nicolson. THE PRIME MINISTER NEEDS KICKING by Oswald Mosley – I desire to vomit.'[36] Nevertheless Raymond's revulsion did not prevent him from contributing an article to *Action* on 'The Reasons why I prefer the Present.'

Harold acknowledged that the paper was a failure. He was depressed, for he was still not reconciled to failure. He knew too that the New Party was a sly little movement. 'I am loyal to Tom since I have an affection for him. But I realise that his ideas are divergent from my own. He has no political judgement. He believes in Fascism. I don't. I loathe it. And I apprehend that the conflict between the intellectual and the physical side of the N.P. may develop into something rather acute.' Undeviating loyalty to friends was one of Harold's strong tenets. But in political life it can be a weakness if put before convictions. Adherence through thick and thin to friends who were irresponsible was to be detrimental to Harold's reputation on more than one future occasion.

At a Party meeting just before Christmas it was decided that *Action* must close down at the end of the year. It was financially bust; and to pay off some of its debts Harold had to borrow from his bank. Without a job his own financial situation was so bleak that it is a wonder the bank allowed him to borrow from them at all.

Still he did not immediately leave the New Party. Instead he begged Sir Oswald not to get muddled up with the Fascist crowd, and advised him to be patient, to wait and meanwhile to travel and write books. As for himself he told Bruce Lockhart that the *Sunday Despatch* had offered him a page on gossip-column lines. He needed the money but felt a little conscience-sore about Beaverbrook, whose contract he had broken. Lockhart told him he need not worry for he was sure Max was far too proud to ask for his return. Beaverbrook for his part told Randolph Churchill that he considered Harold 'cracked'. To his credit Harold turned down the *Sunday Despatch* job flat.

In his diary he summed up the year 1931 with 'Everything has gone wrong. I have lost not only my fortune but much of my reputation.' He had incurred enmities. He had failed with the B.B.C., the *Evening Standard*, *Action*, the Election. He reviled himself and urged upon himself amendment. 'Yet in spite of all this,' he continued, 'what fun life is!' After all he had done nothing to be ashamed of. His conduct had merely been a generous, if ill-judged, example of misguided patriotism.

One good thing had happened to him. He had been elected a member of the London Library committee.

In the last issue of *Action* the editor announced that he and the leader of the New Party were about to visit Germany and Italy in order to study 'new political forces born of crisis, conducted by youth and inspired by completely new ideas of economic and political organisation. This does not mean that we wish to import Italian or German methods and practices into this country.' Not all *Action*'s readers were edified by the announcement. On New Year's Day 1932 Harold Nicolson went by train to Rome where he was to join Tom Mosley and afterwards accompany him to Germany. Harold was met at the Rome railway station by Christopher Hobhouse, one of the defeated New Party candidates, and driven to the Excelsior Hotel where the three men engaged a luxurious suite, with a vast drawing-room, little gilt tables and palms. Christopher, who had just come from Munich, was full of information about Hitler just one year before he came to power and what the Nazis thought of the New Party. He said Hitler contended that 'we British Hitlerites are trying to do things like gentlemen. That will never do. We must be harsh, violent and provocative. I do not care for this aspect of my future functions. I fear it will be very bad for Tom to go to Munich,' Harold wrote to Vita.[37]

Christopher Hobhouse was an extraordinarily bright and erratic young man. He was the orphan son of a mentally unstable Canon of Winchester. His mother died when he was young, and he was brought up, in the holidays from Eton and vacations from Oxford, where he spent his entire patrimony on good living, by a guardian uncle, a parson of the muscular Christian variety. Christopher did not care for this uncle. His unhappy upbringing made him insensitive and disdainful. He was as handsome as he was haughty and held his head high while he delivered rather portentous and outrageous statements in Gibbonian oratory. He was naturally political and attached himself to the New Party soon after going down from Oxford. He had been by far the youngest parliamentary candidate, and his electioneering card bore the slogan, 'Vote for Hobhouse, the Children's Champion.' Whereas few of Christopher's contemporaries took to him at first because of his deplorable rudeness, Harold was interested in his mind and amused by his audacity, which lent him a perverse charm. Hobhouses's views, always emphatic, were often contradictory and usually wrong. As he grew older they became less aggressive. He wrote a brilliant biography of Charles James Fox in passionate sympathy with his hero's reckless character, was called to the Bar, and by 1939 was earning a handsome salary. He was an early victim of the war.

In Rome Sir Oswald had an interview with Mussolini, whom Harold refused to see. The Duce advised him not to try the military stunt in England. Mosley was treated by the Fascists with the utmost deference, being regarded 'as a duce en l'herbe'. The editor of the *Lavoro Fascisto* came to interview him, telling him about the Fascist electoral system, 'which is in fact not electoral at all. We were much impressed.'[38] Their Italian hosts inundated them with Fascist pamphlets with which however Harold was *not* impressed. 'Once a person insists on how you are to think he immediately begins to insist on how you are to behave,' he noted. The three of them were taken to the Pontine Marshes, then in process of reclamation, and lunched at Ninfa, 'amid the waters and the ruins'. Gladwyn Jebb, who was serving at the Embassy, accompanied them.

Having returned to London for a few days Harold set off for Berlin, but without Mosley who was unable to accompany him. Standing on the Friedrichs-Strasse platform, where two years ago he had departed in a blaze of obscure respectability he reflected upon his translation to infamy and degradation. 'I feel rather a scrubby old thing.' He found Christopher Hobhouse already installed in the Prinz Albrecht Hotel. He called on the Ambassador, Sir Horace Rumbold, who told him the Nazis had missed the bus and were losing ground every day, an opinion Harold shared. He sensed that Naziism was a doctrine of despair and that Hitler would fail to satisfy the expectations of the discontented who had rallied to his banner. At the Jockey dive he met Tom Mitford, 'a nice young man', and Peter Rodd, Mitford's future brother-in-law, both of whom were slightly shocked by the warm welcome Harold received from the barman. In the night clubs he noticed that everyone looked hungry, with eyes like wolves, and that Hitler was the sole topic of conversation.

He visited his friend Erich Mendelsohn's villa in the Grünewald, now completed.

Oh my word! It really is very nice indeed. You press a button and the maid appears with a tray; you press another and a taxi emerges from the floor. You pull a string and there you are shaved and manicured. The slight depression of a lever renders one breakfasted, purged, clothed, and ready for bed. But in all truth it is a fine device. And the view in summer must be superb. The whole side of one room glides downwards silently into the floor leaving one out in the garden. It is all as spick and span as a spanner and a spicker. Then we went to see [Stephen] Spender. It was a different atmosphere altogether. A pension room in the Sleist Strasse. A bed with a lace quilt. A cup of tea with a cigarette in it. A bottle of ink and some paper. A hard brass electric light – and in it all Spender, excited and charming, his eyes beaming like a tipsy deer. He leads a life of the greatest asceticism trying to get himself down to the level of his communist protégés. He teaches English at a communist school. I felt that there was something about him. I felt gross in comparison – just Boulestin.[39]

By the end of January Harold was back in England. He allowed Christopher Hobhouse, who had nowhere to live and was without a job, to lodge in King's Bench Walk. They saw much of each other and constantly dined together at their respective clubs the Travellers and the Reform. Hobhouse was one of Harold's few younger friends whom Vita did not much like. And even Harold soon found him a bore because he would contradict for the sake of contradiction. 'He runs about looking for lost causes in order to defend them.'

Harold's situation was scarcely any better than his young companion's. The problem was what should he now do? And how was he to earn badly needed money? In spite of Vita's big sales from *The Edwardians* and *All Passion Spent* the two of them only had £300 in the bank. Their way of life was extremely extravagant. They had three establishments to keep up, and two boys to educate at Eton. Harold's friends urged him to write a second *Some People*. But he sensibly decided he could not recapture the youthful mood when that little masterpiece was composed; and in any case a sequel would be an anticlimax. He was offered the literary editorship of the *New Statesman*, but turned it down because the salary was inadequate and the job would have confined him to London. He also turned down an approach from Sir Robert Vansittart that he might re-join the Foreign Office. It had given him a mischievous satisfaction to pose the unacceptable condition that he be immediately granted ambassadorial rank. For some months he did nothing by way of earning money. Yet he was in a state of inexplicable hubris. He and Vita were busily improving Sissinghurst, preparatory to moving into the place during the summer and letting Long Barn. Then, as though to flout Providence, he began a second novel.

Before embarking on this he had to get clear of the New Party. At a meeting of the Executive Committee on the 5th April 1932 it was decided to dissolve the Party but keep on the youth movement. Harold was violently opposed to the youth movement's retention. Mosley announced that he had refused an invitation from David Margesson to join the Tory party, and an approach from Joseph Kenworthy[40] to become leader of the Labour party. He preferred to stand aside and coordinate all the Fascist groups under his leadership. He said that he had no wish to be tarred with the brush of the old regime,

> that he thinks, as leader of the Fascists, he could accomplish that [sic] as a party back-bencher, and that in fact he is prepared to run the risk of further failure, ridicule and assault, rather than allow the active forces in this country to fall into other hands. I again say that I do not believe this country will ever stand for violence, and that by resorting to violence he will make himself detested by a few and ridiculed by many. He says that may be so but that he is prepared to take the risk. I say that on such paths I cannot follow him . . . The argument, though painful, is perfectly amicable. The ice cracks at no single moment. Nor do I think that Tom was hurt or imagined for one moment that I was deserting him. Yet I hated it all . . .[41]

Next day Harold reiterated these arguments in a friendly letter. In *My Life* Mosley acknowledged that Harold held on longer than others, such as Strachey, Young and Joad, more in loyalty than from conviction. But he complained caustically that Harold simply could not grasp that he, Mosley, had the stark choice of facing violence or closing down. Neither did Harold approve the new men then necessary to the cause any more than they appreciated his literary artistry in writing an article like the one entitled, 'Lift high the Marigold'.

It was high time that Harold reached the conclusion that his and Mosley's paths must separate. There was no place for him in a movement which had turned to provoking violence where violence need never be. Nor is it surprising that he simply could not countenance the sort of thugs whom the British Union of Fascists enlisted. It is hardly surprising that such people could not appreciate the artistry of his prose. Nor was Harold alone in walking out of the New Party at this time. Peter Howard, the tough ex-Captain of the England Rugger XV, prominent Moral Rearmament supporter, and one of the Party's most reputable members, likewise forcibly expressed his abhorrence of the Party's move towards Fascism, and walked out with him.

In order to make his principles perfectly clear Harold wrote the following month in the *Weekend Review* a resounding rebuttal of Fascism, calling it unnecessary in origin, oppressive and untruthful, and constituting a danger to the future of European stability. At the same time he admitted that something could be learned from it, namely, that democracy was not enough; and that duties were more important than rights.

Harold's defection did not sever his friendship with Tom Mosley. In June he wrote him a long considered criticism of his manuscript of *The Greater Britain*; and in July, while dining with him and his wife, gave him a real drubbing. He told him that no constitutional changes in this country could be carried out except at Westminster through the medium of existing institutions.

Harold had written to Vita that when on his way to Berlin in January 1932 his train stopped at Rotterdam. He wanted to go to the Museum. It was shut. So he went for a long walk along the Shiedammdijk, 'and thought of my new novel'. The idea of a second novel, in which events were to revolve round a conscientious, conventional Principal Private Secretary called Peabody, had for years lain fallow in his mind. On the 11th April he confided to his diary that he was about to begin writing. He decided that it should be a dramatic, even a romantic novel, dealing with an international crisis. It turned out to be a satire. Within ten days he had finished the first chapter. He found that the lady assistant-secretary to the Secretary of State, called Jane Campbell, a mixture of Hilda Matheson[42] and Gertrude Bell, was taking over the plot. Soon he was writing 5,000 words a day. In three months he had finished the book. It was published in early October.

For the novel's title he chose *Public Faces* on the basis of Auden's lines, 'Private faces in public places, Are wiser and nicer than public faces in private places.' The story was written to suggest that the atomic bomb would introduce an era of universal peace at a time when most people cherished the notion that peace could only be preserved by pacifism. Harold's contention was that the sole deterrent to an aggressor country from making war was the certainty of losing it; and that the country possessing the exclusive instrument of total destruction was capable of dictating terms to the rest of the world. He had come to see that wars were caused by greed rather than by fear. They would be precipitated by uncertainty. The action of the story was projected into four days of early June 1939. When in 1945 the first atom bomb was exploded *Public Faces* was read again with curiosity. Its revival caused a mild sensation and Harold was pursued by the press anxious to know how he had foreseen so accurately what would happen thirteen years ahead.

No sooner was *Public Faces* sent to the publishers than Harold began work on another book. If *Public Faces* was a sort of *jeu d'esprit*, a tuning in to the new life of freedom from a regular job, *Peacemaking 1919* was a more serious matter. The book was meant to be the second of a trilogy (the first having been *Lord Carnock* and the third to be *Lord Curzon*) recounting the causes of events leading up to the First War, the settlement of the peace terms and, finally, the study of post-war diplomacy.[43] The series was in fact a philosophical survey of international politics, in which the author was bold enough to show how the mistakes of the past might be rectified in the future. *Peacemaking* was written within a single month, between the 8th November and the 8th December, although research had occupied three months of the autumn. The subject was one with which Harold was very familiar, he having played a part in the 1919 Peace Conference from start to finish. It was published in two parts, the first being a narrative of the Conference and discussion of its weaknesses and failures: the second his detailed day-to-day diary kept before and during the Conference. The moral of the sorry tale was that vagueness and imprecision are the causes of failed conferences. In many subsequent articles Harold emphasised this strong conviction. As he wrote to his publisher, Michael Sadleir,

My first idea was to make one book of the whole thing and to illustrate the first part by quotations from my diary. I abandoned that intention. I saw quite clearly, when it came to the point, that my diary was quite valueless as incidental quotation, and valuable only as a cumulative record of atmosphere. I abide by that point of view. I still contend that the diary, shaming as it is, does represent exactly what we all felt and thought and did in Paris.[44]

The book was fortified by the answer to thirty questions which Harold put to Lloyd George, the chief participator in the Peace Conference, at an interview he had with the old statesman at Churt in October 1932.

Harold had re-established himself in his own esteem. He had written two books within six months. He had spent nearly all those six months at Sissinghurst, a record period in his life of uninterrupted country sojourn. He had obliterated from his mind the wretched memories of Fleet Street and the New Party. He had always been able to shake off like a puppy emerging from water, disagreeable incidents of the past, and with his incorrigible optimism and love of life, to look forward to the sweets of the future.

'I feel absurdly happy. The dogs bark in the woods,' he wrote. Sissinghurst had been a joy to both Nicolsons that summer. Together they had been busy paving the courtyard, siting the statuary, planning long axial vistas and marking out hedges; fashioning the *rond-point* in the rose garden; planting acacias, planting buddleia at the end of the moat; planting old-fashioned roses like Souvenir du Docteur Jamain. After dinner Harold was to be seen bent over squared paper, rulers and pencils. A bedroom for him was being added to the South Cottage from his designs. 'God! if only life were ten times longer.'

My first visit to Sissinghurst was on a very hot August evening of that year. I was brought over by friends with whom I was staying nearby, piloted by Christopher Hobhouse. The two Nicolson boys were bathing in the lake. Their clear voices echoed across the water. 'Oh, what a bore, here are visitors!' they complained, while passing unflattering remarks about me and my companions who heard every word. Harold and Vita had finished their writing for the day. In spite of the heat they were both bending over a flower border, he in short sleeves and an old panama hat with a black ribbon, she hatless and wearing a drab cotton skirt. I had first met Harold the previous October during the Election. Having just gone down from Oxford I was canvassing in a very humble capacity for Sir Oswald Mosley at Stoke-on-Trent. Harold had come over to speak at a meeting and stayed the night at the station hotel. I found him brusque, bustling and rapid in movement and speech. He did not address a word to me while we all had supper together at a late hour in the hotel.

Ben was about to take an examination for entry to Balliol. His anxious father was full of advice, as to how he must introduce himself to the porter, how he must not guess the answers to questions, or show off in his papers. Balliol was far more interested, he counselled, in whether a candidate was clever than learned. It loathed the silly-clever type. He hoped Ben was not wretched. If he was he should read *Wuthering Heights*. It was always a good thing to read about others more miserable than oneself.

On the 28th December 1932 Harold and Vita left for a three months lecture tour of America. Hilda Matheson, who, having resigned from her job as Director of Talks at the B.B.C. on account of differences with Sir John Reith's policy of caution, and having assumed the role of part-time secretary and financial adviser to both Nicolsons, saw them off at Waterloo. At Southampton they boarded the Norddeutscher Lloyd boat *Bremen* bound for New York.

'A lovely year for which I thank life heartily,' Harold wrote in his diary. 'I have got rid both of journalism and of politics. All the horrors of 1931 are behind me.'

AMERICA AND IN BETWEEN, 1933–1935

Just before leaving for America Harold had time to contribute to the *Architectural Review* a letter of strong protest against the almost incredibly philistine proposal to demolish Carlton Gardens and Carlton House Terrace, which, he angrily pointed out, constituted one of the sole remaining specimens of intelligent planning and adaptation of site which existed in our bemused London. For the rest of his life he was to be an active defender of the Georgian streets and houses which the authorities of the unprincipled thirties were allowing to be sacrificed wholesale to unscrupulous speculative builders.

The voyage to New York was made memorable by two hurricanes, the worst ever recorded, which lashed the *Bremen* from beam to beam. Battered though they were, neither Harold nor Vita was even seasick. Great excitement greeted their arrival in New York, where they were besieged by reporters, publicity agents, bootleggers – prohibition had not yet been abolished – and invitations from unknown society hostesses. To their relief they were met by their friend of Tehran days, Copley Amory, as they were walking down the gangway. Amory piloted them through ranks of officious photographers on the quay and conducted them to their hotel.

Neither Harold nor Vita had visited America before. As their son Nigel has explained[1] they could not have chosen a worse way of seeing the country for the first time or a worse moment for arrival. America was in the throes of appalling economic depression. The grand hotels and rich apartments were virtually empty. Even the millionaires were retrenching. The important people they met were obsessed with the gravity of the situation. Before they left, the country was almost bankrupt and all the banks closed. Confidence was restored only after Franklin Roosevelt had succeeded President Hoover in March. But the situation did not prevent their hosts and audiences giving them a boisterous reception wherever they went. They were in fact amazed to discover how widely their reputation had preceded them. It transcended anything they had experienced at home. Vita in particular was adulated for her novels, her patrician background, her looks, dignity and, when they saw her in the flesh, her diffidence and shy demeanour.

HAROLD NICOLSON

Harold was renowned for *Some People* and *Public Faces*, and acclaimed as 'one of the cleverest men in England'. From the very day on which they set foot in New York, where they were entertained to dinner to meet Charles Lindbergh, America's greatest living hero ('there is much more in his face than appears in photographs'[2]), until they sailed for home on the 14th April, they were on the move. They went their own ways, Vita lecturing on the modern spirit in literature and the English social life, Harold on diplomacy, the European situation and the future of the world as he foresaw it. They travelled from one end of America to the other, from east to west, and north to south. Vita even lectured in Canada. Most of the time they were separated, to link up again for a brief night or two in some hotel. When apart they were wretched and lonely, and kept up a sad, homesick correspondence, worrying how to get their money out of the country before the crash came, each anxious about the health of the other, and exhausted by the incessant train journeys and, worst of all, the social receptions and the strain of appearing pleased and being polite. Their most successful public occasions were when they met on the same platform and carried on informal discussions about matrimony, how to educate children or just changes in the English domestic scene. For they found that Americans could never hear too much about how the upper classes across the Atlantic lived, and what the entertainment in great country houses amounted to.

From the first Harold was amazed by the American character. He was perplexed by the fundamental differences in American culture from that of Europe. The people lacked background.

> That is what I feel is missing in this country. Nobody seems to have anything behind their front. Poor people, they feel it themselves, and hence all those pitiful gropings after manor-houses in Wiltshire and parish registers . . .[3]

Americans were so slow in conversation, he complained, 'that it is like being held up by a horse dray in a taxi. And they never listen to what one says oneself.'[4] He found their long-winded jokes so naive that he could not raise a smile. What was worse, the adulation to which they were prone was of the slushy sort. Harold was not a gracious recipient of insincere flattery, and he could not disguise his irritation. He was inclined to mock pretensions to culture.

> Rows and rows of aged dames with rimless pince-nez and heaving breasts and complimentary faces. Rows and rows of little autograph

albums tended for signature upon glossy pages of pink and green and blue. Rows and rows of glasses of iced water and celery. The inevitable platform and reading desk . . .[5]

He smiled at their transparent snobbishness and their preconceived assessment of what their visitors ought to be.

Lady West and Mr. Nicolson are not only well reputed representatives of the British nobility, not only authors whose books are on all our tables, but fine man and woman joined in matrimony.[6]

Their odd pronunciation could lead to such awkward misunderstandings. Miss Dennett, or whatever her name was, in Chicago, said,

'Oh, Mr. Nicolson, I took the liberty of asking two girls of the Ellesmere Institoot to come up and be photographed with you.' 'Certainly, Miss Dennett, delighted – but what is the Ellesmere Institute?' 'Oh, they look after tarts.' 'Rescue work, I suppose.' 'Of course not – only tiny tarts.'

It was the 'nice women's' clubs that got him on the raw. The asininity of some of the members moved him to laugh at them mercilessly in letters to his friends. In March he and Vita lectured together to a woman's club in Toledo, Ohio, on marriage. After the lecture a luncheon was held.

There was a high table with daffodils [he wrote to Raymond Mortimer][7] and freesias and several lower tables decorated only with daffodils. Some four hundred neat and chattering women sat down to their pineapple salad. High up in the corner of the room an amplifier bawled out at us, relaying from Washington the ceremonies attendant upon the installation of President Roosevelt. The neat waitresses in dainty print frocks tripped from table to table pouring iced waters into old-world beakers of violet glass. On my right was a fool in purple silk called Mrs. Stinahan. On my left an idiot in biscuit-coloured silk called Mrs. Cranby.
    'And so,' said Mrs. Stinahan, 'you are going right out west, Mr. Nicolson, that will be mighty interesting. You will like California.'
    'I am sure we shall, Mrs. Stinahan, but what we are really looking forward to is the Grand Canyon and Arizona.'
    'You will find the Grand Canyon swell. When first I saw it I said to Mr. Stinahan, "My! how I wish Beethoven could have seen this!" I care so much for music, Mr. Nicolson. I do not understand how

one can view life steadily unless one cares vurry vurry deeply for music.'

At that the man at the microphone raised his voice. He yelled. 'Ladies and gentlemen!' he yelled, 'This is the National Broadcasting Company addressing America from the steps of the Capitol. A supreme moment in our history is approaching. The President and the President Elect are walking down the gangway. The band is about . . .'

The band at Washington then intervened with a spirited rendering of 'Hail to the Chief', and the sound of cheers reached us from the District of Columbia.

'Mr. Stinahan,' whispered my neighbour, 'does not care vurry much for music. American men generally don't. Now in my own case . . .'

At that Chief Justice Hughes administered the oath to Franklin Roosevelt and the latter repeated the formula in firm but majestic tones.

'In my own case,' continued Mrs. Stinahan, 'I just couldn't live without music. I find it to be the language of the stars, if you know what I mean, Mr. Nicolson.'

President Roosevelt by then had embarked upon his inaugural address. During the first few words the women there assembled hushed their chatter, but only for a few seconds. The whisper of Mrs. Stinahan began again over my right shoulder.

'It is a reel pity,' she said, 'that you are only such a short time in Toledo. You should see our Museum. Lord Joseph Duveen says that it is the finest collection outside Noo York. And above all, Mr. Nicolson, you should see our peristyle . . .'

'Small wonder,' came the firm and impassioned voice of Mr. Roosevelt, 'that confidence languished, for it thrives only on honesty, on honour, on the sacredness of obligation, on faithful protection, on unselfish performance: without them it cannot live . . .'

'. . . peristyle,' continued Mrs. Stinahan in her lanoline whisper, 'a thing of simple beauty, Mr. Nicolson. A poem in stone, though it's marble, reely, the finest marble – all white it is reely, only the lights are so arranged that it looks yellow somehow . . .'

'It can be helped,' came the voice of the President, 'by national planning for and supervision of all forms of transport . . .'

'You see, Mr. Nicolson, they have devised hidden lights. By that I mean you cannot see the lights although they cast their glow over the whole peristyle. And the lights change. I mean in the morning you have the glow of sunrise, and at midday, I am told (for I seldom go there at midday), the lights are quite Greek, and then you can get the sunset effect . . .'

'But in the event,' said President Roosevelt, 'that the Congress shall fail to take one of these two courses, I shall not evade the clear course of the duty that will then confront me. I shall ask the Congress for such powers as would be given to me if we were in fact invaded by a foreign foe.'

'. . . and then, at night, it is all blue somehow, all dark, if you see what I mean, Mr. Nicolson – so pure it is, so simple, with all those great columns glimmering – and it's more than a poem in marble – it's a dream come true – I mean that literarily, Mr. Nicolson . . .'

'Mrs. Stinahan,' I said firmly, 'do you realise that your new President has just announced that he will be assuming the dictatorship of this country? Do you realise that you have just heard one of the most startling pronouncements in the whole of American history?'

'Well, isn't that just too interesting. Not that I reely care for the radio myself. Mr. Stinahan insists on having it – so we have put it way out by the bathing pool. You just can't see it because of the ivy. And at night, when we have some boys and girls there in the summer, they turn it on when they have a dip – swim to it if you understand what I mean – it's like Venice, Mr. Nicolson. Have you ever been in Venice, Mr. Nicolson. Have you ever been in Venice? We were there once in the fall of 1928 . . .'

'We aim,' concluded President Roosevelt, 'at the assurance of a rounded and permanent social life. We do not distrust the future of essential democracy. The people of the United States have not failed. In their need they have registered a mandate that they want direct, vigorous action. In the spirit of the gift I take it. In this dedication of a nation we humbly ask the blessing of God . . .'

Mrs. Stinahan at this ceased her whispering and cast submissive eyes upon her plate.

'Now,' she said when the voice had ceased, 'I should like Mrs. Nicolson and you to say a few words to the club. Just stand up and say something pleasant. They expect it, Mr. Nicolson. And don't worry about your train. I have the car here and will see that you arrive at the station on time . . .'

Harold's rather supercilious reactions very soon melted before the warmth of the welcome extended to them in every part of the country. 'The people are so kind here,' he wrote to his son Ben, 'that I simply cannot make fun of them.' – to their faces! Since Harold could never, from extreme youth to extreme old age, refrain from making fun of almost everyone, his oldest friends, and himself included, this laudable intention was certainly not observed within the family circle. In his letters to Vita during their separation he was outspoken:

I think that it is not sufficient merely to *avoid* hurting these peoples' feelings. One must flatter them as well. One's very presence, clothes, assurance, and high rank fill them with agonies of humiliation which have to be screened with lauding if they are not to chafe and smart . . . Dear me, how kind they all are to one![8]

Then it dawned upon him that supposing he and Vita were doing a lecture tour in England they would find the people they had to consort with just as incompatible, and perhaps not quite as nice.

Vita was no less touched by the kindness she received from every American. She reciprocated it in a way that was not natural to Harold. She became genuinely fond of them, just as they admired and grew to love her. They were entranced by her good nature and lack of pomposity. For instance, when the women of one audience could not believe that her cheeks were not rouged, she allowed them to wipe her face with a handkerchief. She liked Americans almost everywhere she met them. When she was told that a gossip-column writer in Chicago had accused the Nicolsons of having abused the United States, she was dumbfounded, and very indignant. She protested vehemently that she would never be so ill-mannered, or so unintelligent as to do such a thing; that on the contrary she found the United States fascinating and congenial.

Certainly she was acclaimed wherever she went. 'Mummy is lionised like nohow,' Harold told Ben. 'She is given orchids and is met by groups of people at stations. You know how modest she is. It will do her good. It is extraordinary . . . how famous she is.'[9] Nevertheless she found the tour taxing. She was amazed by American lack of imagination in not seeing how she needed to be alone at times. The very few respites allowed were immensely welcome. One such was a few days' rest at Mina Curtiss's farm on the Berkshire Hills. Miss Curtiss was a woman of fortune and culture who taught in Northampton College, as Vita put it, just for fun. Her farm was in real country with elm avenues and villages of white clapboard houses. Her own was a homely, rambling, wooden building with pigeons on the roof, Jersey cows in the meadows, and horses in the stables. It was almost a breath of beloved Kent. Harold's respite was a visit which they paid together to the Embassy at Washington with his old chief of Berlin days, Sir Ronald Lindsay, and his wife. Elizabeth. He was enchanted with the beauty of the Massachusetts coast, the indented lagoons, the little wooded islands, the white houses and churches. There was not a trace of the vulgarity and brashness which so often offended him elsewhere. With

Vita's company he felt wholly relaxed. They were driven to Mount Vernon, and stopped on the way to see the Lincoln Memorial and the statue, which he found impressive – 'the sunken eyes and heavy working-man's hands', and the 'angered despair in the face'. On the other hand his visit to the Senate shocked him. The Vice-President was a bleary, tobacco-drugged looking man. The lack of decorum was manifest. Around the tribune sat little messenger boys, wearing black plus-fours. They were giggling and picking their noses. Under each Senator's desk was a green glass spittoon. When speaking the Senators turned their backs on the Vice-President and wandered away from their desks. The proceedings were undignified and ungainly. Before returning to New York in April Harold and Vita arranged a holiday for themselves in Arizona. They were both suitably impressed by the Grand Canyon, where they picked up seeds of unknown plants.

Harold told Bruce Lockhart that together he and Vita took out of the lecture tour £3,000, of which they spent £1,000. The two of them netted about £2,000.

On his return he was commissioned by the *Daily Telegraph* to write six articles on his impressions of America. They were published consecutively in May. He began by outlining what he failed to find. He failed to find Americanism as deep a force as he expected, although Americans had adopted a compelling uniformity of manner. The standard of education was wider though less deep than in England. Notwithstanding the use of the English language, differences in custom between the two countries were perplexing. He noticed an uneasy disinclination to submit quantitative values to qualitative criticism. It was surprising that a country so sensitive about its lack of tradition should systematically be destroying what might, if left undisturbed, become traditional to the children. Americans were very well informed of foreign affairs and deeply suspicious of the motives of the old world, indeed of all foreign countries. This was because of the 'Magnificent Lie', which they were all taught at school, namely that the United States was inspired by ethical conceptions of right and justice, not to be found in the Old World. As he was to write to Lady Colefax ten years later, it was doubtless essential for America to invent a comprehensive and compelling theory in order to boil down the disparate foreign ingredients which it had absorbed, into some uniform condiment. He believed that within the next fifty years the United States would completely alter its character. It would lose the Anglo-Saxon flavour which it had preserved so long and become a country ruled by the dregs of Europe. If he were an American he would view this prospect with considerable alarm. [10]

On the 20th April the *Bremen* with the Nicolsons on board anchored off Cherbourg en route for Southampton. At 5 a.m. Ben who had been learning French at a crammer's on the Loire, and Nigel who had joined him, clambered up the side of the liner from a tender.

At home again Harold was still beset by the problem of how to earn money. One of the first things he did was to engage himself to review for the *Daily Telegraph* five books a week for three weeks in each month. Since this would not bring him enough income to meet his needs he actually considered in the autumn an invitation from the *Evening Standard* to edit the Londoners' Diary on his own. He was much flattered at being asked and in spite of his intense dislike of that column when he wrote for it was about to accept, subject to several conditions. But on Vita discovering that she had £2,500 hidden away in a French bank, and Leonard and Virginia Woolf happening to lunch with them on the 5th May and expressing strong opposition to his re-selling himself to Beaverbrook, Harold declined. He felt relieved.

On the 11th June *Peacemaking* was published. [11] Its general reception was extremely favourable. It was acclaimed as a brilliant book. It was received with more caution by American critics, sensitive about the author's attribution of the breakdown of the 1919 peace terms largely to President Wilson's 'rigidity and spiritual arrogance'. The *Saturday Review of Literature* pronounced Nicolson a British type at once incomprehensible and irritating to the average American mind. He was so clever that it was hard to take him seriously, and so full of instinctive affectation that it was difficult to trust his sincerity.

The Woolfs were still very much in the Nicolsons' lives. Virginia had been seized with gloom when Vita left for America. 'Yes,' she wrote to Ethel Smyth, 'that saddens me; it takes away a lamp and a glow, and a shady leaf and an illuminated hall from my existence.' [12] Vita and Virginia kept up a regular correspondence, the latter's letters being couched in a bantering style that can be maintained only by a person whose own passion, though on the wane, has not yet turned to ashes. It was late in the month of May when Leonard and Virginia were again lunching at Sissinghurst and Ben, aged eighteen, related the story of his grandmother informing him that both his parents were homosexual, that his father had had boys in Tehran and Berlin, and his mother affairs with Violet Trefusis and Virginia, and that they were wicked people. While Ben was speaking Virginia sat in silence, her head bowed. Suddenly she exploded with anger. 'The old woman ought to be shot,' she said. Harold felt sick with rage at his mother-in-law's devilry. Vita courageously went to Ben's bedroom, sat talking to him till long past midnight, admitted that what her mother had said was true, but denied resolutely that there had ever been the slightest risk of Virginia endangering her marriage. The full story of this disgraceful episode was recorded in writing by Ben years later,[13] when he made it clear that his grandmother's mischievous revelations had merely bewildered him at the time but otherwise hardly worried him at all, contrary to what the psychoanalysts would have one believe. Harold derived some comfort from a talk with B.M.'s doctor who told him that she was almost, but not quite, certifiable. At all events Lady Sackville, when taxed by Harold and Vita, showed no penitence whatever. On the contrary she renewed her accusations and turned the two of them out of her house.[14]

Exactly nine years previously Harold had gone to Jonathan Cape's office at the publisher's invitation. Mr. Cape put to him the proposal that he should write Lord Curzon's life. Without being clear whether the idea was Cape's own or Lady Curzon's Harold declined on the ground that he did not know enough about India for an official life. At the same time he left the door open for writing a monograph on the statesman after the official life, which was undertaken by Lord Ronaldshay, had come out. Now he was free and anxious to begin his monograph, but the book was to be, as the sub-title – *The Last Phase, 1919–1925* – indicated, a continuation of the trilogy on events leading up to and following the Great War. With his customary partiality for starting a new job at the beginning of a month, Harold set about his research work on the 1st May. He finished it on the 21st August, and would have done so sooner had there not been a motor jaunt to Florence in June to see Ben who was learning Italian, and acute anxiety over Nigel's serious appendix operation in July. The book was written by the 14th November and delivered to Constable's in January 1934.

Notwithstanding his illness Nigel was acquitting himself with distinction at Eton. He got eight credits in his School Certificate examination. Harold was immensely proud of his younger son's acute mind which he compared to a medical forceps which gripped things quickly, firmly and exactly in the right place. Their relationship was based on complete mutual confidence, and total lack of reserve on either side. Harold's only concern was because Nigel's relations with his mother were not on quite the same carefree basis. On Christmas Eve of 1933 there was a family scene which, perhaps not important in itself, revealed to Harold that whereas Vita and Ben were introverts, he and Nigel were extraverts. At 7.30 they turned on the wireless. Someone was reading in a sing-song voice rhetorical passages from the New Testament. 'Oh God!' said Nigel, 'Poetry!' This produced a nerve-storm in Vita. She switched off the wireless, and they all trooped downstairs to the dining-room with bowed heads. They ate in silence. Then Vita burst into tears and left the room. She wandered sobbing by the lake in the dark. Harold was much upset. Vita returned and said that Nigel was cynical and sneered at things that mattered. He had all Harold's worst qualities. He was hard and cold. He never 'felt' anything. 'Oh, yes, he is kind and affectionate,' she went on, 'and all that, but he has no passion. All with him is cold hard intelligence.'[15] Nigel, aged fifteen, sloped off to bed in self-imposed disgrace, rather puzzled by what the trouble was all about. Harold endeavoured to excuse their younger son to Vita, and Ben with gentle wisdom explained that Nigel was excessively reserved. Vita still maintained that if he suppressed all feelings they would atrophy. Harold's conclusion was, 'Niggs's remorseless logic irritates her as much as Ben's muddle-headedness irritates me.'[16] At the same time he was beginning to worry about Vita's health, especially her emotional outbursts, which though usually controlled, might, he feared, bring her unhappiness in the years to come.

Although the nadir of Harold Nicolson's long life had been reached in 1930 and 1931 with journalism and involvement with the New Party he was not to feel settled, or rather fulfilled, until he got into the House of Commons in 1935. Whereas the intervening years saw him busy with his books, broadcasts, reviews, and occasional lectures – like that at the Sorbonne in December of 1933 while a students' riot was in progress – still he suffered from a sense of guilt that he had no regular profession. The guilt was the consequence of his upbringing and the constant example before his eyes ever since he could remember of his father stepping into the Chancery of some foreign embassy or into the Foreign Office in Whitehall punctually at half past nine every morning, and leaving, when no crisis was on hand, at 5.30, and much, much later if there was one. He could not bring himself to believe that publication of successive books of the highest calibre, and collaboration with Vita in creating a paradisal garden were justification of the intellectual gifts with which Providence – for he attributed nothing to the Almighty – had endowed him.

In his youth Harold had always been closely attached to his sister Gwen, younger than him by ten years, and the wife of Sam St. Aubyn.[17] Owing to the fact that the St. Aubyns lived rather conventional county lives, poles away from Bohemia, and were preoccupied with a large family of children, Harold and Gwen after their respective marriages rarely met, and Vita did not know her sister-in-law at all well. But when the St. Aubyn children began growing up and Mrs. St. Aubyn was less tied to her home she came to realise that there were other functions in life than wifehood and motherhood. Vita warmly espoused what she interpreted as Gwen's intelligent revolt from man's domination. Gwen started paying visits to Sissinghurst. By September 1933 she was to all intents and purposes living there. But her health was very precarious. In January 1934 she had a serious operation on her head after a motor accident, and was in great pain. Vita, who had become attached to her, was in constant attendance at the London Clinic. When Gwen was convalescent Vita rented for a fortnight the Castello, an isolated little villa at the top of a rocky peak at Portofino on the Italian riviera. On the 26th she motored Gwen out there. Harold was slightly concerned. 'I hope,' he wrote to Vita, 'my poor cracked sister is all right.' He dreaded a deferred reaction from the head injuries in this abrupt translation to Mediterranean utopianism.

Before joining wife and sister in Portofino Harold set off for the continent. He went to Paris for a weekend. I accompanied him there. The Channel crossing was hideously rough, and Harold sat on deck in the bitter wind and spray talking ceaselessly to Lady Colefax. In Paris, which he loved and knew intimately, he was a superlative guide.[18] The first night of our arrival we dined at La Perouse and went the rounds of Montmartre and Montparnasse. The next day, which was cold and bright, we lunched at Versailles. The château was practically deserted. In the Galerie des Glaces Harold revived memories of the signing of the Peace Treaty in 1919. At six o'clock in the evening we called by appointment at James Joyce's apartment in the rue Galilée. An account of the strange visit is given in Harold's published diaries under the 4th February. I well remember how when the door-bell was pressed the sound of agitated scuffling from within met our ears. The door was opened by Joyce's son, a young replica of the father. He was a coarse young man wearing an overcoat down to his ankles which he kept on throughout the visit. The sitting-room was like the small *salon* of a provincial hotel. It smelled strongly of celery soup. There were prim little upright mahogany chairs, of the sort of which any French land-lady might be proud. There was an upright piano covered with a crochet cloth and some hideous frames containing photographs of hideous people. Dotted about the small plush-covered tables were baskets of stiffly arranged mimosa tied with broad magenta ribbons.

> Then Joyce glided in. It was evident that he had just been shaving. He was very spruce and nervous and chatty . . . Huge concave glasses which flicked reflections of the lights as he moved his head like a bird, turning it with that definite insistence to the speaker as blind people do who turn to the sound of a voice. Joyce was wearing large bedroom slippers in check, and wearing heavy rings on nervous hands. Ordinary steel specs with one detachable lens . . . He was very courteous as shy people are. His beautiful voice trilled on slowly like Anna Livia Plurabelle. He has the most lovely voice I know – liquid and soft with undercurrents of gurgle.[19]

Joyce told Harold that the ban on *Oolissays* had been removed in America. He hoped it might be removed in England. For half an hour conversation ensued in staccato phrases between embarrassed pauses, not made easier for the two men of letters by the silent presence of the self-conscious son and myself. 'There was a sense about the flat of furtive insanity.'

Harold continued alone to Munich to make arrangements about the translation into German of *Peacemaking*. He found a chill sort of Nazi Calvinism in the air of Munich which he much disliked. In Vienna, his next stop where he had to lecture, there was an undercurrent of revolu-tion. One compensation was the presence in this capital of Alan Pryce-Jones, at that time courting his first wife, Poppy Fould-Springer. Harold had first met Alan two years before and was so bowled over by his charm, intelligence and Greek hedonism as to remark, 'I like him more than I care to think.' He even exhorted his son Ben to consult with this paragon of life-enhancers how to adjust his sex life so as to get the greatest fulfilment out of it with the least disreputability. From Vienna he continued by train to Santa Margherita where Vita met him and motored him to Portofino. For a day or two he stayed with Vita and Gwen in the little fortress-like Castello above the village, its walls inside lined with steel engravings of the Duke of Wellington and Lord John Russell.

They went to luncheon with Max Beerbohm at Rapallo.

It was a shock. He used to be the neatest trimmest little person in the whole world – little tight cuffs with coral links; little tight shoes with silk socks; a little tight waist and huge eyelashes which rose and fell like safety curtains. But since I last saw him two years ago something has happened to his metabolism. He has swollen. His cheeks were rounded like two melons and from between them protruded a thing like a pepper corn which was his nose. Also his neck had given way somewhere and his head hung sideways, a little giving him the look of a stricken starling painted red on the beak. Not that he is an indulgent man. He drinks not nor does he smoke, yet Solomon at his very worst cannot have gone down hill quite so quickly as that.[20]

The party consisted of Gerhart Hauptmann, the German poet and dramatist, who looked like Goethe except that the back of his head was flat, and his slim, dark wife. He was dressed in an enormous grey frock coat and had a tortoishell chain round his neck like the anchor chain of a yacht.

On the 10th February Harold moved to Cap Ferrat near Nice to stay with Somerset Maugham. Here he experienced a taste of Riviera dissipation and luxury. He dined with Michael Arlen, 'a decent, companionable person,' at Cannes,

and then out into the night – pavements strewn with faded narcissus from the battle of flowers and sailors with arms linked making patterns under the palm trees, the stubs of their cigarettes glowing bright occasionally like the flashes from the destroyers in the bay. We went to a villa where the sailors were prepared to dance with the customers. I just sat and drank vermouth, not being a dancing man.[21]

At Cap Ferrat he also conceived the idea of a monumental autobiography, to be called *Mutations*. He wrote that he wanted to talk to me about it. 'I feel ambitious at the moment but I fear it is too huge to contemplate.' It was to be his *magnum opus*, a vast undertaking on a Proustian scale, stretching over ten years. In possibly as many as ten volumes he would group round certain central figures the development either of his own ideas and experiences, or of the general atmosphere of the Victorian, Edwardian, pre-war, war, and post-war epochs up to date. The idea was fathered by a sort of intoxication from his hectic travelling, the memories in the Salle des Glaces at Versailles, the success of his lecture in Vienna, the brief interlude in the romantic little Castello at Portofino on its rock lashed by the winter winds, the long talks with Max Beerbohm and Hauptmann, the descent into the carnival atmosphere of Willie Maugham's villa and the night life at Cannes, the flowers, the sailors, the fun. And then reflection at leisure. A sudden self-revelation, a mood of confidence. 'I may be wrong, but I feel that in the last year I have found myself.'[22] His obsession with what he called THE IDEA disclosed to him – alas, the revelation was short-lived – that his prevailing political ambitions, the presumption that he might become Foreign Secretary, were vain, trivial, laughable and merely an unconscious attempt to solace himself for not writing better. Now he knew he could write better. To his diary he confided the sudden onrush of this new conviction. It followed him to Morocco, where he next went with Vita and Gwen. He began taking notes. The book must at all costs be true, not a collection of half-truths as in Proust's *A La Recherche*. But the moment that doubts entered his head whether he had the ruthlessness to be sufficiently candid about himself, the idea started to wilt. The straightforward autobiography, even the fictional autobiography, was abandoned. Other literary distractions, that did not call for deep heart-searchings, intervened. The idea lay dormant until he embarked upon *Helen's Tower* in 1937, by which time he had lost the first magnificent liberation in this golden February of 1934. *Helen's Tower* is one of Harold Nicolson's most evocative and nostalgic books of reminiscence, but it did not embrace the compass of THE IDEA. And the reason for this was that the pull of politics had in the meantime again overcome the ambition of purest literature. Harold was not now to become a totally dedicated writer in the exclusive sense that Virginia Woolf was, or even Vita. This does not mean that his early promise was not fulfilled, but may mean that his greatest potential was never accomplished.

At Marseilles Harold re-joined Vita and Gwen, and they crossed the sea to Tangier where memories of his happiest days of childhood flooded over him. There in the old Legation was the very same sofa on which he had induced his mother's maid to sit when he was frightened at nights. And there the very bed on which he had slept. The three continued to Marrakesh and Fez. At Fez his ear was stung by an insect and suppurated. When he got back to England he was ill with poisoning and had to recover in a nursing home.

April was spent happily at Sissinghurst, reviewing books for the *Daily Telegraph*, and gardening. He received an invitation, which he accepted, from Paul Morand to contribute a weekly letter to *Figaro*, 'rédigée avec toute la grâce et l'esprit qui vous caractérisent sur les évènements britanniques capables d'interésser au public français'.[23] And in May *Curzon: The Last Phase*, after four instalments had been serialised in the *Times*, was published. It evoked tremendous praise from all quarters. Letters of congratulation came from Lord D'Abernon, Lord Riddell, A. D. Lindsay, the Master of Balliol, Gerald Berners and Bruce Lockhart. The *Times Literary Supplement* pronounced that the philosopher and biographer struggled for the control of his pen; that he was right in pointing out how far the personality of a statesman influenced international events; and that the book repeatedly transcended the bounds to which the subject would have limited a less skilful author. The *Sunday Times* considered that Mr. Nicolson had in writing it rendered a public service.[24]

In May he sailed to Stockholm to lecture on Democratic Diplomacy. On arrival in Sweden he wrote to Vita:

> On the train next to me at luncheon was a young man whom I had seen on the boat . . . all tied up in bandages. He said that he was on his way to stay with a man who belonged to the British Legation. In fact the Honorary Attaché. I said I was also going there. He said, 'Did you know that Harold Nicolson was on the boat with us?' I said, 'That tall, handsome man, was it?' So far so good, but I blushed not scarlet but a dull shade of purple. That spoilt it and I collapsed. 'It's me,' I said. He said that the barman pointed out someone quite different. I think he thought I was spurious.[25]

He stayed at the Legation with his old friend Archie Clark Kerr, and his beautiful Chilean wife, Tina. Both said they hated Stockholm, and Harold suspected that they also hated each other.

> Oh my God! Sweden was not made for you or me [he told Vita]. It is worse than Switzerland for utter smugness and lack of character. It is horrible. Archie has taken to drawing. Gets young Swedes to pose in the nude. To avoid scandal he has a teacher present. Not good.

Yet Harold was much impressed by the architecture of Stockholm town hall. He noticed that the bricks of which it was built were not pointed at all, or rather the mortar was not flush with the brick, so that each brick threw its own little shadow. What however delighted him most of all was finding in the Legation a superb review of Vita's *Collected Poems* by Richard Church. He went about all day with 'a warm doughnut inside, sweet outside, soft-all-round, and with a fid of jam in its little gentle belly'.[26]

In Sweden he met a German who shocked him by saying that all his friends of Berlin days had either been exiled or thrown into concentration camps; all the liberal politicians had bolted or were shut up. The first-class brains had left the universities. The information was confirmed by Heinrich Brüning, whom Harold saw at luncheon in London on his return. The last time they had met Brüning was the powerful Chancellor of the Reich. Now he was a refugee.

> He looks sadly at me from behind his steel clerical glasses. He smiles with all his gold teeth like a flash of Benares ware in the sun. He says a reaction against Hitler is already beginning and the economic position is awful. All the statistics are faked.[27]

He was sure the young were already disillusioned with Naziism, and wanted a Hohenzollern prince back on the throne. When Harold repeated to General Weygand, whom he met soon afterwards, that Brüning believed the only way of maintaining constitutional order in Germany was by reinstating the monarchy, the General remarked, 'Il a bien raison,' adding that Brüning was a noble man. In a *Daily Telegraph* review[28] Harold wrote a vehement indictment of Hitlerism. Even so he cautioned British readers to understand that what would be an extreme neurosis in England or France was in Germany an ordinary method of expressing opinion. For this reason instead of applying interventionist force he advocated an adjustment of the balance of power in Europe so as to prevent Germany from attacking the civilization of other countries. Nevertheless optimists should bear in mind that the worst did frequently come to the worst.

Harold did not have enough work to do. Broadcasting and reviewing did not take up enough of his time. He had lately turned down the offer of a gossip-column from the *Daily Telegraph*. So when an invitation came out of the blue that he should write a life of the American Dwight Morrow, statesman, lawyer, banker, ambassador to Mexico, and senator, he was enthusiastic. He had been chosen directly by

Morrow's widow, who had never met him, through the advice of Thomas Lamont, the chairman of J. P. Morgan and Company, the bank on the board of which Morrow had served. Lamont was Sibyl Colefax's closest American friend, and Harold had met him and his wife at Sibyl's table. It was flattering for an Englishman to be so approached; and Harold took it as a challenge. American resentment was to be expected from some quarters. The difficulties would be formidable, and Harold's knowledge of finance was practically nil. He would have to spend much time in the States, and he would have to have his expenses paid, or he could not afford to leave England and his journalism and broadcasting. But the moment was opportune, and the adventure enticing. It is extraordinary how throughout Harold's entire life some welcome proposition always came to him when it was most needed.

On the 14th September he sailed for the United States in the *Berengaria*. Now it happened that two days before the boat arrived in New York the man, Bruno Hauptmann, who had murdered the Lindberghs' kidnapped baby in 1932, was caught. As Mrs. Lindbergh was the daughter of Mrs. Morrow, with whom Harold was to stay, the episode portended embarrassment. On descending the gangway he was met by Mrs. Morrow's private secretary, by Thomas Lamont's private secretary, and by the embarkation officer of the house of Morgan. Also by a dumpy little youth in pince-nez who said, 'I'm Dwight Morrow.' And so he was – Dwight Morrow jnr., shy and stammering. Two huge cars were waiting where no other cars were allowed to wait. Harold was driven to Next Day Hill at Englewood, New Jersey, twelve miles from New York, one of the Morrow houses where in fact Morrow had died in 1931. It took them forty minutes to get there through country like Epping Forest. Within a glade a big wood of forty acres, dissected by neat, winding paths, surrounded the house. Attached to the modest dwelling was a vast library like a cathedral. The panelled, pile-carpeted rooms were hung with Raeburns and Hoppners. A Miss Schiff who had been cataloguing the Morrow papers was put at Harold's disposal. A housekeeper invited him to choose his own suite. It was there he was to work.

Harold promptly took a night train to Deacon Brown's Point, North Haven, Maine, which was the Morrows' summer house. The train stopped at Rockland, a small seaside place, where it was met by the captain of the Morrows' boat, 'by a man I couldn't make out, by another man whom I could not make out and by a third man whom I could not make out. The retainers who attach themselves to millionaires are disconcerting . . . Anyway I shake hands all round.'[29] A taxi took them to the Copper Kettle where Harold was given breakfast by George Rublee, who had been Morrow's chief assistant in Mexico and at the London Naval Conference of 1930.[30] He was about sixty-three, huge and lank, and Harold described him as 'an angel'. From a little pier the launch took them to an island and, among pine trees, a house with shingled walls. Mrs. Morrow, neat, ugly and extremely friendly, but in a state of nerves, greeted Harold at the gate. She worshipped even the faintest shadow of her husband's memory, but was withal intelligent and very conscientious, determined not to control what Harold wrote. He was soon much impressed by the memory which Morrow inspired in the several friends he met. He spent two days at Deacon Brown's Point before it was shut up for the winter. On his way back to Engle-wood he stayed with Miss Mina Curtiss who gave him information about the Morrow-Lindbergh relationship. Lindbergh, she explained, was really no more than a mechanic and, had it not been for the lone eagle flight across the Atlantic in 1927, would then have been in charge of a gasoline station on the outskirts of St. Louis. Although the Mor-rows were themselves of humble origin yet they were cultured and distinguished people. Thus Lindbergh, who came from a lower social stratum, they treated with aloof politeness. He was himself simple and not easy. His wife Anne had a difficult task. Then Dwight junior was a disappointment. He was backward, heard voices, and had been shut up. Mrs. Morrow was not too nice to him. The press even had the bad taste to suggest that the Lindbergh baby had been despatched by the 'lunatic Morrow son'.

Harold also called on his old friend, Archibald MacLeish, at his farm, a nice wooden house with green shutters and the shadows of vines upon long deck chairs. 'Mrs. MacLeish was in a bathing dress and as she looks like Siegfried, Sigelinda and Odin all rolled into one it was an expansive sight.'[31] Archie was wearing corduroy trousers and a singlet. Having won the Pulitzer Prize he was now a famous man. He explained that America was highly organised for Fascism in the chambers of commerce and every rich city. Harold stayed at the Rublees' farm at Vermont where he met Judge Learned Hand who confided that Mor-row had lacked charm and was physically rather revolting. But he had fascination. Harold was quickly becoming interested in the psycholo-gical problem which the elusive Morrow presented.

On his return to Englewood on 30th September he was for the first time alone with the Lindberghs, Mrs. Morrow being out to dinner. Colonel and Mrs. Lindbergh had, since the murder of their baby, come to live with Mrs. Morrow at Next Day Hill, closely guarded by patrols of armed police, plain clothes detectives and ferocious dogs. Harold was immediately captivated by Anne Lindbergh, small, clever and gentle. He pronounced her adorable. Charles, slim, schoolboyish, with delicate hands which belied the motor mechanic attribute, was diffident and shy until he got used to their guest. He had a dry sense of humour, although inclined to be over-serious. For instance, while Harold was eating his melon at breakfast Lindbergh would reply to a casual question, which was meant merely to cover time, as one to which Harold had come thousands of miles to elicit a reasoned answer. He would deliver himself of a laborious response the intensity of which was hardly justified by the subject.[32] He was not at all stupid, although uneducated. He soon became a sympathetic companion, taking the new guest into his confidence about his hatred of publicity and his persecution by the press and public. He often received 100,000 letters a day. Although the newspapers – and in the house every printed newspaper seemed to be displayed – were packed with news of the murdered baby and Hauptmann, not one word about the subject was mentioned by the family. Harold soon understood that Lindbergh's reputation for sulkiness and bad manners was entirely due to his fear and dislike of society.

Harold was obsessed by what he called the 'infantilism' of the Americans. He wrote to Vita:

If I could understand what causes [it] I should have got some way towards understanding their nice housemaid mentality. I use the word 'housemaid' in the best sense, the sort of nice housemaid whom one meets if one goes too early into the library of Hatfield, Penshurst, Wilton, Longleat or Knole – the rustle of the pink starched dress, the general deftness of it all and yet the sense of being below the salt. They all have it. They all rise to it. They none of them, without years of Paris, rise above it. In England, I suppose, Mrs. Morrow would be a complete bedint and the Morrow sisters would be like Mrs. Woods at the Weald post office (they are rather like her as it is). Yet Mrs. Morrow is far far above that level. She is really an educated, intelligent and wise woman. I like her very much indeed. Yet one feels that even with her there is the housemaids' room atmosphere. She is like the very best type of retired upper servant. (How Gwen will squirm at this snobbishness). Anne is like Emily Booth [wife of the Knole butler], Charles Lindbergh like a bright young chauffeur. I have these feelings only when I meet a European. I feel rather ashamed of putting them down on paper even to you, since nothing could equal the kindness I receive here. But I do not put them down in dispraisal. I merely record an impression which is recurrent and permanent.[33]

He concluded that one explanation for this American infantilism was that they had been taught to think in terms of achievement, which could be measured only quantitatively; and that they were almost incapable of thinking in qualitative or hypothetical terms. Thus all forms of abstract thought, even ordinary intellectual curiosity, were to them 'idealism'; that such things as art, music and poetry were mere attributes to normal human conduct, which people 'ought to have', especially 'nice women', but were not the substance and centre of the stream of human consciousness.

But worse than the Americans' subordination of the abstract things as 'idealism', was their smarminess. The convention that it behoved them to declare that black was white, that sinners were saints, was universal. He had first-hand experience of this tendency when endeavouring to glean information about Morrow from friends and acquaintances. With the single exception of J. P. Morgan[34] hardly one American who had known Morrow told him anything he truly wanted to learn, anything that he could believe to be more than polite gush. It so infuriated Harold that he confessed to Vita he positively wished to bash their faces in. He was seized with a reprehensible desire to be brutal to them.

He soon settled down into a regular, intensive course of research among the Morrow papers. His hosts were quick to understand that nothing and nobody was allowed to interrupt it.

I lead a strange life [he told Sibyl Colefax]. I have two rooms up in the attic which sounds like Chatterton and is really like Lady Mendl. A bedroom with shaded lamp and soft *duvé* softness. A sitting-room with Fragonard engravings, bright chintz chairs, three enormous tables, and a statue of the unknown warrior (from the Avenue de l'Opéra). Between these apartments is encased an American bathroom with lysterine, medicated cotton wool, a shower bath, many towels embroidered with the Morrow initials, two washing basins, a weighing machine (a most outspoken and humiliating contrivance) and a cork thing to sit and stand on. I rise at 8.15. I wash. At 8.45 I depress the telephone receiver at the point where a pink button comes opposite the words 'Breakfast Pantry'. 'Good morning!' I exclaim democratically, 'I'm about to come down.' 'Welcome sure . . .' the voice answers and then I descend, not without a certain awareness of the Lindbergh police dog who never seems to recognize me until he gets quite close.[35]

He worked ten hours a day, apart from meals and one and a half hours' exercise. His leisure reading was confined to Emily Dickinson, whose acute awareness he compared to Virginia Woolf's. His only other distraction was the unfailing daily letter to Vita. To her he poured out the details of his life and intimate thoughts, which his diary covering this American visit did not contain. He wrote to her about his conflicting opinions of Morrow as he advanced his way through the papers and spoke to more and more of the people who had known him. The man was a Protean figure, with the mind of a criminal and the character of a saint.

While he was away Vita's novel, *The Dark Island*, was published. The heroine Shirin was modelled on Gwen St. Aubyn, to whom the book was dedicated. Ben and Nigel did not like the book. Nor for that matter did Harold. He found it 'morbid and distressing'. Virginia Woolf also complained that Vita had failed to get away from the personal zone and view the story from outside herself.[36]

Harold enjoyed a few intervals of light relief. He told Raymond Mortimer that he managed to have three or four affairs with young men in New York. He was intoxicated by the city at night, the skyscrapers above Central Park flashing and winking from a million windows. He felt immensely exhilarated by the explosion of triumphant human energy which made London seem a provincial village by comparison. He considered New York one of the most impressive visions in the world. He spent a weekend with Copley Amory[37] on an island off the coast of Massachusetts which had been in the Amorys' possession since 1814. It had beech woods thick with deer and wild turkeys, and marshes, and bays where the great Atlantic breakers pounded. The two friends rode from one end of the nine-mile-long island to the other. Then there was the incident of Mrs. Woodbridge's stomach which Harold could not resist recounting at length and I cannot resist quoting.

Yesterday Dean and Mrs. Woodbridge came to luncheon. I spent the whole afternoon shut up with him. Poor Mrs. Morrow walked Mrs. Rublee and Mrs. Woodbridge round and round the garden. The effect upon Mrs. Woodbridge was very strange. We sat round the tea table and Mrs. Woodbridge developed internal rumblings such as I have never heard except among the more active types of volcano. They began in the normal fashion – a trifle exaggerated, yet of the ordinary rotary, ruminatory and regurgitant type. This was succeeded by a single, long-drawn note of startling clarity. Rather reedy and sweet the note was, something between a blackbird and a thrush. But so loud, darling. I talked quickly and hilariously, but it was no good; however I might raise my voice, the native wood notes wild of Mrs. Woodbridge pierced through my intervention. I became seriously alarmed. Dean Woodbridge himself is a trifle deaf, and although he must have heard these sounds he may have felt that they came from the Hudson river ferry and not from the inside of his wife. Mrs. Morrow, who was dispensing tea, looked anxiously at the kettle thinking it had gone mad, and then at me. I offered Mrs. Woodbridge a large slice of cake, enough to stifle any blackbird. She took it. She munched hard. I was relieved by this. A person about to explode cannot munch cake. Obviously she was used to giving vent in this way, and may even have come to find the sounds stimulating and pleasurable. The sounds subsided into the sleepy squeak of young birds beneath the eaves. 'Never,' said Mrs. Woodbridge, 'have I seen the trees such a lovely colour as this fall.' We were saved.[38]

Before returning for Christmas Harold went to stay with the British Ambassador, Ronnie Lindsay, at Washington. Charles Lindbergh offered to fly him there, but owing to his promise to Vita, Harold felt obliged to decline. Lady Lindsay was to his regret away. Nevertheless he revelled in the easiness, lack of fuss and false modes of conduct, and above all in the blessed ability to say without offence whatever came into his mind, in the company of this tolerant and engaging friend. He also visited Berkeley College, Yale, where he lectured to three hundred undergraduates about diplomacy. He much admired the gothic architecture of the college – more effective than any he had come across. 'That is the whole thing about America. Things have been made but have not grown.'[39] On the 30th November he embarked at midnight on the *Olympic*, and on the 7th December was in Paris, staying at the Ritz. After seeing some French friends of Morrow he crossed to England on the 9th.

Nigel has described[40] with what method and precision his father had during the autumn filled a huge loose-leafed notebook with extracts taken from the Morrow papers and records of interviews with Dwight's friends. By the time he left America after this first visit the skeleton of the book was ready for the flesh. With none of his biographies did he take more trouble. And none of them was for his English readers less appealing.

For two months Harold had a break from America, to which he was to return three more times before completing *Dwight Morrow*. He actually wrote fifteen out of the eighteen chapters at Sissinghurst.

He was at home where he ought to have been so happy. Yet during this interlude he was not entirely so. He thought his life was without purpose. The books, like the one on which he was engaged, were incidental to what should be a larger, wider purpose. He discussed his condition with his sister, Gwen, who was then living at Sissinghurst. She was wise. She explained that until recently he had remained very youthful and ebullient. Now he was realising that suddenly later middle age had overtaken him. It was a shock to him. She also reminded him that he was naturally a domesticated person, and in fact gave up diplomacy primarily to preserve a home; but that Vita was not a domestic person, and could not therefore supply him with all he needed when he was at home. Moreover Vita had reached a stage of her life, from which she was never to deviate, when she had no real need of more than one person at a time, apart from Harold; and ironically that one person was now his sister. Harold was not made in this way. He was naturally gregarious and at Sissinghurst he missed the companionship of friends, such as used to congregate at Long Barn. Sensing this state of affairs Gwen advised him to return to public life in some way. Harold agreed with her that pleasant though life was at Sissinghurst, it was for him lotus-eating. He could never be content there all the time. If he was not to become morbid, introspective and dissatisfied he must get out into the world again, and do something else besides writing.

Nevertheless the parting with Vita for America in February was as painful as ever. On the 5th Harold went to tea with his Aunt Lal Dufferin in London to say goodbye to her and his mother. He found Lady Dufferin covered in old lace and ninety years of distinction, surrounded by relations who all seemed to know Harold and of whom he recognised few. Lady Carnock, the younger sister, was briskly tripping around, handing buns. Harold sailed for the United States on the *Berengaria*. On landing he was motored straight to Englewood and warmly greeted by Mrs. Morrow as though he were a member of the family. He realised what an affection he had for this good and generous woman. Again he arrived at a critical moment for the Lindberghs. While they sat down to dinner the first evening the Judge was summing up the Hauptmann case in New Jersey. The wireless was kept on at full blast in anticipation of the verdict. After several tense hours an announcement came that Hauptmann had been condemned to death without mercy. After his wife and mother-in-law retired to bed Lindbergh went over the whole case with Harold calmly and entirely without feelings of vengeance.

On the 16th the family left for Mexico in a train which rocked horribly. Before reaching St. Louis they stopped outside a suburban station to avoid reporters, and drove to the Jefferson Memorial which contained the Lindbergh trophies, consisting of old coats, boots and junk associated with the great flight across the Atlantic. The curator, Miss Beauregard, a worshipper of the hero, informed Harold that she had once actually flown with him. 'Since that day,' she said with tears in her eyes, 'I have never quite returned to earth.' Harold's first view of Mexico from the windows of their private carriage on the train was of stumpy aloes dying from the bottom, untidy and ugly. Next, the platform of Monterey station, with the word 'Bienvenidos', and under it 'Welcome', a side of American influence which he deprecated as meaningless and insincere. The train chugged between mountains sharp as razors. The sandy soil was covered with dry scrub like camel-thorn, giving a sort of grey elephant-hide colour to the landscape. The train passed through deep ravines, looking as though they had been scraped by a light rake.

Mexico City was a shabby little Spanish town like Murcia or Alicante. The station was little bigger than the wayside halt of Paddock Wood near Tonbridge. They motored to Cuernavaca, a large village with wide streets, bordered by pink and blue houses, all smothered in puce bougainvillæa. It was dominated by a baroque cathedral and the palace of Cortes who inhabited it after the Conquest, and later of the ill-fated Maximilian and Carlotta. A short lane brought them to the Morrows' house, or rather series of cottages, courtyards and pools. It had been bought by Dwight when he was Ambassador to Mexico towards the end of his career. Harold was given a little pavilion and courtyard to himself at the end of the garden. The next morning he woke up to a blaze of sunshine and the scent of plumbago, datura and banana trees in fruit. Cavalcades of donkeys attached by ropes trotted, thud, thud, thud, beneath his windows.

He instantly resumed writing while Betty Morrow checked facts as he filled the sheets. She was extraordinarily objective, forbearing and sensible. She did not the least mind the few criticisms he made of her husband. By the 8th March he had practically finished the book. Betty

Morrow and Anne Lindbergh both expressed unfeigned satisfaction with it; and their opinion was what Harold cared most about. His own conclusion was that *Dwight Morrow* would make a dull book, and that no one would believe that he had taken trouble or not been paid a huge fee for doing it. In reality he had worked unconscionably hard and accepted no payment from the Morrow family or Morgan Grenfell beyond expenses. The writing had interested him immensely and taught him much. There was no doubt in his mind that Morrow was a great man whom he had grown to love. What was important about Morrow was his character. The actual things he did were heavy as lead. The contrast with his own father was striking. Whereas Lord Carnock had dealt with historic cosmic events Morrow had chiefly dealt with the New York underground railways.

Harold thought Mexico one of the loveliest countries in the world. At the end of February he was taken across an open plain fifty miles broad to Taxco on the foothills of a mountain. He woke during the night,

> when a little moon came over the mountain. Then I slept again and woke to see a blur of green behind the ridge, deepening into pink and then lightening into gold. The datura tree at the end of the terrace was still smelling as dawn came. I saw one of the white bells shaking and found that a huge dragon-fly was poking at it with its nose. Then suddenly I realised that it was a humming-bird. I sat up in bed all excited. It fluttered off shimmering to perch on a poinsettia and at that moment the sun rose with a lance of flame. Now that is one of the moments that I shall never forget.[41]

When March came Harold hated having to say goodbye to Cuerna-vaca and the family. Betty Morrow, Anne and Charles Lindbergh all came to the door in the little lane to see him off. By now he had become devoted to Mrs. Morrow. In this ugly little woman of sixty-five with a disagreeable mouth he found dignity, courage and almost inspiration. She was not brilliant; she was not amusing. But there was something about her which was positively important, something so steadfast that she represented in his eyes several of the best feminine qualities which were to be found only on the far side of the Atlantic. He took a train to Guadalajara, and walked to the cathedral. Peasants with ecstatic faces were creeping up the aisle on their knees 'mumbling all sorts of nice things about Jesus and his mother'. At night the train passed through a fire along the line. 'We stood on the rear platform as we passed through it and the flames lit up the bare brown torsos of a hundred men in huge

Mexican hats.'[42] He again broke his journey at Culiacan in order to visit the dictator President Plutarco Calles, with whom Morrow had established close relations to the great mutual benefit of Mexico and the United States. But all he elicited from the President was the repetitive phrase, 'Señor Morrow was a man of great judgement and friendliness.'

On his way back to England Harold was met in Paris by Ben and myself. The three of us drove to Versailles and visited the Trianon and gardens of the château.

Almost immediately Harold and Vita set out in April taking Nigel on a Henry Lunn cruise to Greece and the Aegean islands. The cruise had been planned long ahead for the benefit of their younger son who had inherited his father's keen interest in the classics. It was a great success. At breakfast-time one morning the ship got stuck on a mudbank at the entrance to the Corinth Canal. At midday all four hundred passengers were made to walk to the stern and jump in unison, but the ship would not budge. The London newspapers cabled Hugh Walpole, who was also on board, and the Nicolsons, for a scoop, but they were warned by Sir Henry Lunn 'not to be naughty children'. When the ship, having been released by tugs, reached the Piraeus, Walpole, pointing to the Parthenon asked, 'Harold, what is that extraordinary building?' After the cruise Vita motored from Marseilles with Gwen through France while Harold, having disembarked with Nigel at Naples, continued to Rome. There he met Axel Munthe. Munthe began the conversation with the phrase, 'Great writers like you', which annoyed Harold who found him gushing. 'The man is a fraud. Now he ought to know that I am not taken in by being called "a great writer". It merely insults me that he should have such an estimate of my vanity. He was half blind and very conceited and unctuous.'[43]

On arrival at Sissinghurst at the very end of April the garden was at its most promising. The early tulips were out; the primroses in full bloom; the bluebells in bud. Various building alterations were in hand. The garden wall was finished and the courtyard wall begun. The bookshelves in Harold's sitting-room were installed, and a new window had been inserted – not too well. But the big room was still incomplete and the end windows not yet put in.

To his chagrin Mrs. Morrow telephoned in a state of agitation on the 16th May to say that the House of Morgan were not satisfied with the book, and he must come over at once. So on the 31st he crossed the Atlantic for the third time, on the *Aquitania*. He reached Englewood very depressed. He cleared off some slight revisions suggested by the Morrow family, but J. P. Morgan's objections were more serious. They were furious with the tone adopted towards their eminent House, which amounted chiefly to an impression Harold had accurately conveyed that Morrow had disliked working for them. They were positively set on diminishing the book's value. After discussions with Thomas Lamont, Walter Lippmann, the political commentator, and George Rublee, Harold adjusted certain offending passages without however entirely giving way to Morgan's desire that the book should be an unqualified eulogy of the Bank. In the adjustments, for which he had to fight inch by inch, he was firmly backed by Lindbergh. Harold found the opinions of people whom he deemed idiotic to be worse than irritating. They drove him to frenzies of anger. Over this issue he did not feel penitent at all. He had sufficient self-confidence to know that he was right and his Morgan critics were ludicrously wrong. He was convinced that the modifications he was obliged to concede had made the book flabby and sugary, a view which was to some extent shared by Vita.

Within five days Harold left for home. He was adamant about returning in time to discuss with Balliol dons Nigel's future at Oxford which, he insisted, was 'far more important to me than any book on Dwight Morrow'.

Just before he had hurriedly left for the States to meet the frivolous comments of J. P. Morgan, Harold heard a rumour that the Conservative Member for Sevenoaks, Sir Edward Hilton Young, was about to be made a peer, as indeed proved to be the case. He asked Vita to inform the leading people in the local Conservative Association that he might submit his own name as a candidate in Hilton Young's place. He ultimately did so, but was not adopted. While he was away he received a cable from Bruce Lockhart asking if he would give a definite reply to a renewed offer from the *Evening Standard* to return to the Londoner's Diary. He replied in the negative.

On the 19th June Harold wrote in his diary a revealing analysis and assessment of his abilities and ambitions. It was sparked off by his friend Christopher Hobhouse telling him that he had not got a political mind. He was too fastidious and too critical to have a burning faith in democracy. Harold admitted that Christopher was right. Then the same day another friend told him that Michael Sadleir, Harold's publisher, had mentioned that Harold would live as one of the leading writers of his time. The two remarks made to him within a few hours of each other set Harold pondering. Christopher's, which he believed to be true, suggested to him that perhaps his desire to enter politics was not supported by political ambition or aptitude. Michael Sadleir's, which he did not believe, urged him to devote his life to his Proust-like *magnum opus*. But he realised that he had not enough confidence in his literary powers. And it was this lack of confidence that was pressing him to enter politics as a distraction from a probable failure to achieve greatness in the literary field. The two remarks filled him with perplexity and aroused doubts in his mind which he never resolved. 'How little,' he complained, 'one knows oneself.' Only recently he had said to Vita, 'One should not worry about being oneself. One should flower spontaneously like the anemone japonica. Only it is a bore when one would like to produce great lotus flowers to burst into little senseless pointless buds.'[44] Harold's mistake was that he did not heed the advice of both Hobhouse and Sadleir.

Harold told Bruce Lockhart that he was disappointed in having, at forty-eight, no place in public life. He did not want to be a journalist. He could not get into Parliament. He would like to go back to the Foreign Office, and wondered how he could best set about it. He even contemplated – he was so depressed – applying for the post of Office librarian. Lockhart told him to aim high, and write to his friend George Clerk, asking for an assistant under-secretaryship at least. This he did not do.

Once again Harold had to make a brief visit to the States because of the Dwight Morrow book. This time he took Ben with him on the *Normandie*.

There are some fifty *liftiers* in bright scarlet who look like the petals of salvias flying about these golden corridors, [he wrote to Vita[45]]. That is the essential effect, gold, lalique glass and scarlet. It is very gay but would drive me mad after a week.

They stayed at Deacon Brown's Point, Maine, where Harold went through the proofs with Morrow's widow. Few corrections were needed. Betty Morrow was absolutely happy because the New York literary agent had told her that it 'was a great work about a great man', which 'assuredly will pass into literature'. Charles Lindbergh too was full of praise. 'What beats me,' he told Harold, 'is how a Britisher could have got the American scene so absolutely correct. I could not have believed that the book was not written by an American.'[46] And he extended to Ben the coveted invitation of piloting him in his little scarlet aeroplane over the sea and the islands. Ben accepted the privilege with his customary nonchalance and lethargy.

The threatened invasion of Abyssinia by Mussolini in August made Harold feel more than ever out of things. It provoked him to ask Lancelot Oliphant privately whether he stood a chance of being allowed back into the Foreign Office. Oliphant bluntly told him that his chances were small; that some of the best ambassadors were having to be retired; and that his record since 1930 would not be a recommendation.

Harold's lack of self-confidence at this time was not mitigated by the receipt of six letters of raving fulmination from Ezra Pound. He had reviewed in the *Daily Telegraph*[47] a book by Pound, entitled *Jefferson and /or Mussolini*, an attempt to draw a parallel between the Italian dictator and the prophet of American democracy, on the preposterous grounds that the two heroes both disliked machinery (which was untrue of Mussolini, because he loved it) and both placed order above liberty (which was untrue of Jefferson who did nothing of the sort). 'Jefferson,' Pound wrote, 'was one genius and Mussolini was another. I am not putting in all the steps of my argument, but that don't mean that they aren't there.' Harold's rejoinder was that it did mean that they weren't there and that their absence destroyed any validity which Pound's argument might contain. He concluded that the book was confused rubbish and one of the silliest he had ever read.

Pound's letters,[48] typewritten with many autograph emendations, were couched in an abusive and scatological vein. 'My dear Nicholson, or masta 'Arold, It is a pleasure to be called confused in a paper like The Telegraph which is hired to lie,' one of the milder letters began in defence of his book. 'The bleeders of England DO NOT want justice at all,' and 'It is the grovelling cowardice of the governing class! The things you blokes WILL NOT FACE that is so disgusting' were merely the random jibes of an unstable Fascist mind. But descending from relatively mild condemnation of the privileged classes, international Jewry and usury, the letters became those of a madman.

May hell shit on all Edens (son of the he/bitch that tried to do down Whistler, rotten stock, Sassoons, assoons, Beckett shops, etc . . . For 14 years there wasn't a daily paper in your buggerd country that wd/

have TRIED to print as fair a statement on economics – MY KHIYIST wot a Kuntry! . . . It's not yr damn fyce I want to kick it is yr/intellect, if you've got one.

When Harold went to stay with Victor Cunard in Venice at the end of August Vita wrote warning him that Pound was also in the city. She advised him to avoid a meeting or the enraged American poet might well challenge him to a duel. Harold in heeding the warning plunged into Venetian dissipations, and his published diaries contain a vivid description of a drunken party held in the Palazzo Vendramin.[49] 'The whole of Venice,' he wrote soberly the following day, 'seems given over to water melons, either gashed into rubicund half-moons, or round and cool and green.' The barges were laden with peaches. The evenings were still, and there were great orange slabs of sunlight upon the houses. 'The beauty of Venice,' he told his son Ben, 'is a constant restorative to all the moral and intellectual squalor to which it gives rise.'[50] He and Victor spent one glorious evening at the Malcontenta, that forlorn and haunting villa on the Brenta, surrounded up to the garden walls by factories and belching flares from oil pipes.

The rooms are architecturally superb but sparsely furnished . . . The remains of frescoes stand out chalkily from the whitewash, and long candles began to stab the vaulting. There was a slight smell of drains about the place and every fifteen minutes a brightly lit tram would scream round the corner and clatter past the portico on the other side of the canal but only 30 yards away. More candles were lit in the great rooms opening on the portico, but we continued to sit out there looking down upon the canal waiting for the sudden scream and clatter of the tram and drinking cold tea with mint in it . . . As darkness descended the perfect proportions of the villa became enhanced and the architecture acquired so intensive a humanism that no trams or factory chimneys could intrude. There is a grave gaiety, a light seriousness about Malcontenta . . . which left me in a very humanistic mood.[51]

He was back in England by mid-September. Disquieting things were happening in Europe. On the 2nd October Italy invaded Abyssinia. Harold felt more restless and at a looser end than before he went to Venice. Then on the 3rd October the telephone rang at Sissinghurst. Lord De La Warr, who was Chairman of the National Labour Party and a cousin of Vita's, informed Harold that there was a fairly safe seat going at West Leicester, and asked if he would contest it. Harold said he would think it over. He did think it over, and consented. The Conservatives promised to lend him their support. By the end of the month he was adopted as the National Government candidate for West Leicester.

3

THE THREAD OF PEACE, 1935–1937

HAROLD NICOLSON was on the eve of achieving what he was always to consider the greatest triumph of his life. His election to Parliament certainly brought him supreme satisfaction. From the start he loved the House of Commons, almost with passion. It was to him more than a club. It was almost more than a home. It was a sort of elysium. He loved the Gothic setting, the endless corridors and galleries, the mock medieval frescoes, the declamatory statues and busts, the leather chairs and settees, the waxed and varnished wainscoting, the dim yellow lights and the crepuscular shadows as though one were perpetually groping in a Victorian fog. He was fascinated by the history of the building and its vivid associations with those political giants of the past, Balfour, Asquith, Gladstone, Disraeli, Palmerston and the frock-coated figures of nineteenth-century men of eminence. He felt proud and humble to be walking and sitting where they had walked and sat. When introduced to the cloak room of the House of Commons he was delighted with the peg allotted to him, dangling from which was a piece of red tape tied in a loop. 'It is through that loop that one places one's sword, such weapons not being allowed in the House,'[1] he told Vita. The policemen were respectful; the attendants in evening dress were friendly. The ringing of bells, the bustle, and the excitement were just what he relished. He felt, and was, at last in the thick of things.

But before he was able to enjoy these delights there were some distasteful preliminaries to be surmounted. Having been adopted as a National Government candidate, and having received the approval and promised support of the Conservative Party in West Leicester, there was the opposition of the Liberals – the last M.P. for the constituency having been a National Liberal who had gone over to the Socialist Opposition – and the straight Socialist candidate, John Morgan by name, to be overcome. In fact the horrible prospect of a General Election fight. This Harold simply loathed.

In the first place the electors of West Leicester were confused. They saw in Harold Nicolson a candidate standing in a Liberal constituency as a straight-forward National Government candidate without prefix or suffix, in support of a Government which was overwhelmingly

Conservative. As such he announced himself in his Election Manifesto. Moreover he was a candidate who proclaimed himself to be a Liberal by inclination, who had actually offered himself earlier in the year as a Conservative to Sevenoaks constituency, and who was tainted by close collaboration with the extremely unpopular Sir Oswald Mosley, now a professed Fascist. What were they to make of Nicolson? He struck them as a decent, affable and withdrawn intellectual, well-intentioned but ill at ease with the proletariat who made up the vast majority of the electors of this industrial zone. In the second place Harold was not a little confused himself. He found himself in a climate which to him was totally unknown and alien. He had never had experience of an industrial town or industrial workers. He was academically interested in foreign affairs, which meant little to the electors whose support he was endeavouring to enlist, and nothing about home affairs which concerned them deeply. He was an ardent supporter of both Mr. Baldwin and Mr. MacDonald. He was also an ardent supporter of the League of Nations in the stand it was adopting against Mussolini's invasion of Abyssinia. The Labour Party under Mr. Attlee's guidance was less enthusiastic about the imposition of sanctions against Italy and what it saw in its blinkered fashion as the first slippery slope to war.

Harold was truly in a muddle. To add to his and the electors of West Leicester's perplexity the London headquarters of the National Labour Party took it upon themselves to announce that he was standing as their candidate after he had been adopted by the constituency as plain National Government candidate. In truth Harold knew nothing about the machinery of electioneering and party manoeuvring.

> I have no idea how these things work. My knowledge of the ethics and the conventions of the whole business is as slight as if a man, sitting down to play bridge, were to ask brightly, 'Tell me, are hearts those red things like clover and do they count more than the black things shaped like spades?'[2]

What then, it may be asked, were the motives which impelled Harold to seek election? First of all it was, as has already been made clear, his desire to be playing an active part in public affairs, a desire not to be confined day in, day out, year by year, to Sissinghurst which he loved, in the company of Vita, whom he adored, but whom he knew he could not satisfy with his exclusive companionship. That was understood. Again, although he dreaded and, when it was experienced, he detested, the unavoidable battle of the hustings and hob-nobbing with the masses, he honestly believed he would be of use to his country in the dark days looming ahead. He was confident that his knowledge of foreign affairs must contribute to the deliberations of Parliament. To this extent his confidence was justified . Finally, he genuinely wished to forward the education of those masses whose company he professed to dislike. He was saddened by their ignorance. 'It just depresses me terribly. I feel so sorry for them and get a dull ache inside.'³ This attitude was not a mere expression of condescension or insincerity. On the contrary Mr. C. G. Tuthill, his parliamentary agent at West Leicester, has recalled Harold's conspicuous compassion and humanity.⁴ Once on learning that the magistrates had ordered a boy in his constituency to be birched Harold went next morning straight to Sir John Simon, the Home Secretary, begging to have the order rescinded. He was successful. Harold said to Mr. Tuthill, 'I will *not* have the children of the working class birched, or thrashed. They get plenty of cuffs and kicks as it is. On the other hand children from the public schools should be beaten because in after life they are given positions of authority, wherein they hand out punishment to other people. They will then learn to appreciate what punishment is like.' Likewise during the war he, with Richard Denman, 'got a prayer' asking for cancellation of the Order compelling children to work on the land. He was persuaded to withdraw it only by the Parliamentary-Secretary to the Ministry of Agriculture, the Labour Tom Williams, who stressed the necessity for getting in the 1942 harvest as quickly as possible.⁵ Again, he told a women's meeting in a residential district of West Leicester that the school-leaving age must be raised; and more facilities must be provided for young people when they were launched upon the world. Democracy, he said, could not survive unless people and children were given decent opportunities in life. One woman asked, 'Who is going to pay for all this?' Harold answered, 'You and I.' Other women murmured, 'But we pay for the education of our children. Then afterwards they have to compete with the scholarship children who have been educated free! Now you propose that we should pay more money for these other children.' In walking away from the meeting Harold was hot with indignation. 'Typical middle-class Tory minds!' he growled to Mr. Tuthill. 'They don't care a damn for the children of the working-class so long as their own are all right.'

The agony of canvassing and platform speaking during the month preceding the Election was made worse by his intense loneliness in unsympathetic lodgings in West Leicester. To his embarrassment and distress Vita absolutely refused to come near the place. Harold's protests and beseechings were of no avail. All October she was touring in Provence with Gwen. Harold wrote vainly begging her to visit him at least once; thereafter she need never come again. The inhabitants of West Leicester were very straight-laced. They might think he and she were divorced if she made no appearance at all.

> Yesterday I went to a whist drive. It took place in a residential district, or to be more exact at Sunny Croft, 258 Hinckley Road, Leicester. In the front room which was the size of our bathroom there were fourteen matrons and a gas stove all steaming together . . . We sat down on wicker chairs and had tea upon the card tables. Strong black tea and cakes covered with sugar and little silver confetti. Mrs. Pearce who is Chairman of the Women's Conservative Association told me that on reading that I was really Labour she cried all night.[6]

Vita was by no means tantalised by this account of the life she was invited to participate in. Harold was hurt.

> Vita says she will not come up to help me at Leicester. She contends that this is a matter of principle. I find it difficult to discover what the principle is. Gwen is equally disagreeable. Not a very pleasant visit home.[7]

Vita was upset that Harold should be hurt; and she wrote him a letter telling him so, while explaining her reasons.[8] They were sensible enough. She reminded him how they had always been in agreement that their two professional lives were to be their own affair. But it was untrue, as he maintained, that she took no interest in his career. On the contrary she had always cared very, very deeply about his writing and even his broadcasting. She rated his rare gifts far higher than he did. Moreover if she were to come to Leicester but once, this would lead to further commitments, opening of bazaars and fêtes, etc., after the Election, things which she was determined not to allow to interfere with her writing. Harold was not entirely convinced by this protestation. In his secret soul he thought her attitude was selfish and unfeeling. So in the constituency he hedged about her not coming to Leicester, pretending to his helpers that his wife was not up to it. Mr. Tuthill, and the Chairman of the Conservative Party Association, Colonel W. B. Jarvis, were infinitely sympathetic and understanding.

Indeed Vita's jealous insistence upon her independence was a basic principle of her being. Without acknowledging or even perhaps knowing it she was a pioneer of Women's Lib. Like Ethel Smyth and

Christopher St. John among friends of an older generation who had been members of the Suffragette movement, she positively flaunted her individualism. Of course it did nothing to diminish her devotion to Harold. Yet the mere mention of being treated simply as his wife drove her to fury. She gravely resented the implication that her femininity implied inferiority, and once rebuked Clive Bell for mentioning the word 'authoress' – 'It ought to be abolished from the language. Art has no sex.'[9] Fully aware of her sensitivity Harold could not refrain from teasing her about this foible. It amused him although he took it seriously. Only a few months before the Election campaign he wrote to her abroad in feigned perplexity about the awkward predicament into which her loathing of being what she called an appendage put him.

> *I have a very difficult task.* Take this addressing business. How on earth am I to address you on the envelope? If I put Mrs. Nicolson then that is an appendage and the startled clerk at the Ritz receives a smart box on the left ear and then a smarter box on the right. But if I put V. S-W – then that does not correspond to your passport and may remain on a green baize rack for years and years. I ought to have asked you about all this.[10]

For three dismal weeks Harold, unaccompanied by Vita, pursued the relentless round of electioneering – walking to the committee room, drafting leaflets, answering thousands of letters, telegrams, queries and messages of abuse; interviewing people and the press; telephoning, visiting factories and addressing meetings. He attended working men's clubs, to be heckled by Communists who, when he was off the plat-form, treated him with kindness and hospitality, as though he were a guest at Knole. He conducted his campaign with scrupulous honesty making every endeavour to prevent his supporters from doing any-thing mean or dirty against his opponents. And in all his letters he begged Vita to care what happened to him. 'I care passionately what happens to you,' she replied.

> The only thing which puts you wrong is that the things which I want to happen to you are not always the things which *you* want to happen to you, e.g. you would like to be Foreign Minister. I should like you to win the Nobel Prize.[11]

The 14th November was Election Day. Harold did not believe he stood a chance of victory. But he defeated the Socialist candidate by 87 votes. It was a narrow shave. His first thought was characteristic. 'Poor

Morgan, I must show no sign of triumph.' The thought was answered by Morgan's aggressive voice from the hall, shouting, 'I claim a recount. I claim a recount.' Of all the congratulations he received that from a reporter of the *Leicester Mercury* pleased him most. The man who had followed him to all his meetings told Harold he had lost £2. 10s. od. in bets. He had laid ten to one against him. Why, Harold asked him? 'Well, you see,' said the reporter, 'I did not believe that a man as decent as you were could ever be elected in so bitter a contest.'

Harold was in the seventh heaven. His agent averred that he gave the impression of a purring tabby cat. Harold told Vita he really had fought a straight fight and had not uttered a single word of which he felt ashamed.

The political party to which he suddenly found that he belonged numbered eight in the House of Commons. Its leader, Ramsay Mac-Donald was so exhausted by the Election in which he himself had been defeated, that for several days he could neither speak nor rise from his chair. When Harold saw him nearly a week after the event the old man was visibly in decline. Yet he was very pleased to welcome the new recruit to his exiguous flock. 'My dear Harrold, that was a grrand fight,' he said, and proceeded to talk about his party's future. 'In your hands rests the future of Tory Socialists. You eight people are the seed-bed of seminal ideas. The young Tories are on your side. Work hard. Think hard. And you will create a classless England.' The Tories, old as well as young, numbered 385 under their leader Stanley Baldwin, Prime Minister once again since June. Harold for his part truly believed that his small group might serve as a leaven of righteousness.

On his entry into the House for the first time he ran into Baldwin, from whom he asked for guiding principles for a new politician. Baldwin's advice was that a political tyro should not mind over much the attribution of false motives. The more he saw of Baldwin the fonder Harold became of him, and the more mystified. The solid, seemingly straightforward English countryman had such strange nervous tricks.

He has an extraordinarily unpleasant habit of smelling at his notes and licking the edges slightly as if they were the flap of an envelope. He scratches himself continuously. There are russet patches of rust across his head and face. And a strange movement of the head, with half-closed eyes, like some tortoise half awake smelling the air – blinking, snuffy, neurotic.[12]

Harold now met for the first time the fellow M.P. who was to become his best friend and ally in the House. Robert, or Rob, Bernays was a gentle, nervous yet stalwart man in his mid-thirties, with a stammer. He had sat as Liberal Member for North Bristol since 1931. In 1936 he was to transfer himself to the National Liberal group. He was a person of shining integrity, unassuming manners and sound views. He became a sort of self-appointed nanny to Harold when he was about to make a speech, advising him what to say and what not to say. He had a far keener understanding of the moods of the House than his friend. And Harold always sought and usually heeded Rob Bernays's advice. On the very first occasion of their meeting Bernays advised Harold to lie low in the House for six months at least. This piece of advice was not followed.

In December the House of Commons was seething over the Hoare-Laval proposals to conclude peace between Mussolini and the League of Nations by conceding to the Italian dictator a large chunk of the Abyssinia he had invaded. Harold felt very unhappy about the pact. He was present when Hoare made his statement of excuses to Parliament, and he witnessed his walking out of the Chamber, humiliated, broken, and looking more than ever like Aunt Tabitha, which was Anthony Eden's nickname for him. He felt impelled by his knowledge of the subject to intervene in the debate which followed. He delivered his maiden speech. His theme was that Parliament ought to care more about the spirit of the League than preservation of an intact Abyssinia. Abyssinia's territorial integrity was of little account because she had acquired large areas by disgraceful means. He then deprecated the whole procedure of the Paris talks. It was a terrible mistake to conduct affairs between Foreign Ministers. He would like to see a constitutional rule made whereby the Foreign Secretary, like the Lord Chancellor, might not leave the country without a vote of both Houses of Parliament. Diplomacy by conference was a mistake. He lamented that this particular conference had been carried out in 'the foetid saloons of the Quai d'Orsay'. He begged the Prime Minister for an assurance that the future handling of this situation would be carried out at Geneva, and not behind the back of the League.

The theme propounded by Harold was one which he was to expatiate upon over and over again – in his book *Diplomacy* (1939), in speeches and numerous learned articles.[13] It was a theme which he had learned from experience and close observation while in the Service. His maiden speech was a great success. Even *The Times* next day called it an attractive speech. Members who had listened gave it warm praise. He received many congratulations. Chips Channon corroborated its generally favourable reception.[14] Harold knew that the speech would have been even better had he been less nervous. Yet he felt that he had won his spurs.

The year 1935 ended on a note of exaltation. Harold was at last in Parliament. He had made his first contribution to an important debate. His book *Dwight Morrow*, which had come out in October, was receiving fulsome praise from the critics. By general consent it was considered less diverting than his previous books. That was hardly surprising, for the subject was not one to interest the average British reader. Yet a clever young contemporary historian, Derek Drinkwater,[15] sees in the book a major diplomatic biography, an extension of the trilogy of *Lord Carnock*, *Peacemaking* and *Curzon* into a tetralogy, as illustrating the function of the 'new' diplomacy, of which the change in pattern had been set by Morrow himself.

Harold however maintained that *Dwight Morrow* was the worst book he wrote. Having been in a sense a command performance, it was as such uninspired.

As for Vita, her refusal to cooperate in his Election campaign had been forgiven. On the 16th December Harold wrote to her that no person had ever been more loved so 'gaily' as she was loved by him. 'But you do not believe all that,' he concluded, 'since what you like is PASSION and not spent in the least. Real good Triana jealousy and knives. That's what Mar likes. Anything else is just your old armchair.'

At the beginning of January 1936 Charles and Anne Lindbergh, with their surviving baby son, fled to England to avoid intolerable persecution by the American press. Harold met them at Southampton. He considered that the precautions to avoid our press were exaggerated. He was not allowed to meet them on board the *Bremen*. They disembarked into a special tender and were spirited away to a remote wharf where they were bundled into a large Rolls Royce. Harold having by then joined them, they motored to Winchester where they lunched, unrecognised, in an hotel. For several weeks they took refuge in Anne's brother-in-law's house in Wales. But they wanted to find a house, relatively remote, for more permanent residence. The Nicolsons offered them Long Barn. Harold invited them to luncheon in the House of Commons, and got Megan Lloyd George to meet them. 'Harold, twinkling and bustling,'[16] conducted them round the House. Then they discussed Long Barn. Harold took care not to over-gild the lily. He merely said it was a very happy place, which just comes out and jumps all over you like a spaniel. The Lindberghs lost no time in inspecting it. They fell for it, finding it secluded and peaceful. Anne particularly loved its crooked, rambling, tipsy floors and slanting walls, the old-fashioned furniture and the zinnia-coloured tapestries. They agreed to rent it for two years. In March they moved in, re-arranged all the furniture and made the rooms, in the Nicolsons' eyes, perfectly hideous.

Their first meeting with Vita, which had been somewhat dreaded, passed off satisfactorily. Vita was wearing what Anne Lindbergh described as riding trousers (*jodhpurs*) and a kind of velvet doublet. She was natural and easy. But she made Anne feel 'curiously feminine, terribly frivolous and feminine, and half the time as if she weren't a woman at all.' During their tenure of Long Barn the Lindberghs and the Nicolsons at first met frequently. Harold was charmed by Charles's diffidence and naiveté, his stories of apotheosis from a simple aviator to a world hero, and his different receptions by heads of state. When received by George V at Buckingham Palace, there was a Lord who told Lindbergh that the King wished to see him alone. He was con-ducted into a room where the King was standing. Having bowed the aviator was told to sit down. 'Now tell me, Captain Lindbergh,' the King asked breathlessly, 'there is one thing I long to know. How did you pee?' Lindbergh explained that he had an 'aloominum container', which he dropped overboard when he reached France. Soon Harold became increasingly disturbed by Lindbergh's impression of German military strength, his pessimism and advice that England should espouse Germany's cause against the decadent French and Communist Russians. The fact was that the murder of his child and his persecution by the American press had led him to despise and detest democracy. He came to believe too that England was effete. When his views turned openly pro-Nazi Harold lost sympathy with him altogether; and when during the war his propaganda became outrageous he wrote a letter of strong protest to Mrs. Morrow, and an even stronger article in the *Spectator*.

Harold plunged into work on behalf of the National Labour Party. He edited the Party's News Letter. He rushed to Ross and Cromarty to support Malcolm MacDonald in a bye-election, Malcolm having like his father lost his seat at the General Election. Ramsay was without delay returned to the House as Member for the Combined Scottish

Universities whereupon he invited Harold to be his Parliamentary Private Secretary. Harold declined on the ground that were he to accept his freedom of action in the House would be curtailed. Ramsay was hurt. Instead Harold consented to help as General Organiser of the Party and to see Ramsay for consultation every day at 12.30 when the House was sitting. Already he and Lord De La Warr were of opinion that now the Tories had worked to get both MacDonalds back into the House there was no future for the National Labour Party. Also, so long as Ramsay remained at the helm, it would never forge ahead.

The month of January 1936 was one of anxiety and mourning. While Harold was at Dingwall in Scotland electioneering for Malcolm Mac-Donald he learned that Rudyard Kipling and King George V had died within two days of one another.[17] On the 23rd he witnessed together with his fellow-Parliamentarians the inauguration of the late King's lying-in-state in Westminster Hall.

> Six huge guardsmen with bared heads carry the coffin which slips quite easily on to the catafalque although its Royal Standard gets caught for a moment underneath it. The officer in command straightens the Standard, clicks his heels and marches off the steps which raise the catafalque. The coffin remains there, just a wreath of flowers and the crown, its diamonds winking in the candle-light.[18]

It was then that he noticed something wrong and inauspicious. The Maltese Cross was missing from the top of the imperial crown, having fallen off during the procession from Trafalgar Square and been deftly retrieved by a Company Sergeant Major. The same thought flashed across the minds of Harold and the new King Edward VIII. In Edward's Memoirs[19] (written fifteen years before the appearance of the *Diaries and Letters*) he wrote that the fall of the Cross 'seemed a strange thing to happen; and, although not superstitious, I wondered whether it was a bad omen'. Harold wrote that it was a 'terrible omen'.

On the 27th of the month Gwen had a serious operation. Vita, much upset, took a room near the nursing-home and remained with her while she regained consciousness. Gwen suffered great pain, but recovered. On the 30th Lady Sackville died in her house, White Lodge, at Roedean. The strangely disturbed and disturbing spirit was at last presumably at rest. A week later Harold and Lady Sackville's secretary, Cecil Rhind, hired an engine-driven fishing smack with two sailors and chugged into an angry sea opposite White Lodge. The engine of the smack was turned off; the two sailors and Cecil Rhind stood up and took off their caps. Harold, kneeling by the gunwale, emptied the ashes into the sea, saying as he did so, 'B. M., all who love you are happy that you should now be at peace. We shall remember always your beauty, your courage and your charm.' It was a fitting farewell. But unfortunately there was an anti-climax to these pious obsequies. A gust of wind blew some of the ashes back into Harold's face. During his return journey to London in the train he found himself shaking his greatcoat free of his mother-in-law's remains. Even in death she gave tit for tat. Lady Sackville left legacies to her two grandsons, enabling them to be independent. Vita at the same time inherited the money which had been settled on her. It amounted to £5,000 a year gross. The Nicolsons, with this inheritance and what they earned between them, were henceforth relatively rich.

Meanwhile the likelihood of another war with Germany was of grave concern to a minority of far-seeing Members of Parliament. Count Albrecht Bernstorff, Counsellor at the German Embassy under Ambassador von Neurath, and a friend of Harold, begged him and his House of Commons friends to use all their influence to prevent Great Britain identifying herself too closely with modern Germany. This perspicacious and extremely courageous diplomat was outspoken in his contempt of Hitler. The man must, he declared, be stood up to at once, before he got too powerful, and he would collapse.[20] In February Anthony Eden told Harold he was prepared to make great concessions to German appetites provided Germany would sign a disarmament treaty and join the League of Nations; after which no further concessions of any kind must be countenanced. Harold associated himself wholeheartedly with Eden's attitude. On the 27th February he gave a brilliant address to the Foreign Affairs Committee of the House of Commons. It won commendation from Chips Channon who wrote, 'It was shrewd but alarming and we almost heard the tramp-tramp of the troops. Harold predicted that the trouble would come from the German source in 1939 or 1940.'[21]

Sure enough Hitler was now set on the predatory course from which he never wavered. On the 7th March he denounced the Locarno Treaty of 1925 and entered the Rhineland zone. For a year he had been preparing for this military gamble against the advice of his generals and the financiers, and he got away with it. From this date Harold's resolution to oppose appeasement in all its forms, and to adhere to whichever political section in the Commons agreed with him, was firmly arrived at. Already the leader of that section appeared in Winston Churchill. More and more Harold was influenced by Churchill's attitude that

Hitler must be checked before it was too late. On the other hand he knew that the mood of the majority of the House was fear. On all sides he heard exclamations of sympathy with Germany. 'There is not going to be a war,' he wrote to Vita. 'Only humiliation and rancour.'[22] Churchill, Eden and Lloyd George made statements to the effect that we should refuse to negotiate with Germany until she evacuated the Rhineland; and that it was essential to demonstrate that treaties could not be torn up with impunity. The lobbies of the Commons were buzzing with Members enlisting signatures to different resolutions, no war at any cost, and honour at all costs. Vita's attitude at this time was typical of the average, peace-loving citizen. 'I am glad about there not being war. It may be neither heroic nor noble to be glad, but I prefer not to think of Hadji being bombed in the House of Commons, or Sissinghurst destroyed from the air.'[23]

The French, gravely disconcerted by the craven attitude of the House of Commons, regarded us as traitors in that we would not commit ourselves to fight for France. At a meeting of the Foreign Affairs Committee Harold protested that we were bound by honour morally to stand by France and Belgium. Furthermore, he firmly believed that, if the crisis arrived, Britain would honour her guarantee to protect France, Belgium and possibly Holland. But he warned his friend, Roland de Margerie,[24] not to expect Great Britain to commit herself to protect any other State than these. He did not believe it was possible to convince the British public of the necessity, so great was their aversion from the risk of involvement in another European conflict.[25]

On the 22nd March Harold went to Brussels to address the Anglo-Belgian Society on diplomacy and public opinion. He spoke for one hour, first in French, and then in English. He received high praise for the liveliness with which he discussed, as in conversation at a London club, this dry subject. Before the ordeal he was received by King Leopold III in Laeken Palace. He was struck by the charm, good looks, apparent sadness and loneliness of the royal widower of thirty-four. He advanced gaily across a long strip of carpet, stopped, bowed, advanced and grasped the young man firmly by the hand. After some polite introductory remarks by the King, such as, 'But you look scarcely older than I am!' Harold, always susceptible to compliments from the young and handsome, was determined to put his royal host at ease. He talked to him about Eton where he had been educated, whereupon Leopold lost his shyness, 'and laughed in a pathetic little way like a faint dash of sunshine through a mist of rain'. And they discussed education. Then, back to Eton, and the King said he had made many friends there, including Eddy Sackville-West who looked like a little mouse, but now it was so difficult to see them. And he sighed.

On the 26th March Harold spoke after Eden and Sinclair to a packed House of Commons and crowded gallery in the debate on the European situation. His theme was that pro-Germanism in England was only apparent when Germany was not weak. Whereas Britain had not helped Stresemann's and Brüning's struggles to save an insecure Liberal Germany, now that Germany was totalitarian and strong we were saying, 'Heil Hitler!' We might disagree with the French over many things, yet they would never be our enemies. Besides we should always remember that their minds were sharper than ours. In 1914 we shilly-shallied. That must never happen again. We must not run away from Locarno. We must let Europe know what we intended to do; and assure France that we would come t ɔ her assistance with our armed forces in the West, but not in the East. The speech was commended by the next speaker, Lloyd George, who said that Harold had a healthy acquaintance with our Foreign policy in Europe. *The Times* conceded that the Speech had made an impression.

By the end of 1935 the Prince of Wales had for about two years been deeply attached to Mrs. Ernest Simpson, a lively and well-born American woman married to a London shipping broker as her second husband. While recognising more than most the nervous exhaustion under which he laboured, Harold had always entertained a certain reserved admiration for the heir to the throne (the Prince in his turn liking Harold, whom he described in his memoirs as having been a mutual friend of Mrs. Simpson and himself). Harold had met the Ernest Simpsons at Sibyl Colefax's on various occasions in 1935, sometimes in the company of the Prince. 'One finds him modest and a good mixer,' he wrote of the Prince after one such meeting in December 1935. 'He talks a good deal about America and diplomacy. He resents the fact that we do not send our best men there. He knows an astonishing amount about it all.'

Harold did not care for the conventional Mr. Simpson. Nor did he find himself personally in sympathy with Mrs. Simpson's somewhat hedonistic and unintellectual social world, but on the whole he found her an estimable character and a good influence on the Prince. On the 13th January 1936 he was invited by Sibyl to see Noël Coward's *Tonight at Eight-Thirty* at the Phoenix Theatre. When he and she met before the play she disclosed that the other guests were to be the Prince and Wallis Simpson. On the little party entering the auditorium Harold was somewhat discomfited to find the seat next to his occupied by the Prince's former favourite, Lady Furness. Afterwards the party had supper at the Savoy. Harold called Mrs. Simpson 'bejewelled, eyebrow-plucked, virtuous and wise. I had already been impressed by the fact that she had forbidden the Prince to smoke during the entr'acte in the theatre itself. She is clearly out to help him.' The Prince himself was 'extremely talkative and charming. I have a sense that he prefers our sort of society to the aristocrats or to the professional highbrows or politicians.' But walking home Harold felt sad. And why did he feel sad? It was surely because Mrs. Simpson was keeping the Prince away from the sort of people he ought to be consorting with; and because the Prince was in a mess and out of tune with his environment.

In April Harold was invited by Mr. and Mrs. Simpson to dine at their flat in Bryanston Court. The King, which the Prince had now become, was present. He sat between Lady Oxford and Mrs. Simpson, and talked to them exclusively. He did not leave till 1 o'clock in the morning. Harold remarked that 'Something snobbish in me is rather saddened by all this. Mrs. Simpson is a perfectly harmless type of American, but the whole thing is slightly second-rate.'

On the 10th June he met the King and Mrs. Simpson again at the last dinner-party which the recently widowed Lady Colefax gave in Argyll House, Chelsea, before selling it. After dinner numerous guests drifted in to hear Artur Rubinstein at the piano. He played Chopin. King Edward endured three performances of the great virtuoso's playing with politeness but no enjoyment. When Rubinstein was about to embark upon a fourth piece the King advanced to him, held out his hand and said, 'We enjoyed that very much, Mr. Rubinstein.' He then said good-night all round, and was preparing to depart when Noël Coward went to the piano and began strumming and singing, 'Mad dogs and Englishmen.' Whereupon the King resumed his seat. This behaviour did not enhance his reputation among the intellectuals present, including Princess Edmond de Polignac, for caring for serious music.[26]

As the summer wore on and persons in high positions became aware how serious was the King's friendship with Mrs. Simpson, there was perturbation. In July Ramsay MacDonald spoke to Harold of what he described as the King's appalling obstinacy in sending his mistress to Ascot in a royal carriage, and of the unfortunate court circulars in which her name repeatedly featured. He contended that if she were a widow it would not matter. 'The people of this country do not mind fornication,' he said, 'but they loathe adultery.'[27] Harold's attitude was turning to one of distress. On the whole he liked Mrs. Simpson but it irritated him that 'that silly little man *en somme* should destroy a great monarchy by giggling into a flirtation with a third-rate American.'[28]

In striking contrast to the hot-house surroundings, the arum lilies and orchids, the butlers in livery and maids in print dresses, and the somewhat brassy and artificial New World atmosphere exhaled by Mrs. Simpson's entourage, were those of the Soviet Embassy in Kensington Palace Gardens. Ivan Maisky had been Russian Ambassador since 1932. During a further seven years stint in London Harold got to know him well, and even to like him. He had frequent interviews and meals with him. Maisky was perhaps the last Soviet Ambassador to a western country with whom it was possible to conduct friendship on mutual cultural terms. Harold gave one of his most observant and penetrating sketches in a letter, which described his first luncheon party with Maisky on the 6th April. Everything about the Kensington Palace Gardens house was horribly grim.

> The door was opened by a gentleman in a soft collar and a stubby yellow moustache. I was ushered into a room of unexampled horror where I was greeted with effusion by Mr. Maisky the Ambassador, Mr. Pavloff the Counsellor, Mr. Vinogradoff the first Secretary, and the correspondent of *Pravda*.

The other guests were Lord Camrose, the editor of the *Daily Telegraph*, and the Foreign Editor of the *Daily Mail*.

> What a foolish thing to have done to have asked us in a bunch like that! We stood in this grim ante-room while we were given corked sherry, during which time the man with a yellow moustache and a moujik's unappetising daughter carried tableware and bananas into the room beyond.
>   We then went into luncheon, which was held in a winter-garden, more wintry than gardeny. We began with caviare, which was all to the good. We then had a little wet dead trout. We then had chicken in slabs surrounded by a lavish display of water-cress. We then had what in nursing-homes is called 'fruit jelly'. There was vodka and red wine and white wine and curaçao. Maisky filled his glass with each

separate form of liquor but never drank anything but water. Why did he do this? Was it to manifest his self-control, or to put us at our ease, or to show the lavish temperament of the commissar? I sat next to Vinogradoff who has an inferiority complex. I asked him if he was any relation of the celebrated professor of that name. 'We have in Russia,' he answered, 'no genealogies.' 'Yes, but surely you must know whether a person is your uncle or not?' 'We take no interest in such matters.' What a good idea! Such a help it would be to Jessica and Piers [Harold's St. Aubyn niece and nephew]. During the whole meal, I felt that there was something terribly familiar about it all. It was certainly not the Russia of my memory. And then suddenly I realised it was the East. They were playing at being Europeans, just as Djemal and Kemal used to play at it. They have gone oriental. The propaganda which the Ambassador tried to put across was childish to a degree. One felt sorry for the little beast.[29]

On closer aquaintance Harold was able to have perfectly frank discussions with Maisky, who found him safe as well as sympathetic. They exchanged gifts of books. During the war Harold often succeeded in eliciting explanations from the Ambassador of Stalin's cryptic movements, and Russia's ambivalent attitude towards Britain.

During the summer session Harold Nicolson played the most active role in his ten years' membership of the House of Commons. Because the main preoccupation of Parliament was foreign affairs he was frequently on his feet in the Chamber. His views were listened to with interest and respect. He took part in a debate on the 23rd June on Britain and sanctions. He applauded Eden's courage in abandoning the sanctions which he had previously imposed on Italy. Sanctions were an emotion, not a policy, he said, and certainly not a deterrent. Only force could restrain aggressive action; and he supported Eden in pledging himself to restore to the League the plenitude of its powers. James Maxton, the I.L.P. Member, retorted that Harold's proposals were Utopian, futile and illogical; and he described Harold as a dancing dervish going round and round the Treasury bench. On the other hand Eden was grateful for his speech, and Chamberlain and Baldwin expressed pleasure.

On the 29th Harold was urgently summoned back to the Commons from Chatham House, where he was billed to give an address, in order to support Duff Cooper, who was being taxed by the Opposition for having, while in Paris, encouraged the French to rely upon British armed intervention in the event of war with Germany. While claiming that Duff Cooper merely meant to impart sympathy and encouragement to the French who were undergoing a moment of great internal stress, he once again deplored the dangers of diplomacy by personal mission of Ministers overseas. It was the first speech Harold made in which he was seriously interrupted – and by Lloyd George too. He wrote to Vita that his speech had been a *succès de scandale*.[30] He was thought audacious. The letter provoked a reply[31] from Vita which shows that she followed his activities closely, and was able to proffer wise advice. She cautioned him not to let Members have reason for thinking him unbalanced. Considered judgment was what counted in the long run. It was what won respect in public life, not brilliance and wit, which he had in abundance. He should build his house first, and then add the ornamentation.

Harold continued to work at high pressure. He paid a flying visit to Paris in order to reassure the Under-Secretary Pierre Viénot, a French politician he greatly respected, that parliamentary opinion in Britain was swinging away from Germany. He was made Vice-Chairman of the Foreign Affairs Committee. He worried about Germany, agreeing with Winston Churchill's views that we were then strong enough to defend ourselves and should therefore organise a coalition against her in the shape of the League. He worried about the outbreak of the Spanish Civil War, which would mean the division of Europe into left and right and would fortify the pro-German and anti-Russian tendencies of the Tories at home.

In August 1936 he met a young friend and Balliol contemporary of his son Nigel, whom he took to immediately and to whom he remained deeply attached. James Pope-Hennessy was not yet twenty. He was very attractive if not strictly handsome. He had abundant raven black hair, a pale complexion, large protuberant brown eyes and an alert expression. He was bright, observant, mischievous and amusing. His charm was annihilating. The younger son of Major-General and Dame Una Pope-Hennessy he had been brought up in Catholic intellectual circles. But he had no money; and he wanted to leave Oxford and get a job. Harold was, to James's acute intelligence, the obvious person to find him one. They met often and started a prolonged correspondence, which at once assumed an intimate, mutually teasing quality. In spite of the disparity of ages their friendship was absolutely unaffected by the generation gap. Each was perfectly frank with the other. James, whose friendships were apt to be erratic and staccato – he quarrelled with and dropped those nearest and dearest to him with lightning rapidity – remained, if not consistently loyal, then consistently devoted to Harold. When he trumped up a grievance against Harold he expressed it brutally to his face. Harold unashamedly loved James without being under any illusions about his standards, ethical, moral, political or social. He always forgave James for the most outrageous behaviour, for he was too kind to do more than gently reprimand him. In fact he spoilt him more than any other of his young friends. He lent him money which he could seldom afford (and which was never repaid), got him out of scrapes, encouraged his writing which he admired unstintedly, and lavished praise when often criticism would have been more fitting.

Having failed to get his new young friend a job in the National Portrait Gallery Harold was directed by James to make enquiries on his behalf with the Foreign Office. Would not the Diplomatic Service be a suitable career for someone with his protean gifts? 'My dear James,' Harold wrote on the 12th October in that vein of semi-seriousness, semi-badinage, which characterised all his letters henceforth:

> James could easily get into the Foreign Service irrespective of family budgets were he not James. That's where the snag comes. A lazy little beast. That's what he is. And the shame of it, that my son should have such a friend, sends the blood coursing to my cheeks.
>
> Seriously James, you may want a life like Harry Cust. What a thing to want. He was a man of independent income, extreme brilliance, looks in comparison to which your face is just a sad little muzzle, enormous energy, vast erudition and the immense privilege of living in the nineteenth century. In spite of these advantages he put an innocent girl into the family way and died (if I may say so) of drink.[32]

James was not fooled into supposing that these admonitions were serious. As things turned out he worked – for a short time – in a publishing firm. But his ambition had always been to write, and it was by writing that he achieved distinction. In 1940 he won the Hawthornden Prize for his first book, *London Fabric*. By then the Army beckoned. But what regiment was he to join? Again Harold was called upon for advice. 'Does the idea of a kilt,' he answered, 'produce the ground-swirl of the perished leaves of hope?'[33]

It was in August also that Harold began his book, *Helen's Tower*. He wrote to James Pope-Hennessy from Sissinghurst that he was trying to write two chapters a week, at ten hours each day. For relaxation he bathed in the lake every morning and gardened for an hour every evening, while eschewing all wines, spirits, starches, sugars and fats, with the result that he looked and felt exactly as he did a month ago. The book, ostensibly autobiographical in accordance with the *magnum opus* project of 1934, virtually amounted to a life of his uncle by marriage, the 1st Marquess of Dufferin and Ava. In order to revive his memories of Lord Dufferin's house, Clandeboye in County Down, where he had spent so many of his school holidays, Harold went to Ireland at the end of the month. He was the guest of his cousin Basil, the 4th Marquess, of whom he was very fond.

Yet the visit was more melancholy than pleasurable. He found the house rather dolled up since the old days, the drab lincrusta having been scraped from the walls and smart papers substituted. In other respects it was much the same. There were still the armorial bearings and the Greek gods, and the gaunt plate glass windows, through which one gazed upon the heavy green park trees. He wrote to Vita:

> The whole place is peopled for me with 'des voix chères qui se sont tues', or even if they have not been hushed have ceased to be happy voices . . . All of which gives one a sad sense of the mutability of human nature as compared with the immutability of the unorganic . . . And yet everything Clandeboye [once] meant to me has disappeared beyond capture, and it now seems a muggy, ugly place entirely hedged in by damp overgrown trees.

He was obsessed by the transitoriness of human life and the fallibility of memory.

> This à la recherche business is not really much fun when the *temps* is as *perdu* as all that . . . It is strange [he went on] how patchy the memory is. I could put my hand on most books in the library here and yet I get slightly muddled about passages. The books also are strangely familiar. A two-volume life of Don John of Austria stirs memories in me like the smell of some old cupboard . . . I shall be glad to get away from this cemetery of dead associations . . . I feel as if I had been very frightened and had lost all my self-confidence and bounce.[34]

Analysing on his return his acute depression at Clandeboye he decided that it was caused by the twenty-five years which had passed since his last visit, the gap representing the peak of his life, whereas now he was descending to the deep valley of late middle age, which he could not expect to be sunlit.

Harold had not been home for three weeks before he left, rather reluctantly, to stay with Chips Channon and his wife Lady Honor at Schloss St. Martin, Im Innkreis, Upper Austria, which they had rented from the Arco Vallées. From the station he was driven in Chips's grey Rolls Royce through sun-bathed meadows and dense pine forests to the huge castle, with a long yellow façade and two footmen bowing at the front door. The whole tenour of the rich and luxurious establishment annoyed him. He was provoked to feel caustic and spoke his mind very freely about the Channons' seduction by the 'champagne-like influence' of Ribbentrop and the socialite Nazis they consorted with. Harold's old friend, Lali Horstmann, who was also staying, agreed with him. While Chips was recording in his diary[35] that 'dear, sentimental, hard-working, gentle Harold, who [was] always a victim of his loyalties', to the extent of refusing to pass through Germany because of Nazi rule, had just arrived to stay, Harold was writing to Vita about Chips's peculiar brand of snobbishness. It was that of a man who collected keys for keys' sake. There they hung in the corridors of his mind, French keys, English keys, American keys, Italian keys, and now a whole housekeeper's-roomful of Central European keys.

> So all is Fritzy Lichtenstein and Tutti Festitics and Windisch Grätz twins and Cuno Auersperg ('My favourite man, absolutely my favourite man!') . . . Chips calls Honor Frau Gräfin to the servants . . . Well, I suppose that's all right . . . All I know is that it would never occur to me to call you Frau Baronin.[36]

From Austria, where he had felt acutely uncomfortable in the meretricious atmosphere of Schloss St. Martin, he went to Venice to stay with Victor Cunard. He resumed writing *Helen's Tower*. He was taken to tea at the Palazzo Polignac on the Grand Canal.

> A huge *salone* with vast furniture and tapestries, and then an inner music room where the Princess [Winaretta de Polignac] was seated. There she was – all teeth and sewing machines. She started to talk to me about Mozart but I soon put a stop to that.[37]

While Vita was touring the Highlands of Scotland with Gwen in the first half of October Harold was conducting a frenzied performance of

speeches, lectures, broadcasts, attendance at public luncheons and dinners, and the taking of chairs at meetings in London and the provinces.
On a single day he gave three addresses. He was to keep up this hectic
pace of engagements throughout the year.

On the 3rd November King Edward VIII opened Parliament. 'He
looked like a boy of eighteen and did it well.' Harold was invited by
David Margesson, the Tory Chief Whip, to second the Address in
Reply to the King's Speech. This was looked upon as a signal honour
for a new Member. Miss Florence Horsburgh moved the Address. She
was the first woman to do so. Wearing a long evening gown of brown
velvet and white gloves she spoke charmingly and amusingly. She
congratulated herself that no woman had yet done it better than she,
and that she was at least making history. She was followed by Harold,
dressed in the uniform of the Diplomatic Corps hired from Moss Bros,
which did not fit or become him. He began his speech in somewhat
highfalutin' praise of his leader, Ramsay MacDonald, which at once
forfeited him the sympathy of the House. He referred to Ramsay's
peculiar vision, unsullied integrity, dignity, sturdy Scottish tradition
and faith. It provoked hoots of derision from the Labour Opposition.
After stumbling, and at one moment appearing to break down, he
recovered himself. He went on to express in a seemingly desperate
fashion a few pious hopes that Russia, Germany and Italy would show
more understanding of the British people; welcomed the assurances
that the Government's foreign policy was based, not on entangling
alliances, but on regional agreements negotiated on the Locarno model,
and sat down in complete silence. It was indeed a rambling and sad
performance. Chips Channon felt sick with embarrassment for him.
Margesson rather cruelly told him afterwards that it was no good
pretending his speech had been a success. Harold was not at once
abashed. He considered that the tribute to his discredited and unpopular
leader had been an act of courage. It certainly was that, but it was
misplaced on such a non-political occasion. The general opinion of the
House was that he had not been brave and noble, but silly and tactless.
This view was soon borne in upon him, and he came to fear that his
floater speech would prevent his getting a job in the spring when a
Government re-shuffle was due. 'Three minutes of blindness and a
ruined career!' he ruminated sadly.[38]

Harold's speech in seconding the Address to the Throne was a missed
opportunity. It was the first definite reverse he had so far suffered in the
House of Commons. He was to recover his reputation as a parliamentarian, and again to lose it after the outbreak of war. Only the toughest

Harold and Vita in her tower-room
at Sissinghurst, 1932.

2(a) l. to r.: Raymond Mortimer, Edward Sackville-West, Harold, Nigel, Vita, Ben. Photographed by Raymond's time-triggered camera, so that he could include himself in it. Sissinghurst, 1932.

(b) The rose-garden at Sissinghurst seen from the top of the tower. Harold's formal design was planted romantically by Vita.

parliamentarians push their way through reverses to the top, and remain there. Now although Harold was ambitious he was not tough; nor did the actual delivery of his speech give an impression of virility. And so he never reached the top. His maiden speech on the Hoare-Laval affair had, as we have seen, been a distinct winner. It made a favourable impact on the House in spite of coming immediately after Lloyd George's speech which was a *tour de force* of oratory in that it stirred Members to sit up and turn white. But then Lloyd George possessed the spirit of leadership. Harold did not possess that quality. He was too soft and sentimental. Nevertheless Members eagerly awaited his second speech. When it came (on the 26th March) it struck them as too like the first to be arresting.[39] The consequence was that whenever it was known that Harold was speaking the Chamber seldom filled as it filled when Churchill or Bevan spoke, even though he was generally acknowledged to be an expert on European affairs.[40] Moreover the whips, without whose regard no Member can make headway in his Party, tended to look upon him as a clever man gone astray, even as a traitor to his class. They sensed that there was something wrong with a man of his intellect and known traditionalist views belonging to a party, which in spite of its leader's defection from Labour, still paraded Labour's banner. They did not quite question his sincerity, but they considered him slightly odd in the head. They deemed him brilliant but misguided.[41]

Mr. Harold Macmillan has compared him with Arthur Balfour, in that both men were highly civilized and cultivated. But although Balfour was extremely languid he was far from soft. 'He was lethargic but he was ruthless. Unlike Harold's his spine was made of steel. He would sacrifice a friend of forty years without a murmur, without a moment's hesitation, if he decided that it was necessary to get rid of him. That was the difference. Besides Balfour did not care a damn what people said or thought about him. Harold did. He worried if he was criticized. He wanted to be liked. A fatal propensity.'[42]

At the beginning of December gossip about the King and Mrs. Simpson was building up to a crisis which exploded first in the pulpit, then in the press, and finally in Parliament. Harold was deeply distressed by the turn of events. Bruce Lockhart, his ear always close to the ground, assured Harold on the 4th that the majority of 'serious' people in Parliament, Whitehall and the City (in other words the Establishment) wanted the King to go because he had already proved himself to be irresponsible. In the days that followed society was in the throes of hysteria. Lady Colefax, in the light of what Mrs. Simpson had told her but three weeks previously, was convinced that the King had not actually proposed marriage, and rushed to ask Mrs Chamberlain to pass the information on to the Prime Minister. It was not true that the ordinary people welcomed the idea of abdication. For them the King was still the Prince Charming of his not so remote youth. Those for whom the monarchy stood as an institution inviolable and perdurable, viewed the romantic unorthodoxies of God's anointed as no excuse for toppling that representative from the throne of his fathers, and substituting another. Vita, a born romantic, wrote on the 8th: 'I really mind more than I could have believed possible.' Others, more extreme, regarded Mr. Baldwin as an arch-Puritan and little better than a regicide. Others again, no less monarchist, put the Crown's interests before those of its wearer. A leading Labour Member said to Harold, 'Thank God, we have S.B. at the top. No other man in England could have coped with this situation.' Harold was present in the House during the tense and emotional announcement of the Speaker, in a quavering voice, of King Edward's abdication, followed by Baldwin's masterly exposition of how the calamity had come about. Broken with sorrow and sympathy the Members filed out of the Chamber in deadly silence. In the corridor Harold bumped into Baldwin. 'You see, Nicolson,' he said, gripping him by the arm, 'the man is mad. MAD.' And then in an unwonted expansion of the moment, he went on:

> He could see nothing but that woman. He did not realise that any other considerations avail. He lacks religion. I told his mother so. I said to her, 'Ma'am, the King has no religious sense.' I do not by that mean his atheism. I suppose that you are an atheist or an agnostic. But you have a religious sense. I noticed it the other day (that meant my sticking up for Ramsay). You realise that there is something more than the opportune (what a good phrase that is). *He* doesn't realise that there is anything beyond. I told his mother so. The Duke of York has always been bothered about it. I love the man. But he must go.'[43]

Much the same feelings were expressed to Harold by a great friend who had been in the King's service when he was Prince of Wales, had never liked his master and now rejoiced in his fall. This courtier actually believed that Edward and Mrs. Simpson had laid plans to run away together in February, and that only King George V's death prevented it. He said the King was like the child in the fairy story who was given every gift except a soul. There was nothing in him which even understood the intellectual or spiritual sides of life. All art, music, poetry were dead to him. Even nature meant nothing, and his garden at Fort Belvedere meant nothing beyond a form of exercise. He enjoyed nothing at all except through the senses. He had no real friends for whom he cared a straw. His private secretaries had a devil of a time. He would disappear every Thursday to Tuesday to the Fort where none of them was allowed to follow. Despatch boxes were actually lost when not attended to. Even when in London he shut himself up in Buckingham Palace giggling with Mrs. Simpson for hours on end, while the royal footmen would say to the waiting secretaries, 'The lady is still there'. Harold's friend disclosed that he once told him exactly what he thought of him. 'Yes,' was the reply, 'I was not made to be Prince of Wales.'

> He was without a soul, [Harold's interlocutor kept on repeating], and this has made him a trifle mad. He will probably be quite happy in Austria. He will get a small *Schloss*; play golf in the park; go to night-clubs in Vienna; and in the summer bathe in the Adriatic. There is no need to be sorry for him. He will be quite happy wearing his silly little Tyrolese costumes (there was a note of fury at that) and he never cared for England or the English. That was all eyewash. He rather hated this country . . . and did not like being reminded of his duties.

After this somewhat hysterical tirade against the unfortunate ex-King, he added, 'The new King will be first class – no doubt about it.'[44] Thus encouraged Harold went down to the House and took his oath to King George VI.

In November of 1936 Harold reached his fiftieth birthday. Most people dislike passing this irrecoverable bourne after which no assumption of youth can ever deceive man or woman, no matter how fit and energetic the semi-centenarian may inwardly feel. Harold simply hated it. It was a deep sorrow to him. He would not have minded quite so much had he not dispersed his energies in life, and done too many different things without reaching any harbour. He was still thought of as promising, with his jaunty air, his unsuitably flamboyant tie and his carnation in button-hole. 'Fifty, filthy fifty,' he expostulated. It was a great gallows standing upon his primrose path. God didn't understand somehow that he was not intended to grow old. He was young by nature. He could not make God see that. God allowed him to get old just as if he were Lord Salisbury, which he wasn't. The appalling effrontery first struck him as he returned from a Bloomsbury party at 1.15 on a December morning. 'I am fifty,' he said to himself, and then realised that it was a jubilee and required a procession. It was difficult to organize a procession in the Strand at 1.15 a.m. when one was all by oneself. Nevertheless he walked with dignity towards Temple Bar, bowed as he imagined the Lord Mayor was handing him the keys of the City, and then walked onwards down the middle of Fleet Street, bowing again to left and right until he reached Bouverie Street, where he dismissed his escort with a wave of the hand, and returned in his black trilby hat and shabby greatcoat to the Gate of Middle Temple in Tudor Street.

1937 was a comparatively quiescent year. The dictators, temporarily hushed, were building up their military strength, whereas Great Britain was merely turning her thoughts to a gentle re-armament. The only overt evidence of the dictators' activity was the civil war in Spain.

Harold had been asked to go on a commission under the chairman-ship of the Parliamentary Under-Secretary of State for the Colonies, Lord De La Warr, to the Sudan and Uganda to report on the state of African native education, and in particular of Makarere College in Uganda. The Commission was to consist in from four to five educa-tional experts, plus Robert Bernays and himself. He accepted with alacrity. Buck De La Warr was an easy-going, extravert charmer. Rob Bernays was Harold's most intimate confidant and companion in arms in the House. Their friendship could not be on a happier basis. The task was novel and African problems were something he had never before experienced. On New Year's Day Harold and his colleagues were speed-ing across France to embark upon the *Viceroy of India* at Marseilles. Crossing the Mediterranean he wrote a chapter of *Helen's Tower*. In Cairo he spent a night at the Residency, peeped into the room which he and Vita shared on their honeymoon when staying with Lord Kitchener, and was reminded of the little pattering feet of their dog, Mikki across the floor. From Cairo the party took an aeroplane to Khartoum. Harold begged forgiveness from Vita (who was displeased) that he had broken his promise to her not to fly. He stayed in the Palace, a vast structure of three storeys built on the site of General Gordon's rather ramshackle smaller house. He stood above the loop of river where Gordon watched and waited for the relief ship which came forty-eight hours too late. He was shown by Gordon's old servant the exact spot on the steps where the General was hacked to death. From Khartoum the party flew on to Entebbe. At Ujiji they were met and entertained by Sir Harold MacMichael, the Governor of Tanganyika Territory, and a nephew of Curzon. They watched him present an ebony-and-silver walking-stick to an aged cripple who as a young man had been one of Dr. Livingstone's servants. The little ceremony took place under the very mango tree which had echoed Stanley's famous remark on greeting the Doctor. At Kampala Harold received letters from Vita. She informed him that Ben was extremely happy in his new job as an attaché at the National Gallery, and was about to share furnished rooms in Gloucester Place with me, who had moved out of the spare-room at King's Bench Walk. Vita was very concerned because our rooms at £3 a week each seemed to her 'terribly expensive'.

One evening Harold stood on the little knoll in the centre of Kampala on which fifty years before the first white man had established his stockade. Now the Catholic and Protestant cathedrals crowned the neighbouring hills. Red roads ran between neat trees and houses. There were schools, hospitals, hotels, shops, gardens and a golf course where so short a time ago was dense scrub. Harold was joined by young Africa in the shape of eight boy scouts. Darkness fell suddenly and on the edge of the earthwork the scouts lit a fire. The flames danced upon their ebony knees and smiling faces. They sang their songs and laughed gaily.[45] And yet, pleased though he was by the improvement in the natives' lot, Harold felt no affinity with the dark races, being unable to believe that civilisation existed anywhere outside western Europe.

He worked extremely hard on the Commission's Report, of which most of the recommendations were ultimately adopted. The outcome was that Makerere College became the inter-territorial and inter-racial University of East Africa, with a handsome new white building, crowned by an arcaded tower.[46]

When Harold got home to Sissinghurst he was suffering from acute mental, rather than physical exhaustion, as the result of his flying and continuous movements over the past ten weeks. Parliament was already in session. The Spanish Civil War was uppermost in the minds of politicians. He threw himself into parliamentary work and spoke in the debate on Propaganda on the 25th March, urging that we, who were naturally bad at it, should not attempt to indulge in it on totalitarian lines, but spend the equivalent money on sound British education abroad. On the 7th April he had a slight seizure, which the doctor put down to too much whisky and brandy, while attributing his chronic cough to excessive smoking. Harold dismissed his trouble as a slight *crise de foie.*

On the 14th April he was well enough to take part in the debate on the Government and Bilbao. Attlee had moved a motion deploring the failure of the Government to give protection to British merchant ships entering the port of Bilbao, which Franco was blockading. The inaction, he said, was encouragement of Mussolini's interference in Spain. The Government retorted that they were deliberately pursuing a strict policy of non-intervention. Harold in a short speech pointed out that the difficulty which had arisen was due to our not having recognised either side in the Civil War as belligerents. Franco was not able to carry Bilbao by storm – only by starvation. To provide one side with arms and deprive the other of what military advantage it might obtain by a campaign of starvation would be definite intervention. To allow British vessels to carry food to Bilbao would be assisting the Basque Government and be intervention. Intervention would provide Italy with a good excuse for tearing up all non-intervention treaties, and would merely strengthen the Fascist Powers. Attlee's motion was defeated by the Government. The Spanish Civil War worried Harold considerably. In discussing it with Lloyd George, the leonine old statesman said to him, 'If I had been Prime Minister we should still be the most powerful country in the world, and none of these crimes would have happened.' Harold considered this an arrogant thing to say, but nonetheless probably true.

On the 23rd he delivered the Rede Lecture at Cambridge, on *The Meaning of Prestige.* This important lecture was published in pamphlet form later in the year. It was prompted by a survey of the whole colonial problem which a Chatham House committee, chaired by him, was circulating. The lecture was prefaced by an analysis of the different meanings of the word *prestige* in different countries. It went on to raise a number of pertinent questions, and, without providing definite answers, left the intelligent auditor to reach the conclusions obliquely propounded. The first, formulated while Harold was on the educational mission in Africa, was this. How was a handful of unarmed Englishmen miles from the mother country to wield authority over obedient millions? Could power based upon reputation maintain itself any longer against reputation based on power? He thought not. A German's spiritual loneliness prompted him to place confidence in quantitative values, exaggerated erudition, or exaggerated force. He tended therefore to surrender his own individuality to the State. He came to regard the State with a passion that was unreasonable. His personal honour became confused with national honour. During Great Britain's years of immeasurable power she could afford to be gentle, tolerant and kind, because of her security. Now that she had lost her sense of security, should she always retain her good humour and her objectivity? Would her honesty, candour and truthfulness survive undiminished? For without them, no matter how fast Britain re-armed herself, her prestige would perish from the earth. The lecture ended as it had begun on a note of negative interrogation.

In July Harold involved himself in a sudden, quixotic and romantic escapade.[47] The Duke of Windsor and Mrs. Simpson had been married on the 3rd June. A few weeks later Stephen King-Hall told Harold that he had happened to lunch recently in an hotel at Evreux. The proprietor showed him a sheet of paper containing important personal notes written by the future Duchess during her dash to the South of France, which she had, after telephoning to the Duke at Fort Belvedere, inadvertently left behind. King-Hall remarked that the notes reflected greatly to her credit: one of them, he remembered, being, 'Think only of your own position and duties, and do not consider me.' Harold at once decided that these notes must be recovered and returned to the Duchess. So he wrote and asked for her permission to retrieve them. She readily granted it. He then wrote to his friend Roland de Margerie, First Secretary at the French Embassy in London, asking for an official letter on Embassy paper instructing all French authorities to assist him. Margerie at once supplied one. Harold left for France.

He crossed the Channel to Le Havre where he took a train to Rouen. At Rouen he hired a car and motored to Evreux. He went to the Hôtellerie du Grand Cerf and asked to see the proprietor. The man was at first suspicious lest Harold might be a member of the press, but after being shown the letters signed by the Duchess of Windsor and Monsieur de Margerie, he finally handed over the sheet of notes. Harold, with the scrupulosity peculiar to him, held the sheet at arm's length so that he might just identify the handwriting as the Duchess's without reading what it contained. Having thanked the proprietor warmly Harold walked across to the Cathedral to give thanks, and returned to lunch at the inn. The following morning he was back in London where he wrote a letter to the Duchess, returning her notes. The Windsors (and in particular – since it showed consideration for his wife – the Duke) never forgot this generous act. In their memoirs, *A King's Story*

(1951) and *The Heart has its Reasons* (1956) the Duke and Duchess, in acknowledging Harold's kindness, referred to the proprietor as a chivalrous man who knew Harold to be a distinguished man of letters. Actually this interpretation was incorrect. The proprietor had to be submitted to a good deal of persuasion before consenting to surrender the paper; and he had not the least idea who Harold Nicolson was.

On the 19th July Harold took part in the debate on Foreign Affairs. It was brought about by Parliament's anxiety over Franco's installation of howitzers, which he trained across the Straits of Gibraltar. Eden gave a long survey of world affairs, and reiterated his determination to protect British interests in the Mediterranean. Harold paid tribute to the Foreign Secretary as a man who desperately desired to prolong peace, and would best be able to preserve it. The speech was rather too long, with a protracted dissertation on the nature of democracy. Nevertheless Harold received congratulations at a luncheon party given by Lady Spears,[48] at which he sat next to Mrs. Ronnie Greville. He was always amazed how this mischievous and venomous woman managed to command the affection of so many friends. 'How comes it,' he wrote, 'that this plump but virulent little bitch should hold such social power?' Then at dinner he sat next to Margot Oxford. She was not venomous; she merely made a concatenation of gaffes. He far and away preferred her to 'Maggot Greville'.[49]

After lecturing in Cambridge to the Summer School, and in Oxford to the Examination School where he was given a guest room in Balliol next to Nigel's, which was full of his things and books – 'Oh, how I love that boy!' – and had a swim in Parson's Pleasure, thinking on his past youth and managing to conceal himself under the waters as he had seen the hippopotami do in Lake Tanganyika, Harold spent the whole of August at Sissinghurst. He worked contentedly at *Helen's Tower*, which like Vita's *Pepita* was to be published in the autumn. One afternoon Auden, looking as scruffy as ever, and Spender, looking as much like Shelley as ever, came to tea. Another day Vita was stung on the heel by a wasp. It seemed nothing at the time and they applied an onion to the sting. Five minutes later her leg flared up, swelled, and she felt queer. She was hurriedly taken to Harold's bed by Gwen. She was violently sick, had a heart attack, and lost breath. Alarmed, they sent for the doctor. By the evening she was better, but her heart-beats remained irregular for twenty-four hours. The same distressing symptoms accompanied all future wasp-stings. In October she and Gwen went on a motoring tour to the Dordogne and the Lot.

That month Harold saw himself for the first time on a film. Having dined with me he took me to the first night of the Gas Light and Coke Company's film on schools.

As a film it was superb but my appearance in it was lamentable. Suddenly on the screen was flung a shot of my committee . . . In the centre of this powerful group sat Lady Astor and Monsieur de Charlus. Lady Astor launched off into a passionate harangue which had got nothing whatever to do with school buildings. M. de Charlus could not conceal his impatience and irritation and drummed upon the table with his pencil the whole time. Then when Lady Astor paused to gain a fresh gulp of breath M. de Charlus intervened. 'Yes,' he boomed, 'we all know about that, but the point is what are we to do about bad school buildings?' It was so odd to see this mild old gentleman suddenly bursting out in rage and bellowing with the voice of a young bull, that we all laughed out loud. There was a cheer from the whole theatre. 'Jim,' I said, 'you agree that that cross old gentleman is not really like me?' 'Exactly like you,' he answered. 'Damn, damn, damn!'[50]

A fortnight later he was televised for the first time at the Alexandra Palace.

It really is an ordeal and a nervous person would not stand it . . . One is made up by a deft little lady and then one goes into a studio as vast as Paddington station, and great reflectors on trucks are manoeuvred like tanks around one and a howitzer on rubber wheels is sidled up and one is just expected to talk quite airily without a manuscript or a subject or anything but this glaring hot light between yourself and panic. I enjoyed it, because it was an experience. But it is certainly an ordeal.[51]

On the 10th November Harold on returning from his constituency by train took a taxi from the hotel. The porter, as he handed him his luggage told him that Ramsay MacDonald was dead. Harold was so shocked by the information that he ordered the driver to take him to the Central Station in Leicester instead of the L.M.S. A few days later one of the directors of Constable's invited him to write Ramsay's biography. Rather surprisingly in view of his too fulsome praise of Ramsay during his reply to the Royal Address the previous October Harold told him that he did not admire him morally or intellectually enough to justify so much labour. One could not write the life of someone for whom one did not have real enthusiasm. Affection was not enough. Ramsay's death again gave rise to Harold's disappointment that he had received no promotion. Vita's counsel that he should not be impatient provoked him to reply:

> You always say that you know nothing of politics but I should never take any important decision without consulting you, since your general principles and instincts are so sound.[52]

In December he had breakfast with Lord Baldwin in his house at 69 Eaton Square. They talked of literature and politics for an hour and a half. Baldwin spoke generously about everyone whose name cropped up, save Lloyd George, who, he said, had done his best to debauch British politics and 'had never led a party or kept a friend'. When the Lloyd George coalition broke up in 1922 he, Baldwin, and Halifax never expected to win but were determined, if they failed, to leave politics. They were convinced that Lloyd George and his cronies were degrading English public life. Baldwin felt after every Cabinet meeting that he needed 'a bath of disinfectant'. He told Harold that he was leaving the note – such a childish scribble – which King Edward sent him after the abdication, to the British Museum. There were patches in that King's brain which were those of a boy of thirteen. 'I have never enjoyed a breakfast more,' Harold concluded. 'I take back everything I have ever said against that man. He is a man of the utmost simplicity and therefore greatness.'[53]

Just before Christmas Harold was obliged to get rid of his male secretary. He had lost the man's predecessor, Charles Pulley, whom he liked, only a few months before. He was going to interview a lady secretary, a Miss Niggeman. 'I shall not engage her without much thought. No more Niggers in wood piles for me,' he wrote.[54] He did not feel over sanguine that the interview would be a success. He need not have worried. Elvira Niggeman not only consented to work for him but remained with him for the rest of his working days. She was efficient, clever, a shrewd judge of character, and quickly learned how to manage Harold without seeming to do anything of the sort. She was to become a close friend of the whole Nicolson family, and was respected and liked by all their friends.

In summing up his achievements during the past year Harold was not altogether satisfied with himself. He was conscious that his political career had suffered a decline. He did not possess enough combatant qualities to impress his personality upon the House. One good speech, he decided, might restore the reputation he had enjoyed before his unfortunate speech on the Address in October 1936. And that he was determined to bring about.

Yet he had achieved a great deal of literary work. He had published three books – *The Meaning of Prestige*, his Rede Lecture, and *Small Talk*, a collection of what he called fugitive essays, mostly culled from periodicals and broadcasts. A few appeared for the first time. *Helen's Tower*, which was published in November, was of a distinctly higher calibre than the other two. It contains some of Harold's finest writing. The passages about his childhood memories, about the five senses, about Early Victorian privileges (now things of the past), about the old St. Petersburg Embassy, about Lord Dufferin's too gentle and over-civilised character (not unlike his own) are written with sensitivity, humour and delicious irony. Yet he was not satisfied. The dust-jacket announced that the book was to be the first of a series of volumes under the title, *In Search of the Past*, with the object of recording the transition in social, political and ethical conditions; and that it was meant to be a new method of autobiographical biography. Indeed Harold hung the picture of his own childhood upon the peg of Lord Dufferin's career and character. The first chapter, in describing the little Harold's arrival at the Embassy in Paris, starts off in a nostalgic manner suggested to the author when he was conceiving his 'Great Idea' in Morocco in 1934. But the ensuing chapters do not follow in the Proustian vein, and the advertised series were not to materialise. Harold recognised this falling off at the time, and so did at least one reviewer. Harold told his son Ben before the book came out that the method which he had thought so ingenious, had failed.[55] He meant to write the life of his uncle through a child's eyes. Thus he described him as he remembered him, and that part was all right in a *Some People* sort of way. Then came those parts of him when the author had not been present, such as Canada and India, and he found himself describing the Canadian Pacific Railway Enquiry and the Oudh Rent Act much as he described the Ruhr Occupation in his Curzon book. The two manners did not coalesce, and the result was a book half a history and half a magazine article. He was of course far too self-depreciatory. Standing on its own *Helen's Tower* is, as the majority of reviewers agreed, enchanting. Desmond MacCarthy could hardly fault it. The author's humour had never played over the surface of sentiment more revealingly, nor had his sentiment blended better with his intellect and his comprehension of history.

The single reviewer who judged the book, not on its own but as part of an intended series, was Evelyn Waugh.[56] He seized upon the vaunted claims of the dust-jacket. There was nothing, he said, remotely Proustian about the venture. Proust was a literary man as only the French understood the word. His work was his life. Harold Nicolson was a man of multifarious interests, and Waugh, with exaggerated irony, saw his writing as merely a profitable recreation. He went on to say that the book gave the impression of having been tossed off rapidly between other more pressing occupations. No talent could survive such treatment. Whereas in Nicolson's former books:

> one felt that one was reading someone with an almost effortless grace of expression and humour, there is now a feeling that the writer is obliged from time to time to remind himself, 'I am writing a *book*. This is a personal possession of my own. I am working for myself. No man has hired me. I am writing for a small, critical public and for posterity.' Even so, the result is not always harmonious. Some passages are painfully slick. The opening sentence, 'At breakfast the next morning, each of the three footmen wore powdered hair.' Why 'the next'?

If Harold read this review it did not impel him to refrain from dissipating his energies (that fault for which he had so often reproached himself) and concentrate exclusively upon writing. By now he was far too gripped by the political fever. He knew that world affairs were in so parlous a state that he might even have to lay aside his pen altogether, and take up some more aggressive instrument. After all he was not, like Proust, a sensitive plant that could turn its face away from catastrophe and exhale sweet perfume from an ivory tower. When the storm actually burst Evelyn Waugh was also among the first to leave his desk and put on battle dress. Henceforth *In Search of the Past* had to surrender to bitter conflicts of the present.

4

THE BRINK OF CATASTROPHE, 1938–1939

Vita's book *Pepita*, the life story of her maternal grandmother, the Spanish peasant dancer, was no less tumultuously received than Harold's *Helen's Tower* about his uncle, Lord Dufferin. Pepita's nature, tender and passionate, protective and savage by turns, could be traced in both her daughter Lady Sackville, and her grand-daughter, Vita. Harold's pride in the conflicting ingredients of his wife's character did not abate one iota as the years went by, although they never ceased to surprise him.

> Oh my God in heaven I do love you so and you do not really care a hoot whether I do or don't. But my dearest you are the person whom I admire most in the world. That I think is really the basis. All my standards are mere firewood compared to the great trees of your ideals. I love you so, dearest. I love you dreadfully. It is very odd.[1]

It was odd, as he candidly acknowledged in a letter to Ben:

> I am not the least 'in love' with Mummy. But I love her more than anything on this earth because I respect her character and intelligence. She is not an easy wife in the conventional way. She is a difficult wife. Yet she is everything on earth to me as you know. And why?? Because although we have many tastes which are different, many activities which we do not share, essentially she and I are one. And why again? Because we are each a trifle afraid of the other. We each regard the other with deep respect.[2]

The Nicolsons were an amazingly united family. Harold had slowly come to find in his elder son a confidant, although he was never to be on quite the intimate terms he quickly established with the younger, Nigel. Gone however were the days when he feared Ben might turn out a 'rotter'. Still he never could reconcile himself to what he considered Ben's lethargy, which was really a congenital slowness, a ruminative vagueness. He mistook his total lack of *savoir faire* for stupidity. And he was to remain perplexed by Ben's left-wing propensities and his dislike of being reminded of his patrician origins. Oddly enough Vita, whom

Ben loved in his remote fashion and yet with whom he never got on very well – he was repelled by her built-in conservativeness and her pride in Knole and her Sackville blood – understood him better than did his doting if critical father. She saw in his detached soul a sort of innocence, idealism and purity which were endearing, even when most irritating.

Even so I do not think that either of his parents fully understood or appreciated Ben. Indeed his apparent coldness, aloofness, moroseness, taciturnity, not to mention his left-wing bias, were often disturbing and sometimes antipathetic to casual acquaintances whose principles, if not their conduct, were conventional. It took a long time to win Ben's intimacy. He did not wear his heart on his sleeve. He was censorious of those whom he regarded as flippant or wrong-headed, and would not bother to charm them. On the contrary his censoriousness took the form of a positive and rather rebarbative reticence. But with his own select circle he would expand in a manner which was warm and even enchanting, because of a disposition which was naturally benignant and transparently guileless. He became entertaining, amusing, amused and, when totally relaxed, among the most convivial of companions. Proof of this assertion is surely found in the number of friends who loved him for his esoteric qualities, and of acquaintances who respected his high standards, strong intellect and his fine scholastic achievements.

The consequence of Ben's guilelessness was that his parents were inclined to treat him like a child of fourteen when he was twenty-four. And it was astonishing that Ben bore his father absolutely no resentment for this treatment. For instance, when Harold learned that Ben had taken a fancy to an American girl in Florence, where he was studying art, Harold wrote pouring cold water on the attachment. The girl's letters would, Harold averred, although he had not set eyes on her, grow thinner and thinner after she returned to America, and Ben's more and more perfunctory. Vita even sent him a questionnaire about the girl. It was followed by Harold rebuking him for tampering with her feelings and – for this was the point – for not realising how desirable and handsome he, Ben, was. He assumed that the girl was his son's social and cultural inferior. When Nigel reached the same age during the Second World War and also fancied a girl the parents exchanged a flood of letters about her qualities, weighing them up to see if they would suit their younger son, regardless of the fact that all the time the young lady was engaged to somebody else. Harold actually made a list of the twenty virtues he considered paramount in a wife for Nigel.

★　　★　　★　　★

The year 1938 marked the beginning of the landslide which was to culminate in world catastrophe. It also witnessed a resurgence of Harold Nicolson's activity in Parliament. On the 12th February Chancellor Schuschnigg of Austria was summoned to Berchtesgaden, where he was bullied by Hitler into making disgraceful concessions. On the 17th Harold made a stiff upper-lip speech to the Foreign Affairs Committee, exhorting them to stand up to Mussolini and Hitler. It was well received. On the 21st Eden, the Foreign Secretary, and Cranborne, the Parliamentary Under-Secretary of State for Foreign Affairs, resigned from the Government and gave their reasons for doing so in the House of Commons. The prevailing one was an attitude towards the dictators diametrically opposed to the Prime Minister's. Theirs was uncompromising; his was conciliatory. Harold spoke to a full house in defence of Eden. He insisted that the Government before parleying ought to demand Italy's withdrawal from Spain, a cessation of her anti-British propaganda, and withdrawal of her large forces from Libya. He praised the late Foreign Secretary for his struggle to preserve the rule of law and the principles of the League of Nations. Sir Archibald Southby,[3] a Conservative diehard, deplored Harold Nicolson's spirit of non-cooperation. If that was the way in which the Hon. Member for West Leicester had conducted negotiations when he was in the Diplomatic Service no wonder he had met with failure! Southby's view fairly summarised that of the Parliamentary right wing which hated Communism so much that it was prepared to tolerate anti-British Fascism from Italy. *The Times* leader next day took the typically pusillanimous view that the Italian talks should proceed unconditionally, for if they broke down we would at any rate be no worse off than we were at present. And Chips Channon who hero-worshipped Chamberlain deprecated Harold's attack on Italy in what Chips called violent and foolish terms, thus doing the cause of peace as much harm as he could.[4] On the other hand Harold received congratulations from Lloyd George (who crossed the floor of the Chamber to shake his hand) and Winston Churchill for his courage and outspokenness; also a personal letter of thanks from Eden. The approval of these three independent statesmen was welcome compensation for the odium he had fallen into with the Government. By now Harold had absolutely made up his mind to which group in the House he was committed. When at the end of the debate the National Labour Party joined in a vote of confidence in the Prime Minister, Harold was the only one of that Party to abstain. He immediately went to his constituency to explain his conduct. He received their unqualified approval.

Disastrous events followed one another rapidly. On the 12th March Hitler presented an ultimatum to Schuschnigg to call off his plebiscite to resolve whether his countrymen were in favour of a free, independent and united Austria; and without waiting for a reply, marched into Vienna. By now the British man in the street, always slow to face up to disagreeable realities, was at last beginning to realise that future chances of negotiating with Italy and Germany seemed futile.

On the 16th March Harold took part in a debate on Spain and Intervention by Foreign Powers. He urged the Government to consider what would be the effect of a victory by General Franco on British interests and security. He made an impassioned appeal not to let Gilbraltar and the Straits slip into Mussolini's and so Hitler's control. And when the Government voted not to depart from its policy of non-intervention, Harold began seriously to question whether he could continue supporting it. He discussed his predicament with Malcolm MacDonald whom he liked and respected. MacDonald advised him to continue criticising in detail but to support the Government in general because Britain's defences were so inadequate that London could be blown to pieces in a matter of hours. Harold's dissatisfaction with the Government was not mitigated by his being asked to resign the vice-chairmanship of the Foreign Affairs Committee.

In the second half of April Harold was officially invited by the British Council to give a lecture tour in the Balkan States on such subjects as 'Are the English Hypocrites?', 'The British Empire Today', and 'The Foundations of British Policy'. The first was a subject very much after his heart, one about which he held positive views. It was a thing foreigners could not understand. And yet it was so simple. It was also important that they should understand it. The charge arose from our optimism, our laziness, our distrust of logic and our belief in instinct. 'You see,' he once told his French friend Roland de Margerie, 'Englishmen really do imagine that they are noble, just and truthful. When circumstances cause them to behave in an ignoble or insincere manner they just pretend that it has not happened. This deception is however primarily self-deception. It is what in sexual matters is called "sublimation". And what is interesting is that they really do succeed in convincing themselves.'[5] A Frenchman, and one so well acquainted with the English, and so exceptionally intelligent as de Margerie, would fathom this perplexing Anglican weakness; but could Roumanians, Hungarians and Yugoslavs be expected to do so? It was doubtful.

Sir Robert Vansittart of the Foreign Office begged Harold to bolster Balkan morale to withstand Hitler, yet warned him against making any public pronouncements. He might however speak his mind to the Kings of Roumania and Bulgaria, and the Regent of Hungary. At the same time Sir Robert confided in him that the Foreign Office did not trust Nevile Henderson, our Ambassador to Berlin. Henderson was a complete Nazi: stupid and vain, and almost hysterical. Unfortunately he could not be recalled at this sensitive juncture.

On the 11th Harold and Nigel listened to a speech by Hitler over the wireless announcing that he had been sent by God to save Germany and Europe, while the crowds howled their approval. Two days later Harold took the train to Bucharest accompanied by Nigel as far as Venice where he was to join Ben. By pre-arrangement Ben was to meet them and talk to his father while the train remained in the station at Venice. Rather typically he arrived just as the train was steaming from the platform.

In Bucharest Harold stayed at the Legation with Sir Reginald and Lady Hoare. At the station he was greeted by a battery of cameras and representatives of the Anglo-Roumanian Society and the Roumanian Foreign Office. He was worried lest the Roumanians might be attributing to his visit greater importance than it warranted. He feared they were already interpreting it as a promise of British support against Hitler, whom they held in mortal dread.

King Carol invited him to luncheon. To the consternation of the British Minister Harold had brought with him no tail coat or top hat. He was obliged to borrow both these accoutrements from his host. The coat could not be brought to button across the front. When he went upstairs to dress he felt giddy, so, remembering that he had with him a small bottle of sal volatile, he put it in a pocket of his trousers, which were his own. At the Palace he was warmly greeted by the King. Accompanied by an aide-de-camp in stays and aiguillettes, host and guest passed to the dining-room. Sitting on a pink plush chair on King Carol's right Harold ate an enormous and delicious luncheon of Roumanian dishes. They talked intelligently of current affairs, at first keeping off controversial topics. Gradually Harold edged his way to tackling the King's dictatorial powers, which he had been urged to do by the Foreign Office. The King explained the difficulties that had confronted him. It had been necessary for him to get rid of the old party politicians, a poor lot, and he hoped soon to set up three parties.

'Why three?' I asked, my mouth full of *lutchanika*, 'Your Majesty,' I added. He replied that two parties were apt to share the spoils between themselves, and a third party was necessary to restore the balance. Quite a good idea.[6]

Then Harold asked him why he did not pay one of his surprise visits to the Hungarian regions and find out how the Hungarians were really being treated. Throughout the conversation the King retained a wistful look behind his blue eyes, which suggested loneliness and conscientiousness.

I was beginning to enjoy my conversation when I became aware of a cold trickle and the smell of ammonia. I thrust my hand into my pocket. It was too late. The sal had indeed proved volatile and my trousers were rapidly drenched. I seized my napkin and began mopping surreptitiously. My remarks became bright and rather fevered, but quite uninterrupted. I mopped secretly while the aroma of sal volatile rose above the smell of gruzhenkoia.

This was agony. I scarcely heard what he was saying. 'Have you,' he was asking, 'recovered your land-legs as yet? After three days in the train one feels the room rocking like after three days at sea.' So that was it! Why on earth had he not told me before, and now it was too late. I recovered my composure and dropped my sodden napkin. The conversation followed normal lines. At 2.45 he rose abruptly. I rose, too, casting a terrified glance at the plush seat of my chair. It bore a deep wet stain. What, oh what, will the butler think? He will think only one thing, and that is too shaming even to imagine. Luckily the King, as is the way with Kings, walked very briskly to the door; entered the central hall; swung round; shook hands and was off. 'Come back again,' he called from the lift. I entered the car and sat gingerly at the edge in order not to stain the seat. I returned to my room, with dripping trousers and a completely empty bottle of sal volatile. Why do such things happen to me?[7]

He was much impressed by Carol's intelligence, knowledge and seriousness, which his undeniable bounderishness belied. Harold's luncheon two days later with Virgil Tilea was not accompanied by any embarrassing accidents. When he first knew Tilea this Transylvanian was a shy, serious young man who could speak only German. He was a junior secretary in the Roumanian Legation in London. Now he was a swell and a power. He was King Carol's chief adviser. He created Governments and was adulated by Prime Ministers. He was also rich with a house in the suburbs, a large garden, a swimming pool, crazy paving, pots and flowering shrubs. His house was in the Byzantine bungalow style, with Boyar ceilings and curved arches. Little tables groaned with photographs of royal personages. Harold was given a succulent luncheon with purée de caviare and the richest Roumanian delicacies, and met a host of politicians and ex-Prime Ministers. When war broke out Tilea behaved well. He became leader of the Free Roumanians and was given asylum in Oxfordshire. When his country was finally occupied by the Russians, his career was ruined, his fortune confiscated, and he was a broken man.

The remainder of Harold's visit to Roumania was occupied by lectures, broadcasts and dinner-parties given for him by Sir Reginald Hoare. He was driven to Princess Marthe Bibesco's house, Mangosoia, seven miles from Bucharest, through dead flat, featureless country, planted with conifers. An avenue of plane trees led to a clearing, with lakes and willows. A little church stood beside a group of Muscovite buildings, which the Princess had transformed from a ruin into a fake. The house had polished floors of marble, rough beige-plastered walls, iron-work grilles and gates. 'From outside came the constant yell of peacocks calling me by my Christian name.'[8]

On the 20th Harold embarked on a little ferry steamer which plied up the cold Danube to Ruschuk. There he was met by the Mayor, the Prefect of Police and the Chief Officer of the Douane, each of whom made a speech of welcome to Bulgaria. He was put into a victoria drawn by two horses, seated beside the Mayor. He found Sofia dull and the Bulgarians ugly. All they thought about was the territories they had lost in 1913 and 1919 through their own fault. Dozens of them called on Harold with their complaints. They hated the Germans and Italians, and would prefer to recover their lost possessions under our aegis. But since they would be unable to, they would doubtless turn to the Germans. Of all the Bulgarians he met the only one he liked, and he liked him very much indeed, was King Boris. At an audience they talked for two hours. The King delighted him with stories of his adventures and threats to abdicate. It did him good, he told Harold, to let off steam. He said he hated having to act as a dictator and participate in constant coups d'état, but he was driven to do it. 'His charm is enormous and his virtue great.'[9]

At Beli Dvor, in a park a mile outside Belgrade, Harold lunched with Prince Paul of Yugoslavia. The Palace, surrounded by police and detectives, was a lovely building with views over hills and woods. Princess Nicholas of Greece was present, dressed in widow's weeds, and looking heart-broken. She talked of the old days and Harold's father. When luncheon was over the host took his guest to see his art treasures – pictures by El Greco, Gainsborough, Poussin, a magnificent Savonerie carpet from Lord Curzon's house, and bookshelves and over-doors from Chesterfield House. He talked about his English friends and art, keeping off politics except to say that the English press always seized upon the least creditable things connected with his country.

On the return journey Harold wrote a report of his Balkan tour (dated the 30th April) which he handed to Vansittart at the Foreign Office. He received from him a letter praising his self-sacrificing integrity. On four successive evenings he made speeches on his Balkan experiences, and in none of them did he disguise his depression about the future. His report and his speeches were widely disseminated, and won credence. He had become one of those backbench M.P.s of very specialised knowledge, whose opinions and advice were sought, regarded and evaluated. Both David Margesson, the Chief Whip, and W. S. Morrison separately told him that the Government was worried about its foreign policy. Could Harold suggest what they ought to do? He replied that the honourable course was to return to their election pledge, the League. 'You know how reserved Father was,' he wrote to Vita.[10] 'Once he said to me, "The only thing that counts in life is integrity." That is always my watchword. It sounds so silly when typed out. But, dearest, you *know* it is my watchword.' Eden too confided in him his worry that foreign affairs were splitting the country into two halves and asked his opinion of the feeling of the House.

Harold was asked by the Foreign Office to invite Konrad Henlein, the leader of the Czech Sudeten Germans, to meet a few members of the Eden group. Henlein had been instructed by Hitler to reorganise the Sudeten Germans on Nazi lines and to convince all the Germans in Czechoslovakia how brutally they were being treated. In fact the Sudeten Germans had never belonged to Germany, but to Austria; and did not wish to join Germany. Harold arranged a tea-party at King's Bench Walk which lasted for two hours. He thought it did some good and made his guest realise that if he went too far there would be general war. Henlein was a solid, solemn man with vague empty eyes and a faculty for clear expression. He had a slight sense of humour and leered painfully at any joke.[11]

When at the close of the discussion, I helped this stout schoolmaster into his enormous and ungainly greatcoat, I said to him: 'I hope that you will not allow Hitler to render you the Seyss-Inquart of Czechoslovakia.' He answered, '*Gott bewahre!*'[12]

But Harold did not then know that the previous day Henlein had been secretly in Berlin receiving instructions from Ribbentrop how to hoodwink the English. Before May was out Hitler was threatening Czechoslovakia.

Towards the end of the month the two Lindberghs and Mrs. Morrow paid a farewell visit to Sissinghurst. Their lease of Long Barn had come to an end by their own arrangement. It was on this occasion that Charles Lindbergh shocked Harold by telling him that Britain's air force and defences were so inferior to Germany's that we had far better give way and make an alliance with Hitler. Anne Lindbergh described the discussion in milder terms than Harold. 'C gets Harold Nicolson and evidently pummels him hard with gloomy aviation data.' And she finished with the words, 'I feel rather sad . . . A cloud has descended on us.'[13] It certainly had.

While Lord Halifax was intimating that Goebbels would greatly appreciate an invitation to Sandringham and was surprised by the opposition of the King and Queen to the proposal, Mussolini, in spite of Chamberlain's Anglo-Italian Agreement, was sending more troops to Spain, and the Germans were rounding up people walking in the Prater in Vienna. They were forcing Jewish men to take off their clothes and walk on all fours, Jewish women to climb trees and chirp like birds, and Princess Stahremberg, the present Prince's mother, to wash out the men's urinals in the railway station. The British public were profoundly disgusted. In the light of these and similar happenings Harold came to believe that the country was passing out of the zone of fear into a zone of anger. 'The great drama begins to shape itself towards its close.'[14]

Although Harold was temporarily lying low[15] in the House of Commons because he could not support the Government's foreign policy and did not consider the time had yet come to say so openly, he gave in July the first of a series of thirteen extremely outspoken weekly talks on the wireless, entitled *The Past Week*. At 10 p.m. on each occasion he addressed himself to twenty million people. One of his listeners was Anne Lindbergh. She was fond of Harold and, whatever her husband thought of the talks, was impressed.

He still speaks in that pleasant, half-humorous, and rather effeminate accent of cynical sideline detachment, but you can feel his emotions. He speaks of Chamberlain as pleading, 'Do not shoot this bird (Czechoslovakia) and in a short time we will bring it to you in a cage.' And then of the Germans, having the bird in a cage, not being satisfied, wanting a dead bird.[16]

Vita followed each broadcast with intense interest. She advised him to appear to be impartial, and to stick to the announcement he made in the first of his series of talks, namely to put forward all sides of every question and then to sum up with a balanced view.

While spending a weekend at Waddesdon Manor in Buckinghamshire, which belonged to the James Rothschilds and resembled a château on the Loire, Harold fully realised that the experience marked the end of an age of grandeur whose apogee had been in King Edward VII's reign. In this archaic mansion where in every square inch jostled fabulous art treasures, in which French furniture and porcelain predominated, the party consisted exclusively of racing people – hardly, one would suppose, Harold's choice of company. There were the Hillingdons, the Bessboroughs, Lady Linlithgow, Richard Molyneux, Lord Harewood and the Princess Royal. Harold loved every minute. He was fascinated by the contrast of extreme luxury with discomfort, the gigantic bowls of roses in every passage, and no hot water in the bedrooms. The gardens, stuffed with bedded plants, were, in his opinion, hell on earth, and must have cost £20,000 a year to keep up. He wrote in the morning, ate a gargantuan luncheon, ambled in the afternoon to the acres of greenhouses, and had long talks with Princess Mary who remembered his father with affection because in the old Balmoral days he was so nice to the royal children. At dinner all the women were draped with pearls and diamonds, exactly as in 1910. After dinner they played poker and he took £2 off Princess Mary.

Bitterly distressed that Nigel only got a third degree in his History Finals at Oxford – he could think of nothing else for four days – Harold, having condoled with his son, left for a visit to Somerset Maugham at Cap Ferrat on the 2nd August. One night the Windsors came to dinner. As usual Harold was responsive to the Duke's glamour from the moment when, on entering the room with his swinging naval gait, he exclaimed, 'Oi'm sorry we are a little loite, but Her Royal Hoighness couldn't drag herself awoy from the Amurrican orficers.' The Duke's face and neck were burnt brick-red by the Mediterranean sun, against which his fair hair showed up as if it were stuck on with glue, or were a wig. The pathos of him never failed to strike in Harold a chord of sadness about the things which perhaps did not sadden the Duke – the harping on the glories of his past, the pretension to his being so very busy and, in truth, the enforced frivolity of his present existence.

La Cröe on Cap d'Antibes had been rented by the Windsors for three years. It was a great white villa with rounded front set in a pine forest. Two days later Willie Maugham and his party lunched with the Duke and Duchess. Harold gave a description of the visit which has not been published.[17]

We are met on arrival by Forwood, at one time honorary Attaché at Vienna, and now Equerry to H.R.H. . . We then walk down to the sea. One goes through the pine wood and there are the rocks and the Mediterranean all neatly arranged. A space has been scooped out of the rocks and it has been terraced and smoothed with cement. In the middle is a large red and white tent surmounted with the Prince of Wales's feathers in which one undresses. This tent is continued as a wide awning over the rocks. Underneath it are all imaginable shapes and forms of cushions, mattresses, sunshades, little low tables, cigarettes, scent-bottles, etc. From there it is only a few steps down to the sea.

When we arrive the only people there are Lord Sefton and Mrs. Colin Buist. But in a few minutes the Duchess arrives. She is very simply dressed in blue linen with a huge spray of rubies at her corsage. Then he comes dressed in blue linen also. We undress and leap into the sea. The Duke's little dog dives in with us and we swim round and round. Then we get out, dry ourselves and smoke cigarettes. We then return to the house for luncheon. Over the house flies a flag bearing the Prince of Wales's feathers. I make no comment on that.

The Duke takes me into the gents' lavatory which is large and well furnished. He is full of chat. It is rather pathetic. On the wall is a map of the world with all his journeys marked. He points them out to me. On the table below are bagpipes.

We then join the rest of the party. It is terribly hot – over 100 in the shade. The Brownlows are there and the Colin Buists and Sefton . . . There are very elaborate drinks, pine-apple and orange-juice in great jars and bunches of mint. We then go into luncheon. I sit on the Duchess's right. The dining-room is high and painted white and yellow with the Munnings picture of the King over the mantelpiece. We have very elaborate food. Melon with tomato ice in it, eggs with crab sauce, chicken with avocado pear salad, a pudding which only Queen Alexandra knew how to make. Fruits. The Duchess is servant-conscious. Apparently they have a mixed bag of French and Austrian servants and their major-domo has been sacked. Thus the serving is none too good and two different sorts of *vin rosé* are produced. The Duchess cannot speak French or German and thus her signs to the servants become wild gestures, and as such noticeable.

He sitting opposite is as gay as a cricket and does not seem to notice this ungainly business on the part of his *hausfrau*.

We then have coffee outside. I talk to H.R.H. He is very full of past reminiscences. His visit to Turkey. Mustapha Kemal. How he never managed to see the old Emperor Franz Josef. What a *poseur* the Kaiser was and how he used to receive people sitting on a saddle at his desk to give the impression that he was a cavalry officer. He talked about Father whom he remembered perfectly. He had had no luncheon as usual and was waiting for his tea. It never came. I must say he was most patient about it. He then showed us the other rooms. A large drawing-room, his own study with a picture of Queen Mary over the mantelpiece in Garter robes, many books bound in morocco, red chintz chairs. In his hall is his Prince of Wales's banner from his stall at Windsor. 'When Oi became King,' he said, 'they had to toik it down as there was no Prince of Woiles. So I did not see whoy Oi shouldn't have it here.' I saw why. But he didn't. It is his insensitiveness to such things which brought on all the trouble.

Then we take our leave. He sees us to the door. He is very gushy to me. Asks about Leicester and all that. Very ostentatiously calls me by my christian name. All this is owing to Evreux. When I say I go back to London tomorrow his eye twitches in pain. Otherwise no sign of anything but complete happiness.

Can a picture of an ageing Prince Charming exiled in lotus land, deprived of authority, duty and honours, yet endowed with every luxury, and having nothing whatever to do, be anything but infinitely tragic?

After the sybaritic style of life on the French Riviera the primitive existence of a Hebridean island was a bracing contrast. Harold went straight from Willie Maugham's Villa Mauresque to the Highlands of Scotland, reaching Mallaig on the 9th September. Nigel had bought with money inherited from his grandmother the small group of Shiant Islands between Skye and Lewis. Harold was delighted by his son's quixotic action, which he interpreted as a hidden romantic streak emerging from an aloof and severely practical mind. After all, were not the Nicolsons an ancient family which had been settled in Skye in the sixteenth century? Had they been called Vandeleur or Trevelyan people would overlook the fact that they were dispossessed of land. But since they were called Nicolson nobody realised that they enjoyed one of the earliest baronetcies and could trace their ancestry to the 9th century on emigrating from Norway. So Nigel by acquiring his own land in the Hebrides was restoring the Nicolson family to its historic past of

'vikings, clans, chielfs, slchuals, crhoneths, and other Celtic mystics.'
For some extraordinary reason Harold had always been sensitive about
the Nicolsons' lack of territorial possession and felt humiliated by
and resentful of the Sackvilles' strong sense of possession and lineal
superiority.

At Mallaig he hired a yacht which took him to Portree on Skye. It
was his first view of Skye and he was thrilled by the great mountain-
tops looming above a vapoury mist. He felt he had come home. He
thought that perhaps his ill-adjustment to English life was due to his
Celtic strain. At Portree he chartered a small ketch to take him to the
Shiants. There he was met by Nigel and his Balliol friend Rohan Butler,
and spent a few blissful days in a primitive shieling. Never had he felt
happier than with Nigel among the puffins and the seals, isolated
between sea and sky, leading the simplest *al fresco* life, and eating
porridge and pickled herrings off a flat stone.

The visit to the Shiants was the last absolutely carefree holiday
Harold was to have for many a year. On his return to England he was
plunged into the mounting crisis which led to Munich. The events of
the autumn of 1938 are by now minutely documented history. They are
also recorded day by day in Harold Nicolson's diaries. It would be
superfluous and tedious to detail them again in these pages. Harold, as
well as recording, played if not a prominent, then an active part in
them. One of the first things he did in London was to lunch with his
friend the Russian Ambassador Maisky, with whom he was now on
remarkably close terms. Maisky made plain to Harold that, were Great
Britain to join with France in assisting Czechoslovakia, Russia would
come to their assistance. If Britain were to abandon Czechoslovakia,
Russia would become isolationist. Harold was impressed by and
believed in Maisky's assurances which he passed on to Vansittart.

He was still delivering his broadcast talks on *The Past Week*. They
became more and more premonitory of war. The B.B.C. cautioned
him not to alarm the public unduly. Harold retorted in a letter to the
Director-General: 'I feel strongly that the public, at this juncture, has
got to be alarmed.'[18] *The Times*, in view of its appeasing stance, was
surprisingly laudatory of the series. It referred to Harold's light but sure
touch in reviewing events, his eschewing of condescension and didac-
ticism. It praised his courage when dealing with the thorny problems of
the Sudeten Germans. But when the Czech crisis loomed dangerously

near and Harold submitted the script of a talk on that subject to the
B.B.C., they in concert with the Foreign Office asked him to omit
certain passages criticizing the behaviour of the Nazis. Harold was
incensed, particularly with the Foreign Office. At this time he also
recorded a newsreel speech for release in the cinemas, protesting in the
most outspoken and unequivocal terms against Hitler's threat to
Czechoslovakia. The speech ended with the words: 'We must warn
Hitler that if he invades we shall fight. If he says, "But surely you won't
fight for Czechoslovakia," we will answer, "Yes, we shall."' This
splendid performance was prohibited by the censor and not released.

When Harold heard on the late night news of the 14th September that
Chamberlain had gone to Berchtesgaden his first emotion was one of
enormous relief. It would be magnificent if the Prime Minister managed to obtain concessions from Hitler. Harold's inmost feelings were
passionately against war, which would mean the loss of all the things,
and worse than the things, the persons he loved. But should his feelings
be personal? Patriotism should come before them. 'I admire the P.M.
for going and I shall be one of his most fervent admirers if he brings
back something which does not constitute a Hitler triumph.'[19] Vita on
the other hand maintained that Czechoslovakia was an artificial State
anyway, and reminded Harold that he had been on the Committee of
the Paris Peace Conference which defined the Czech frontiers, and at
the time deemed them inequitable. Hitler did of course triumph at the
Berchtesgaden meeting, in that Chamberlain agreed to the cession of
the Sudetenland to Germany. On the morning of the 19th the Anglo-
French plans for handing over the German-speaking areas were published. Harold went to see Eden, who was in despair and convinced that
war was now inevitable.

At the Beefsteak Club on the following day there was general indignation over *The Times*'s appeasement attitude. Harold said loudly in
front of Robert Barrington-Ward, the assistant editor, that the paper's
leader was 'a masterpiece of unctuous ambiguity, and I do not in the
least mind repeating that in the presence of its author'. Vernon Bartlett
told the assembled company that he had learned in Berchtesgaden that
only the defeatist attitude in Britain had prevented the German Army
from arresting Goering and Ribbentrop and facing Hitler with an
ultimatum. Harold was summoned to Winston Churchill's flat to meet
other anti-appeaser M.P.s. They decided to attack Chamberlain only if
he returned from Godesberg, where he flew next, and again brought
back Peace with Dishonour. While gas-masks were being issued and
trenches dug in the London parks, and the big room at Sissinghurst was

being made gas-proof, Harold wrote to Ben, then studying in the Fogg Museum, Cambridge, U.S.A., urging him, if war broke out, to remain there and get a much needed job in the British Embassy until he was called upon to join the forces at home. He then turned to his book, *Diplomacy*, which for the past two distressing months had occupied him. Vita when she read it was amazed how by his little twists of phrase he had made a dull subject so alive, unpompous and lucid.

On the evening of the 26th September Harold listened in Broadcasting House to Hitler's speech before delivering his own weekly talk, having brought with him alternative drafts to suit the occasion. He spoke bitterly and sarcastically about Germany. Rex Leeper asked Harold to take charge of the South Eastern Department of the Foreign Office if war came. Harold consented.

On the 28th he went down to the House of Commons to listen to Chamberlain's speech on his return from Godesberg. The dictated account which he recorded that night is perhaps the best known and most moving of all the entries of those critical days in the Diaries.[20] With deft touches, pauses, and parenthetical irrelevancies, Harold conjured up the expectancy, the anxiety, and the dawning hope of the Members assembled on the historic occasion. The Prime Minister on entering the Chamber was greeted with wild cheers, his supporters rising from their seats. 'The Labour opposition, the Liberal opposition, and certain of the National supporters remained seated.' Harold was one of these. He described the Prime Minister's long speech in which he recounted his flight and conversations with Hitler. Chamberlain had spoken for an hour when he was handed a telegram, announcing Hitler's postponement of mobilisation for twenty-four hours and invitation to himself, Mussolini and Daladier to meet him in Munich. 'That, I think,' Harold wrote, 'was one of the most dramatic moments which I have ever witnessed.' There were roars of applause. The House rose almost as a man, waving their order papers in the air. Harold did not mention in his broadcast that he, Churchill and Duff Cooper were the only three Members on the Government side who refused to budge. It was an act of consummate courage on Harold's part, for he was a junior back-bencher. Liddall, the Conservative Member for Lincoln, seated behind him, hissed out, 'Stand up, you brute!' Harold's action, or rather inaction, made a great impression upon his friends.

Vansittart[21] summoned Harold and told him, just as Malcolm MacDonald had done, that it was his duty to rally to Chamberlain and even serve under him if asked. This instruction might at first seem uncharacteristic of that lion-hearted man and hater of Germans and Germany.

But in fact it was given in the conviction that before long the Prime Minister would be driven to repudiate Munich, and enlist the support of every enlightened parliamentarian, including Harold. It did not prevent Harold from telling an audience in Manchester on the 2nd October that Chamberlain had disregarded the advice of the experts like Vansittart who was consistently right, and listened to Sir Horace Wilson, whose advice was never inconvenient,[22] a remark for which *The Times* took him strongly to task. It was an unwritten rule that civil servants did not defend themselves, and Mr. Nicolson having been one himself, ought not to have made this unjustifiable attack against the highly respected Sir Horace. Besides, how could he possibly know what Wilson's advice to the Prime Minister had actually been? On his return to London Harold learned that Duff Cooper had resigned as First Lord of the Admiralty over the Munich Agreement.

During the debate of the 5th on the Agreement that followed Harold kept leaping to his feet. At 9.25 he was called by the Speaker. There was a burst of applause and Members moved in to hear him. He said that having been on the Committee of the Paris Peace Conference which drew up the Czech frontiers he would never advocate going to war over the Sudeten issue alone. But he was prepared to go to war to prevent a large country from crushing a small one. In Czechoslovakia there was a well organized democracy standing in the way of Germany's *Drang nach Osten*. He did not think that any Member of the Government could be quite sincere in hiding from his conscience what this Munich defeat, this humiliating defeat, this terrible Munich retreat, meant to the fortunes and future of our country. We had given away the whole key to Europe. The Prime Minister had put his signature to a paper which committed Great Britain to friendship with the strong against the weak.

> I know that in these days of realism principles are considered as rather eccentric; and ideals are identified with hysteria. I know that those of us who believe in the traditions of our policy, who believe in the precepts which we have inherited from our ancestors, who believe that one great function of this country is to maintain moral standards in Europe, to maintain a settled pattern of international relations, not to make friends with people whose conduct is demonstrably evil . . . but to set up some sort of standard by which the smaller Powers can test what is good in international conduct and what is not – I know that those who hold such beliefs are accused of possessing the Foreign Office mind. I thank God that I possess the Foreign Office mind.

The speech went down well with those comparatively few who were of his opinion. Eden wrote him a letter of congratulation on a very courageous and brilliant performance. 'I have never heard you to better advantage.' Indeed of all the speeches made in this debate Harold's was the most telling criticism of Chamberlain's tragic abasement before the monstrous behaviour of Hitler.[23]

In the voting at the end of the Munich Agreement debate Harold abstained. He was obliged to persuade his constituency to support him, which they did, largely thanks to his admirable and loyal chairman and friend, Colonel Jarvis. They gave him their confidence, with reluctance, although the women were almost wholly against him.

In a bold gesture of defiance of fortune, considering how desperate world affairs were, Harold now did something which for years he had wanted to do and which at a time of settled peace he would have been sensible to do. He acquired a yacht, or yawl, with a 9ft draft, which he christened the *Mar*, her father's nickname for Vita; or to be accurate, Vita raised by mortgage £2,000 to enable him to buy it. Sailing had been one of the few outdoor recreations which he really loved, and he recalled with delight the voyages in Lord Sackville's yacht, *Sumerun*, in the early twenties. The *Mar* had to be laid up at Southampton until the spring.

During the last half of 1938 and the first half of 1939 Harold was tireless in lecturing and delivering speeches all over England, besides serving on numerous committees.[24] He was never at Sissinghurst for more than three days at a time; and when he was, he wrote countless articles on the international situation for weekly periodicals and learned magazines. During October he made eighteen speeches in eleven consecutive days, trying to explain to his audiences what Munich really meant, an awkward task when Chamberlain was regarded by most people as the great peace-maker and saviour of his country. In between this work he allied himself to a small inner group of wise, sensible friends in the House, consisting of Eden (its leader), Cranborne, Sidney Herbert, Macmillan, Spears and Cartland (to his distress Robert Bernays supported Chamberlain at this juncture) who, distinct from Churchill, 'do not give the impression, which Winston does, of being more bitter than determined, and more out for a fight than reform.'[25] The inner group was appalled when it learned the full extent of Britain's unpreparedness, and that had she gone to war in September she would have been knocked out in three weeks. Perhaps after all there was something to be said for Chamberlain's deferment of the conflict until the country had time to re-arm, if only it had not been inspired by fear.

At all events the Prime Minister made a good speech just before Christmas, Harold noted, and seemed to be coming round to the group's point of view. He was glad he had not committed himself to Churchill's provocative group, and had lain low; glad too that he had not resigned his seat as an opponent of the Government, a thing he had seriously contemplated doing in order to fight a bye-election, which he might well have lost under a new label.

What was the impression made upon a very observant writer, and at the time a stranger to him, by Harold Nicolson while he was fighting an unpopular, and often lonely battle, against the entrenched Conservative party behind Chamberlain just after Munich? At a dinner of the Junior Constitutional Club on the 30th November Harold sat next to Freya Stark, whom he described succinctly as 'a nice little foreign thing'. While he was thinking of what to say during the discussion on Mr. Chamberlain's policy that was to follow, she had the opportunity to take stock of him. She pronounced him:

> quiet and unemphatic, with the look of a dignified and serious small boy, so much more grown-up than the adults about him . . . He was silent and absorbed in his thoughts till I made some comparison of Greece with Persia. 'Oh, let us talk about them,' he said, turning his chair a little round, as if the whole Conservative party and all it was interested in were to be forgotten. 'Those are such nice countries to talk about.' It was only near the end of the meal that I discovered how much we felt the same about this moment in England.

In the debate Harold was, she noted – except for their silent alliance – in a minority of one. He never wavered once

> from that clear and sharp Mediterranean standard, the cool merciless flicker of wit, the clear disinterested verity, which is still the norm of civilization, even to us who fear it and carry half the barbarian in our hearts. Whenever I can, I meet him, and every meeting is made memorable by this impression of *civilitas* – as if it were a talk with Boethius or Cassiodorus in the days of Theodoric the Goth.[26]

In fact the Munich crisis had made a stalwart man of Harold. He now knew exactly where he stood, what were his beliefs, and how he was going to implement them with all the force of his authority. He knew too that, although in the House of Commons his authority was limited, as a commentator on world affairs over the air and through the press it was not negligible. Lunching in December at the Reform Club with

Wilson Harris, editor of the *Spectator*, he agreed to write a weekly article for that journal under the title of *People and Things*. The series was to start with the New Year. It soon turned into the famous page, known as *Marginal Comment*, which was to endure, subject to a few intervals, until December 1952.

When the year 1938 drew to its inglorious close Harold in his wretchedness and anxiety turned, as a respite from his political work, to Byron. He re-read *Childe Harold*, with greater appreciation than before.

> His great flow of energy, the passionate rhetoric which is not poetry exactly but the flash of a great character. Behind all his desire to catch the ear of his age there was something serious and sincere. It may have been little more than rage, but it was a fine rage.[27]

He felt happier after reading it. The poet's rapidity of composition, his patrician indifference to literary excellence, his wit, and his lack of prejudices had always greatly attracted him. Besides, Byron epitomised those qualities which Harold in advancing middle age would most dearly have liked to possess – youth, beauty, hauteur, genius, and heroism. Aging people often see Narcissus-like the image of their lost promise falsely reflected in the distorting mirror of another. Once again Harold drew inspiration from the magnitude of Byron's understanding and the nobility of his fight for Greek Independence. Like the poet he affected to depreciate his writing and aspire to action. Like him he was ill-equipped to be a warrior. If his parliamentary efforts were less glorious than the poet's military posturing, they were no less earnest and in the long run hardly less influential upon public opinion.

Harold proceeded to examine the real nature of his own anxieties. Was it dread of war? Fear of losing his sons, and the destruction of his cherished way of life? Horror over the prospect of world carnage? Loathing of the evil of Naziism triumphing over western civilisation? Or did it come from his own lack of power and, as he wrongly surmised, of authority? He was certainly not alone in questioning the causes of the misery which gripped most decent Englishmen and Frenchmen at this terrible moment of history. In their underlying, gnawing anxiety lay the knowledge that, whereas the Axis Powers wanted to fight for a new and positive creed, nauseating though it was, they, knowing full well that war was inevitable, had no positive creed, no ideal to fight for over and above preservation of the *status quo*, which does not inspire the same fanatical will to victory. Moreover they were deeply unhappy that in the forthcoming struggle the ally – Russia –

upon whom they might have to depend for victory was no less diabolical than the declared enemy.

The opening of the year 1939 witnessed further sinister activities on the part of the Axis. While Harold was lecturing to Amsterdam University in January Hitler was bringing pressure upon Hungary and Roumania. In Rome Chamberlain and Halifax were being hoodwinked by Mussolini into a conviction of the good intentions of the Italian Government. Franco was advancing towards Barcelona. And the Irish Republican Army – with that readiness to stab England in the back which characterises the Irish race – began bombing our power-stations. Mr. Chamberlain was returning from Rome to announce to his Cabinet that he found Mussolini and Countess Ciano charming, and was assured of the good faith and intention of the Italian Government. Lord Lloyd instantly confronted the Prime Minister in an interview. He told him that Mussolini was simply out for loot. Chamberlain replied that he did not agree. In a fury Lloyd retorted, 'But surely you cannot disagree with the views of every expert? After all I had two hours with Pacelli [the future Pope Pius XII], the best brain in Italy, and he preached to me nothing but that Musso was out for conquest. Surely you cannot close your mind to such advice?' Chamberlain remarked tersely, 'You and I do not see eye to eye.'[28]

But the scales were to drop from Chamberlain's eyes; and very swiftly. Before January was out Vansittart confided to Harold that the Prime Minister would not let France down if Germany forced an issue upon her. And on the 7th February Harold was startled to hear Chamberlain proclaim in the House an offensive alliance between us and France, just as though this had been his intention all along. Harold at once decided that he must support Chamberlain and refrain from recriminations. On the 17th he referred in *Marginal Comment* to this volte-face. 'The mood of the Government has altered from one of evasive optimism to one of almost resolute vigilance,' he wrote. Meanwhile Vita, who had returned from Paris where she had delivered in French a triumphal lecture and broadcast on Pepita, bought forty additional acres of orchard land at Sissinghurst, and a television set. It was the sort of extravagance, like Harold's acquiring a yacht, which overtakes people on the brink of calamity. They feel they may as well spend any money they have before it is taken away from them, and enjoy while they can what may be lost to them for ever. The Nicolsons

3(a) The sitting-room at 4 King's Bench Walk, Harold's London flat from 1930 till 1945.

(b) Harold acclaimed by his supporters after his election as MP for West Leicester, November 14 1935.

4(a) At his work-table seen through the South Cottage window.

(b) The South Cottage at Sissinghurst.

were early addicts of television long before most people showed interest. Harold always considered it a tremendous invention of vast potentialities, capable, he foretold, of altering the whole basis of democracy.

In February *Diplomacy*[29] was published by Thornton Butterworth in the Home University Library of Modern Knowledge. Considering that monographs of a series usually attract few or no reviews *Diplomacy* got good notices. It was subsequently reprinted, a third edition coming out in 1969 with an introduction by Lord Butler. It is still regarded as essential reading by aspirants to the Service. The book had been written while Harold was learning first hand from current affairs the lesson that diplomacy was based upon a knowledge of foreign psychology, and that owing to lack of such knowledge Chamberlain's Government had landed the country in its present terrible mess.[30] Harold maintained that negotiation ought to be left to the professionals, whose training and career diplomacy was. He strongly deprecated the notion that diplomacy was the art of conversation. It was the art of negotiating agreements in precise and ratifiable form, in which the politician was unversed, particularly the British politician whose ignorance of foreign psychology was abysmal, whose optimism was often crass stupidity, and whose dislike of facing unpleasant facts was common knowledge among astuter nations. Harold's main contention in writing this little book was that of the many qualities which the ideal negotiator ought to possess the most essential was reliability. The reason why Britain's successful relations with Europe between 1814 and 1914 had been phenomenal was the superlative technique of her diplomatic service and its irreproachable standards of honour. This technique had first been established at the Congress of Vienna.

Until the fateful September of this year Harold was constantly travelling. At the beginning of March he was staying at the British Embassy in Brussels with the Clives.[31] He paid a visit to the Archduke Otto[32] at Steenockerzeel, set in damp, drab suburbs and ugly fields. It was a miniature baronial castle on a lake, approached by a drawbridge. He rang a bell at the postern. A neat Austrian maid opened the door. She led him to a tiny, shabby sitting-room and then to a drawing-room, empty save for a piano and a few rep-covered chairs. Windows and doors rattled in the gale. The Archduke wore a grey suit. He was a handsome and vigorous youth, with a Hapsburg chin which he stuck out. He had mobile and eloquent lips, and showed his teeth. He told Harold he would like to see a revival of the Holy Roman Empire, but with its capital removed from Berlin. He said that Gestapo agents were active in every country, even England. He believed in the inevitability of war unless a revolution in Germany could be organized beforehand. Harold was left with the impression of a clever man, of charm and character, and a reservoir of information.[33]

Sir Robert Clive showed Harold reports from our Consuls-general in Germany testifying how young Nazis made Jews pee into each others' mouths, and when they were sick, wipe up the vomit with their own hair.

The Czechoslovakian news was increasingly grave. Under German pressure the Slovaks demanded autonomy. The House of Commons was in a cleft stick. By the Munich Agreement Great Britain was morally obliged to go to the Czechs' assistance. Geographically it was impossible for her to do so. And Hitler knew it. He flagrantly tore up the Agreement, reached with so much humiliation by Chamberlain, and at the same time tore off the mask from his own face. He walked into Prague, took over all the defences, most of the industrial areas, and the vital railway junctions in Bohemia and Moravia. What Harold had been foretelling day in and day out over the past six months, had come to pass. The *Manchester Guardian* bore a leader, headed *The Gift of Prophecy*, quoting a passage from his Munich speech. Henceforth no one of whatsoever party in the House of Commons believed any further in appeasement; and those who thought as Harold did refrained from speaking, unwilling to rub salt into the Prime Minister's wounds. Harold merely felt profoundly sorry for him.

Germany next turned her attention to Poland. The Eden group issued a joint resolution supporting the Foreign Secretary, Lord Halifax, and calling for a united front, to the fury of the whips. On the 31st March Chamberlain, gaunt and yellow, declared in the House of Commons that if Poland were attacked we would go to war. In the debate on support for a pledge to Poland on the 3rd April Harold supported the Prime Minister. He praised his courage in reversing his policy since Munich. He paid tribute to his total dedication to the cause of peace which neither the British nor, in future years, the German people would gainsay. He believed the German people were disgusted by the invasion of Czechoslovakia and the treatment of the Jews; but they would not at this stage do anything to reverse Nazi policy. The result of the debate was that the Franco-British guarantee of assistance to Poland was converted into an Anglo-Polish mutual assistance pact.

Four days later, on Good Friday of all days, Mussolini, the dictator of a great Christian country which contained the seat of the Papacy, invaded Albania. Britain and France countered this unprovoked action by guaranteeing the integrity of Greece and Roumania. Harold spent Easter on the Hamble river getting his yawl, the *Mar*, out of her winter dock, revelling in the preparations, the scrubbing, polishing and unfurling of sails in brilliant sunshine, and thinking how happy he would be were it not for the cloud on the horizon far bigger than a man's hand. He was tremendously pleased that Ben had, through Kenneth Clark's assistance, got the job of Deputy-Surveyor of the King's Pictures, and proud that Nigel was working in Newcastle with the Tyneside Council of Social Service. Throughout the rest of the summer he spent every weekend he could spare from Sissinghurst with his yacht and its crew of three. Like all small yachts the *Mar* was unable to leave harbour half the time its owner wanted to sail, owing to foul weather. If Vita deprecated these too frequent absences, she never complained. In any case she could not sail with her husband for she was kept at Sissinghurst all the summer by another of Gwen St. Aubyn's illnesses.

While the press was speculating who was to be sent to Washington as Ambassador, the *Manchester Guardian* strongly advocated Harold Nicolson as pre-eminently suitable. The post was given to Lord Lothian. Again when in July the press was campaigning for Eden and Churchill to join the Cabinet the *Manchester Guardian* urged that Harold should be included as well.

During the debate on Foreign Affairs on the 31st July Harold surprised himself by suddenly intervening. When Sir Archibald Southby declared that there was a group in the House which lacked restraint, desiring rather destruction of the Nazi regime than world peace, and mentioned Eden and R. S. Hudson[34] (the Secretary of State for Overseas Trade) by name, Harold lost his temper and jumped into the fray. He stressed how moderate Eden's speeches had been since his resignation, and defended Hudson from charges of indiscretion in meeting and talking outspokenly with his opposite number in Germany. He was uncertain afterwards how pleased Eden and Hudson actually were with his intervention on their behalf. In the debate on the 2nd August on whether the House should adjourn for the summer recess Eden, whom Harold had been gingering to protest against its doing so, gave way to the Prime Minister. This change of tactics caused Harold to question why he was always left out on a limb and to indulge in one of his repeated bouts of self-deprecation. But he was in an honourable minority. When the Prime Minister categorically insisted on adjournment and foolishly declared that the very suggestion that Parliament should continue sitting was tantamount to an attack upon himself, young Ronnie Cartland in an outburst of indignation rose to his feet and said,

'We are in the situation that within a month we may be going to fight and we may be going to die.' Whereupon an injudicious older Member laughed. 'It is all very well for you to laugh,' Cartland shouted at him:

> There are thousands of young men at this moment in training camps, and giving up their holiday, and the least that we can do here . . . is to show that we have immense faith in the democratic institution. I cannot imagine why the Prime Minister could not have made a great gesture in the interests of national unity. It is much more important to get the whole country behind you rather than make jeering, pettifogging party speeches which divide the nation.

Rob Bernays leant across to Harold and whispered, 'Ronnie has ruined his chances with the Party but he has made his parliamentary reputation.' It was only too true. He had no further chances inside the Party. Within nine months of his impassioned outburst Ronnie, who joined up the instant war was declared, died fighting at the age of thirty-three.

Parliament adjourned for the summer recess on the understanding, extracted from the reluctant Prime Minister, that it would reassemble should an emergency arise. Harold spent three weeks of August sailing in the *Mar*. In any other month than the last one of peace for a harassed\ and apprehensive Europe, it would have been a holiday of undiluted happiness.

On the 4th he embarked with his friend John Sparrow on the *Mar* at Plymouth. They had a superb sail to Falmouth. Harold wrote reviews and read a detective novel. At Falmouth they bathed, and two St. Aubyn nephews[35] from St. Michael's Mount joined them in a long boat. Off Penzance they encountered bad weather. They had intended to sail round Land's End to the west of Scotland. But high seas caused them to change their plans. They decided to abandon Scotland and make for France instead. So they doubled back to Weymouth where Nigel joined them on board. By now it was pouring with relentless rain. They crossed the Channel to Cherbourg, where the French would not allow them to tie up in the Avant-Port. They were obliged to pass through the lock gates into the Bassin de Commerce, which was heavy with the scent of herrings and the grime of coal-dust. They were glad to leave Cherbourg, an ugly town. Sailing west past Cap de la Hague they sighted Alderney on their starboard side, and anchored in St. Peter Port, Guernsey. They visited Victor Hugo's house:

> the most fantastic thing you can imagine with tapestries nailed on to the ceiling and a great mass of carved woodwork and bad stained glass. His working room in the roof contains two little standing

desks by each window and great *étagères* where he used to spread his wet sheets, rather than blot them.[36]

On leaving St. Peter Port

It was a marvellous day and we sailed away happily past the island and away towards France. How gay and happy we were! Sea and sunlight and an expedition in front of us. The sails tautened, the sea sparkled into foam at our bows, the dim islands slid behind us. We were young and adventurous. And as the sun turned round the sky, the day continued to be lovely and the sun sank in a purple sea and the new moon hung in the air and the stars came out. Tomorrow morning, we thought, we shall wake up outside Brest.[37]

In this passage there are echoes of Childe Harold's description of his sense of freedom and adventure on leaving the shores of England.[38] In the company of his young companions, did the eternal child in Harold Nicolson, see for a delirious moment himself as his homonymous hero, breasting the waves, attended by a little page and stout yeoman?

> The sails were filled, and fair the light winds blew,
> As glad to waft him from his native home;
> And fast the white rocks faded from his view,
> And soon were lost in circumambient foam . . .
> While flew the vessel on her snowy wing,
> And fleeting shores receded from his sight,
> Thus to the elements he poured his last 'Good Night'.

They meant to continue to Brest, but mist descended off Brittany. The surly, sullen bell-buoy off Ushant warned them that it would be wiser to return to Plymouth. They re-crossed the Channel, and entering the Pool tied up opposite a little ketch, called *The Outward Bound*. Harold went down to the cabin and turned on the news. It told that Ribbentrop had left Berlin for an unspecified mission to Moscow. This news was to be followed on the 22nd August by a German and Russian announcement that the two Powers were about to sign a non-aggression pact. For some minutes Harold felt stricken to the dust. The pact would render any chances of Britain honouring her guarantees to Poland, Roumania and Greece out of the question. On board *The Outward Bound* two boys and a girl were gaily swabbing the decks, polishing the brasswork, and singing as though they had not a care in the world.[39] In watching and listening to them Harold was overcome by the poignancy of these unknown young victims, ignorant of their impending doom. Next morning the newspapers announced that the

House of Commons was to be summoned. Harold changed into his London clothes, and leaving John and Nigel in Plymouth walked sadly to the station where he took the train to Waterloo. He was never to sail in the *Mar* again. She was laid up in the Hamble river and later damaged by a bomb.

In London he dined with members of the Eden group. Everyone was in the depth of dejection. Only Winston Churchill, they were told, was in high fettle. The smell of powder in his nostrils never failed to intoxicate the old war-horse. Rapidly the international situation deteriorated. Having thoroughly turned the tables on the French and British Hitler was free to dispose of Poland. With his customary tactic of issuing totally unfounded accusations of provocation by his prey, and demanding reparations within twenty-four hours without offering any terms whatsoever, he marched into Poland on the 1st September.

On that autumn morning Harold was sitting in the sun on a deck-chair outside the South Cottage at Sissinghurst, and reading, when Vita walked quickly along the path. 'It has begun,' she said.[40]

In the hours that followed Harold chafed under the enforced wait for England and France's declaration of war against Germany. He felt powerless and inarticulate. Yet he had said his say. His *Marginal Comments*, read weekly by thousands, had been just as admonitory as all the pious words spoken by M.P.s in the House of Commons during that wretched session, and just as powerful. He had been outspoken in telling his readers that Britain must fight to re-establish among the nations the rule of law and the sanctity of contracts; that until order and honesty were again imposed upon the people of Europe we could never re-attain that tranquillity of mind and conscience under which alone the good life could be lived.[41]

That afternoon Harold went post-haste to London and listened to the Prime Minister's heart-broken speech to the House. The responsibility for the terrible catastrophe lay, Chamberlain announced with unwonted anger, upon the shoulders of one man, the Chancellor of the German Republic. 'He is evidently in real moral agony,' Harold commented, 'and the general feeling in the House is one of deep sympathy for him and of utter misery for ourselves.'[42] On Sunday, the 3rd, while waiting in Ronald Tree's house in Queen Anne's Gate, he heard Chamberlain's announcement over the wireless that our ultimatum to Germany had expired. Then he walked to Parliament beside Eden, Duff Cooper and Leo Amery; and the sirens wailed.

5

THE SECOND WORLD WAR – STRUGGLE FOR SURVIVAL, 1939–1942

ALTHOUGH he had long foreseen that war was inevitable, yet, now the actual declaration had been made, Harold was stunned. What made the reality more difficult to comprehend, and the situation so heart-rending, was the unadulterated beauty of that September of 1939. As he walked down to the lake at Sissinghurst in the early morning of the 4th, the absolute calm of the water, the unruffled movement of the swans and the languid disinterest of the poplar trees were almost unendurable. That nature could be so unmoved by impending catastrophe of such magnitude was a cruel reproach to man, and almost unforgivable for its cynicism.

Whereas in 1914 the young Harold's duties in the Foreign Office were cut and dried, dictated from above, not to be wondered why, and obediently to be carried out, in 1939, although the middle-aged Harold was a Member of Parliament, they had largely to be sought. His constituency duties were not in themselves enough. Yet he was not idle. One of his earliest activities was to become chairman of the back-bench Air Raids Precautions Committee and a member of Duff Cooper's Committee on German Refugees. To his credit Harold in a *Marginal Comment* article appealed for a just treatment of those Germans who had escaped from Germany to seek asylum in our country. They could not return home, he said, and must not be regarded as undesirable aliens here.[1]

In his heart of hearts Harold Nicolson could not see how this war was to be won. If we lost it, we were finished. Of that he was in 1939 quite convinced. But he was buoyed up by the certainty that this time we were fighting against something so diabolical that defeat and extinction were preferable to compromise and survival. The certainty however did not detract from his conviction (which, as the war advanced, he was to revise) that, whether we won or lost, the outcome would bring the end of everything he cared for. 'Thus,' he admitted to himself, 'there is a little timid selfish side of myself that tempts me by still murmurings to hope that we shall reach a form of appeasement after the Germans have occupied Poland.'[2] He quickly brushed aside the ignoble thought. Even so, a visit to Vansittart at the Foreign Office, at the time when Hitler's army was surrounding Warsaw, did not encourage him to believe victory for the Allies was going to be possible. And a visit to Lloyd George was even less encouraging. This aged lion actually suggested that, if the chances were positively against us – and only the Government knew – then we should make peace at the earliest opportunity. He contended that the Government's guarantee of Poland and Roumania without an understanding with Russia had been an act of incredible and reprehensible folly. And Harold did not derive much solace from his friend the Soviet Ambassador, with whom he lunched alone. Ivan Maisky went into a long dissertation on why Russia had thrown us over and joined Germany. Britain had betrayed the League of Nations by her weakness and shown herself consistently opposed to left-wing countries; had insulted Russia at the time of the Czech crisis and treated her with contempt. Russia was bound to protect herself in the Black Sea and the Baltic, having lost all confidence in the western countries. Her only alternative therefore had been to make terms with the strongest Power. Nonetheless Russia would remain neutral in the conflict provided the Allies did nothing to provoke her. These typically vague and disingenuous excuses merely spurred Harold to gird his loins. The odds against us were so terrible and unpropitious that we could only behave like David towards Goliath, and put our trust in miracles.

Harold was far too old to join the fighting forces, unlike his colleagues in the House of Commons, Jack Macnamara and Ronnie Cartland; his friends, John Sparrow who enlisted as a private in the Oxford and Bucks Light Infantry, and Christopher Hobhouse in the Marines; and his sons, Ben who joined an Anti-Aircraft Battery as a private, and Nigel who went to Sandhurst. For Harold not the sword, but the pen was his appropriate weapon. He wrote numerous articles as well as *Marginal Comments* on the causes and purposes of the war.[3] On the 29th September Allen Lane asked him to write a 50,000 word Penguin Special, to be called *Why Britain is at War*. With astonishing rapidity he completed the book within a fortnight and sent it to Penguins on the 12th October. Within a month it was on sale; and by the end of November 5,000 copies a day were being printed. Its success was phenomenal. No one disparaged it. The Under-Secretary of State for Foreign Affairs, R. A. Butler, pronounced it a work of art, which factually could not be faulted; and Eden gave it praise, with only one small technical reservation.

Harold argued that, whereas it was frequently stated that Hitler was put into power by the Treaty of Versailles, it was more correct to say he owed his success to Poincaré. By the end of 1922 the German people had come to accept the 1919 Peace Treaty. The following year however Poincaré insisted, in spite of the advice of the British, upon occupying the Ruhr and obtaining a stranglehold on German industry. Thus the German middle classes saw their savings swept away in a week and were faced with ruin. Hence their misguided reliance upon Hitler as their saviour. 'It must be remembered,' Harold emphasised, 'that the German people are more gullible and neurotic than other peoples.' He stressed that this war was against Hitler, and not the German people.[4] Finally he advocated, once the war was over, a sort of defensive European Union as a substitute for the League of Nations which had demonstrably failed. His Union would however have to lay down mutual tariff and currency arrangements as well as establish a cultural patriotism, since patriotism appealed to humans before economics. In fact Harold was advocating what to some extent came about in the European Community.

Why Britain is at War was read and its arguments were accepted by millions of people. Yet today we may well wonder why none of Harold Nicolson's readers pressed the Government to make greater endeavour between 1939 and 1945 to wean the German people away from Hitler; and why the author did not emphasise – for he made no mention of it – that Soviet Russia was just as great an enemy of our liberties, unless of course he identified her with Germany, whose ally she had become at the time of writing.

One unfortunate sequel of *Why Britain is at War* was that the Foreign Office rescinded an offer made to Harold to work in the Political Intelligence Department, having previously persuaded the Prime Minister to allow him, although an M.P., to rejoin them. Harold had welcomed the offer. But the Permanent Head of the Civil Service, Sir Horace Wilson, was so infuriated by the author's reference to his bad influence upon Neville Chamberlain that he had the proposal cancelled.

Harold was very worried at this time by anti-British feeling in France. He wrote to Roland de Margerie, who, no longer a young man, had managed to join the Army, begging him to convince his country-men that Britain was really doing everything within her power to come to France's assistance. The general public was deeply distressed and worried by Russia's agreement with Germany and very alive to the gravest danger that would confront both England and France 'once the third German war begins,' by which Harold meant once the 'phoney war' phase had ended and the Allies had rejected the peace 'threats' which Hitler was bound to proffer. As though to assuage any doubts and fears as to our intentions which de Margerie might be labouring under, Harold assured him that Chamberlain was the best man we could have at the moment.

> He has great courage and strength of will and his record as an appeaser is an advantage . . . I think that when the great peace offensive begins, he is exactly the person to carry through our resistance and that it would be unfortunate if any other man were to take his place until we have passed from the second into the third German war. During the agonies and ordeals of the opening stages of that war it is probable that public opinion in this country will be deeply roused and angered and will call for a complete change of Government. Chamberlain will then disappear with all honour and a coalition Government will be formed. At the present moment the idea is that Halifax should head such a Government and Churchill lead the House of Commons. The latter's stocks are rising so rapidly that I should not be surprised if he became Prime Minister immediately.'[5]

Harold's prognostications were not far out. Meanwhile he seized an opportunity to go to France.

On the 28th October he flew to Paris with a party of eight back-bench M.P.s, led by Edward Spears, to exchange views with French *Députés* and inspect the 'impregnable' Maginot Line. The party descended in a lift 300 ft below ground as though entering the tube. Harold was suitably impressed by the apparent efficiency, the scientific precision, the optimism and the camaraderie of the clinical men below the Maginot Line. He had talks with Paul Reynaud, the Minister of Finance who was to succeed Daladier as Prime Minister in 1940, and with Daladier likewise. He did not find the latter an attractive man. He looked like a drunken peasant. Giraudoux, the playwright Minister of Information, and Léon Blum, the ex-Prime Minister, expressed to Harold their utmost confidence in ultimate victory.

At home the anticlimax of the 'phoney' war was having its ill effect upon forces and civilians alike. People were idle. Disillusion and grumbling and a tendency to defeatism were in evidence. If however others were obliged to do nothing Harold was in great demand to address public meetings. The Penguin book had brought him wide publicity and renown. He was invited to Oxford. At Balliol he put on an M.A. gown and walked across to the Sheldonian. The auditorium and the galleries were packed. He was escorted to the platform by the Vice-Chancellor, who bowed to him on the rostrum. For an hour he spoke. During the pauses between sentences one could have heard a pin drop. He then dined with officers of the Oxford Conservative Association, and spoke on war aims to a hall filled to overflowing, with people sitting on the floor. For three quarters of an hour he was submitted to a barrage of questions. No wonder that he was tired at the end of the day. When a nice old lady got into his railway carriage he heard himself politely asking her, 'Do you mind if I smike a pope?' Tired though he was, he was no longer depressed. He had come to accept the inevitable fact that we were in for a very long war. His initial acute pessimism had evaporated. But of course he was still apprehensive about the future. If the death of Princess Louise merely evoked from him the remark, 'My God! How the past slides like a great mass of vegetable matter down the sluice,' he was easily moved to compassion. The fate hanging over 800 gallant sailors of the *Graf Spee*[6] induced him to write:

> I hate it all . . . Few things have convinced me so much of the idiocy of modern warfare. It is no more than blood sports . . . There will be no sense of triumph or defeat whatever happens to the *Spee*. Merely a dull sense of the ineptitude of the human mind.[7]

These were not of course the words of a tough leader of men, but rather of a sensitive humanist philosopher.

Hostilities were suddenly to get cracking. 1940 became a terrible and critical year, made supportable to Harold only by absolute reliance upon Vita's love and positive sympathy with his views and ideals. A steady progress of disasters was launched in mid-March by the capitulation of Finland to Russia. In April Denmark was invaded by Hitler within a matter of hours. Norway's defeat quickly followed. These reverses were a forecast that Chamberlain would simply have to go. In May Hitler advanced into Holland and Belgium. While German troops were rapidly marching westwards Neville Chamberlain resigned the premiership, to be succeeded by Winston Churchill. On the 17th German armoured divisions swept across the Ardennes, broke through the French lines and quickly reached the Channel Ports. The Belgian army capitulated. The B.E.F. were cut off from the French armies. At the end of May they began evacuating Dunkirk. On the 14th June the Germans entered Paris. France fell. Daily England expected invasion. From August to September ensued the aerial Battle of Britain; and from early September until early November London was subjected to devastating bombardment every single night. At the end of the year conditions took on a slightly favourable turn in that the Italians, who had entered the war against us, suffered reverses in the Adriatic from the Greeks and were driven out of Egypt by Wavell. Throughout these world-stirring events Harold Nicolson kept a detailed record of the war as witnessed day by day within Parliament and even from the fringe of Government.

The winter of 1939–1940 had been climatically one of the severest experienced within living memory. Harold, barely recovered from a bad attack of influenza, spent a fortnight in March lecturing in France on war aims for the Ministry of Information. He was obliged to stand in a railway corridor all the way from Paris to Dijon by night. At Grenoble University he threw away his notes and spoke extempore for fifty minutes in French to a packed audience, receiving at the end a prolonged ovation from the students who stamped their feet and roared their approval. He spoke at Lyons. He addressed the Sorbonne in Paris, receiving afterwards a letter of congratulation from Herriot.[8] While in Paris he learned that the war in Finland had ended, with the imposition of severe peace terms upon that country by Russia. Georges Mandel at the Colonial Ministry told him that the effect upon the French was one of extreme dejection. Harold dined at Maxim's with his friend Robert Boothby who had just returned from Switzerland where he had gathered first-hand news of Germany from German refugees. The two friends agreed that the British and French policy of wait and see what happens next was madness, and that instead of letting Hitler attack when it suited him, we should immediately take the offensive by seizing Narvik in Norway and Baku on the Caspian, in order to interrupt supplies of Swedish ore to Russia and Russian oil to Germany. Five days later Harold listened to Neville Chamberlain's remarkably vigorous speech in the House of Commons. He was persuaded that the old man was at last out to win the war.

Harold put all his combatancy into his weekly *Spectator* articles, which he really believed to be doing good. He was persuaded by Somerset Maugham to write a *Marginal Comment* rebuking his literary friends Aldous Huxley, Gerald Heard, Wystan Auden and Christopher Isherwood for having emigrated to America at a time of crisis to their own country. It happened that a personable young American of twenty-one called Alastair Forbes, who had suffered frostbite in Finland, called on him. He said he had decided to devote all his efforts to the Finnish cause. 'The best way I can help Finland is by having a whack at the Germans.' Harold said, 'But you are American.' 'Well,' he answered, 'that is a slight difficulty. But I think I can get over that if I lie a bit.' 'My God!' Harold wrote, 'I thought of Auden and Isherwood and felt ashamed.'[9]

When Denmark and Norway were invaded he wrote: 'The House is extremely calm and the general line is that Hitler has made a terrible mistake. I feel myself that I wish we could sometimes commit mistakes of such magnitude.'[10] The phoney war was indeed over. Henceforward there was to be sweat and tears.

Harold joined the Watching Committee, or re-cast Eden group of Members of both Houses under the chairmanship of Lord Salisbury. The Watching Committee's task was to needle the Government into action. It urged the Foreign Secretary Lord Halifax to take the initiative and bomb German cities. Halifax replied that the Government must abide by the advice of the service departments. The Watching Committee were in despair. On the 7th May Sir Roger Keyes in full uniform with six rows of medals dangling upon his chest delivered a devastating broadside in the House against the Naval General Staff for assuring him that action at Trondheim, recently captured by the Germans, would be easy enough but was unnecessary. In the debate denunciations were hurled against Chamberlain, ending with Leo Amery's famous quotation from Cromwell's address to the Long Parliament, 'In the name of God, go!' At the end of the Norway debate Harold was one of forty-four who voted against the Government.

When on the 10th May the morning posters announced that Holland and Belgium had been overrun, Lord Dunglass[11] warned the Watching Committee that at such a crisis as this the Prime Minister must not on any account resign. But he was wrong. Harold on his return to Sissinghurst, where the garden was flaunting the full flowering of its spring beauty, heard on the 9 o'clock news Chamberlain broadcast his resignation speech, and announce that a Coalition would be formed. He, Chamberlain, would agree to serve under Churchill. The retiring Premier then made a fierce denunciation of the invasion of Holland and Belgium.

It is a magnificent statement [Harold remarked], and all the hatred that I have felt for Chamberlain subsides as if a piece of bread were dropped into a glass of champagne.[12]

Churchill lost no time in forming his Government. By the 17th May practically every post had been filled. Just before luncheon at Sissinghurst the telephone rang and the Prime Minister came on the line.

'Harold,' he said, 'I think it would be very nice if you joined the Government and helped Duff at the Ministry of Information.' Harold, who had already been alerted by Sibyl Colefax and Buck De La Warr, accepted without hesitation. He was thrilled to be in office at last. He was very fond of Duff Cooper, admired his sharp intelligence, and enjoyed working for him as Parliamentary Secretary, finding him sturdy, quick and imaginative. Yet as Minister Duff was not popular with his personnel, especially those in the lower-paid jobs. In the regional offices, where Harold sometimes accompanied him, they found him arrogant, aloof and short-tempered. Vita was delighted that Harold had finally got a job in the Government, although she thought his position and Duff's ought to be reversed. 'I like Duff, as you know,' she wrote, 'but he's a white mouse compared with you.'

Within two days of his appointment Harold was installed in a sunny room of the Ministry of Information, which occupied the Senate House of London University Building in Malet Street, W.C.1. His ostensible duty was to promote British propaganda abroad. However, the very first thing he did was to write to Vita on Ministry paper to tell her how warmly he had been greeted and how pleased he was to be amongst so many old friends. Among those with whom he worked closely were the Deputy Director-General Walter Monckton, Charles Peake, Kenneth Clark, Ivison MacAdam and Osbert Lancaster. From the start the new Ministry was riddled with jealousies and intrigues. The fortunes of Great Britain were at their lowest ebb in our long history. Harold in his privileged position knew that there was panic within the senior ranks of the services, and that France showed no fighting spirit. All those working in the Ministry were tense, anxious and nervy. Moreover seldom have so many literary intellectuals been assembled under one roof. For them to pull in harness at such a time was a lot to expect. And they did not pull in harness. Apart from antagonistic personalities the Ministry was not favoured by the press, the B.B.C. or the public. The two media regarded the Ministry as an unnecessary channel, through which they were supplied sparingly with Government news, and by which their freedom of selection and publication was restricted. The public which regarded it as the fount of news, which it was not, resented the morale-boosting demeanour of the Ministry in treating them like children. And like children they rightly suspected that unpleasant truths were frequently being kept from them. Duff Cooper frankly disliked his job. He despised the journalists, was in frequent disagreement with the Foreign Office and continually frustrated by the service departments. One of Harold's rôles in this maelstrom of hatreds and resentments turned out to be that of mediator. As his son has put it:

> He was his Minister's lightning-conductor. Since British relations with defeated France were the dominant topic of these weeks and France was the country which he knew best after his own, he was a key person in the right job. Many of Harold Nicolson's own friends were among those people, British and exiled, who stormed the Ministry with offers of their services and ideas for influencing British and neutral opinion. A great deal of his time was spent in such interviews, and in attending Standing Committees at the Ministry several times a day. He drafted the Cabinet statement on British war aims, advocating a Federal structure for post-war Europe and increasingly Socialist measures at home.[13]

Throughout the summer of 1940 the new Parliamentary Secretary of the Ministry of Information was constantly answering questions in the House of Commons.

Harold was so busy with his new job that he could only occasionally get away from London to Sissinghurst for the odd night. Vita was left alone to look after house and garden, as well as serve on local committees connected with the war, in particular the Women's Land Army. Not only was Sissinghurst directly on the route of German bombers to London but, in the event of the expected German invasion, within the path of the advancing armies. She and Harold had worked out what she should do if the invasion started.

> You are a brave person and you have a sense of responsibility [he wrote to her on June 4th]. It would not be you to run away and leave your people behind. If you are told to go then you must go. But I see and you see that you must stick it out if you are allowed to.[14]

Should the invasion come and Kent be ordered to evacuate then she must be prepared to flee at a moment's notice, which he imagined he would be able to give her. She was to keep their Buick car with a full petrol tank in running order. She was to store in it enough food to keep her for twenty-four hours. She was to pack in the boot her jewels, his diaries, and any small thing very precious.[15] She was to take what clothes she could make do with. He added that she must also take with her Gwen St. Aubyn, then living in a nearby cottage,[16] and Copper, the chauffeur-handyman and his wife. Everything else must be left behind. She would drive straight to Devon, presumably to seek refuge with his brother Eric and his wife. On the 27th May Vita wrote that she supposed they might never meet again, and had decided to send straightway Harold's diaries and her will to Eric's.

By the end of May it was clear that Vita could never bear to leave the garden, come what Germans might. 'I find that things become more endurable in ratio to their seriousness,' she wrote to him. It was a merciful dispensation to bear the unbearable. In the second week of June she was having an Anderson shelter constructed in the orchard to share with the Beale family from the farm next door. The brew-house was being kept as a decontamination centre against gas-attacks which were then anticipated.

Both Harold and Vita decided without any hesitation that rather than fall into German hands they would commit suicide. So they settled to take poison. But how to get it? Harold undertook to consult friends. Through Raymond Mortimer Dr. Pierre Lansel, a Swiss doctor, soon obliged with a lethal pill. Henceforth the Nicolsons referred to it in their letters as 'the bare bodkin', which on the 18th June Raymond handed over to Harold. Vita was not very pleased to learn that the bare bodkin took a quarter of an hour to work. Nevertheless the Dunkirk spirit had entered into both of them.

I think that things just now do lift one on to a different plane [Vita wrote to him[17]] from one's previous life. This sounds high-falutin' perhaps, but I mean it perfectly soberly. Love, courage, resolve, and even a fatalistic resignation, gain increase in times of high trial. It even gives one a sort of vanity; one discovers oneself to be of a finer mettle than one had even suspected. This sounds awful, but you know what I mean.

Harold too experienced a sort of elation during these most hazardous weeks. Fear and sorrow had given way to anger and pride. He felt almost anaesthetised as he wrote, quite collectedly, 'In three weeks from now Sissinghurst may be a waste and Vita and I both dead.'[18] While walking to the Temple one summer night under the stars he tried to analyse his feelings. Did he think we should win? No, not really. We might with luck achieve some compromise. Did he believe that he would survive? No, he did not think that either Vita or he would survive. He had even chosen a plot of ground in Withyham churchyard where his ashes might repose, if they could be recovered, and if there were anyone to recover them.[19] Was he in gloom with these thoughts? Not in the least. He was exhilarated. 'I never knew how much my pride and my deep love of my country can give courage. I always imagined that I was a cowardly man. I am not cowardly in these days.'[20] During the raids on London he succeeded in practising a sort of suspension of the imagination,[21] a total concentration, illogical if you like, upon – victory. His elation and optimism at this nadir of British fortunes was so marked that it actually irritated some of his friends. 'It was impossible to make out,' Clive Bell wrote to Frances Partridge on his return to Charleston on the 21st June, 'what people were thinking or feeling in London. Only Harold Nicolson was painfully confident, & after all he's paid to be that.'

Busy as he was Harold made time to see his younger friends, usually in the evenings. He would often snatch an hour or two to give them dinner at the Travellers, before slogging back in the black-out to Malet Street. There he would attend to some urgent business before retiring to a camp bed in the comparative safety of the stalwart University tower, which stood up to several direct hits while he was sleeping below it. And he would walk across St. James's Park each Thursday to spend the night in less comfort on firewatching duty in the House of Commons. He dossed down on a pallet with unclean blankets in a stuffy room with waiters and boiler-stokers who spat and snored. A little paraffin lamp made two eye-holes on the ceiling. It spluttered and added to the general fug. The next day he always felt unrested. During the height of the bombing he did not sleep in King's Bench Walk, going there each morning by bus or on foot for a bath and breakfast and to collect his letters.

On the 11th June he attended Christopher Hobhouse's wedding in Chelsea Old Church to a beautiful girl, Gavrelle Thomas. Christopher looked very slim and smart in his blue uniform. It was a last-minute affair because he was allowed only the day off from his duties, and there were a mere handful of guests present. Harold found the little ceremony moving. He hurriedly left to plunge back into the vortex of his Ministry work. He was not to see Christopher again. Less than two and a half months later Christopher was blown to pieces during a raid on Portsmouth, leaving his widow pregnant and penniless. Harold undertook to be the child's godfather.[22]

Other young friends would turn up unexpectedly at King's Bench Walk, either on leave or in transit from one service post to another in England or abroad. There was Robin Maugham, Willie's nephew, whom he first got to know as a Cambridge undergraduate in 1936. He became an intimate friend who charmed Harold with his astonishing, often hair-raising tales of adventures, his uninhibited enjoyment of life and his romantic temperament. Harold would visit him at his flat, back from the front with shrapnel in his head and the threat of a tumour on the brain; or in hospital recovering from appalling injuries sustained in an earthquake. He would read through his manuscripts and offer advice on his novels which usually shocked him. 'I wish Robin were a little more proper and discreet. He seems to regard any reticence as hypocrisy.' His trouble in Harold's eyes was that he could not dissociate his body from his mind. But Harold relished his companionship and would refer to him as 'my beloved Robin Maugham.'

Then there was Richard Rumbold, one of Harold's extremely lame ducks and often a heavy cross to bear. The son of an eccentric and cruel father, of a gentle mother who committed suicide, and brother of a devoted sister who also took her own life, Richard was a psychological case, 'mad, good and dangerous to know.'[23] Born a Roman Catholic and by temperament devout, he managed to get himself excommunicated for some provocation of the Church more silly than serious. Subject to deep fits of melancholia and driven to desperate acts of bravery in the Air Force while ill-advisedly in charge of a bomber crew, or of foolhardy bravado such as flying under the Menai Bridge, for which he was court-martialled, haunted by the horrors of war, and brooding over slights offered and imagined, he was a perpetual anxiety to Harold who was constantly getting him out of scrapes and intervening with the authorities and pleading with his doctors. Richard, who in his sanity was a gifted writer, always declared that Harold was the one person whom he depended on and worshipped. Having survived years of suffering from tuberculosis and periods of near-madness he finally threw himself out of a window in Palermo.

On the 12th September we read in Harold's diary: 'Dine with Guy Burgess at the Reform and have the best cooked grouse that I have ever eaten.' Harold had first met Burgess in 1936 and got to know him well two years later. In November 1938 while he was working for the B.B.C. Guy told Harold that he was in a rage with his employers for refusing to allow Admiral Richmond to broadcast about Britain's strategic weakness in the Mediterranean. He threatened to resign. Harold persuaded this violent and emotional young man to do nothing of the sort. He had been attracted, not by his person – he had the look of an inquisitive rodent emerging into daylight from a drain – which was already grubby and drink-sodden, but by his extremely nimble mind, his passionate interest in politics and genuine loathing of Naziism. He was amused too by his outrageous views and contentious statements. It is likely that Harold knew about his membership of the Communist Party while a Cambridge undergraduate. He would not have known that Guy resigned in order to further the Marxist cause by methods of infiltration, which could best be done through entering public services, but could never be done by an avowed Party member. He would have been appalled by such perfidy. Yet he recorded on the 21st August 1940 that Guy, who had just come back from America, confided in him a determination to get in touch with the Comintern to create disturb-ances in occupied territories. He had no idea that his friend was already working for that nefarious body. Like many other of Burgess's friends and acquaintances he was taken in by his mendacity and plausibility. He did not know how many of his portentous rhodomontades to believe. Yet he valued his opinions on politics as, not necessarily sound, but thought-provoking. This does not mean that he did not consider Guy a scamp, and he deplored his affair with James Pope-Hennessy, whom he considered far too sensitive and affectionate for so ruthless and promiscuous a partner. There can be little doubt that Guy Burgess extracted from Harold inside information which he passed on to his masters in Moscow.

James was the one young friend with whom Harold found time to keep up a regular correspondence. He was serving in an anti-aircraft battery at Chatham with Ben. Harold's letters to him were alternately laudatory and expostulatory. James's attitude to the war was equivocal. Sometimes he raged against the Germans as the disturbers of what would but for them have been the pleasantest of worlds for him, James, aged twenty-three with an unquenchable thirst for devoting his life to literature and love. Sometimes he blamed England for having pro-voked unnecessary hostilities and railed against Harold's generation for its responsibility for the impasse in which he found himself. At times these pinpricks so exasperated Harold that he mildly rebuked him.

> I don't mind your views about the war so long as you do not air them to people who might get you into trouble. I know it does you good to be able to abuse a person of my generation especially when he is in an official job. And it does me good in a way to hear you voicing thoughts that I half think myself. But why you should abuse me who

have always warned people against this nightmare I am not quite clear. My line has been perfectly consistent . . . I wish I could really understand your frame of mind. It seems to me to be based upon a purely instinctive sense of anger and panic. You feel frightened and furious at this interruption of your life. You have no sense of history, only an acute liking for historical anecdotes. And you are like a hurt animal biting at the hands of your friends.[24]

It really was intolerable to listen to James's petulant tirades while London was being submitted to an average of 200 German bombers every night for 57 nights in succession; while our Fighter Command was losing a quarter of its pilots and 466 Hurricanes and Spitfires in the Battle of Britain; while Inner Temple Hall was burnt out and in Mitre Court the clock tower was destroyed. 'I should shake James till his teeth rattled,' he told Vita, 'if I lived with him, much as I like seeing him from time to time.'[25] But he always forgave him. When in October James won the Hawthornden Prize for his first book, *London Fabric*, Harold was in ecstasies. He was touched that, having got some money for the first time in his life, James spent it on giving him an expensive present.

And then by contrast Eve Curie came into his life. This gallant musician and writer escaped from France with nothing but a small handbag. At the request of General de Gaulle she went to America to tell them what France meant to the world. She returned to England and joined up as a private in the French W.R.A.A.F., scrubbing floors. 'She is one of the most remarkable women I ever met,' Harold told Vita,[26] 'and if I were able to fall in love I might fall in love. But the thing can't be done.'

As usual Harold felt that he was not pulling his weight in the Ministry, or had not enough weight to pull. Yet he was kept busy without relief. He represented the Ministry on the Civil Defence Committee of the Cabinet. He was largely responsible for a Memorandum by the War Aims Committee which anticipated the Beveridge social reforms. He was constantly answering questions in the House of Commons. On the 18th December he made a long statement on the policy of his Ministry, which was not to imitate the tactics of Goebbels, but to aim at creating and maintaining Great Britain's credit. He informed the House that whereas a year ago broadcasts were given in sixteen foreign languages, now they were given in thirty.

He was much upset by Lord Lothian's sudden death at the Embassy in Washington. Harold's name was bandied in the papers as a suitable successor. But nothing came of what might have been a most suitable appointment. And the reason was that Winston Churchill did not really care for Harold. The two men had known each other for many years without ever becoming intimate. Harold's admiration for Churchill exceeded that for any other man, even, as his son has pointed out, Lloyd George at the time of the 1919 Peace Conference. To him Winston stood the impregnable rock of defiance against the most evil philosophy in the history of the civilized world, Naziism. Any failings he may have had faded in Harold's eyes before this one factor. Winston was of heroic stature. Harold was so captivated by him that he observed and noted down his slightest gestures and moods. None was unworthy of record. He described how he would, when deeply concentrating on a speech in the House of Commons, rub the palms of his hands with five fingers extended up and down the front of his coat. He described his eyes when he was talking to him in the Smoking Room as:

> glaucous, vigilant, angry, combative, visionary and tragic. In a way they are the eyes of a man who is much preoccupied and is unable to rivet his attention on minor things (such as me). But in another sense they are the eyes of a man faced by an ordeal or tragedy, and combining vision, truculence, resolution and great unhappiness.[27]

He had got it right. Churchill's eyes were unable to rivet their attention upon Harold's, which were too adoring, too spaniel-like. Had Harold's attitude towards Churchill been less adulatory, more easy and egalitarian, then his splendid intelligence, discernment and knowledge of foreign affairs might have won him a position of greater authority in the Second World War.

The winter of 1940–1941 was as severe as the previous one. And it saw the worst excesses of the German blitz on London. Harold was an impotent spectator and sufferer of most of the worst raids on the capital. They aroused in him a love of London and England and a pride in his countrymen of which he had hitherto been unaware. His diaries and letters were inspired by the devastating and dramatic scenes he witnessed, and the courage of the bombed and wounded inhabitants. They gave vent to some of the most vivid descriptions by eye-witnesses of these terrible and terrifying months. They showed that he was just as courageous and uncomplaining as his fellow citizens. And they kindled in him a sympathy and understanding of the ordinary man and woman in the street which he had never experienced before.

While he was touring the provinces on morale-boosting missions, often in the most uncomfortable circumstances, carrying his heavy luggage to a London terminus in the pitch dark, and standing in the corridors of late, unheated trains, the Temple was being flattened by land mines. Miss Niggeman wrote to him that the window-frames of his chambers had been torn out, and the original convex panes had gone for ever – 'We are fighting devils.' Vita sadly lamented the old panes which were irreplaceable. She loved those windows which made the messenger boys' reflections look like his pot-bellied brother Freddy. Harold enjoyed his tours on the whole, for he felt he was doing good in encouraging hard-pressed war-workers in the industrial regions and ironing out their grievances. Always fascinated by the vagaries of the rich he was amused when his host Lord Stamford of Dunham Massey Hall complained that the B.B.C. would not play the Abyssinian National Anthem on Sunday evenings, and Evan Morgan of Tredegar Park showed him his bedside table littered with photographs of royalty in silver frames, and one of the late Pope cheek by jowl with that of an able-bodied sailor.

At Nottingham he made a stirring speech, saying, 'What you need to do is to clear out some of the dead wood.' Whereupon there was a slight moan from the audience and an old gentleman fell back dead in his chair with his chin pointing to the ceiling.

Vita meanwhile was marooned by snowdrifts at Sissinghurst where the cold was appalling. Yet she rather enjoyed the rigours. They prevented her getting soft. She liked being in contact with the elements, bringing the swans into shelter, and tending the sheep. She positively relished being cut off from the outside world. By now her anti-social stand was confirmed. She hated pompous parties. The slightest social effort made her nervous and unhappy. Harold finally realised that the world considered her neurotic. But he knew that she had found all she now wanted from life – her flowers, books, dogs, family and few intimate friends – and got out of it more than most people did in a hectic pursuit of diversions away from home. He rejoiced that her neurosis took so negative and harmless a form, and not some positive form to disturb her emotions. Vita admitted rather touchingly that people bothered her, scattered her. They made her say silly things because she became confused and then everything went to pieces. She felt decreased. At the same time Harold warned her not to concentrate too much on a love of loneliness. As winter turned to spring he worried about her health and state of mind. She had become blotchy in the face. She often tottered when she walked and spoke with unwonted slowness. Her heart, probably owing to the physical work to which she was not accustomed, in addition to intensified writing, was weakening.

And then suddenly Violet Trefusis, driven out of France, was in England, and got in touch. Vita had met her in London, and Violet was considering taking a house in nearby Sussex. Although Vita assured Harold that wild horses would not get her involved with Violet again, yet the renewal of correspondence had undoubtedly prodded old wounds.

Harold was aware of this cause of Vita's dejection. Her muddles, as he called them, and consequently his troubles always seemed to assail them when he was at his busiest, during critical moments of his career. He deplored the fact that he never seemed really able to help her when she most needed help.

> I just moon about feeling wretched myself [he wrote to her], and when I look back on my life I see that the only times I have been really unhappy are when you have been unhappy too. In fact since I was a little boy, I have never been unhappy at all except in connection with you – either when I was at Resht wretched at leaving you or bothered to death by your being unhappy about things I could not manage or control. Or even understand.

And he continued:

> I wonder if you would have been happier if married to a more determined and less sensitive man. On the other hand you would have hated any sense of control or management, and other men might not have understood your desire for independence. I have always respected that, and you have often mistaken it for aloofness on my part. What bothers me is whether I have given way too much to your eccentricities (even as Dada gave way too much to B.M.'s eccentricities . . .). But what has always worried me is your dual personality. The one, tender, wise, and with such a sense of responsibility. And the other rather cruel and extravagant. The former has always been what I have clung to as the essential you, but the latter has always alarmed me and I have tried to dismiss it from my mind. Or rather I have always accepted that as the inevitable counterpart of your remarkable personality. I have felt that this side of you was beyond my understanding, and when you have got into a real mess because of it you have been angry with me for not coping with the more violent side in yourself. I do not think you have ever quite realised how deeply unhappy your eccentric side has often rendered me. When I am unhappy I shut up like an oyster.[28]

What these words convey is that Harold needed a strong prop against which to lean. Most human beings do. Some find it in religion; others in art; most in a stable love. Vita was his prop. On the few occasions when he saw the prop threatened he panicked like the small boy he never ceased to be.

The very day, March 31st 1941, that Harold wrote admitting how much Vita's eccentric side distressed him and expressing rather unnecessary concern about Violet she was writing him a letter, which crossed his. It was to announce Virginia Woolf's suicide. This came as a tremendous shock and grief to her. Virginia's friendship may not have transcended in passion Vita's for Violet, but it had certainly been the most influential as it was the most literary one of her life. Barely more than a month before Vita had stayed at Rodmell. While Leonard went to the market laden with baskets of apples and carrots she sat alone with Virginia in her cosy room with its incredible clutter of objects which made her terrified of knocking something over.

Vita's letter to Harold in answer to his worried one of the 31st, misunderstood what he meant by her eccentricities. She dismissed it by supposing he referred to her becoming a recluse. As it was, Harold rushed down to Sissinghurst for the night. It was in the middle of the week, and he was at his busiest. Neither made any allusion to his reason for coming, which was of course to bring her comfort. Yet each understood it. Spoken words between them were on this occasion, as on many others, unnecessary. Vita wrote later to tell him how grateful she had been. 'My dearest,' Harold wrote back to her, 'I know that Virginia meant something to you which nobody else can ever mean and that you will feel deprived of a particular sort of haven which was a background comfort and strength. I have felt sad about it every hour of the day.'[29] And every hour of that day he had also been worried to sickness by our troops' withdrawal from Libya.

Having sifted through the problems of the regions Harold returned to London full of ideas for improvements which Duff Cooper was always ready to consider, and usually to adopt. This is what made working under him so satisfactory. The Parliamentary Secretary was also specially fitted to act as liaison between the Ministry of Information and the Free French. He had recently met General de Gaulle for the first time. He was not favourably impressed by this conceited and prickly man, who never for one instant prefaced his opinions, which were often intensely critical, with blandishments. During luncheon, at which Clement Attlee and Hugh Dalton were present, de Gaulle accused Harold's Ministry of being Pétainiste. 'Mais, non, Monsieur le Général,' Harold expostulated. 'Enfin, Pétainisant,' the General conceded ungraciously. 'Nous travaillons,' Harold insisted, 'pour la France entière.' 'La France entière,' shouted de Gaulle, in his best Louis Quatorze manner, 'c'est la France Libre. C'est moi!' 'Oh, le Roi Soleil!', Harold replied impertinently. There was a hush. De Gaulle smiled wanly.

They were to meet on many subsequent occasions. Gradually Harold overcame his distaste. He made allowances for the General's abusiveness, argumentativeness, vanity. De Gaulle had something to be vain about. At first Harold thought his arrogance was Fascist. Later he decided it was the essential quality of leadership. He noticed his tired retriever-dog-like eyes and curiously effeminate hands. But though Harold managed to dislike him less he could not altogether admire him. He never considered him responsible enough to have sole charge of a great nation, because he was possessed of rancour and sheer bad manners. As he got to know him better in the course of the war he dared to advise him not to dwell on his dignity. He begged him occasionally to *faire le grand geste*. De Gaulle was almost amused. He wagged a roguish finger like a human being.

In collaboration with Lord Halifax before his appointment as Ambassador to Washington in December 1940 Harold had with much trouble prepared the statement on war aims, advocating a European federation and increased Socialism at home, which his son has called his greatest contribution to British policy while he was at the Ministry of Information.[30] To Harold's disappointment Winston Churchill on the 22nd January rejected it on the grounds that the announcement of precise aims would be compromising, and imprecise statements were bound to be disappointing. Days of work and pages of drafts had thus been in vain. Yet Harold bore his leader no resentment whatever and magnanimously praised as authoritative, conciliatory and amusing Churchill's replies in a debate on man-power delivered the same afternoon.

He was not at all happy about the situation at the Ministry. He was worried that Churchill had got his knife into Duff Cooper. Churchill did not like the Ministry, nor in fact did Duff, who consequently did not fight sufficiently for it in Cabinet. Lack of confidence by the Prime Minister in his chief meant that Harold also felt his authority in the office to be undermined. Then he too got into trouble. A talk which he had given six months before to a private meeting of the Fabian Society about the forbidden subject of war aims was published in the Society's year book and in a roundabout way, via America, reached the eye of the Prime Minister. Churchill blew up and sent a highly critical letter to Duff Cooper, asking by what right he had allowed the subject to be publicly ventilated. Harold drafted a minute explaining what had happened, and was touchingly pleased when Churchill wrote to Duff, 'Thank Mr. Nicolson for his explanation.' Chamberlain, Harold remarked, would merely have written, 'I accept Mr. Nicolson's explanation.' So readily, and no doubt too servilely, did the Parliamentary Secretary accept the slightest mark of condescension from the great leader, who in fact rather liked being stood up to on occasion. 'I love Winston and would not mind if he were to be unjust to me. But one does like these delicate pats that he gives,' was Harold's reaction. As for his own status in the Ministry, he regretted that what he called the chicken food jobs allotted to him prevented him giving serious broadcasts and writing articles untrammelled by governmental vetoes. Moreover although he had supposed his particular job to be a stepping-stone to Cabinet rank, yet now he felt certain that he would never be admitted to the front bench.

In May destruction of the City and the Temple went on apace. Nevertheless King's Bench Walk still stood. The House of Commons was burnt out, Westminster Hall badly damaged and the Abbey injured.

> I go to see the ruins of the old Chamber. It is impossible to get through the Members' Lobby which is a mass of twisted girders. So I went up by the staircase to the Ladies' Gallery and then suddenly, when I turned the corridor, there was the open air and a sort of Tintern Abbey gaping before me. The little Ministers' rooms to the right and left of the Speaker's Lobby were still intact, but from there onwards was absolutely nothing. No sign of anything but *murs calcinés* and twisted girders. I went away with a heavy weight on my heart.[31]

Bombardment of London always seemed to coincide with bad news elsewhere. The Yugoslavs and the Greeks collapsed. The Germans took Crete. Panic seized Egypt. Winston cheered the House at the worst moment and received a vote of confidence of 447 against 3. Harold again gave up smoking as a gesture of atonement as well as for economy reasons. Rudolph Hess chose to fly to Scotland. The incident caused ructions in the Ministry of Information, which was told nothing of what had happened. The Press were furious with the Ministry which laid blame upon the Air Ministry. The Director-General, Walter Monckton, threatened resignation. He was persuaded by the Prime Minister not to behave like a prima donna, but the whole affair led to drastic changes in the Ministry.

At first Harold judged Hess a fine fellow disgusted by the people (like Ribbentrop), whom Hitler had round him, people who in Hess's eyes were fighting for their own purposes and leading Hitler astray from the Holy Gospel of *Mein Kampf*. He was soon disillusioned with the man and his mission. He lunched with the Churchills in a tiny flat given them in the Office of Works, which was done up very prettily and contained some of the Prime Minister's own paintings. Churchill would not be drawn to talk about Hess but purred gently like an old cat. On June 22nd the news at breakfast announced that Germany had invaded Russia. Harold was not sure whether it was good or bad – 'Not that I have the slightest objection to Russian Communism,' he wrote rather surprisingly in his diary.[32] On the 25th he dined alone with Rob Bernays who cursed him for his prevailing weakness, a lack of assertiveness. Rob told him frankly and brutally that he had more desire to please than to dominate. Harold took his rebuke much to heart, for Rob was one of the few friends in the House who through affection would speak his mind candidly.

With the Prime Minister's affability fresh in mind Harold was deeply distressed and offended to receive out of the blue a curt letter from him, dated the 18th July and beginning, 'My dear Harold Nicolson, The changes at the Ministry of Information lead me to ask you to place your Office as Parliamentary Secretary at my disposal.' It went on to ask him to give his services to the public as a Member of the Board of Governors of the B.B.C. This ungracious note – 'I think it might have been more politely worded,' was Harold's only comment – was followed by a telephone message from the Prime Minister's Secretary that he wanted a reply at once. The ostensible reason for Harold's sacking (and he accepted it as nothing less) was that his office was needed for a Labour Member of Parliament, the replacement being Ernest Thurtle, a comparative nonentity with absolutely no knowledge of the important tasks of overseas persuasion. At the same time Duff Cooper was replaced by Brendan Bracken, a firebrand in the Prime Minister's close confidence.

Needless to say Harold agreed to become a Governor of the B.B.C. although this meant for a time at least prohibition of his broadcasting.

Harold's removal from the Ministry of Information was a severe blow to his pride and self-esteem, from which he never recovered. He fully realised that it could mean the end of any political ambitions he had ever cherished.[33] It was little consolation to him that Duff Cooper wrote commiserating sympathetically over his shabby treatment. The same treatment had been meted out to him, with the difference that he was promoted to be Chancellor of the Duchy of Lancaster. Quite 120 colleagues in the House, Harold calculated, told him how well he had done at the job and how shockingly he had been dealt with. He also received numerous letters of condolence from unknown sympathisers. His colleagues in the Ministry were genuinely sorry to see him go. Sadly he packed up his personal belongings in the office. He was touched by Osbert Lancaster's kindness in giving him a parting luncheon. 'After luncheon I went down the street with nothing to do. I went to a dull film . . . I have too heavy a heart to write more.'[34] He left a space in his diary to indicate the end of his ambitions in life; and then added a line from Tacitus: *Omnium consensu capax imperii nisi imperasset* – had he never been invested with authority no one would have questioned his capacity for it.

How unsuccessful had Harold Nicolson been at the Ministry of Information? There was curiously little comment on his dismissal in the press. But the periodical, *Truth*,[35] announced that his departure was no great loss to the Department; that the qualities which had assured him so successful a career under the Foreign Office were not necessarily those best suited to present Britain's case to advantage in a world at war; and that it was probably not his fault that the manners of the Foreign Office were ridiculed by neutral countries as lacking in virility. 'All the same this impression,' *Truth* went on, 'for lack of a better word, let us call it Edenesque – undoubtedly exists, and many have felt that it is a mistake when Britain is fighting for her very survival, that she should speak in a voice in which there is even a trace of the mincing accents of a Paris salon.' Did these pejorative words contain an oblique suggestion that Harold's homosexuality was prejudicial to his work? If so, they were totally unwarranted. But in implying a certain softness when important and instant decisions were required even by a junior Minister they were not entirely without justification. It was the inability to be conclusive that made Harold an indifferent administrator. Professor P. N. S. Mansergh, who was in the Dominions Office during the War recalls seeing occasional minutes of Harold's which 'were elegantly phrased, a bit discursive, and not . . . leading on to a decision.' On the other hand conversation with him was no more rewarding 'because he was . . . too much given to reflecting or refining, when decisions were being looked for, to be even a reasonably good administrator.'[36] Walter Monckton told Brendan Bracken bluntly that Nicolson was 'not of sufficient calibre'. Lord Clark, who was his colleague in the Ministry and a friend, is even more severe with his strictures. 'There was a curious air of futility in Harold,' he has written.[37] 'He had absolutely no gift for politics at all and was equally useless at what one might call the preliminaries of politics, meetings, interviews, etc . . . There was something in his attitude towards public events which gave an impression of irresponsibility.' This shrewd observer may have taken too seriously the flippancy and wit, under which Harold was at times too much given to disguising his true opinions. There is no disputing that Harold Nicolson showed abnormal sensitivity while in office. He was quite frankly in terror of getting into trouble with Churchill, the cat which, when it ceased purring, could show very formidable claws indeed. And when it came to standing up to a barrage of hostile questions and heckling in the Commons, to which he was constantly subjected, often under the baleful eye of Churchill, he showed not fear, but confusion.[38] One of the last of such miserable experiences arose when he was obliged to grovel in the House on the Ministry's behalf for having released news of the Hess affair before getting consent from the Secret Service Department.

On the other hand Sir Kenneth Grubb,[39] a Controller in the Ministry under Harold, declared that his departure was a real loss to those concerned with overseas publicity. He had been an invaluable ally because of his knowledge of foreign affairs, especially in all things French. Sir Kenneth categorically states that his dismissal was simply a political deal, in that the Labour Party felt it did not have a fair share of Under-Secretaryships and nourished a certain political prejudice against him.

When all is said and done Harold Nicolson was in office and close to the centre of Government throughout the worst twelve months of the war. It may be true that during that time he was unable to introduce many spectacular measures while in office. His authority as Parliamentary Secretary to the costive Ministry of Information was greatly circumscribed by power beyond his control. But he brought to bear upon the Ministry an influence which was beneficial and civilised. He was strongly opposed to heartless internment of harmless aliens, and helped relieve the plight of many unfortunate internees on the Isle of

Man. He was opposed to the Ministry's Anti-Rumour campaign and prosecution of individuals for gossiping. He was right, for soon the absurd and totalitarian measures proposed had to be rescinded. He was more aware than others in the Ministry of the necessity for formulating peace-time plans, on the ground that the old pre-war social order had collapsed and a new order was needed. And he strove harder than any of his colleagues to implement them. He made his colleagues realise the necessity for Britain to eschew the crude methods of propaganda practised by the enemy and to adopt subtler attitudes becoming to a democratic nation. When his friend Maynard Keynes refused a request to broadcast a rebuttal of the economic policies of the Nazis because he considered them on the whole sound, Harold was delighted. He had the sense and the courage to write to Keynes that he agreed with him and that he too hated sham propaganda.[40]

For a time Harold felt, not only hurt, but at a loose end. He was also very hard up, and had to borrow £500 from his son Ben. Again he tried to give up smoking in order to economise. It was an agony for him. What, apart from the B.B.C. governorship, was he to do to earn money? Where too was he to stay during bad spells of bombing now that his safe shelter in the Ministry building was denied him? He arranged things so that he need spend only three nights a week in King's Bench Walk, and a fourth firewatching in the House of Commons. As for another job, Wilson Harris of the *Spectator* at once engaged him to resume his weekly *Marginal Comment* articles at ten guineas a time. Harold then set about editing his diary of 1939 for publication. Constable's, to whom he submitted it, accepted it; but Lord Cranborne, whom he consulted, advised that it was premature, and that so much of interest would for reasons of secrecy, not to mention causing offence to living people, have to be left out. Cranborne feared that it would re-open too recently inflicted wounds among the Conservatives in being reminded that Chamberlain was wrong and Churchill right. So Harold abandoned that idea.[41]

If the duties of the B.B.C. board were slight in comparison with those of the Ministry of Information, they nevertheless interested him very much. After all he was a very well known and popular broadcaster. He had the greatest respect, almost affection for the B.B.C. Ten years previously he came to disapprove of Sir John Reith's dictum that the B.B.C. must not give voice to opinions that might offend anybody. It is what made distinguished writers like E. M. Forster complain that the Corporation was becoming far too cautious. But now, although Harold thought the B.B.C. still a trifle flabby at the top he saw it as

representing a certain moral and intellectual dignity, a certain gentleness of mind which were in accord with the standards of the British
race. He told Lady Violet Bonham-Carter:

> We are about to enter an age when all the old values will be called into
> question and many of the most precious of them discarded, not
> because they lack validity, but because they are old. We cannot hope
> that the Press as a whole will swim against the tide of vulgarisation
> which will sweep in from the west. Only the B.B.C. can teach the
> public to think correctly, to feel nobly, to enjoy themselves intel-
> ligently and to have some conception of what is meant by the good
> life [42]

Such over-optimistic sentiments envisaged the B.B.C. exercising a
corrective, almost paternalistic influence upon the British people.
Things did not turn out quite like that. But on the expiry of his term as
Governor in 1946 Harold still felt, when paying tribute to the B.B.C.,
that they might. It was one of the reasons why he believed the Press was
jealous and took every opportunity of criticising the B.B.C. Another
was their sense of the superiority of the read over the spoken word.
They looked down upon the B.B.C. just as professional pianists looked
down upon the pianola.

Harold found a valiant ally on the Board in his old friend, Lady Violet
Bonham-Carter, who had made it quite plain from the start that she
was not going to be treated as a mere figurehead, which Harold learnt
from his friend Harman Grisewood was just what the then Director-
General, Sir Frederick Ogilvie, wanted. [43] For Ogilvie claimed that he
had the Governors in the palm of his hand and could manipulate them
like puppets. Lady Violet and Harold soon disabused him. The two of
them working as a pair, often to the irritation of their Conservative
colleagues, brought a breath of liberalism to Broadcasting House. They
agreed over principles and worked together in great harmony over
particular issues. Harold made a point during his five years' service of
forwarding to the Chairman criticisms and comments he received from
individuals regarding broadcasts to enemy countries. It was his strong
belief that whereas the German radio treated its listeners to a *Blitzkrieg*
of propaganda, the B.B.C. should endeavour to convey confidence and
establish credit. He insisted that the traditional role of the Chairman
and Governors was 'to maintain truth and virtue', not to ascertain
whether the housewives of Leeds or Godalming preferred the Home
Service to the Forces Programme. [44]

He was always fascinated by the conflict of personalities; and when told by Grisewood that the controllers of the B.B.C. were not on speaking terms with one another, insisted on investigating the causes and endeavouring to set them to rights. When Dylan Thomas, whom he described as 'a fat little man, puffy and pinkish dressed in very dirty trousers and a loud check coat', applied to him for a war job on the B.B.C. Harold told him that if he was employed he must promise not to get drunk. He dismissed him with the loan of £1 for which Thomas had asked and which he never paid back! 'He does not look as if he had been cradled into poetry by wrong. He looks as if he would be washed out of poetry by whisky,'[45] Harold observed. He was not an unqualified admirer of his writings. He was disgusted by Thomas having to drag in urine and copulation into *Portrait of the Artist as a Young Dog*, and when on the eve of his 70th birthday he went to see *Under Milkwood*, he disliked the lack of drama and thought the whole performance boring.

Harold was again concerned (and not for the last time) with the question of what should be done with the National Labour Party. When in February 1941 Malcolm MacDonald was appointed High Commissioner in Canada, Lord De La Warr wanted Harold to succeed him as Leader. Harold wisely refused, thinking that the best thing was to let the Party die a natural death. But the moral problem of actually closing down the Party which had elected him to Parliament was a tricky one. Finally he wrote a summary of the position of the Party for De La Warr. After much argument and counter-argument the two of them decided that the best course was to continue until the end of the present Parliament as if nothing had happened since 1935.

December 1941 was another critical month for Britain. The Japanese had the effrontery to attack the American Fleet in Pearl Harbour, and the Germans and Italians to declare war against America. Ultimate victory for the Allies was thus assured. Germany was meeting with stiff resistance from Russia and her casualties were hugely mounting. But the sinking of the *Prince of Wales* and the *Repulse*, the capture of Hong Kong and the Japanese advance on Singapore, so disturbed the British public that they could find in the optimistic prognoses little to cheer them.

That Harold was still smarting six months later from his dismissal from the Ministry of Information was made evident by his response to a provocative remark made by James Pope-Hennessy on the second day of the year 1942. James had brought Guy Burgess to dine with Harold and me at Brooks's, which seemed somehow to have survived the war better than most clubs, although Harold's description of liveried foot-men slowly carrying Queen Anne silver across thick carpets was a slight exaggeration. Nevertheless it was a jolly little dinner-party.

> We had a lovely talk all the time [Harold told Vita[46]]. I do so enjoy talking with people who are intelligent about things and to whom one can say things which would be misunderstood by others. I talked about the frustration of wartime.

We talked about success; and James said, 'It is ridiculous of you, Harold, not to realise that it does not matter your having been a failure at the Ministry of Information, since you have written such good books.' The remark annoyed Harold,

> since I was not a failure at the M of I [he told his Diary], merely politically inconvenient. I say that I would rather be able to send 100 tons of grain to Greece than write an immortal book. This impresses them, as they agree. What does even the *Symposium* matter compared to the death by hunger of 200 Greeks a day.[47]

We may have been impressed; but James and I begged to differ from these noble sentiments, and, what is more, we could not then believe that Harold was being sincere. Guy Burgess remained silent, thus expressing an opinion contrary to ours. And it was Guy's opinions, rather than James's and mine, that Harold heeded in those days.

The year 1942 opened inauspiciously. Everything on the war-front seemed to be going wrong. Japan was sweeping the board in the Far East, gobbling up Singapore and taking 60,000 prisoners. Rommel drove our troops out of Cyrenaica, regaining all the territory they had won in November. Our loss of ships in the Atlantic was catastrophic. At home Churchill was being strongly criticised for a blind reliance on the mercurial Beaverbrook, then Minister of Supply. A section of National M.P.s wanted to get rid of him. Harold was disgusted with this disloyalty. His confidence and faith in the Prime Minister remained steadfast. 'Winston is the embodiment of the nation's will,' he main-tained. And the moment Churchill addressed the House of Commons, taking them into his confidence and warning them of worse times to come, they gave him a resounding vote of confidence. 'My God, my love and admiration of Winston surge round me like a tide!' Harold wrote.[48]

Worse times did come, as soon as February. Our troops were not fighting well in Malaya or in Libya. Churchill was deeply disconcerted by the lack of spirit and morale among the Forces. And Harold felt the ice-cold grip of defeat around his heart. In this condition he flew to Dublin where he addressed The Law Society's Inaugural Session and participated in a debate with undergraduates in University College. Owing to mischievous reporting in the Irish papers he got into trouble. His mistake had been not to weigh his words carefully enough. He did not sufficiently heed the warning of his friend Daniel Binchy[49] who had called to see him when he arrived in Dublin. Binchy told him that the visiting Englishman was apt to be taken in by the blarney and imagine that native feelings towards him were friendly, whereas in fact at the bottom of every Irish heart was a little bag of bile. Irish neutrality, he said, was a holy motive, and that it had so far been honoured was in the minds of Irishmen attributable, not to English efforts and good faith, but to de Valera's genius. Harold's Dublin speeches were a little too calculated to please the unpleasable.

On his return to London the Conservative M.P. for Lincoln, W. S. Liddall, tabled a motion that the House deplored a statement made in Dublin by the Member for West Leicester to the effect that our imperialism had gone, that our military power might go and that we should probably emerge from the war in a very battered and bedraggled condition. In view of the generally defeatist character of the speech the Member for West Leicester should be removed from the Board of the British Broadcasting Corporation. On the 26th March Harold, much upset, made a personal statement in the House in reply to Mr. Liddall's motion. Such motions were customarily tabled by Members as a means of expostulation but were seldom debated. Harold took the motion too much to heart, and replied to it at too great length. The alleged brick he dropped was, he explained, in a debate with the undergraduates of University College. One undergraduate spoke with venom of the imperialist ambitions of the British, claiming that the war was really being fought by us for imperialist ends. When it came to Harold's turn to take part in the debate he felt incensed by this extraordinary account of our war effort. He told the University that the old nineteenth-century imperialism was dead and buried, and that if, at the solicitations of this brilliant young man, they pictured the British lion as a rampant beast red in tooth and claw, they had got a completely distorted view. It would be much more sensible to regard the British lion as an elderly, replete and somewhat moth-eaten animal, whose tail had been twisted so frequently in the last twenty years that very few hairs remained. But that animal was, nonetheless, at the moment, up, alert and angry. He told the undergraduates that we must expect further disasters in the future; that defeats and rebuffs had not only diminished our conceit and destroyed our self-complacency; they had increased our pride.

Harold then pulled the notes of that speech from his pocket. He informed the House of Commons that he believed it was the best speech he had ever made, and proceeded to read out further quotations from it about our fighting on our own and other people's beaches. In self-exculpation he described how he had been cheered in a way unexpected from a thousand Irish undergraduates. To cries from Members, 'Don't overdo it!' Harold asked Mr. Liddall to withdraw his motion and express some contrition. Mr. Liddall withdrew the motion, but refused to qualify his justification for having tabled it.

Before leaving Dublin Harold had an interview with de Valera. The man's appearance was unexpected. Instead of being sallow, lined and severe, with lank, black Spanish hair, de Valera was almost puffy, pale, with benevolent cold eyes and soft, brown hair. An agreeable smile lit up his face and eyes 'very quickly, like an electric light bulb that doesn't fit and flashed on and off. Yet not an insincere smile. A happy smile.'[50] His manner was gentle, but his conversation uninteresting.

Ben, now a 2nd Lieutenant in the Intelligence Corps, gave his father to understand that he might be posted to Ulster. So Harold wrote him a long letter[51] about his Irish relations and their houses, about whom he imagined rightly that Ben knew nothing whatever, but in whom he might be interested. Not at all. Ben, in spite of his profession as an art historian, was not the least interested in relationships, considering them a snobbish fad.

During the summer Harold had a first-hand experience of the amazing incompetence in all manual matters of those who devote their lives to intellectual pursuits. Having some spare time he went to a training centre for munitions work in Vincent Square, and clad in overalls, filed things at a bench. His ineptitude at this work left him 'with a sense, not so much of humiliation, as of blank astonishment.'[52] He had never in all his life met with such patience and kindness as he received from his fellow-workers.

There were two of them and they each discovered that in me they had found a whole-time job. While one of them would repair the tool that

I had damaged, the other, with sweet forgiveness, would re-adjust the belt that I had displaced. The objects, which with great care and much exhaustion I would manufacture, were at the end of the evening's class placed by themselves in a cardboard box, marked N.G., signifying (I have little doubt) 'No Good'. I would leave the shop with my muscles twisting in pain, with my feet throbbing with flat-footedness, with my eyes thick in oil, and in my hair large pools or splashes of that viscous fluid with which machine-tools are cooled. Fifty years of study and action had been taken from me; I was back at school soiled and humiliated by physical incompetence. Grimly I reflected that I had missed my true vocation in life; my true vocation was that of *saboteur*.

Harold was undeniably a butter-fingers. He was incapable even of unscrewing the cap off a bottle of cider, and during Vita's last illness his deeply concentrated attempts at being practical by her bedside were pitiable to behold.

In July he spoke in the debate on Criticism of our Propaganda. Nobly he gave praise to the remarkable work done by the Ministry of Information during the past twelve months since his departure from that scene. But what he advocated as British methods of propaganda were too vague to have much effect on the House. That month he was cheered by his first sight of the pork-pie hats of the American sailors walking the streets of London. But he felt tired. The raids on London which had started again were taking their toll. He still did firewatching on Thursdays. On the 30th there were two alerts during the night. He dressed and patrolled with his torch. 'In and out of the Prince's Chamber and the Royal Gallery I go, and into the dark House of Lords.'[53] He sat on the Woolsack with his tin hat on, his torch giving the sole illumination while the guns thundered outside. In August he received a telegram that his nephew Peter Nicolson, his brother Eric's twenty-year-old son, a sub-Lieutenant in the Royal Naval Reserve, had been killed.

Early in September Harold paid his first visit to St. Michael's Mount, which since the death of Sam St. Aubyn's uncle in 1940, was now his sister's home. Harold greatly admired the proud and handsome stronghold on a prominence of the South Cornish coast, amongst granite rocks, pines and ilexes. The Mount had to be approached by a causeway.

I should be driven mad by the fuss about boats and tides [he wrote to Vita[54]]. Their lives are dominated by that strip of water. It would drive me quite mad – as if not only the big room and the dining-room [at Sissinghurst] were permanently locked, but as if the key of my own sitting-room were kept at the top of the tower and I had to climb up every time. I kept on wondering how you would have taken to it were you Lady Mountiful or the Dame de Serq. If you had been born to it you would have become a sea-gull, perching on rocks and screaming sea-gull cries. You would have gazed from your parapets at the causeway being covered with water and at the world being sundered. I should have wished to run down to Bridglands for some cigarettes – but, no – it meant boatmen and being carried on their backs to the shore. Or else you would have been permanently in a boat rowing against angry seas like Grace Darling, but I am glad I am not the Dame de Serq's husband.

Harold was quick to notice the inconvenience of other people's houses whereas it did not occur to him that anyone would find any in the extraordinary living conditions, a central tower, two detached cottages, converted stables and outbuildings, which comprised Sissinghurst Castle. Vita was slightly resentful of his visiting the Mount, for she feared he might like it better than Sissinghurst. She called him a quisling.

In October of this year both the boys were sent on service overseas. Nigel was the first to leave home although the last to sail from his depot. Harold and Vita hated losing them. 'I did not enjoy saying goodbye to Niggs,' Vita wrote on the 1st. 'But fortunately his train started moving out of the station just as he got into it.' Harold was much impressed by the assumed nonchalance with which the brothers, who were devoted, parted from each other, whereas his heart was full. 'Well, goodbye Niggs. We may meet somewhere,' Ben said. Then Nigel left. 'I may not see him again,' Harold wrote. 'I feel quite sick with sorrow. I watch Niggs walk away and pass the railings by the corner towards Mitre Court.'[55] Then came the other's turn to go to the Middle East. Harold dreaded losing Ben, he confided in Vita. 'I love his quiet, sleepy affection and his intelligent attitude. I also value his intelligence and his guts. These truly are the bravest, those who dread war deeply and yet face it without a whimper.'[56] Harold too was brave in that he never betrayed to his friends what he felt, and only to Vita. When Ben left for Paddington Harold accompanied him in the underground from the Temple station as far as Charing Cross. They sat beside each other, Ben clutching his fibre suit-case and funny little hand-bag. Harold could not speak. When the train stopped at Charing Cross he got up to go. 'Goodbye, Benzie.' 'Goodbye, Daddy.' Harold closed the carriage doors behind him. He stood on the platform waiting for the train to move. It jerked away. 'My eyes are blinded with tears.'

That very afternoon Harold wrote Ben a letter:

> This is the first of what I trust will not be more than a short series beginning this Sunday and continuing every Sunday until you come home. When Nigel leaves I shall address an identical letter more or less to each of you . . . I shall keep carbon copies in case you wish to refer to them.[57]

Indeed he wrote 130 joint diary-letters of about 3,000 words each to his two sons. The first few were addressed to Ben alone since he was the first to leave, the last to Nigel in 1945 since he was the last to return. This weekly task was additional to his daily letter to Vita when they were apart during the week, and his diary. They contained a store of information of what went on in Parliament, what he was doing, what reading, whom seeing, and what thinking. Although their content had to be discreet he wonderfully managed to convey intimate information about the conduct of the war, adroitly phrased so as to avoid the suspicions of the censor. All of them have been preserved. They are enchanting letters of a father to his sons. Whatever came into Harold's head was typed out by him, without forethought. And yet it was always interesting. The tone of the letters is perhaps set by a passage in the very first to Ben the day he left. After telling him he had no news since he saw him three hours and forty-four minutes ago, he remarked that the problem of displacement had never been well expressed.

> It seems unaccountable to me that I should still be using the same cardboard box of cigarettes as I used at the club last night, and that when I bought it you bought a fountain pen. The box will go to salvage in a few hours and the pen will go to hazards whence no tears can win it. It seems unaccountable to me that the present should so suddenly become the past and that rapidly the familiarity of K.B.W. should be succeeded by the unfamiliarity of a cabin and that the voices you know should be merged into voices that you do not know. It is a theme which never ceases to perplex me and to seek for expression.[58]

No wonder that until his death Ben treasured his father's war-time letters as the most precious of his possessions, more valued than all the pictures and works of art he inherited and was to collect in after years.

6

THE SECOND WORLD WAR – SURVIVAL TO VICTORY, 1942–1945

HAROLD had prefaced his diary for the year 1942 with the words, 'A year, I hope, of recovery.' His prognosis was correct. Events made it increasingly clear that the Allies had overwhelming long-term superiority, and November 1942 marked the turning-point of the war. A number of incidents favourable to the Allied cause happened on different fronts, incidents which, subject to inevitable reverses, were to lead to ultimate victory. It is true that during this month the Germans occupied Vichy France. But that, in view of French collapse under Pétain, was only to be expected even if certain consequences, like the scuttling of the Navy and the Allies' deal with the traitor Admiral Darlan, were unforeseen. The heartening news however was Montgomery's victory of Alamein. It was followed by the landing of American and British forces in Morocco and Algeria. And before November was over, the Russians outflanked the German army in Stalingrad.

While the church bells were ringing – the cautious thought somewhat prematurely – Vita was writing to Harold that her new novel, *Grand Canyon*, not yet out, had already sold nearly 8,000 copies.[1] By now she was such an established author that a sale of this magnitude was accepted by the Nicolsons as her due. But *Grand Canyon* was by no means her best novel, and it received some carping reviews.

With *Grand Canyon* published Vita was having an uphill struggle with her second long bucolic poem, *The Garden*. Her complaint that anyway nothing in life mattered very much in those days drew a rebuke from Harold who declared that everything in life mattered more than it ever did before, so great was his pride in the courage of his countrymen and confidence in England's future. He really believed England was setting an example to the world by tackling the social and economic problems of the twentieth century. He had in mind the recommendations of Sir William Beveridge's Report that had just been published.

In August Harold went to see Sir William[2] in order to put to him several National Labour proposals about medical services being taken over by the State, an increase in old-age pensions and encouragement to old people to retire. Although his recommendations were not received with much enthusiasm Harold came away greatly encouraged by what

Beveridge was propounding. It was the congenital Liberal in Harold that warmed to the provision of social services and improvement in living conditions for the masses. Although he never made close contact with the working classes, yet he believed passionately, if academically, in the betterment of their living conditions, so long as this did not mean the lowering of standards generally. He was delighted with the Report and felt confident that through it we should get a new England without revolution. Certainly the Beveridge proposals were of immense importance in that, when adopted, they became the first of a series of post-war Acts of Parliament to redress the worst social abuses of the capitalist thirties. Vita on the other hand took a predictably Tory view of them.

> I think it sounds dreadful [she wrote[3]]. The proletariat being encouraged to breed like rabbits because each new little rabbit means 8/– a week, as though there weren't too many of them already and not enough work to go round . . . and everybody being given anything for nothing. Lloyd George gave them pensions, and what do they do? Grumble about having to contribute to the stamps, and then grumble because they don't get money enough. Oh no, I don't hold with Sir William Beveridge, and it all makes me very pre-1792.

The recovery of the Allied cause in November coincided with an accident which all but brought about Harold's extinction. He was on his way in the black-out from the Travellers' Club to Buckingham Palace, in order to read Nigel's official diary of the Grenadier Guards, of which he was Intelligence Officer in the 3rd Battalion. The diary was in the custody of Sir Arthur Penn, Nigel's Regimental Adjutant as well as the Queen's Private Secretary. In crossing the road opposite St. James's Palace in the pitch dark Harold was knocked down by a taxi. He was lucky to escape with only a cracked rib, and the loss of his torch and spectacles. The taxi-driver before picking him up thought he must have killed him. He was deeply concerned and asked Harold where he would like to be taken. 'Buckingham Palace,' Harold answered. 'Come, come,' the cabby replied, 'Surely, sir, I had better take you to hospital.' When convinced that his fare was not suffering from delusions he did what he was asked. Arrived at Sir Arthur's office, his clothes torn, his face bleeding and his back in agony, Harold was in a state of shock. Sir Arthur just had time to give him a stiff whisky and soda before being rung for by the Queen, who sent him back with a message begging Harold to stay the night at the Palace. Gratefully Harold declined. Spectacleless he somehow managed to read the diary. As the result of the accident he had to go about for several weeks swathed, as he put it, like Amenothep the Second.

The year 1943 was marked by several very important events in which Harold played no direct part. In January our troops pursued Rommel for 1400 miles across the North African desert and entered Tripoli. In February the Germans under Field Marshal Paulus surrendered at Stalingrad. After much anxiety over the way affairs were going in Tunisia and understandable worry about Nigel who was in the thick of the fighting, Harold rejoiced when Tunis and Bizerta fell to the Allies in May. By July the collapse of Italy was imminent. One night Harold was in bed asleep. He was woken by Vita standing at his bedside, announcing dramatically that Mussolini had fallen from power. After weeks of confusion Italy surrendered in September. Then came the Battle of Salerno following the Allied invasion of southern Italy, and the pursuit of German forces up the peninsula. November was made memorable by the Teheran Conference, at which the disastrous decision was made to allocate Poland and East Prussia to Soviet Russia. All these events were closely followed and commented upon in the diaries and letters.

Although he bitterly lamented that he held no government post Harold did not complain that he lacked occupation. On the contrary, he complained to Vita how every morning at King's Bench Walk his telephone would relentlessly ring.

> Would I write an article for the *Daily Express?* Would I take the chair at a Jewish meeting? Would I lecture to the Free Austrians? Would I write an introduction to a book by an American? Would I dine with Lady Oxford? And Lady Kemsley? And Lady Cunard? Tinkle, tinkle little bell.[4]

No doubt he accepted all these invitations, which were incidental to his parliamentary responsibilities, his B.B.C. Board work, his weekly *Spectator* article, his *Daily Telegraph* reviews – and his current book. In all conscience one would suppose they were enough for any man of fifty-seven, even in wartime. And in addition to these occupations he was in touch with leading members of the Free French movement.

Not surprisingly perhaps he was overtaken by a bad attack of nerves during the summer. He was present at a debate in the Commons about the Colonies. He felt he ought to speak about African education. Physically he could not rise to his feet. A blinding loss of self-confidence overwhelmed him. He was absolutely convinced that he was a dud. He was appalled afterwards by what he considered his lack of guts, and told Vita so. She instantly replied that she was not the least astonished. For some time she had been suspecting that something of the sort was going on in his mind. What the hell did African education matter to him, with all his other interests? That was his trouble. She did not worry about a temporary lapse of self-confidence. What she worried about was his tendency to dispersal. There was a tide in the affairs of men when they should go in for a little stock-taking. 'You are now floating on that tide, but instead of bobbing like a cork on different waves,' she wrote,[5] 'I feel that it is time that you made an invasion, landing on some definite beach.' Wisely she advised him to give up his endless committees, speeches and articles, and concentrate on his *Marginal Comment*, the B.B.C., the Free French and his book. Her counsel was in fact similar to what she had given when he was in Berlin, when he was a journalist and when he was mixed up with the New Party. Alas, it was not heeded. Harold went on obstinately dispersing his interests and his talents as before.

In March he took part in a debate[6] in the Commons on reforms in the Foreign Office, chiefly instigated by Anthony Eden. In Eden's absence the Under-Secretary of State for Foreign Affairs, Richard Law, announced that his superior's intention was not so much to reform the service as to bring it up to date. The main purpose was to fuse the Diplomatic with the Consular and Commercial services. It was no longer proper that entry to the Foreign Office should be restricted to members of the 'governing classes'. Representatives should henceforth be drawn from all classes. Lack of candidates' means should be no bar to their acceptance. What was needed was greater efficiency. With these proposals Harold, when his turn came to speak, was ostensibly in full agreement. He said that if the new scheme were adopted it would be essential that men were filtered through as it were a staff college, so that by the age of thirty to thirty-five they reached the department at which the abilities of each would be most valuable. He also begged the Secretary of State not to carry out the rule of enforced retirement at sixty. 'Diplomatists were, like wine, improved with age.' His speech was constantly interrupted by Lady Astor who complained that women had never been given chances to prove their capacity in the foreign service. Harold retorted that they might not have been *given* chances, but from the days of Helen of Troy to those of the Noble Lady the Member for Plymouth they had *taken* them, and the results had been disastrous. In a letter to his sons he explained that debating with Lady Astor was like playing squash racquets with a dish of scrambled eggs.

By virtue of his friendship with Pierre Viénot and his knowledge of France Harold became deeply involved in the unseemly struggle for power being waged between Generals de Gaulle and Giraud for leadership of the Free French. Harold's role, which was self-imposed, was to pour oil on troubled waters. Viénot, having twice been imprisoned by Vichy, was now de Gaulle's Diplomatic Representative with the British Government. Harold lunched with him in May when he had been in England only ten days. Viénot sought to convince Harold that there was no question but that the issue between the two generals must rest with de Gaulle, whose name was already a legend, and who represented France's leadership in the eyes of all resistance workers. Harold in that case beseeched Viénot to persuade de Gaulle to modify his churlish attitude towards Churchill. In June he found Viénot deeply depressed because Eisenhower as Commander-in-Chief had summoned the two French generals and insisted that Giraud should be in supreme command. The effect on fighting France, Viénot said, would be disastrous. By their intervention the Americans were facing France with civil war. They were also, which was far more dangerous, on the way to bringing about the only rift between the United States and Great Britain.

It was in aid of the Free French Movement that a poetry reading was organised by Osbert and Edith Sitwell in April. It took place in the Aeolian Hall and was attended by the Queen and the two young Princesses. Those taking part included John Masefield, T. S. Eliot, Arthur Waley, Edmund Blunden and Vita. Each poet read from his own verse. Vita, 'serene as a swan', declaimed passages from *The Land*. Dorothy Wellesley had also been invited to read but in the interval of the performance it was discovered that she was in no condition to appear on the platform. Alarm had already overtaken the organizers when at the rehearsal she swayed around the other performers exclaiming, 'Don't think there is anything wrong with me. I am completely within my *elephant*.' Fortunately, since her name began with W, her turn was to have been the last. But towards the end of the performance the royal party were tactfully hustled from the platform before it dawned upon Dorothy that she was not to recite. Frustration and rage seized her. Casting her walking-stick aside she accosted Edith Sitwell with, 'You beast! You brute! You have humiliated me. I have never been so insulted in my life!' Edith Sitwell burst into tears. Harold tried to pull Dorothy away. She turned on him. 'Take your bloody hand off my shoulder! Who are you anyway?' she yelled. They managed to drag her downstairs, and while waiting for a taxi she sat on the pavement, banging it with her stick, and threatening to bring an action against the Sitwells.

In May 1943 *The Desire to Please* appeared in the bookshops. The whole first impression of 4,000 was sold out before publication and another 3,000 had to be printed. The public's appetite for new books during the war was insatiable and every author of renown had the certainty of satisfactory sales. *The Desire to Please* was a continuation of Harold Nicolson's search into his own past as centred in the life of his maternal great-great-grandfather, Hamilton Rowan, the Irish Nationalist. It was meant to be a sequel to *Helen's Tower*, but in that respect did not quite fulfil its purpose. For whereas Lord Dufferin's life could be said to form a fraction of the author's autobiography, Rowan's was too remote. Besides Rowan was not a very important character in spite of the fact that Harold claimed to see in him a foretaste of himself. Apart from a gentle rebelliousness Harold shared no other qualities with his rumbustious forebear, however much he detected in his present circumstances a reflection of the outcast failure which Hamilton became. Indeed the accounts of his hero's activities form the least interesting parts of the book. The deliberately parenthetical recollections of his own early childhood are far more rewarding. There are some splendid sections, notably the introductory paragraphs, beautiful and nostalgic, on memory, and descriptive vignettes like the one of an aunt – 'Her eyelashes would flutter absently as the wings of a butterfly which has settled on a flower which it does not really like' – more arresting than syntactical. Raymond Mortimer was shocked by the amount of careless writing in *The Desire to Please*, which betokened too great hurry in its composition. Nevertheless what makes the book so attractive is the glimpses it affords of the author's quick perceptions and fastidious tastes.

One of Harold's bizarre friendships was with the last representatives of the deposed Persian dynasty of Qajar. He loved Persians even when their evasions and circumlocutions drove him to distraction. In 1937 he met, through Sir Denison Ross, Prince Hassan Mirza Qajar, the last of the dynasty actually to sit on the Peacock Throne. Had fate, principally in the person of Reza Pahlavi, been less unkind Prince Hassan might have proved one of the best loved and enlightened of Persia's rulers. During a difficult moment of the First War his brother Ahmed Shah retired to Paris. Prince Hassan succeeded him and exercised his responsibilities and duties with integrity and skill. Yet when Reza Pahlavi consented to found his own dynasty, Hassan was despatched to the west in exile. He was a good Moslem, a person of refinement and culture, though not a man of action. He hated politics. In London he loved to consort with those people who, like Harold, were devoted to Persia. In his homesickness he would recite to them long passages from the Shahnama or the poems of Hafiz.

When in 1941 Reza Shah was in his turn deposed Harold introduced Prince Hassan to Sir Horace Seymour, Assistant Under-Secretary of State at the Foreign Office, to see if he would be worth restoring to the throne. Prince Hassan was very charming but inconsequent. Sir Horace asked him how long he intended to stay in London. He replied, for as short a time as possible because the raids might begin again, 'et j'ai tellement peur, mon ami'. Harold abruptly changed the subject to that of his family. What was his eldest son, the Valiahd, doing? He had just passed out of H.M.S. *Worcester*. 'Il s'appelle Drummond,' the Prince murmured. But why on earth, Harold asked? 'C'est un nom écossais,' the plump little man explained. 'Does he speak Persian?' Harold enquired anxiously. 'Pas un mot,' came the delighted reply. This did not go down very well with Sir Horace. 'Mais il pouvait bien l'apprendre,' the King of Kings added. The meeting was not exactly a political success.

In 1943 Prince Hassan died at Maidenhead. In May Harold invited his son and heir to lunch at the Travellers' Club. He was a nice, simple, modest sailor with an extremely common accent. He called Harold 'Sir', which coming from the rightful King of Kings Harold found comical. His host reproached the boy for not knowing a word of Persian. 'But I am told, Sir, that it is very easy to learn.' He asked him what he was going to do after the war. 'Well, first,' he said, 'I must go to Kerbala with him.' 'With whom?' 'Yes, Sir, I must take my father to the Qajar vault at Kerbala.' 'And then?' Harold asked. 'Well, Sir, the Perkies will get bored by that Pahlavi boy, who is, believe me, Sir, a stinker and then I shall become Shah.' Harold shook his head sadly, and begged him not to believe in any such destiny. It would clearly be a mistake.

More rewarding was breakfast over a kipper alone with Lord Baldwin, who spoke generously of Churchill; and also a meeting with Lord Wavell. Far from being elegant and sophisticated Wavell was stocky, silent, unworldly and of undistinguished appearance. When a week or so later Harold heard the Field Marshal talk about the continuation of the war in the East he was impressed by his solid, determined and powerful reasoning.

In October he was sent by the Ministry of Information to lecture in Sweden. He was obliged to fly from Leuchars near Dundee in a bomber. Vita was racked with anxiety. For several days he was stranded in Dundee waiting for the gales to subside. Twice he was driven to the aerodrome, and back again. He spent a Sunday of pouring rain in the town. The streets were empty but for a few lonely figures battling against wind and wet. Shops and cinemas were closed. With no books to hand he wrote articles for the *Spectator* out of his head, sitting in an hotel bedroom 'which no tweenie could be given without a prosecution on the part of the local council.' In a funny way he was not depressed because he was able to reflect at leisure on his happiness with his home and family.

Trussed up in a padded dressing-gown and mae west, complete with parachute harness, a life-belt, torch and whistle, and provided with a supply of oxygen, he eventually took off. He stayed in the Grand Hotel in Stockholm before moving to the Embassy as guest of Sir Victor Mallet. He dined with Roger Hinks, who was working in the Press Attaché's office. Hinks expounded to him his views that the Swedes were narrow, obstinate, conceited and materialistic. They were not the least ashamed of being neutral. On the contrary they believed that when the war was over Europe would want so much from them that they would become a great Power.

Harold lectured about the British Empire to an immense audience in a concert hall. He met several Swedes who having been in Germany told him about the terrible conditions in that country. He met a Member of the Riksdag who said that two German Ministers in Berlin wished to come to terms with Western Europe. They begged the Swedish M.P. to get in touch with an English M.P. and make soundings. Would England be ready to abandon Russia? 'Never!' was Harold's curt reply. He also met Doctor Benedek, former editor of the *Neue Freie Presse* of Vienna, a journalist of J. L. Garvin's high standing. This distinguished Austrian disclosed that in Vienna the Nazis had knocked out all his front teeth. Apart from this he was not ill-treated; but his companion, an extremely clever Jewish lawyer, had knives dug

into him by Nazi youths. 'Never as long as I live,' he said, 'shall I forget
the faces of those Nazi youths,' as they jabbed with their pen-knives.
His companion was pouring with blood and screaming. The youths
wore the grin of extreme sexual excitement. Dr. Benedek said that the
older Germans knew about the behaviour of their sons and were
terribly ashamed, but also afraid of remonstrating with them.

We all drove in the pouring rain to Ulriksdal Palace to lunch with the
Crown Prince [Harold wrote to Vita[7]]. It is a large 1750 building in a
wet park beside a wet lake. We were met in the hall by an equerry and
taken up the huge wooden staircase where we were received by a
Lady-in-Waiting. We were then conducted into the drawing-room,
a large, light room with heavy wooded furniture and presented to the
Crown Prince and his wife. He reminds me vaguely of Geoffrey
Scott – at 60 – grey and with his head slightly on one side, pince-nez
being continually adjusted. She is like a nice Miss Battiscombe[8] sort
of person. Why she should be so English (since she is pure German on
both sides) I do not know. She is Dicky Mountbatten's sister.
    We went into luncheon. I sat next to the Crown Princess.
Although there had been many footmen about they all disappeared
and we served ourselves from a side-table as if at breakfast in an
English country house. The Princess is very agreeable. She talked
about Dicky and said how much they all adored Edwina. She had
been down (as President of the Swedish Red Cross) to Gothenburg to
witness the exchange of prisoners. She had had to behave exactly the
same to the German prisoners as to our own men. She said the
difference was incredible. Our own lads simply roared with laughter
and kept on bursting into song. The Germans were sullen, silent,
dour. She said she had cried when the band played Home Sweet
Home and our men took up the song. She said that she did not cry at
all about the Germans; they filled her with despair. Afterwards I had
a long tête-à-tête with the Crown Prince. Not for repetition.

After luncheon the Crown Prince's brother, Prince Wilhelm, remarked
to Harold with typical royal mateyness, 'Cheerio! How d'you like our
Swedish grub?'.
    Harold visited Axel Munthe, then aged eighty-eight, who was living
in the royal palace as the guest of the King, aged eighty-six. Munthe
was sitting in a little dark room with one eye-shaped window. He had
two rugs over his knees. He was blind, ailing, miserable and pathetic.
His dream was to return to San Michele on Capri and die there. But the
King would not allow it. 'I am unhappy here,' he said. 'I am alone. In
the evenings I go upstairs and sit with the King. He is as old as I am. He

is not an intelligent companion. We sit together for hours.' While the King embroidered copes to present to churches Munthe sat in silence, listening to the rain outside, and the sound of stitching. He was not kind about the King. He complained that he had homosexual instincts which the Queen was worried about. And before Harold left the querulous old man took his arm and begged him, 'Cannot England, who has won her prestige now, be generous and offer peace to a distracted Europe? I know that Germany would be willing to make terms.' To which plea Harold gave him a sharp rebuff. The old man dropped his arm.

Harold visited a refugee camp containing people who had escaped from Denmark. When they first saw him they looked frightened. When they heard him speak English they broke into broad grins. He met with more than kindness in Sweden. He met with enthusiasm. The Swedes admired our country. It was a fine thing to be British those days. He was tremendously pleased he had come.

On the 11th November he spoke in the House of Commons in the debate on famine in Europe. He considered his speech one of the best he had made. The Chamber filled up and he was cheered. He begged the Ministry of Economic Warfare to reconsider the argument that by relaxing the blockade and sending relief to starving Europe we should be helping the enemy. Such a notion was preposterous. All the benefit Germany would derive from this act of humanity would amount to the equivalent of two or three grains of chaff. Whereas it was Germany's declared policy to debilitate generations yet unborn, our duty was to defy that policy. The Minister replied that it was not true the Germans sought to starve the countries under their domination from which they intended to derive much free labour. It might be just possible for us to relieve Greece, but no other country.

There now arose one of those moral problems which were constantly perplexing Harold. Without consulting Parliament, Herbert Morrison, the Home Secretary, whom Harold greatly esteemed, let Sir Oswald and Lady Mosley out of prison where they had been detained in horrible conditions under Defence Regulation 18B. He did it on the grounds that once a national emergency was over no one ought to be detained without fair trial. The Labour Party were enraged. Even Herbert Morrison was appalled by the savage, vindictive attitude of the proletariat towards Mosley. Members of Parliament received deputations of protesters from all over the country. The constituents of West Leicester were not backward with their remonstrances. They were impervious to argument and devoid of generous understanding. Harold was in a quandary. Should he speak out in the House on behalf of his erstwhile political colleague and friend? He consulted Raymond Mortimer, his closest mentor. Raymond counselled him to leave it to Morrison to defend his action and not to rush into the fray, but keep his, Harold's, powder for better causes. No one would think him a coward. Harold accepted his advice and refrained from taking part in the debate, which was acrimonious. The reason he gave his sons for refraining was that he had been too closely associated with Mosley for any words of his to have helped support Morrison.[9] This was undoubtedly his honest conclusion, but it may not have the right one. It was a pity he did not speak, for thereby his reputation for probity and courage would have been enhanced. As it happened when Sir Oswald was first imprisoned Harold made a journey to Brixton and would have seen him had not the detainee declined the honour. Mosley subsequently acknowledged Harold's courageous act of friendship while explaining his reason for the repulse, which was that only the previous night Harold had broadcast something about him which he thought disobliging. Nevertheless Harold's abstention from the debate made him uneasy. 'I hate discretion,' he wrote to Vita. 'I loathe it. I abominate it. It makes me feel a worm.'[10]

In December he spoke in the House on another matter which was much nearer his heart than the Mosleys.[11] In the debate on support for France Harold expressed acute anxiety about our attitude towards that country. It was physically as well as morally essential that France's boundaries were maintained. He could not understand why the Government, having accepted that premise, now seemed to be running counter to it. We had neglected to adopt towards France the delicacy of touch which we had done towards the United States and Soviet Russia. Harold went on to deplore General Smuts's recent remarks about France.[12] They were both cruel and untrue. The Government should have censored Smuts's speech. If he had made similar insulting remarks about America or Russia they would not have been published. As for the Lebanon and Syria we should remember that French ascendancy in those Near Eastern countries had been traditional for a thousand years. The case for making France abandon the mandate over them was not tactful.

Eden in answering various points of dubiety raised by other Members during the debate made no reference to Harold's strictures. He was in fact displeased. Indeed it was rarely that Harold ventured to criticise the Government in wartime, and his words on this occasion proved that he lacked no courage or loyalty to France. Left wing Members, like Gallacher and Aneurin Bevan, congratulated him; and the Liberal Rob

Bernays, who really cared for his parliamentary repute, approved wholeheartedly. 'Very formidable,' he called it. Most gratifying of all was his friend Viénot's approval. He showed Harold a handful of telegrams from de Gaulle's National Committee in Algiers expressing their delight.

Considering how severely Harold taxed his strength it was remarkable that he kept so well. Whenever he received warnings that he was overdoing it, he paid them no attention. On the 28th December he was dining with Guy Burgess in the Reform Club before catching a night-train for Cornwall. In the lavatory he had a slight fall and fainted four times. On recovering consciousness he said, 'I did not expect to die in the place where I first met Robbie Ross.' Yet he insisted on going to the station. Burgess accompanied him to Paddington and put him in his sleeper. He borrowed an aspirin from a soldier travelling on the train and made Harold take it. Worried, he telephoned to Vita, who ever afterwards felt a tenderness for him and was sorry when he absconded with Maclean.

Within forty-eight hours Harold was back again in London, apparently none the worse and his spirits as ebullient as ever.

I dined yesterday at the Travellers [he wrote to his sons on the last day of the year 1943[13]] and sat next to a friend of mine and yours called James Langley, who, as you know, has a most dreadful stammer. An elderly gentleman came in just as we had begun and took the table on my other side. James told me that he had had a letter from Nigel. He added that Nigel had had himself photographed in order to please Mummy and me. But when the photograph was developed it was too awful to send. 'He told me,' James continued, 'that it made him look so beastly -m-m-m-m-m-m-m-m-m.' The man on the other side finished his soup and started on some hashed chicken. 'So beastly,' persisted James, 'M-m-m-m-m-m-m-m-m.' The man finished his chicken and was given (as I saw out of my left eye) some cold Christmas pudding. 'So beastly m-m-m-m-m-m-m-m-m.' 'Fat?' I tried, not wishing to be hard on Nigel, but hoping somehow to bring this umming to an end. James again indicated dissent. The gentleman beside me finished his Christmas pudding, and said he thought he would like to try an apple. 'So beastly m-m-m-m-m-m-m-m-m – MMMMM – STOUT,' he ejaculated at last. The old gentleman by then had paid his bill and left.

★　★　★　★

'Perhaps the beginning of the end.' With these words Harold Nicolson prefaced his diary for 1944. But there was still much suffering and sorrow to be endured before the end of the end. He began at this time to feel deep concern about the intentions of our ally, Soviet Russia. He feared that the lesser countries of Eastern Europe might not enjoy the right to preserve their identity after the war. He saw signs of the terms of the Atlantic Charter of 1941 (in which Great Britain and the United States renounced all desire for aggrandisement while offering the enemy countries, large and small, equitable economic treatment) being abrogated. His concern was first aroused by a Russian communiqué to Poland insinuating that the Soviets would annex the eastern provinces of that country. The situation was not made less menacing by Eden's persuasion of the Polish Prime Minister to tone down his resentment in replying to the communiqué. The truth was that Britain was physically powerless to restrain her Russian ally's brutal treatment of the Poles. Churchill was taken in by Stalin's pretence that he wanted a strong, independent Poland. Stalin wanted nothing of the sort. When his Russian troops reached the outskirts of Warsaw he encouraged the citizens to rise against the Nazis. He then deliberately halted his troops' advance in order to allow the citizens to be butchered by the enraged Germans. Thus he eliminated thousands of Poles who had looked to the west for support in the coming peace. When Molotov played a similar dastardly trick in annexing the Baltic States and a piece of Roumania Harold felt sick with disgust and impotence. Prospects of gross injustices after the war spurred him to prepare notes for an article for the Army Bureau of Currrent Affairs on *The Last Peace and the Next*. He found it good practice having to put the subject into language which a lance-corporal could understand. In this endeavour he received encouragement from Eden, who urged him to give a series of B.B.C. talks on the peace. Although B.B.C. governors were prohibited from broadcasting Eden arranged with Bracken that an exception should be made in Harold's case. Furthermore he invited him to attend his weekly conferences so that he could learn all there was to know about foreign affairs.

The Italian battle front was also causing tense anxiety. At first it was thought we had made a mess of the Anzio beach-head landing. There was fierce fighting when our troops advanced towards Monte Cassino Monastery where the battle raged for weeks. Nigel's regiment was in the thick of it, and the Nicolsons were worried about his safety. The thought of him was a perpetual ache in the back of both their minds. And Vita was so unhappy envisaging his suffering from the cold of the

Italian mountains that she turned off the small stove in her writing-room in a sort of anguished sympathy.

Meanwhile the air-raids on London were stepped up, and the flying bomb made its first unwelcome visitations. Londoners were beginning to feel the strain of the war acutely. Vita begged Harold to take a room in the Savoy Hotel (for which she would willingly pay) rather than spend nights in fragile King's Bench Walk. But he refused to move. Then a bomb was dropped in the park at Knole. Little damage was done to the house beyond the breaking of a few windows, but the heraldic leopards on the gable finials merely turned their backs on the scene of outrage. Vita was infuriated. 'Those filthy Germans!' she wrote. 'Let us level every town in Germany to the ground!'[14] The affront to Knole prompted Harold to write a *Marginal Comment* about the bombing of works of art. He announced that he was prepared to be shot against a wall if that would preserve the Giotto frescoes;

> nor should I hesitate for an instant (were such a decision ever open to me) to save St. Mark's even if I were aware that by so doing I should bring death to my sons. I should know that in a hundred years from now it would matter not at all if I or my children had survived; whereas it would matter seriously and permanently if the Piazza at Venice had been reduced to dust and ashes either by the Americans or ourselves.[15]

And he went on to say that the British public were not merely unaware of artistic values, but were actually prejudiced against them. To the ordinary British citizen the treasures of Italy represented, either nothing at all, or else the curious pleasures of the idle rich.

The reaction among his constituents to these highbrow sentiments was predictable. Mrs. Jones complained ruefully to Harold's agent, 'It's no use my trying to understand Mr. Nicolson. I don't. He seems a kind-hearted sort of man, but he cannot really be even human if he thinks bricks and mortar are more important than human lives. Either he is putting on a pose or else he can have no heart at all.'[16] Mrs. Jones's objurgation convinced Harold that the gulf between the educated and the uneducated was unbridgeable. Had Mrs. Jones known that only four months previously her M.P. had privately asked the Minister for Air to beg our bomber pilots to spare Italian monuments whenever possible she would doubtless have decided that he lacked soul as well as heart.

Harold's attitude to art was that of the highly civilised amateur. It was definitely not that of the expert. The latter assured him that if the contemplation of pictures in a gallery produced in the visitor evidence of the perfectibility of mankind, he was undergoing an amateur experience. In that case then he, Harold, was an amateur. The expert assured him that to derive pleasure from a visit to a gallery meant that one could not know much about art. In that case he knew nothing about art. He did not care what the expert thought. He merely speculated why art experts should be so cantankerous. Was it because art criticism, being a parasitic rather than a creative form of energy, raised a special neurosis of its own? Yet literary critics were by comparison with many other experts equable and mild people. The problem was confusing. Harold was humble about his own artistic likes and dislikes. When Ben bought a Picasso portrait of a woman entirely composed of grey cubes he thought it distasteful. He liked art to be a relief and not a challenge. Ben regretted this sentimental approach; and his father admitted that, since Ben knew more about pictures than he did, Ben must be right. Nevertheless at an exhibition of Sir Michael Sadler's pictures in the Leicester Galleries in January he bought for £75 a picture by Frélaut of a Regatta in Brittany which took his fancy. And when after the war he found himself in Paris for a day, what did he do? He went to the Louvre and looked at what he wanted to see – the Géricaults and Davids – and derived pleasure from them, and found in them evidence of the perfectability of mankind.

He was naturally more sensitive about criticism of his writing, since literature was his craft. And when he was shown a hostile review in the *New Yorker*[17] of *The Desire to Please* by the American critic Edmund Wilson, he minded very much indeed. The title of the review, *Through the Embassy Window*, indicated its theme. Wilson having passed over *The Desire to Please* as a vague chronicle, proceeded to analyse Harold's limitations as an imparter of information and a judge of men. 'In spite of his travels he has only resided in one country – the British Foreign Office, approaching foreigners from a special caste . . . Whatever was happening Harold Nicolson did not know much about it,' he wrote. 'The great social groups and movements of which the pressures are felt . . . seem to exist for him only remotely; they are merely the armies and "mobs" – "mob" is a favourite word of his for any kind of popular demonstration.' Wilson admitted him to be a real connoisseur of verse, but thought it priggish of him to be shocked by Verlaine and Swinburne. He detached himself socially from the poets' company 'by a quiet but well placed accent of amusement, disapproval, disdain.' He was too concerned with maintaining a correct official attitude. There was an element of coy and sly humour in his writing. Wilson praised *Some People* for being by far his best book.

Wilson's charges were then exclusiveness, snobbishness, priggishness and facetiousness. Harold, while believing that Wilson had got the symptoms wrong, had a nasty feeling that he had got the illness right, in that there was something which rendered most of his writing superficial.[18] Vita put her finger on it by attributing whatever shortcomings he had as a writer to his morbid dislike of emotion. She thought it absurd of Wilson to criticise him adversely for belonging by birth to a certain class. He should have recognised it as a fact.[19] Wilson's distaste was reciprocated. When Harold met him in 1945 he found him "a puggy, podgy, puddingy man. Sulky also . . . He said that London appeared to him to be exactly like Moscow. 'Shabby?' I asked. 'Why, that's it!' A most unattractive man he was.'"

Of course Harold was not the least shocked by Verlaine and Swinburne. It merely happened that, given his Embassy upbringing, his public school training and the universally respected convention of his class and generation not to call a spade a spade, he could not bring himself to put in print what he could very readily put in conversation. He never learned positively to let himself go in his writing, even when he had practically outlived the restraints of Victorianism. Just as in *Verlaine* he glossed over the poet's relationship with Rimbaud, so in *Journey to Java* he was too delicate to come clean over Sidney Culpeper's homosexuality. His patrician background made him fastidious. He was frightened of squalor, physical and spiritual. Raymond Mortimer, who knew Harold better than any other writer, considered Edmund Wilson's diagnosis an over-simplification of his complicated and highly intelligent nature. Rather he attributed Harold's slightly over-delicate approach to literature to his having been too much in youth under the sway of Edmund Gosse, whom he called 'that erudite, snobbish, long-winded, busy-bodying, wet-blanket of English letters'. Gosse may have imparted to his admiring junior a whiff of that Puritanism which does not mingle comfortably with the exotic essence of aristocracy. Harold's contemporary Lord Berners saw something else. In a rather cruel lampoon of Harold as Mr. 'Lollipop' Jenkins, M.P., he saw pomposity creeping upon the trail of lost youth. In *Far From the Madding War*[20] Berners wrote of Mr. Jenkins:

In the eyes of the world he was a success. Yet as he approached middle age his more thoughtful friends began to suspect that something was going a little wrong. Although outwardly the rose retained its rubicund exterior intact, they scented the presence of the invisible worm.

It was to be expected, of course, that as he grew more successful and more important he should put aside something of the sparkle and gaiety of youth. He seemed, however, reluctant to abandon altogether the rôle of *enfant terrible* that, as a young man, he had played in so engaging a manner, and people began to feel that there was something really rather terrible about an *enfant terrible* who was growing middle aged and slightly pompous . . .

But Berners must have known that Harold never in his own eyes became successful and important; that in those of his friends he never became pompous, just as he never put aside the sparkle and gaiety of youth. Harold was wounded by Berners's inexact imputations.

As it was, he was so sought after by hostesses and acquaintances that he became a victim of their demands upon his time and energy. The hostesses knew that if they succeeded in luring him to their tables it was a practical certainty that their luncheon or dinner parties would be a success. If another conversationalist as fertile in ideas as himself was present, an edifying and entertaining dialogue would take place. If there was no rival present worthy the name, he would, once launched, embark upon a monologue. But he was never assertive. By instinct he would feel his way by sly, questing interrogations. On finding the company sympathetic, that is to say intelligent and stimulating, he would shine and sparkle. But if he suspected that he had been invited to show off he would shut up like a clam, and a militant silence would ensue. To a pretentious hostess or fellow guest he could snarl. But he never snubbed the young and shy. With three or four intimate old friends in a club, after a good dinner, he was always at his best. Then he would blossom and let himself go. The words would tumble out in a torrent of felicitous phrases as they do unrehearsed in his diaries. Opinions on topical events and anecdotes of historical scandals would come fast and free without any inhibitions. All that was needed from the audience was appreciative attention and occasional prompting by means of downright contradiction or outrageous teasing. Such encouragement he relished. After a short rather high-pitched, whinny-like laugh, he would pause, take a sip of port and a puff at his cigarette, cough, splutter, and continue as before. His eyes were by far the most expressive features of an otherwise impassive, almost Pickwickian face. Small, alert and penetrating, they were indicative of what he was about to relate, infallible signals anticipating the appropriate emotions of indignation, disdain, affection or amusement. In repose they were bland and benign.

Old Lady Carnock, who since her husband's death had inhabited a small house in Tedworth Square, Chelsea, with her eldest and unmarried son Lord Carnock, left London during the blitz to live near her daughter at St. Michael's Mount. In her eighties she had become like many old people gloomy and fault-finding. She naturally wanted to see Harold more often than was possible, and from time to time made it clear that she expected him to visit her. Vita much resented these demands upon Harold's precious leisure. 'She is a damned selfish, grasping old woman,' she complained. Harold on the other hand, who was devoted to his mother, was made to feel guilty and remorseful. Whenever his duties took him to the west country he would extend his journey into Cornwall in order to stay with her. He would bring his work with him.

> Mummy begged me to take my typewriter into her room and to sit there [he wrote to Vita²¹]. 'But you mustn't interrupt,' I said. 'No, but I like looking at you.' Well, I suppose one should be pleased by that – but I was enraged. Whenever I stopped typing she would look up from her knitting and say, 'Thinking what to write?' At which my poor little thoughts were scattered like dead leaves in the wind.

One of his oldest and most intimate friends was Sibyl Colefax. He had known her before his marriage. Well read and much travelled she could talk to him intelligently about books and far countries. For years they corresponded. The earliest letter from Harold to Sibyl to survive, written in 1913, discusses with her at great length the meaning of a passage in the *Odyssey* relating to the equivalent of the married state. If he did not quite take her into his confidence about his own marriage he certainly did about his career. He once promised that he would never take a drastic decision concerning his future or an important step in Parliament without first consulting her. Vita too grew to love her. She made it clear that there were two Sibyls, one the society hostess with a mask of determined bossiness, the other the gentle, generous, garden-loving, plant-knowing Sibyl who rejoiced in country life and country ways. Indeed Sibyl almost became a member of the Nicolson family, would propose herself to stay, contentedly occupying herself and being no trouble to anyone. The interests of Harold and Vita and their two sons were hers. Ben and Nigel wrote her long letters during the war, telling her of their adventures in the Army and, in particular, news of Italy, Florence and Bernard Berenson. In return she sent them chocolates, books and little presents. She undoubtedly loved them all, and they had a special place for her in their affections. After her death in 1950 Harold missed her continuously.

He was fond, very fond of many friends, especially the young. When he lost one of these through death he would mind at the time, but would not grieve for long. In March of 1944 one of the choice circle who availed themselves of the privilege of the letterbox key at King's Bench Walk and who on passing through London on leave would walk into the flat, whether Harold were there or not, was killed fighting. John Strick was in his early twenties. Fair, extremely handsome, a mystic and man of action, poet and soldier, traveller and ascetic, he greatly revered Harold whom he treated as a sort of Nestor. Harold in return encouraged his writing and on his last leave endeavoured successfully to restore his courage, for he had recently gone through such terrible fighting as temporarily to lose his nerve.

> I had an airgraph from him saying that he had recovered his nerves and was now looking forward to going back to the lines. He must have been killed almost immediately. Poor boy, he did not get much out of life. Wellington and then a year at the University and then the London Irish . . . His feather from his cap that he left here when he came to say goodbye is something of a coffee cup.[22] 'Keep this,' he said, 'till I come back.' And there it is on my mantelpiece, a little fluff of green.[23]

In 1949 John Strick's poems were published with an introduction by Harold. Another young poet, whom Harold never met but admired so much that he was impelled to write a *Marginal Comment* about him, was Sidney Keyes. He was killed in Africa in April 1943 at the age of twenty. 'There was genius,' Harold wrote to Vita about him, 'like the rush of an eagle's wing.'[24]

In April 1944 he flew to Algiers on a speaking tour for the benefit of the Free French forces. He stayed with Duff Cooper at the British Representative's villa. He dined with de Gaulle, lunched with General

Catroux and listened to the Resistance people's anti-British and anti-American views. He was entranced by the bravery and spirit of the French officers and men whom he talked to. Most of his speeches were political, but one lecture about Proust, which had been a great success when delivered in Paris in 1936, was a failure. The troops mistook Proust for an English novelist of a very decadent description, who wrote about Sodom and Gomorrah. He flew to Tunis where he addressed a packed theatre on *The Last Peace Treaty and the Next*; and in Oran addressed officers of the 1st French Armoured Division among the pine trees. On his return he received a letter from Brendan Braken enthusiastically congratulating him on his remarkable progress through North Africa.

On the 24th May Harold was called upon by the Speaker to make an unprepared speech in the debate on Foreign Policy. He immediately followed Churchill in an emptying Chamber. Pulling himself together and feeling very nervous he spoke up for the rights, interests and independence of the smaller Powers of Western Europe, and deplored the Government's negative attitude towards France merely because they found General de Gaulle so tiresome. At the end of the month he went by train to Scapa Flow where he delivered twenty-two lectures within seven days, mainly about *Lessons of the Last Peace Conference*, to the Fleet on ships and shore.

Meanwhile the Allies were making headway in Europe. In Italy General Alexander was sweeping the Germans up Italy. On the 4th June Rome was captured. On the 6th the landing in Normandy began.

The abortive attempt by Graf von Stauffenberg on Hitler's life and the consequent reprisals in July were an indication that the Nazi leaders and German people were on the verge of despair. The general feeling in England, which Harold shared, was that it was a good thing von Stauffenberg's plot did not succeed. Had it done so the German Army would have offered to surrender and the Allies could not very well have refused acceptance. That would have meant, so it was argued, the German Army remaining intact to start war all over again at a future date.

Harold spent August and the beginning of September at Sissing-hurst. It was the first long holiday, away from political work, that he had had since the war began. Even so he could not prevent himself from making occasional jaunts to London for the day. In September Constable's published *Friday Mornings*. This little book was a selection of Harold's *Marginal Comment* articles which had appeared in the *Spectator* between August 1941 and March 1944. They embraced every sort of subject, historical, literary, anecdotal, and of course topical. The political entries had had great influence on a wide circle of readers, being eagerly looked forward to week by week. It was typical of Harold to regret, when the proofs arrived for correction, that he had ever agreed to reprint them because they used up paper which might have been allocated to some young writer publishing his first book.[25]

The question inevitably arose what book should he write now. One morning he paced up and down the lime-walk before breakfast pondering. He did not feel in tune to tackle a sequel to his *In Search of the Past* series, of which *The Desire to Please* had been in a sense the second. Such an occupation seemed meaningless in face of current events and the actual suspension of not only past but present and future. He vaguely thought he might write about the Vienna Congress of 1815. Then at breakfast he opened a letter from his agent, Curtis Brown, informing him that Doubleday Doran, his American publishers, wanted a book on Metternich. Would he tackle it? He decided he would not, but the receipt of the letter confirmed his determination to write about that period, 'and I am happy starting at once on a new notebook.'[26] So he bought a large loose-leaved notebook into which he inserted typed sheets, trusting that by this method he would get his facts in the right order. Harold always found the process of absorption quicker and easier than the process of creation. Therefore by taking special trouble about the absorbing process he thought he might overcome his growing diffidence about the task itself. Having accumulated his facts he proceeded to write the main skeleton narrative on the right-hand margin, leaving the left-hand margin and the opposite page blank for subsequent additions of detail. It was his view that in writing a book in which he hoped to render a continuous and lucid narrative, it was essential to have all his material in the same place. It was a mistake to make lazy references to sources, if he wished the digestive process, which was the essential of clarity, to work smoothly. He forced himself to copy out the substance and vital text in the notebook, so as to have it available in the form he would eventually use in the book.

Raymond Mortimer took the opportunity of giving Harold one of his periodic scoldings about his writings. He told him that he had never written a book, except *Lord Carnock*, worthy of his gifts. He begged him to go through *The Congress of Vienna* in the mood of Flaubert, not allowing a single meaningless word to remain or a single unbalanced sentence to go unchecked.[27]

When on the 23rd August Harold reached that stage of *The Congress of Vienna* when the Allies entered Paris in 1814 he looked up to see it was

1 o'clock. He ran to turn on the news. The wireless announcer declared that the French Resistance fighters were that very day freeing Paris. With much excitement Harold, Vita and Mrs. Staples, the cook, toasted Paris in gin.

Back in London for the autumn session Harold took part in the second day's debate on the Prime Minister's War Survey. In pleading for recognition of the French Provisional Government Harold's twenty-minute speech was from the practical point of view the most successful he had made. France must, he emphasised, become as soon as possible an equal and potent partner in the discussions on Europe. But his advice to the Poles that they should not be provocative and should put their relationship with Russia on a realistic basis, and to the Russians that they should behave towards Poland with the grandeur which they had shown on the field of battle was, following the appalling behaviour of the Soviets within the past months, to say the least, unrealistic, and to say the worst, a cruel misunderstanding of the Polish predicament. At a luncheon party a few days later Eden rapped the table, silenced the guests and announced that Harold had made the best speech he had heard him make.

In October Harold lunched with his friend René Massigli who had been made French Ambassador to London, to meet Paul Claudel, the Catholic poet and diplomatist. Harold did not find Claudel at all attractive. The vain old man told him a story of how the *Figaro* was suppressed by the Pétain Government because it published a poem of his in which he congratulated his granddaughter on being christened Victoire. 'C'était,' he said, 'le lendemain de la victoire de Tel-el-Alamein.' He was not agreeable about his fellow-Academicians. '*Ah, celui-là ne compte pas,*' he repeatedly said. He was positively disagreeable about André Gide for exposing his vices like a monkey on monkey hill.

At the end of the year Harold joined the Historic Buildings Committee of the National Trust, thus embarking upon an association with the Trust which lasted for several years. The Committee, of which I was secretary, was responsible for all the Trust's historic buildings and the contents of the houses which it owned. The Committee also negotiated with owners who intended to make over or devise their country houses to the Trust. At that date it was compiling, in concert with the Ministry of Works, a list of the 200 most important country houses in England and Wales. Within six months Harold declared that of all the twenty committees he sat on the Historic Buildings Committee was the one he enjoyed most. Under the chairmanship of Lord Esher it was lively, interesting and amusing. Among its members was Harold's old friend

Gerald Wellesley, now the 7th Duke of Wellington, an excellent committee man in that he held extremely positive opinions on the merits and demerits of buildings. Moreover his knowledge of architecture was prodigious. 'Gerry was particularly firm, precise, sneery, and offensive,' and 'Gerry is so funny. He is rude to and snubs everybody and Oliver Esher teases him,' are some of Harold's references to the Duke's behaviour. Harold also became a member of the Trust's General Purposes and Executive Committees. From 1947–61 he was Vice-Chairman of the Executive Committee. The interests of the Trust meant a great deal to him, and he was popular with his fellow-members and the staff whom he never snubbed but always treated with respect, friendliness and dry humour.

The catalogue of Soviet infamies in 1944 ended with Stalin's invasion of Bulgaria while that country was negotiating with Britain for an armistice. Thus Russia in flagrant disregard of an ally's activities, to which she was privy, drew yet another Balkan kingdom within her orbit. Greece was thereby thrown into perturbation lest Yugoslavia, profiting from this addition to the Communist Balkan bloc, should demand Salonika. On the Germans' withdrawal from Greece Britain was faced with the problem whether or not to go to the assistance of the Provisional Government under Papandreou against the strong Communist element in the country. In the debate on British Policy in Greece Harold spoke. He upheld the decision to send troops to Greece. After all our conscience was clear. Our motives were to enable the Greek people to choose the Government they wanted by democratic means. In fact our motives were to be quickly realised. Winston Churchill, in the face of heavy disapproval from the United States, ordered British troops to take severe measures to restore order. With much difficulty and danger they achieved it. And so one Balkan country was saved from the Communist maw. For his part in the debate Harold received the commendation of Churchill and the Speaker, whom he met walking in Pall Mall. 'I wish to God,' the latter said, 'that all members could speak as you do, really contributing to a debate and not merely airing party views.'

On the 21st December a young Captain, just back from Italy, telephoned the Nicolsons to say that Ben having been knocked down by a lorry, was suffering from concussion and would be in hospital for a month. Harold's reaction was one of cool, silent perturbation; Vita's one of anger and vengeance. The tigress mother in her, inherited through Pepita, asserted itself in violent words since action, which doubtless would have been lethal, was out of the question. 'I wish I could lay hands on that driver. I would take all his clothes off and tie him to a tree in the snow till he died. And would set Martha [her Alsatian bitch] on to bite him while he still lived.' In fact Ben was kept in hospital for several months, and when released was sent home to England. Vita too was in poor health. As the result of an injury to her spine fifteen years before she was suffering from arthritis which hence-forth was never to leave her for long. This ailment, coupled with war weariness, induced acute depression and a temporary inability to write poetry.

It was only temporary. With the return of spring and some allevia-tion of her arthritis Vita was well away with *The Garden*, which had been put aside for several months in favour of a war duty – a book about the Women's Land Army. Now her trouble was an alarming facility of writing which, she feared, might mean loss of quality. 'Flatness has come with increasing competence,' she wrote.

When on the last anniversary of their wedding Vita had presented Harold with a poem beginning, 'I must not tell, how dear you are to me,' he was struck absolutely dumb with emotion, incapable of utter-ing a word of appreciation or gratitude. He was totally unable to express what he felt. 'I hate myself for this side of my nature,' he wrote to her afterwards. The three things which she cared for most, she told Harold in the New Year of 1945, were him, her writing and Knole.

> Then I went on sifting. Knole would have to go in the last resort. But Hadji and my writing? Supposing God appeared (and I thanked God he wasn't given to playing such tricks) and said to me, 'You shall write such poetry as Shakespeare and Dante put together never wrote, but your poor Hadji shall go blind. Choose!' Well, yes, you will be flattered to know that my whole being – my subliminal self – screamed, 'No, no, no!' and I never wrote another line.[28]

The remarkable part of this sifting is the Knole situation. What had for years been the first love of her life was still the last love to be jettisoned. And she went on to wonder which of the pair of them, Harold and Vita, was set on the right path. He with his important committees, or she with her preoccupations with more permanent things. If she were religious – and she thought she was not – she supposed she would be quite certain that her preoccupations were of more ultimate conse-quence than his. But she did not have that consolation.

Harold spent a whole week of January 1945 at Sissinghurst. Having finished his researches he started writing *The Congress of Vienna*. He completed three chapters. He told Nigel that the book would be very long and very dull. It was not a work of historical scholarship, or of original interpretation of events. Its main purpose, linked to the new peace that was impending, was to show the difficulty of maintaining an alliance when once the danger which had called that alliance into existence, was removed. 'There are a number of analogies between the situation after the defeat of Napoleon and that which will arise after this war.'[29]

On the 25th January Harold received a letter from Nigel who had just seen and talked to Rob Bernays about his chances of entering Parliament. Bernays was on a parliamentary delegation visiting troops in Italy and had spent a night with Nigel's Brigade in the front line. The next day Harold read in the *Evening Standard* that Rob was missing in a light plane which had been flying to Athens. 'This knocks me silly . . .' he wrote. 'I feel crushed by this. All my best House of Commons friends are now dead – Rob, Ronnie Cartland, Jack Macnamara.'[30] And the most intimate of these was Rob. Vita was dreadfully upset on his behalf and wished he were with her. 'These hellish aeroplanes,' she wrote. 'We do not hear of the ordinary people whom they destroy in thousands; only of the eminent.'[31] A few days later another plane, carrying Foreign Office personnel, War Cabinet Staff and documents to the Three Power Conference at Yalta, crashed near Lampedusa, thus confirming all Vita's diatribes against flying.

Harold was devoted to 'my beloved Rob' as he termed his friend in letters to Vita. Rob was absolutely sound about the war. He always gave Harold a candid opinion, and was outspoken in his criticism and exposition of his friend's political weaknesses, notably his incapacity to be consistently 'formidable'. Above all he was the perfect travelling companion. Harold was likewise devoted to his widow, Nancy, or Nan. 'I like her very much indeed, and so would you. She is immensely competent.' She was in fact appointed Chief of Staff in the Women's Army with the rank of Colonel. At the christening of the Bernays' two-months old son Robert which took place in Bristol Cathedral after a memorial service to Rob, Harold stood as godfather, thinking all the time of his dead friend.

A gentle ghost, a loving, laughing ghost, a ghost whose memory for me will never fade. More vivid to me than all the hours of the House of Commons are those days and nights we spent together slowly steaming down the Nile [in 1937]. How entranced he was in those days by the rich life which opened before him! And he was killed so needlessly; there was no need for him to have been killed.[32]

Harold took part in the debate on the rebuilding of the new House of Commons on the 25th January. He was in favour of the Gothic style for the new chamber which was to replace the old one destroyed by a bomb. He advocated an advisory panel of Members to support the Minister of Works and the architect, Sir Giles Gilbert Scott.

> We do not want a repetition of those terrible interferences, interjections, interventions and bright ideas which brought Barry and Pugin to their graves.

He wished to reject the offer of Dominion gifts. Uniformity would be destroyed by the introduction of Empire woods, for 'this Chamber will cease to be the parlour of the Mother of Parliaments and will become like a dining-car on the Canadian Pacific Railway.'[33] When the new Chamber was opened in 1950 he attended the ceremony. He considered the finished thing not pretty, but a compromise, a fake of Barry's fake, and lacking spirit. He found the green which they had chosen for the benches arsenical, and the faint olive with which they had toned down the oak dyspeptic.

In February the fateful and disastrous Conference between Roosevelt, Churchill and Stalin was held at Yalta. The principles it established may truly be held responsible for the unsettled state of Europe and the preponderance of strength in favour of Soviet Russia against the disunited West today. It would be wrong to suppose that the British Government and those intelligent and compassionate Members of Parliament like Harold Nicolson, who supported the terms of the Conference at the time, were not deeply apprehensive about Russia's intentions. Of course they were. But it is difficult not to blame them for their blind confidence in the honourable intentions of Uncle Joe. Without our hindsight since 1945 they ought to have known from experience of the past twenty-five years of Sovietism that that system was unscrupulous, ruthless and mendacious. In February 1945 Vita, who had no pretensions to political judgement and hated politics, was nevertheless more right and far-seeing than Harold in the matter at issue. 'I can't understand why you are pleased over Poland,' she wrote to him,[34] 'It seems to me that Great Britain and America have meekly agreed to let Russia take half the country. The Polish Government in London seems to think so too.' Harold of course was disturbed that 1,230,000 Poles, including all the educated and most vociferous Catholic nationalists, and those wretched prisoners of war who had been forced by the Germans to don Nazi uniforms, were being put into

Labour camps in Siberia, to be tortured and exterminated. 'All this is convincing and profoundly disturbing,' he wrote.[35] There is a touch of naiveté in the remark. Nor did he like the idea of Germans being hounded out of Silesia and East Prussia, and Balts out of the Baltic States. Yet Harold would not associate with the group of extreme Tories in the House who were getting signatures for an amendment expressing regrets at the Polish provisions. He felt he must abide by his hero Churchill's conviction that there was simply nothing we could do to stand up to the Russians, who not only were on the spot, a spot which our troops could not then reach, but were infinitely too powerful to be dislodged. 'The massed majesty of the British Empire would not avail to turn them off that spot,' Churchill told Harold in the smoking-room of the House of Commons.

In the debate on The Crimea Decision on Poland on the 28th February the Labour M.P. Pethick-Lawrence put down an amendment. He reminded the House that Great Britain took up arms in a war of which the immediate cause was the defence of Poland against German aggression. He deplored the decision to transfer to another Power the territory of an ally contrary to the terms of the Atlantic Charter and the Anglo-Polish Treaty of Mutual Assistance of 1939, thus leading to the deprivation of free elections in Poland. The Prime Minister replying to the amendment in a speech which swayed the House, pretended that the Yalta principles were a fair and just settlement. Harold supported him. He told a full House it was amazing that so much had been accomplished at Yalta. It was a matter of immense relief that Russia had agreed to make an independent Poland, and not demanded to have her old frontier of 1912 restored. The real question was whether we could trust Marshal Stalin. Throughout the war Stalin had behaved with loyalty. He had demonstrated that he was about the most reliable man in Europe. If the House voted for the amendment in any large numbers the effect abroad would not be good. The House did not indeed vote for it in large numbers. Instead Great Britain betrayed the prime purpose for which she entered the war in 1939. Churchill warmly congratulated Harold afterwards on the tenour of his speech. Thus patted on the head like a little dog, he wagged his tail with inordinate joy.

Harold, let us remember, was one of the large majority in the House of Commons to abide by Churchill's and Eden's contentment to let things be. Did his conscience not trouble him? Apparently not, although emotionally he was all for the Poles. Rationally, he thought that Churchill and Eden had saved Poland from a fate more terrible than might *otherwise* have been, whatever 'otherwise' exactly signified. 'I was absolutely sure,' he told Vita, 'in my own inner heart and mind that the Yalta decisions were not only expedient but ultimately to the benefit of the Poles and mankind. So I supported these decisions (in the House of Commons) with complete ease of mind and conscience.'[36] Vita made no comment on Harold's speech, but she was outspoken in condemning Churchill's. 'I remain unconvinced about Poland . . .' she wrote. 'I thought Winston talked a lot of hypocritical rubbish about not yielding to force. Of course it is force – *force majeure*. I felt ashamed of him over that.'[37] Brave words. She was not the only English person to feel ashamed during the nadir of British shame. Even a communiqué issued by the Americans and ourselves that, once the Nazis were disposed of, Polish wrongs must be redressed, would have gone some way to register our abhorrence of Russia's behaviour, and our good and honourable intentions.

Harold's attitude in the Yalta Conference debate was somehow untypical of his acute sense of right and justice. It is sadly understandable that at such a moment of the war expediency should dictate turning a blind eye to an ally's nefarious conduct. But outright condonation was another matter. That was going too far. Is there an explanation for Harold's volte-face? I think there may be. In his diary under the date 26th February he noted, 'I dine with Guy Burgess, who shows me the telegrams exchanged with Moscow.' These telegrams (and we may well wonder on what grounds this mischievous spy had the right, while working in the Far Eastern Department of the Foreign Office, to take such papers out to dinner), implied that the Commission of Ambassadors set up to determine the composition of the new Polish Provisional Government was 'not to be a farce in the least'. Now Guy Burgess was, like all traitors, extremely cunning, and he had already more than once successfully pulled the wool over Harold's eyes. He probably on this occasion showed Harold telegrams which assured him of Russia's good intentions while withholding others that did not. At all events Harold in writing to Vita the following day told her that, having seen the papers relating to the Polish settlement, 'whatever doubts and pangs I may have had were removed by this perusal'. To the extent of winning over Harold's sanction of Stalin's disgusting actions Burgess had achieved yet another point.

Early in March Harold was sent to lecture in Paris. He was so moved to be back in France after four years that on stepping ashore at Dieppe he bent down and with a sacerdotal gesture touched the soil with his hand. '*Monsieur a laissé tomber quelquechose?*' the porter carrying his luggage asked him. '*Non,*' Harold replied, '*J'ai retrouvé quelquechose.*' The story got about and was broadcast on the French radio. It was a happy, successful, emotional visit. He stayed with the Duff Coopers, now installed at the British Embassy in Paris. He walked in the undamaged streets of the city, practically empty of traffic, with the great sweep of her boulevards and avenues unimpeded by motor-cars, and lovely in the early spring sunshine. He delivered two lectures on what the British thought of the French. They were received with rapture, the students from the Left Bank yelling their appreciation. Receptions and dinners were held in his honour and luncheons given him by Paul Valéry and André Siegfried. His old friend Cocteau called to see him – '*mon cher petit Harold*' – at the Embassy. On his return to England Harold was made chairman of the Anglo-French Inter-Parliamentary Committee.

Then Ben arrived from Italy. He was encased from head to waist in plaster which was rather grubby after weeks of wear and travel. It covered his chin and the back of his head. But he was suffering from no pain. 'Thin and enormous he stalks through the streets of London, arousing pity and terror.'[38]

Once in April and twice in May Harold spoke in the House of Commons. The April speech on the Dumbarton Oaks proposals[39] was the last of his major speeches in Parliament. He praised the proposals as a vast improvement on President Wilson's idealist principles of the League of Nations, in that they restricted and thereby intensified the responsibilities of the new United Nations Charter. But he strongly criticised the use of the Veto. He foresaw – very accurately as things transpired – that the Russians' flagrant use of it would negative whatever power the Charter otherwise possessed. In May he spoke in the debate on family allowances, strongly rebuking a Tory Member for suggesting that aliens, some of enemy origin, were having a much better time in the war than native-born workers and were enjoying privileges to which they were not entitled. Again the same week he spoke briefly in defence of the Civil Service. These two last interventions may not have been highly important, but they set a seal upon Harold's fundamentally Liberal instincts and his loyalty to his old profession.

The end of his parliamentary career, like the end of the war, was in sight. On the 27th April news came that the Russians had completely surrounded Berlin. On the 1st May the deaths of Mussolini[40] and Hitler were announced. On the 2nd all the Italian and German forces in Italy and the Tirol surrendered. On the 3rd Harold learned of the abominable treatment by the Russians of our prisoners in Germany whom they had liberated. 'But what are we to do? We simply must practise appeasement,'[41] he wrote to his son, Nigel. These words came hardly from him who had said the very opposite about the Nazis in 1938, words which he anticipated might be raised against him. Well, his excuse was, 'First, the Nazi system was more evil than the Soviet system. Secondly, because, whereas Hitler used every surrender on our part as a stepping-off place for further aggression, there does exist a line beyond which Stalin will not go . . . If we are firm and patient, the tide of Russian aggressiveness will sooner or later recede.'[42] In the light of subsequent events we may well question whether either of Harold's two statements was correct. And as for his caveat that we should be patient and firm, the pity of it is that we have been the one without being the other.

On the 7th May the Germans surrendered unconditionally. Harold, Vita and Ben (for Nigel was still overseas) flew the flag from the tower at Sissinghurst for the first time in five years.

7

NOSTALGIA FOR PARLIAMENT, 1945–1948

THE interval between the Armistice and the General Election which Churchill had fixed for the 5th July was an uneasy and unhappy time for Harold. He felt that he had lost his bearings and was floating in a sea of uncertainty. Attendance at the House of Commons was made sad for him by an inward conviction that his parliamentary term was set. His political status was also slightly nebulous. The National Labour Party was now petering out from inanition. There was no longer any need for its existence. Lord Elton having resigned and Malcolm Mac-Donald having refused to stand at the Election the party was reduced to four Members. The gallant runt therefore decided to dissolve itself and assume the banner of the National Campaign Committee. Harold spent the suspended interval mostly at Sissinghurst. He occupied himself in writing *The Congress of Vienna* and editing jointly with Vita a poetry anthology. He visited Wellington College to address a discussion group,

> and to smell again those pine trees which cast such a blight across my early youth . . . I am haunted by the picture of myself at thirteen . . . Lack of any self-assertiveness has always been my main disability, and I believe that it was born (or perhaps only intensified) in the grim methodical discipline of Wellington College.[1]

Each return to his old public school was a sort of masochistic penance, for he derived a macabre pleasure from retracing the exaggerated unhappiness of his boyhood and fabricating excuses for his short-comings as a public figure. But a genuine wish to help make the lot of the average schoolboy less wretched than his induced him to accept a governorship of the College in the following year.

He was having great difficulty in framing his Election Address to his old constituents of West Leicester. Whereas normally he found that words of exhortation flew from his typewriter like chaff from a win-nowing fan, the falsity, artificiality and bogus bonhomie of self-puffing was abhorrent to him. To win reluctant votes from constituents by heartiness and comradeliness was wholly contrary to his nature.

85

Besides he had lost his old combativeness of ten years ago. He no longer got a kick out of the prospect of being confronted on the hustings by hostile crowds. Even so an element of the burlesque did not fail to enter the programme. He had to have an election photograph of himself taken. He decided to have it done by a Leicester supporter rather than a fashionable Bond Street specialist. On the way to the studio he remembered that he had that morning put on a most unsuitable shirt of dark butcher-blue. The photographer, on seeing it, told him he could not possibly be photographed in that shirt. 'Not for the Election you can't. It will come out black and make you look like Lord Haw-Haw or Sir Oswald Mosley.' Now the photograph was required instantly. So Harold persuaded the embarrassed photographer to take off and lend him his own striped collar. He put it on. It did not fit, being horribly tight. But it did the trick in taking attention away from the brief expanse of shirt which sure enough in the print looks black. 'I sat on the stool,' Harold wrote, 'and put on an expression suggesting hope, love and charity, combined with deep experience and alert intelligence. Combined also, I fear, with a lurking anxiety lest the photographer's collar might suddenly detach itself from its moorings and float in the air.'[2]

On the eve of the Election campaign Harold wrote a rather desperate letter to William Mabane, the Minister of State for Foreign Affairs in Churchill's Caretaker Government, asking that he might be considered as Chairman of the British Council on certain conditions. Nothing was to come of this approach. He then attended the dissolution of one of the longest Parliaments in history. He was profoundly moved by the simple ceremony: Black Rod knocking on the Chamber door; the scramble into the House of Lords; the Speaker's return to the Chamber without the mace; the shaking hands with the Speaker; and the final good-byes to the friendly policemen at the entrance. The tradition, the history of the Mother of Parliaments was something he was immensely proud of. How happy he had been at Westminster! How he had revelled in being a legislator, however humble a one!

The immediate question in mind was for what Party was he to stand in the General Election. He would not stand as a Conservative, having never forgiven the Tories for their attitude at Munich; and he would not stand against Churchill. He could not stand as a Liberal, for there was already an adopted Liberal candidate at West Leicester. So he decided to stand as National Candidate. The decision was a fatal one, for British voters dislike Independents of whatever colour. Besides they suspect, and seldom re-elect, candidates who in their view keep changing their allegiance. Nevertheless under this alien and equivocal label the Conservative Central Office agreed to support him.

Vita was not at all pleased. 'I don't look forward to this election and your absence,' she wrote to him at the Grand Hotel, Leicester, where he stayed throughout the campaign. 'Why on earth you want to go and get mixed up in politics when you could stay here and write books passes my comprehension. Idiot!'[3] Still, she consented to pay her first and only visit to Leicester, even making a short speech at a women's meeting. Her audience were enraptured. Harold counted the days until the business was over. He hated every minute of the campaign, the tedium of which was relieved only by the occasional help of friends like Robin Maugham and Richard Rumbold who canvassed for him. The chicanery of the whole business affronted his sense of decency. Hecklers in his audiences would try to catch him out by asking him why before the war he voted against certain bills, which he had entirely forgotten about. After making enquiries he would find, when it was too late, that he had never done anything of the sort, but had voted with the Labour opposition for them. He received deputations from cranks, antivivisectionists and even anti-vaccinists. In vain he would protest that the lives of ten thousand guinea pigs were less important than the life of one human. The protesters would contend that we had imposed 'untold misery' on millions of guinea-pigs without having discovered the cure for cancer. At one meeting an intoxicated worker kept yelling, 'You're a liar, you are!' At another a demented woman rose to her feet and, waving her arms, uttered incantations like one of the witches in Macbeth. She accused him of being a bloated landowner who lived in a castle and ground the faces of his tenants to dust. It was no good his retorting that Sissinghurst was only the remains of a castle, that it didn't belong to him anyway, and that their friend Ozzy Beale was not ground to anything but was a flourishing farmer, far more affluent than they were themselves. Admittedly the majority of his audiences were friendly, but what depressed Harold inordinately was the preponderating silent mass of factory-workers in his constituency, 'who just read nothing, hear nothing, see nothing, don't even know my name, but vote' solidly for his Labour opponent, Barnett Janner. It was the same old story; democracy meant majority rule by the uneducated which, to his logical mind, was neither right nor desirable. Moreover, he was no match for the tough and unscrupulous. He fought his campaign with clean hands in kid gloves. He would not demean himself to take unfair advantages over his opponents. When he learned that one of his supporters had said publicly something that was not strictly true, he contradicted him at the first opportunity.

Polling day came on the 5th July. After which the home votes were sealed for three weeks to allow the service men's votes to be collected from overseas. While awaiting the outcome and working at his book one evening at Sissinghurst the telephone tinkled. It was Nigel back, speaking from London. His safe return was a most welcome compensation for the defeat which Harold knew was in store for him. On the 24th he went to Leicester to witness the counting of the votes. Vita, Ben and Nigel accompanied him. He was beaten by Janner who received a large majority. He was one of many victims of the national swing to Labour, chiefly brought about by the Forces' vote and desire for a change after fourteen years' virtual Tory rule.

Harold received many letters of condolence and congratulation for his long political service from Winston Churchill, Gilbert Murray ('The disgust I feel about your case'), Hinchingbrooke ('a calamity'), Vernon Bartlett ('a tragedy'), Massigli ('*la France perd un ami fervent*'), Charles Morgan, Eleanor Rathbone, Walter Elliot, and numerous prominent constituents. What gave him most pleasure of all was Robin Maugham's quotation of Churchill's remark made in his hearing. 'The House,' he said, 'will be a sadder place without him,' and, after a pause – 'and a smaller.'⁴ Harold was flattered but could not help wishing that the man whom he had so loyally and consistently served had done more to recognize his worth while he was in Parliament.

The day following his electoral defeat Harold received notice that he must leave King's Bench Walk by Christmas. This was a hard blow, but not unexpected. The chambers of no. 4 were held in the name of his eldest brother, Freddy Carnock, who had been a barrister but was no longer practising; and the authorities rightly decided that chambers in the Temple should henceforth be occupied preferentially by members of the Bar. Harold was made very sad, for he dearly loved these sympathetic Queen Anne rooms with their sombre panelling which had sheltered him through so many years of activity, joy and anxiety.

On the 6th August the wireless announced that the Americans had split the atom after four years' preparation and dropped an atomic bomb on the Japanese town of Hiroshima. At first Harold did not appreciate the extent of the damage caused or the implications of the appalling weapon. 'It is to be used eventually for domestic purposes,' he noted succinctly in his diary.[5] Vita was thrilled by the atomic bomb, thinking that it would open a whole new era for mankind by rendering conventional warfare obsolete. Harold was at once besieged by the press who telephoned to ask how, when he wrote *Public Faces* in 1932, he already knew of its existence and foresaw its use, for in that novel he had written that the discharge of a bomb no larger than an inkstand could destroy New York City. He had obtained the idea from his scientist friend, Gerald Heard. Two days later the Americans dropped a second, even more devastating atomic bomb over Nagasaki. It brought about the instant surrender of the Japanese. The Second World War was now really over. Yet there was little further jubilation. The English, who are not inclined to gloat over the misfortunes of their enemies, were left pondering the devastation caused by the atomic bomb and its terrifying implications.

The post-war months brought many other barbarities to be appraised by sensitive minds. Harold was deeply shocked by reports of brutalities committed by Czechs and Poles in driving the German populations off their frontiers. The wretched aliens strove to get into the British zone and were shuttled backwards and forwards, until they died of starvation and ill-treatment. How could it be that we, who had fought honourably and well for certain principles and ideals, could be perpetrating or condoning crimes greater than even the Germans themselves committed? Harold was doubtful too about the trial and execution of war criminals. The Belsen thugs, even Ribbentrop, yes. But to clothe summary executions in the ermine and velvet of judicial procedures was to him extremely unpalatable.

It took a long time before he got over the disappointment of not being re-elected to Parliament. But he derived a vicarious satisfaction out of Nigel's efforts to be accepted as Conservative candidate for his old constituency of West Leicester. He wrote his son a letter of advice, begging him to bear in mind his own political mistakes.[6] It is a touching letter of which the moral was that Nigel must not be influenced by personal affections and associations. Harold admitted that he had blundered in allowing himself to be persuaded by his friendship for Tom and Cynthia Mosley into joining the New Party when he had 'not the knowledge of political factors to form an independent judgement.' He had repeated his error through his friendship with Ramsay MacDonald and Buck De La Warr when they persuaded him to join the National Labour Party. Thus he cautioned his son not to follow his sad example, but to be tough and resistant to the blandishments and persuasions of friends.

It was now that Harold turned his endeavours to obtaining for himself a peerage. Since the publication of the third volume of his *Diaries and Letters* in 1968 Harold's critics have derided and even misjudged these endeavours. They have accused him of blatant social snobbery, and desire to ennoble himself. These jibes are grotesque. Harold was only a snob judged retrospectively. For, born as he was in the purple when Queen Victoria still had fifteen more years to reign, he, like all men of his class, accepted his social position in the world as superior to that of the middle and lower classes. And with this sense of superiority went, in his view and the view of his contemporaries, certain responsibilities and privileges. Now that social position and privilege are at a discount, it is easy to misjudge people of Harold's generation for accepting them as part of the natural order of things. In fact Harold was far too well born to set store by the acquisition of a peerage for himself. He was inclined to regard a new peerage as rather a joke, and his references to the title he might adopt, if he were made a peer, whether Lord Cranfield (an old Sackville title), or Lord Sissinghurst (no, his dear friends would call him Lord Pansyhurst), were made in private to Vita and his sons. He was never heard to mention the subject among his friends. What he wanted – and what a Government of any sense of the fitting would have granted him – was a seat in the Upper House. He wished to be a senator, and had he been made one he would have been an exceptionally useful senator. Harold was not suited to the hustings. The rough and tumble of elections did not bring out the best in him. Nor was he a good party man. He was far too intelligent to feel bound by the Whips to rigid party dogmas and principles. In truth he belonged to no Party. He was a natural independent. In the House of Lords he would have been able to pursue his own convictions of what was right, and sit on the cross benches. He would have been able to contribute to debates on foreign affairs, education, the environment, the preservation of architectural monuments and beautiful landscape, and many other matters on which his extraordinarily diverse talents were centred. That he was not made a peer is an indictment of those statesmen who held the power to make him one. The fact that they did not give him the opportunity of serving his country by this means certainly brought him frustration and distress.

The first reference in Harold Nicolson's diaries to his desire for a peerage was in July 1945 after the Election. He regretted the unlikelihood of his being offered a safe seat to contest because so many Conservative front-benchers had lost theirs. For the same reason, with so many claimants for consolation honours he did not suppose a peerage would be offered to him by a Labour Government. In September he did an unwise thing. He wrote to Sir William Jowitt, who had just been made Lord Chancellor by Mr. Attlee. He told him that he would like to go to the House of Lords, but warned him that although he was in full accord with Labour's domestic policy he could not be sure that he would remain so within the next crucial years. Moreover, as he had always supported Churchill and Eden, he would not like to find himself on the opposite side to theirs. He wished to maintain his political independence. Would the Prime Minister elevate him on these conditions? The naiveté of this approach was not calculated to appeal to the Lord Chancellor. Harold sent a copy of his letter to Vita, telling her that he had had to take a large gulp of pride before sending it off. Vita approved of the letter, calling it clear, dignified and all that it should be. Meanwhile a Labour man, in whom Harold confided what he had done, warned him that if he did not accept the Party Whip he would not stand a chance in hell of getting what he wanted.

On the 26th of the month Harold met Lord Jowitt (as he had become) at a luncheon party. Jowitt told him that the only one of his colleagues to whom he had referred Harold's approach was enthusiastic. Harold when he got home thereupon wrote in an access of excitement to Jowitt telling him he would be glad if he would show his original letter to the Prime Minister. He cautioned his family that, now the matter had become rather more than a Sissinghurst joke, they should be discreet if questioned by friends on the subject. Again they began speculating what title Harold should choose. All the Scottish names of places associated with the Nicolsons were a bit artificial, besides being ugly. Lasswade, for example, was not really a place pertaining to his branch of the family. He decided that a name beginning with 'S' would be preferable because of the engraved cigarette-case of his father-in-law which Vita had given him, and the letter 'S' embroidered on her towels. It was a pity, for instance, that the names of fields round Sissinghurst were suitable for fields, but not for persons. For instance, Frogsmead and Plague-spot would hardly do. Then Vita, having raked through an old map of the Sissinghurst property, came upon another field, which she suggested might not be inappropriate. It was called Lower Bottom. By now Harold had worked himself into a state of nerves. He had cold feet about having to dress in white fur and an Admiral's hat and bow three times to William Jowitt. He dreaded being addressed as 'My Lord'. He dreaded Mrs. Staples saying, 'His lordship is weeding in the nuttery'.[7] He did not feel, or look, or think like a lord. 'Anyway it may come to nothing.' That of course is all it did come to. But it was riling when two months later Hugh Sherwood told him he was an idiot to have refused a peerage when he had not in fact been offered one. Finally Harold learned in December from the egregious Guy Burgess, (through what authority he did not know for certain, but he suspected Hector McNeil whose private secretary Guy now was) that Ernest Bevin, the Foreign Secretary, had turned him down for the post of Chairman of the British Council; and that since in some way his peerage was involved in that appointment, it too had disappeared. 'I am sorry about Cranfield,' he wrote to Vita. 'There is a Cranfield far away, without a city wall.'[8]

How he longed to be able to make speeches about the Greek situation, if only there were a platform available to him. The situation in that country was extremely tense. The Greeks, threatened by Communism, and terrified of Russia and Tito, were in a mood of almost hysterical anxiety and uncertainty how to act. Their situation was complicated by the appalling state of the economy. Harold, whose love of Greeks was constant, saw plainly that their only hope of salvation lay in moderation. He longed to be able to tell them so. When towards the end of October the opportunity of his lecturing to them about Byron and Democracy arose, he seized upon it. Plans for his journey had to be made without delay. He kept them from Vita until the last moment in order to cause her the least amount of pain, since he was obliged to fly. She took his casual announcement badly. They wrote each other letters on the subject, he excusing himself because he recognised himself as a long-standing friend of Greece, and his journey a duty; she accusing him of allowing himself to be bossed around by Labour people to whom he did not properly belong. 'This damnable expedition,' she called it. He was as much upset as she.

Flying just after the war was still a hazardous business. There were no regular inter-continental flights. At a moment's notice Harold was whisked off to an aerodrome near Bagshot. He was made to stay in an olde worlde manor-house, a kind of R.A.F. hostel, sleeping in a dormitory with others. Two mornings running he was called at 4.15 on false pretences. Finally he set off in a Dakota machine, sitting on a metal bench which faced another. He stayed the night in Naples, again sharing an hotel bedroom, this time with an elderly Greek. Again he was called at 4.15 in the morning. On arrival in Athens he was transported to the British Embassy to stay in utmost comfort with the Rex Leepers. Seated in a lovely bedroom at an open window, through which the sun was pouring, and overlooking a view of Hymettus, he wrote to Vita about his adoration of Greece. It was, he had no need to assure her, the loveliest country in the world.

I am drunk with its beauty and swallow great drafts . . . Hot it is, as never in England, with that light upon the marble hills which truly never was on sea or land. I brood over the definition of that colour. One says 'violet' or 'amethyst', but these words are meaningless. The beauty of Greece is the amazing fusion of sharpness with gentleness. Everything has an outline, and yet within that outline the shadows and colours are gentle and delicate . . . I do not agree that the Acropolis looks best by moonlight. It wants the blazing Attic sun, and when I was up there making my *prière sur l'Acropole*, the sun blazed indeed and my eyes squiggled up in the glare.[9]

The Leepers took him to luncheon with some Greeks on the coast opposite Euboea.

All around the cottage were the sharp green Mediterranean pines, and the air was sparkling (that is the exact word I mean) with the smell of thyme and sage and gum-cystus. My God! My God! I shall hold that picture as tight in my mind as long as I can. The great mass of Euboea, the colour on the distant mountains, the lapis sea, the little bridge at Chalcis thirty miles below us, where Aristotle was drowned testing the currents which sway there.

As always, Harold found that the British, who take their own politics so calmly, caught some of the Hellenic fever of the politics around them. Certainly the Greek situation was grim. Everyone was frightened of the Communists under various guises. Harold saw at a glance what should be done. He persuaded Leeper strongly to advise Hector McNeil at the Foreign Office that Great Britain should cease to be passive and should help to constitute the best Government available for Greece. We should assist it by appointing British advisers to the Greek Ministry of Finance. Harold actually drafted the Ambassador's telegram for him. McNeil agreed but Ernest Bevin was too chary of interference in Greek affairs to implement Harold's suggestion.

The Osbert Lancasters who were in Athens were a great comfort to him. 'They are so charming and one can talk to them as one might to Ben or Niggs.'[10] But Vita was not assuaged by these rhapsodies. She was making herself ill with anxiety because he would have to fly back, and there were gales, and she was unable to communicate with him. She was finishing *The Garden*, that long poem which was an appendage to *The Land*, and the strain and emotion were telling upon her nerves. It was the first of her writings which she ever showed to Harold before publication. He was impressed but considered that it did not contain passages of purest poetry like *The Land*.[11] Vita too realised that the toils and processes of gardening did not have the dignity of agricultural themes. Seed-packets and wooden labels and hand trowels lacked the wide gesture of dung and marl.

In December the Nicolsons' joint anthology, *Another World Than This*, was published. It had been Vita's venture. She conducted all the business with the publishers. For a year the editors had been assembling their pieces from notes made on the endpapers of books which they had read over the years. They purposely omitted familiar quotations. They included nothing by Shakespeare, Shelley, Keats or Swinburne, and only one extract from Byron. The great majority of the quotations were from the Elizabethan and Jacobean poets (Vita's), with a liberal sprinkling from the Greek and Latin classics (Harold's). By the middle of the month the 10,000 copies of the anthology were almost all sold.

If Vita was shy of letting Harold read her books in manuscript Harold never suffered from a like inhibition. In December of 1945 he gave her to read the proofs of *The Congress of Vienna*. She marvelled over the manner in which he so admirably marshalled his facts, and the wisdom of his comments on men and their muddles. Raymond Mortimer, however, always censorious, found the book stiff, 'with only a flower or two here and there'. He thought it too chatty for a work of history and too historical for a work of literature. But Vita's friend Christopher St. John agreed with her. She praised his masterly arrangement of the huge mass of facts, his wonderful ability in bringing to life the characters in the European drama, and his infallible command of the right words, which made the story so lucid. Moreover the way he never insisted on the moral, and merely implied it, was masterly too.[12]

The fact that the publication of *The Congress* coincided with the opening of the Paris Peace Conference in midsummer 1946 was not fortuitous. The story it told of 1815 emerged from the parallel with 1945. Europe had been at the mercy of a tyrant. Many states had been obliged to capitulate and even to collaborate with that tyrant. Great Britain alone maintained her independence. In the end Napoleon's hubris induced him to launch an attack on Russia. He was driven back. Russia was thereby led to believe that his defeat was solely her doing. There was no limit to her ambitions. She began a process of infiltration. But Tsar Alexander I was a weak man and not an autocrat like Stalin. The comparison thereafter had its limitations.[13]

Readers were meant to derive a lesson from the 1815 Congress story. They were meant to understand with apprehension the immense part played by chance and the moods, vices, and eccentricities of the participants; also the influence upon the outcome of discussion brought about by personal affection and dislike, misunderstanding, the incomplete command of language, even deafness and the lassitude and affability of the distinguished individuals. Harold's hero of the Congress was undoubtedly Castlereagh, who received from him praise instead of customary rebuke and revilement. For 'in placing the ultimate interests of Europe above the immediate advantage of England [he] displayed qualities of imagination and understanding such as have not been sufficiently applauded either by foreign or by British historians'.[14] Castlereagh throughout the Congress endeavoured to follow Pitt's precept that alteration of frontiers could be effected only by superior force and was therefore inadvisable. Order in Europe could be maintained only by concerted agreement of the Powers. Castlereagh's striving not to administer retribution to the vanquished but to bring back Europe to peaceful habits endowed him with nobility and goodness.

No sooner had Harold sent *The Congress of Vienna* to the press than he began another book, to be called *The English Sense of Humour*. He worked on it throughout 1946. This year he also began reviewing for the *Observer* one book every other Sunday, alternating with George Orwell; and in October he started reviewing again for the *Daily Telegraph* at £20 a review. As against these new undertakings retirement from his five years' governorship of the B.B.C. slightly alleviated the pressure of work. But even this respite was counterbalanced by his agreeing to write a fortnightly article for the *Figaro*. The contract lasted for two years.

In January 1946 Harold and his two sons were installed in no. 10 Neville Terrace. There was a floor for each of them, plus a basement. Although the importation of Ben's beautiful furniture which he had inherited from Lady Sackville, and of Nigel's soldier servant and his wife to look after them all, made the house attractive and comfortable – and Vita when she saw it thought it charming – Harold was determined not to like it. Devil Terrace he called it. 'My hatred of Neville Terrace knows no bounds,' he wrote. The very name infuriated him, with its association with Nevile Henderson and Neville Chamberlain. The winter was also extremely severe and the house was not yet properly wired for heat. These reasons for discontent were made worse by the animadversions of friends who lamented the translation from bohemian King's Bench Walk to the prim respectability of South Kensington.

James Pope-Hennessy, whose strongly expressed opinions always affected, if they did not always convince Harold, was loud in disparagement of Neville Terrace. He compared it to a boarding house turned into a reception centre for bombed-out Indian students. It was, he said, the sort of house a conjuror would have taken. And Ben pronounced it the ugliest little house he had ever seen outside, resembling a miniature replica of the Charing Cross Hotel. And then the vision of Harold's seat in the House of Lords was no nearer realisation. The Lord Chancellor told him that Lord Addison, leader of the House, would not consent to his being given a peerage because it was Labour's principle to give peerages only to members of their own party, with the exception of war heroes. Harold's predicament was not made more palatable by his old friend Archie Clark Kerr being created Lord Inverchapel although he was not a Socialist. This rubbed salt into the wound. So he put his name down tentatively for the Combined English Universities seat, vacated by Eleanor Rathbone, notwithstanding his unsuccessful attempt for one in 1931. It was a more attractive alternative for him even than a peerage.

Finally, Harold made another unwise political move. Meeting the Lord Chancellor one April day at a luncheon party of Lady Colefax's he told him too quixotically that he would gladly accept the Labour Whip. He was heart and soul with the Government in its foreign and domestic policies. Jowitt replied without much enthusiasm that perhaps it was a wise and dignified decision to come to. He would mention it to Lord Addison. And Harold went away worried, saying to himself that he had asked for a peerage and been turned down for not being Labour; and when he found he could not get one as an Independent he was ready to change his party coat. Even so he waited almost a year before taking the irrevocable step.

By an arrangement of the Foreign Office Harold accompanied Sir George Clerk on a four-day visit to Nuremberg to witness the trials of the Nazi leaders. The International Military Tribunal had been sitting since the previous November. He felt he must go for the purpose of writing about the trials in the British and French press. Yet he dreaded them. Although he had disliked Ribbentrop he disliked still more the prospect of witnessing his discomfiture. Schacht had been a friend, and his humiliation would be distressing. The scene was as horrid as he had foreseen, and he described it at length in his diaries. The defendants sat in the dock, the headphones disarranging their hair. They had 'the appearance of people who have travelled in a third-class railway carriage for three successive nights. It seems incredible that such a dim set of men should or could have done such huge and dreadful things.'[15] When Harold first entered the court-room Schacht's barrister happened to be defending him. The prisoner acquitted himself well, answering questions loudly and clearly, and vehemently denouncing the Nazi philosophy. When the court rose Harold drove with Sir Norman Birkett, one of the judges, to his villa. Birkett showed him a letter from Frank, one of the leading Nazis, to Hitler suggesting that good propaganda could be made out of the massacre by the Russians of 10,000 Polish officers at Katyn.[16] That was pretty conclusive evidence of where responsibility lay for that appalling incident which the Russians insisted was committed by the Germans. The next day Harold inspected the prisoners' cells and was moved by their pitiable belongings – Ribbentrop's photographs of his wife and handsome sons, Goering's fat suitcase of imitation leather. But feelings of pity were soon dispelled by a visit to the room wherein were kept the horror exhibits – a head, treated as the Borneo head-hunters treat their trophies, reduced to the size of an orange, with a mop of reddish hair; soap made of human fat and looking like cheese; and a lamp-shade made of human skin, showing the marks of two nipples. But by far the worst exhibit was a series of still photographs depicting the mass murder of Jewish women. A huge trench, as large as a small valley, had been dug. The women had been taken out in batches and shot so that they fell back into the trench.

> One could see the line of twelve women standing at the edge of the trench and the corpses of their predecessors filling the upper half of the trench like sprats spilled from a full fishing smack. But the horrible thing was that these women were all stark naked. There was another photograph of them being herded to the place where they were to be shot. At first glance one might have taken this photograph from *Picture Post* depicting girls running down to the sea. But when one looked carefully one saw that they were crouching forward in terror, holding on to each other, staggering together, with their breasts hanging pitiably, their fat bellies protruding above the pubic hair. That was the worst of all the countless atrocity photographs that I have seen. There was another of a pile of heads – a close up – and the head on the top of the pile had a grim smile on its face.[17]

Evidently there had been some idea that Harold might write a book about the Nuremberg trials, but Birkett decided, to Harold's relief, that it should be written by someone who had been present throughout. Instead he wrote a *Spectator* article on his brief Nuremberg experiences which caused a sensation.

In May Sir William Haley, the Director-General of the B.B.C., called on him. His appointment, thrust upon the Governors during the war without their connivance, had almost driven Harold and Lady Violet Bonham-Carter to resign from the Board, but which Harold quickly came to approve. Sir William invited him to go to Paris for the B.B.C. and give two weekly talks on the Home Service, plus one in French and one for the Overseas Service, on the course of the forthcoming Conference, in which texts of the peace treaties with Italy, Roumania, Hungary, Bulgaria and Finland were to be drafted. Conditions of payment were a minimum fee of 60 guineas a week for the four talks, and 15 guineas a time for any additional talk, the B.B.C. to defray all reasonable expenses. Harold jumped at the idea, and on the 23rd July set off for Paris on what was to be one of the most successful enterprises of his life.

Vita did not at all look forward to his temporary absence and when the actual departure came, Harold almost regretted that he had pledged his word to Haley. He wrote to her:

I hated leaving home today. I do not at all like having a barrier of sea between us. I do love you so my dearest Mar and it is an emptiness to me not to see you regularly. I feel unlike myself when I am separated from you.[18]

And she to him:

How well I know this heavy heart-ache always attendant on your many departures! I walk about looking quite usual to other people, but inside me is a lump of lead, which is partly composed of the actual *missing* of you, and partly of anxiety over the dangers you will run – Paris taxis, and so on.[19]

He stayed at the Ritz until he discovered that his room cost him as much as his salary, when he moved to a more modest hotel, the Grand in the Boulevard des Capucines. He was delighted with the two adjutants provided for him, Gibson Parker and Donald Hall. Parker was intelligent, active and a perfect French linguist. Hall was in close touch with the Embassy. Parker ran the whole show as Secretary-General; Hall ran the European Service no less efficiently. Harold was thrilled at the prospect of addressing 20 million people over the air, and was confident that he could make his fifteen-minute broadcasts from Paris as useful and influential as the B.B.C. broadcasts during the war. He was to give his Home Service talks every Sunday and Wednesday after the six o'clock news, which was a peak hour.

With this happy prospect of agreeable work before him Harold sat on the terrace of the Café de la Paix, drinking beer. He reflected upon his love of Paris pavement life. The terraces seemed always to retain a special atmosphere, linking them with Manet and Toulouse-Lautrec, and distinguishing them from all other outdoor cafés on the continent. He attributed their special quality to the busy ambience of a large capital; the sense of many houses stretching all around; the surge of people passing up and down the pavement; the extremely bright lights and awnings with which the terraces were lit and protected; and, above all, the relation between the space set apart for the tables and the width of pavement dotted with large trees. In fact, he decided, the proportion was unique.[20]

He was given a studio in that part of the Luxembourg Palace which was reserved for the delegates. Thus he could mingle and converse with them almost as an equal, and retire through a closed door to give his talk under the statue of a Greek ephebe. His old friend Pierre de Lacretelle once again rallied to him. Harold submitted to him the scripts of his French broadcasts which Pierre assured him needed no alterations.

It was soon rumoured that Harold Nicolson was the only person covering the Peace Conference who had played a part in the Conference of 1919. It brought him fame among hostesses and the press. He assured a reporter that the leading delegates of 1946 were even greater men than those of 1919. But he was depressed to think how much more influence he had twenty-seven years ago. At this Conference he counted for nothing at all. Only the ex-enemies wanted to see him, like Gregore Gafencu, the Roumanian delegate, and then he consistently threw cold water on Harold's optimism about Russia. In Russia, Gafencu assured him, we were faced with our greatest danger in that she was set on creating a military system in Europe. Nowhere was that danger more acute than in Germany. The Germans, themselves always prone to unity, might well find it in Communism. The Allies' only hope, this wise former Foreign Minister opined, was speedily to create a federated Germany within a new Federal Europe, on a liberal basis.

The Paris Conference opened on the 29th in inauspicious circumstances, for Russia controlled six votes (i.e. those of Soviet Russia,

White Russia, the Ukraine, Poland, Czechoslovakia and Yugoslavia), and by exercising them could wreck the proceedings. Whereas the 1919 Peace Conference may ultimately have achieved little, at least it opened in faith and optimism. In 1946 there was no faith and little optimism. No delegates believed in what they were doing. Nor did they believe in themselves or in each other. Harold soon concluded that as an experiment in open diplomacy the Conference was bound to fail. Diplomacy by loud speaker induced delegates to address, not their colleagues round the table, but their electorates at home. This method was inimical to all compromise and all agreement. The system of openly counting votes created unnecessary friction and lobbying. It reduced the Conference to the level of a charade. And, now that Winston Churchill was out of office, there was no leader. The nearest approach to a great leader among the delegates was Ernest Bevin, for whom Harold came to have profound admiration. Unfortunately he was a sick man. Nevertheless he stood up to the Russians, manfully, massively. He never minced his words and scolded them as severely as he scolded the Tories in the House of Commons. Whereas Harold applauded this attitude by Britain's Labour Foreign Secretary, he in his own broadcast talks adopted different tactics. It was his belief that our team should take the side of the Russians when they did right, so that when they were in the wrong (which was usual) we could speak to them with effect. The Russians should be given credit when credit was due. Allowances should be made for the fact that they were not trained in the courtesies of international intercourse. Thomas Cadett, *The Times* correspondent confirmed that Harold's attitude was the correct one. On the other hand the leading British delegates, A. V. Alexander, Gladwyn Jebb and Oliver Harvey, were indignant with what they deemed Harold's attitude of appeasement. Harold defended himself by saying that the Russians might well become our enemies, but until they were, we should treat them as reasonable beings.

In theory this was all very fine. But the Russians were using deliberate steam-roller tactics. And Harold lent too far backwards in reproving Byrnes, the American delegate, for deploring the abuse and misrepresentation to which Molotov was exposing America with charges that she had made money out of the war by her methods of lease-lend to Russia. By the time the Conference was ending Harold recognised that we could never convince the Russians by argument; but he still maintained that the only thing we should do was to behave as well as possible and convince them by the example of our immense moral power. For instance, we still had nearly half a million German prisoners not yet repatriated. We should send them home as soon as possible, and thus influence the Russians to behave with similar mercy and generosity.

At the end of August Vita, with Raymond Mortimer and Eardley Knollys, motored through Paris on their way to the Lot. They stayed one night with Harold at the Grand Hotel. Next morning all three took their breakfast-trays into his bedroom. Together they went to look at the superlative Unicorn tapestries from the Musée de Cluny then on exhibition. Too soon the happy little party left him. He was alone again. Having watched Vita's Buick turn the street corner he walked into the Luxembourg gardens with tears stinging his eyes. He sat on a bench by the octagonal pond. On its surface children were sailing little boats. Their shrill cries reached him, '*Tu vois, André, tu vois, le foc comme il se gonfle.*' The boat heeled over, the mainsail flapped and the jib swelled into pretty curves. He moved into the Conference chamber of the palace. There the delegates were behaving in exactly the same manner as the children. They launched out on a gentle breeze of self-satisfaction. Then they drove round and round in eddies, returning to the very place from which they had started, gusts of indignation and squalls of passion vibrating their voices. They were engendering storms in a slightly larger pond, while far out beyond the Luxembourg were real ships encountering real peril upon dangerous seas.[21]

In September he went with Janet Leeper to see Gordon Craig.[22] Craig lived in a flat and studio with his secretary and their daughter, a pert child of eight or nine. The high studio was covered with innumerable maps of old Paris, old Rome and old Florence. On bookshelves were rows of vellum-bound folios. Craig came in. He was venerable and impressive, and looked like Liszt. He had the face of a very ancient, and the movements of a very young, man. He was interested and alert, his eyes peering, his head thrust forward.[23]

The strain on Harold of the broadcast talks was immense. We must bear in mind that in addition to these talks he was writing three articles a week – for the *Spectator*, the Paris *Figaro* and a book-review for the *Observer*. But the B.B.C. assured him they could not find anyone of his stature to take his place. They begged him to continue until the bitter end of the Conference. After a week's leave in England – in Vita's absence he was met by Ben and myself at Victoria station – he returned to Paris on the 24th. The Big Four decided that all commissions must finish their reports by October 5th. There would then be a series of plenary sessions, culminating on October 15th. Harold would be released on the 17th. The German Conference would take place at the end of November.

While he was still in Paris the recordings of the Nuremberg verdicts were released. Through headphones Harold listened to the Judge pronouncing the defendants guilty and condemning them one by one to long years' imprisonment, or instant death by hanging. It made him feel sick to hear these men being bumped off one by one. He took off his earphones, and walked away.

There is no doubt that the series, of unprecedented length in B.B.C. annals, of broadcast comments which Harold gave, were phenomenally successful. They were more than direct reportage. They were extremely shrewd speculation upon the outcome of events. They were looked forward to with eagerness and heard by millions. Alan Moorhead told him that the British public interpreted the Conference only through his talks. Rab Butler assured him that they had taught the British common man to take his first interest in foreign affairs. Vita wrote that she had never known anything on the wireless which people were so determined not to miss. A friend said to her, 'It is his absolute honesty and moral courage. One feels he would never say a word he did not believe to be true.' Indeed, if his apologies for the Russians did not meet with universal agreement, it was impossible not to admire his fearlessness in trying to make out a fair case for them.

Before the year was out Harold was engaged upon a weekly broadcast on the General Overseas Service about international affairs from a diplomatic standpoint. He addressed millions in India, Persia and China.

In November Ben was offered and accepted the editorship of the *Burlington Magazine*, which he took up the following April and retained until his death in 1978. He was already recognised as an art historian of international repute. He had identified an unknown Raphael and with his boss, Professor Anthony Blunt, the Surveyor of the King's Pictures, organized an important exhibition of paintings by Lawrence. He was now obliged to offer his resignation as Deputy-Surveyor of the King's Pictures. It was accepted to Ben's satisfaction for he was not by nature a courtier. The formalities and etiquette which went with the job were irksome and distasteful to him. His parents had always been nervous how Ben, with his absent-mindedness and indifference to clothes and appearance, would conduct himself in the royal circle. Once when commanded to attend a court ball he informed his parents that he was going to refuse because he had a more congenial invitation.

His father told him sternly that he couldn't possibly do such a thing. A royal command to a royal servant was something which had to be obeyed. 'But, Daddy, I shall be so bored,' was Ben's instant retort. At the same time Nigel, having finished his history of the Grenadier Guards in the war, joined the staff of George Weidenfeld's *Contact Magazine*, soon to develop into the successful publishing firm of Weidenfeld & Nicolson, with which he is associated to this day.

Two events affected Harold closely. On the 21st November he had his sixtieth birthday. It was a landmark which brought him only distress. He hated getting old. He was conscious of a decline in his physical powers. He was becoming deaf. His hair, though grey and still curly at the back, was thin on top. He was fattish. Yet the air of sprightliness, enhanced by the customary carnation which he wore in his button-hole, in spite of the rather casual clothes, had not deserted him. As for his clothes, he discovered one day in Paris during high pressure of work that his only pair of trousers had a huge rent in the seat, and one sole of his only pair of shoes had come off in the street. He bought a needle and cotton and mended the rent in the trousers himself. His clothes always looked from a distance smarter than they turned out to be on close inspection. His American friend, Mina Curtiss, meeting him in London about this time, took note of his Anthony Eden-style black hat, splendid frogged top-coat with Persian lamb collar, well tailored, double-breasted blue serge suit and blue shirt. The effect was somewhat spoilt by his fly buttons being wide open, displaying two prominent shirt-tails.[24] Intellectually however there was no decline. He wrote with the same facility as of old, which he thought might be a fault. And his capacity for work was unabated. On the 9th December he recorded that over one weekend he had written eight articles and reviews, and read two books. But what was sad about reaching sixty was that one lost all opportunity of adventure. It was unlikely now that the unexpected would happen, sexually or even emotionally.

The second event was publication of *The English Sense of Humour*. It did not mitigate what Harold, assessing his successes and failures on his birthday, considered his literary shortcomings. Ben unkindly remarked that the exterior of the book (it was published by the Dropmore Press in a handsome format) was superior to the interior; and Raymond with his usual astringency called it very bad and sham philosophy, which he hoped his friend would not try his hand at another time. Yet most reviews were favourable. Some questioned his exclusive right to determine what was a sense of humour; and others deprecated his claim that the proletariat failed to have it. The book abounded in pertinent and amusing comments. It illustrated the startling premise that humour as a sense was not discovered or discussed a hundred years before. It pointed out that Mr. Gladstone was the first statesman about whom a contemporary thought fit to remark that he was devoid of it. Lack of humour was not mentioned by the contemporaries of Milton, Dr. Johnson or even Shelley.

One of the coldest winters on record set in with the New Year of 1947. The shortage of fuel was so acute that Emanuel Shinwell, the Minister of Fuel and Power, was obliged to ration heat and light. In London the public galleries had never been so well attended by people who crowded into them merely to keep warm. Harold, having run out of his exiguous supply of coal, sat in Neville Terrace with a charcoal hand-warmer and a rug over his knees preparing notes for his regular Brains Trust talks over the air and those lectures on diplomacy, which he was constantly being called upon to deliver. At Sissinghurst Vita, who was beginning her book, *Daughter of France*, was perished with cold in her tower, while blizzards raged outside and drifts of fine snow crept through the lattice window-panes. The two bars of her electric fire barely kept her hands from being frost-bitten. 'If Mr. Shinwell wasn't Labour, I might put one of them out,' she wrote characteristically, 'but as it is, I don't.' And to make life more depressing the news, domestic and international, was as bad as could be. Strikes and subversion were rampant. Industry was practically at a standstill. Exports were deplorably low. The lights were out in the shops. The threat of Communism over France, Greece and Germany was very real. It looked as though the United States and Russia were on the verge of war; and that the British Empire was about to break up.

Harold was wretched at not being in Parliament and at being out of the swim. No longer in the thick of politics his advice on affairs was seldom sought. It was therefore flattering to be asked by his friend Sir Alan Lascelles to write to Prince Paul of Yugoslavia, who with his wife was living in the suburbs of Johannesburg, and urge him to absent himself when our King and Queen visited the Transvaal. Harold had always tried to explain in articles and talks the delicate situation in which the much maligned Prince found himself during the war. On these grounds he was persuaded to tender advice which could not very well come from the King's Secretary. Harold received a sad and touching letter from Prince Paul, assuring him that he would never dream of pushing himself forward when the King and Queen arrived.

In February he left for Paris, the purpose of his visit being to witness the signature of the Peace Treaties with Italy, Roumania, Bulgaria, Hungary and Finland, concluded after the interminable wrangling throughout 1946. Feeling ill with a bad cold Harold, spluttering and coughing, broadcast an account of the event. It was not one of his best talks. He remarked upon the friendly attitude of the victorious Powers towards the vanquished, compared with that of 1919. When the Italian delegates were ushered into the Salon d'Horloge of the Quai d'Orsay, Monsieur Bidault, chairman of the Conference, smiled upon them and said, 'I bid you welcome.' It was in pleasant contrast with Clemenceau's short, sharp barks, 'Sit down! And keep quiet!'

On the 28th February Harold took a political plunge. He wrote to the Secretary of the South Kensington Labour Party seeking to enrol as a member. His letter was acknowledged on the 3rd March by a typist who evidently did not know who the signatory, H. Nicolson, was. His action was the result of months of painful deliberation. It was not impulsive, but it was quixotic.[25] His motives were muddled as he freely confessed. He knew the Labour Party was in a bad way, and honestly believed that by joining it at that moment he would be an encouragement. Of course his basic reason was that in doing so he might further his chances of being made a peer and acquire a seat in the Upper House. Before taking the step he had consulted no friends and none of his family. When he learned that Nigel was preparing an address to the Leicester Conservatives begging for their support he was overcome with embarrassment and guilt. How awful if the press released the two pieces of news at the same time. On the 5th March he summoned his two sons. It was a strange little meeting, the father owning up like a culpable schoolboy to something of which they might strongly disapprove. Nigel recorded the occasion in his diary. 'Now I am going to tell you the awful thing I've done,' Harold said. 'Have a glass of sherry first, each of you.' Nigel was struck dumb. Ben's reaction was not recorded. Doubtless he did not mind in the least, for if he voted at all he certainly voted Labour. Nigel asked his father if he really believed in all the Socialist principles. 'Well, yes, on the whole,' Harold answered, admitting that his only fear was of the extreme left wing. If they gained control, then he would leave the Party. Nigel could not but admire his father's enthusiasm and candour. Then Harold wrote to tell Vita, who took it calmly. She did not, she said, relish his association with people like Aneurin Bevan and Shinwell. 'I do not like people who cannot speak the King's English . . .' omitting from this category Ernie Bevin whom she held in high esteem. 'I long to see you, darling, and find out more about this strange political move of yours; *petit cachottier!*' Finally the press got hold of it. The voters of Leicester, Harold's ex-constituents whom Nigel was now wooing, were indeed shocked to the core.

His mother's and brother Freddy's, reaction was not tolerant. Old Lady Carnock was outraged. In her eyes her son had betrayed his country. Freddy tartly observed that he supposed Harold would resign from all his clubs. Among his friends the Liberal Lady Violet deplored it. She told him that fundamentally he was far less Labour than she was. Besides, the values which Socialists ignored and despised were the most important values in life. And after all, he was far nearer in his philosophy to Conservatives like Eden and Macmillan than to Attlee and Gaitskell. As for his Labour acquaintances the reaction of Richard Crossman was fairly typical. It was not unspiced with contempt. 'I hear you have joined the Labour Party. Which bit of it have you joined?' Another Labour acquaintance assured him he would not accuse him of moral turpitude, unless of course he took a peerage. Only Anthony Eden upheld him. When Emerald Cunard started scolding him Eden said to her, 'No, he is quite right. He is a person apart and has every right to his own decisions. He will do a world of good in the Labour Party.'[26] Harold *was* a person apart. And as such he would have been invaluable in Parliament again, if only the mass of politicians had had the sense to realise it. But they didn't. If they had, they would have given him a Combined Universities seat, or a seat in the Lords. Of the two Harold would have preferred the first, for then he would have remained in his beloved Commons without the incubus of a constituency.

When Harold had his first experience of an undiluted Labour gathering he simply loathed it. He went with two charming men of his own sort, Charles Fletcher-Cooke and Noel Annan, to a dinner of the Haldane Society. They were given vegetable soup, liver, onions, and beer. There were speeches about Law Reform. At the end the Red Flag was sung. Throughout there was a terrible atmosphere of comradely fifth-rateness which nauseated him. Harold was a theoretical Socialist. He believed in planned social economy without the destruction of individual freedom. But the Red Flag and trumped-up mateyness were to him anathema. Another dinner about this time, given by the Omar Khayyám Club (of which he was a member) and the first held since 1939, was a very different affair. The fact that Swinburne and Richard Burton had once been members lent it a spice of exoticism. Sustained by a sympathetic confederation of literary members, and inspired by the memory of Philip Guedalla's wit, the speeches were remarkable for erudition and humorous disputation.

Harold spent much of the summer at Sissinghurst immersed in further plans for the garden and consulting Vita on the planting of the moat walk. Should they have a row of trained apples above the pink magnolia? Or would that be too pink? He felt very strongly that henceforth they should eschew all plants like annuals and biennials which made work. They should keep to a war-style garden. They should have more forsythia, magnolia, kerria, fuchsia – all the things that were least trouble in upkeep. Whatever they planted should be uniform, large and what he called 'not bothersome'. He did not care for rhododendrons which reminded him of Sunningdale. 'They are to us like large stockbrokers whom we do not want to have to dinner.' Vita was in full agreement with these sentiments. It was seldom that they had disagreements about the garden. Only occasionally Harold with his more orderly mind would stress the necessity for forethought in design; and he would reprimand Vita for wanting to jab in plants which she had left over. Occasionally she reproved him for not stopping to examine flowers closely enough. His cursory glances would not do. He never resented spending lavishly on plants because he believed from the very first that they would make of Sissinghurst the most beautiful garden in England. So he would rush off and extravagantly buy quantities of Barr parrot tulips that looked like Battersea china and masses of the finest delphiniums ever seen, Eton blue with a dash of Oxford blue. And always he would attribute his successes to her, and she hers to him.

He rejoiced as much for Vita's sake as for his own when appreciative visitors, like Mina Curtiss, were intoxicated by the beauty of the garden. There were lovely May mornings when he bathed in the lake and had breakfast in the Erectheum, and not a leaf stirred upon the sun-lit poplars; and lovely evenings when he would climb the Tower after sunset and rhapsodise over the garden, and the shadows lengthened and the moon rose into the violet sky.

He was doing some preparatory work on a new book, *Benjamin Constant*. The happy months were interrupted only by voluntary jaunts to London, from which he could never keep away for long. He called on Sibyl Colefax, where he found the Windsors.

> When I come into the room, I find Osbert Lancaster there, and a young man with his back to the window. He says, 'Not recognize an old friend?' It is the Duke of Windsor. He is thin but more healthy-looking than when I last saw him. He has lost the fried-egg look around the eyes. He is very affable and chatty . . . I have an impression that he is happier.[27]

He found the Duchess much improved. 'That taut, predatory look has gone; she has softened.' She told Harold that the Duke was longing to live in England and have a job. '"You see," she said, "he was born to be a salesman. He would be an admirable representative of Rolls Royce. But an ex-King cannot start selling motor-cars."' Harold felt really sorry for them. 'They were so simple and sincere.' He lunched at the French Embassy to meet André Gide who was to be given an LL.D. at Oxford. Would the undergraduates demonstrate against him for political or moral reasons? Harold thought not. They might merely shout '*Corydon!*' in a friendly, but not mocking spirit. He dined with the Hugh Daltons at 11 Downing Street. Best of all, he was made a Member of the Legion of Honour, with Cyril Connolly, at the French Embassy. His old friend, Ambassador Réné Massigli, made a citation. He called Harold '*écrivain, diplomate, et homme politique de renommé mondiale, qui n'a pas cessé un instant de croire en la France et en sa destinée. La France possède en lui un magnifique champion de sa cause.*' He kissed him on both cheeks. Harold, embarrassed, did not know where to look.

> Then we had a *vin d'honneur* [he told Vita[28]], followed by luncheon. The latter consisted of cold eggs, tongue and stewed cherries. Does that sound dull? Well, it wasn't. The eggs were enclosed in jelly and rested upon a thick mattress of foie gras; the tongue was *braisée* and surrounded by every vegetable known to God, and man, including the tips of asperges and the bums of artichokes. The cherries had been stewed in brandy and had little bits of toffee in them. And with it Mersault, and Veuve Clicquot.

At the beginning of August Harold and Vita, escorted by me, went on a ten-day tour of National Trust properties in the West Country. The object of the tour was for Harold, who had just been appointed

Vice-Chairman of the Trust's Executive Committee, to see as many of its historic buildings as possible, and Vita to give advice on the gardens. Altogether we visited some forty houses, and included several cathedrals. Harold made brief notes on the condition of the properties – 'West Wycombe Park: whole place terribly dilapidated, paper peeling from walls, and no servants. Montacute: the house a credit to the Trust. Bradley Manor: the donor is poor, has many children and the house is shabby. Corsham Court: the pictures admirable but the picture gallery too pompous for my taste.' Both Harold's and Vita's taste was for the simple, preferably Elizabethan, Caroline or Queen Anne houses. The symmetry and grandeur of the classical Georgian was not for them. Other privately owned houses not belonging to the Trust, which en route struck their fancy, were visited. Vita, greatly to Harold's concern, would, on spying lodges and gates which betokened a seat, swirl up the drive with the intention of having a good look round. She regarded such unsolicited visits as within her right. 'After all,' she replied to Harold's remonstrances, 'we always allowed strangers, provided their carriages looked respectable, to see round Knole ever since the eighteenth century.' Once only we met with a well merited rebuff. At Ramsbury Manor Vita drove round and round the sweep of the drive extolling the beauties of this exquisite red brick house. It was early in the morning. The owner, Sir Francis Burdett, who had been breakfasting, rushed down the steps, brandishing a newspaper in one hand and a piece of toast in the other. Puce in the face with indignation he shouted to us to stop and explain our extraordinary behaviour. Overcome with shame Harold tried to hide himself on the floorboards. He pleaded with Vita either to obey or drive away. Not until she had finished her disquisition did she draw up. With exquisite courtesy she pretended she had mistaken the house for Littlecote Manor, which it in no way resembled. The incident greatly upset Harold for four reasons: 'intruding upon the privacy of others; telling lies; being scolded; being made to look foolish'.[29] The rest of the morning we drove in painful silence.

At Wilton we had drinks with David Herbert, 'looking young and charming, dressed in Lederhosen, and a maroon shirt,' in his enchanting garden house. On the last day of the tour we listened on the wireless to Lord Mountbatten transferring power to India and Pakistan. Harold was irritated by this example of our national inability to see things as they really were, and our rendering to God the things that were Caesar's. Here we were behaving as though the loss of 400 million citizens and the surrender of our imperial power were some tremendous triumph, and not the final eclipse of the greatest empire in history.

During this highly concentrated tour Harold devoted one morning a week to writing his weekly article and reviews; and Vita her 'In your Garden' column for the *Observer*.

One night of our tour was spent at Wells. The following morning having breakfasted we were about to visit the Cathedral when Vita said she must go to the post office. She told Harold and me to wait for her on the pavement outside the hotel for she would only be away five minutes. She began crossing the street. Just after the war there was not a great deal of traffic on the roads. Nevertheless Vita looked carefully to left and right before crossing. Harold kept a close watch on her movements. It was then that his astonishing concern for her safety struck me as being exaggerated, even slightly absurd. She was as far as I remember in no danger whatsoever. Nevertheless Harold gripped my arm like a vice, turned his head away, and practically sobbing, cried out, 'Oh Viti, Viti, she's going to get run over. I know she'll be killed. Oh God! Oh God!' Vita glided across the street, upright and leisurely. Having despatched her telegram she returned unruffled and unscathed. Harold's behaviour on this occasion was certainly far more irrational than her veto on his flying, which he so much resented. Was it, I asked myself, put on? Was it possible that after thirty-four years of married life a loving husband of unusual intelligence could work himself into such a frenzy because his equally sensible wife was crossing the street of an uncongested provincial town in broad daylight? Quite simply the answer was Yes. He really did at that particular moment, and on hundreds, if not thousands of similar moments, go through real agony lest she might come to harm, be killed and leave him a striken widower. Although Vita was more restrained in the expression of her dreads, she felt the same way about him. Their dependence upon one another transcended the normal relationship between a husband and wife. It was something so fundamental, so integral that it had to be accepted if one was to understand the character of either.

On the 2nd of September Harold left London by the Golden Arrow for Switzerland in search of Benjamin Constant.

I slid in the Arrow through Kent. They were gathering apples in the Paddock Wood orchards. They were picking the hops – so Balkan they looked, all tangled in the byres. Staplehurst flashed past me without a word.[30]

In Paris he lost his return ticket which had slipped through the torn lining of his greatcoat pocket. In Geneva he was met by friends who were passionately keen and knowledgeable about Madame de Stael and her circle. They took him to Sécheron on the western shore of the lake opposite the Villa Diodati which Byron had rented in 1816. Through a public telescope (20 centimes) they looked at the villa and could see nothing, which contradicted Byron's complaints that he was spied upon by the British tourists. They visited the Diodati, with its elaborate ironwork balcony from which the foolish Dr. Polidori threw himself for effect. Its walls were overgrown and fine rooms deserted. Back at dusk in the old town of Geneva, which smelled of drains and Calvinism, Harold watched two youths, brown and muscular, jump laughing into the icy water from the bridge over the Rhone.

Mrs. Ronald Armstrong, the Dutch wife of the retired British Consul, accompanied him to Neuchâtel by train. At Neuchâtel they changed into a tram and went clanking through the suburbs into the vineyards beside the lake. At Les Vergers they got out. They walked through clover-fields towards a seat embowered in trees. Here a formidable lady, Madame Dorette Berthoud, the greatest authority on Constant, limped towards them on a stick. She told Harold how the old Baroness de Rebecque, the widow of a descendant of Benjamin, had allowed her to take a list of the Constant papers from the family archives. She showed Harold that list. It was made, she said, before she became a Constant expert, so she did not really know at the time what to look for. But it suggested that among those papers was the missing portion of the *Journal Intime*. Inspired by this she began her first book on Benjamin. Then the Baroness died. Her son, *'un ours mal léché'*, refused to let her see the family papers ever again, because he had read in a book that one of his ancestors had sold oranges.

At last they visited Colombier, the home of Madame de Charrière, the Egeria of Constant's early life.

It is a little village mounting on one side to a large castle and on the other side rising in vineyards to the foothills. The *manoir* of the Charrière family is stuck in a little hole between these two eminences, with the result that it is like living in a basement, always something in front of one's face when one is looking out. It is completely unchanged, and as such, moving. There was the fountain where she did the family washing and there her music-room and there her bedroom. All so badly designed . . . Dark little windows giving on the village through which, poor woman, she could hear the church clock sounding the empty hours. But you will read all about Colombier one day . . . It is a truly horrible house, so dark, so inelegant, no rooms the right proportion, cold passages, meagre, mingy, mean, and the village clock striking.[31]

Harold was acutely depressed, and having in a lightning-flash formed an indelible impression of Colombier was longing to get away. To his annoyance Madame Berthoud, who 'like Jim has no sense of time' when she found herself in an old house, persisted in showing him every nook and cranny of the place.

The next day he was taken to Lausanne, visiting other existing Constant houses or sites. It was difficult to ascertain in which house the family had lived. Did they go from one to the other? Did they keep servants in each? Or bring the same lot on each peregrination? How remote and unknown was the everyday manner of life in the late eighteenth century. In each house

there was a fountain somewhere, or a spurt of clear cold water from a pipe into a large stone trough. Each of these falls of water has a different note, and speaks, now sturdy, now mincing, in a voice that it spoke to Benjamin all those long years ago. But they can tell me nothing about how many cooks they had or gardeners.[32]

In Lausanne Harold and Ronald Armstrong were shown the herbal of Rosalie de Constant, the spinster first cousin who loved Benjamin. It consisted of fourteen bound volumes of some 1,200 neat water-colours of alpine plants, each with a description written so meticulously in that old maid hand. They were told how once Madame de Staël burst into the room when Rosalie was painting arduously with her sharp little tongue out, and the plant itself spread before her. She must have worked with a magnifying glass. Madame de Staël, who loathed seeing anyone doing things she was unable to do herself, was enraged by Rosalie's occupation. 'It amuses you, all that nonsense, Mademoiselle. It would bore me to tears,' she said brutally.[33]

Harold spent another day in the University Library at Geneva pouring over Constant manuscripts. He did not allow himself time to read all the letters from and to Constant. He did not intend his book to be one of laborious research. He meant it to be a study, an interpretation. Since childhood Constant had been a precise calligraphist. Each letter

5(a) Harold on his yawl *Mar*, March 1939.

(b) Ben Nicolson and Nigel in 1938.

6 The entrance to the White Garden, Sissinghurst. The marble plaque of the three oriental bishops was bought by them in Constantinople in 1913.

that Harold picked up gave him an insight into his subject's character, even when he did not read it.

He visited Coppet, Madame de Staël's house on the lake of Geneva which her father, Jacques Necker, bought in 1784. He walked there from the station, along the park wall. It was only five feet high, and pierced in the middle by an iron grille. Through this grille Harold fancied that Constant had his clandestine interview with Charlotte de Hardenberg, whom he ultimately married to the fury of Madame de Staël. The house stands much as it looked when Germaine de Staël lived there after her exile from France by Napoleon, a substantial *manoir* with brown tiles and woodwork of faded jade green. The ladies of the house, descendants of Necker, were sitting in the garden under an immense cedar. They were typical *gratins*, speaking, as Harold put it, with the accents of the rue de Varenne. He was given tea in a small room upstairs next to the big *salon*, with its tapestries and fine chairs. They ate off blue china embossed with an S and a baronial coronet. The small room was lined with portraits of de Staëls, and the Gérard portrait of Germaine. After tea his hostess showed him the library, Germaine's bedroom, and beyond it the bedroom of her closest friend, Madame de Recamier, whom Constant also loved in vain.[34]

The following day Harold returned by train to Colombier by himself. For Colombier seemed to him the key to the Constant story, and he wanted to be alone and immerse himself in the whole distressing, melancholy surroundings. The more he thought of Geoffrey Scott's *Portrait of Zélide*, the worse the book struck him. 'It is not only written as if he were putting pistachio nuts into a coffee cake, but he has got her out of focus.'[35]

I have given the above account of Harold's search for Benjamin Constant at somewhat undue length in order to show how he set about preparing a biography. In this particular book, which was a literary and not an historical life, his actual documentary research was, as he frankly confessed, negligible. On the other hand he took immense pains in environmental exploration. He soaked himself in atmosphere. He noticed with his keen eye every small detail that might bring to mind the subject he was studying, the sound of running water and the fountain, the repetitive chime of the church clock which reminded Madame de Charrière so poignantly of her receding middle age, the sight of poor Rosalie's flower paintings, and the calligraphy of Constant's letters, all of which revealed to him more than the words themselves glimpses of Benjamin's sharp and mercurial character. Harold did not however start serious writing of the book for another year.

Switzerland was not devoted exclusively to the pursuit of Constant. One Sunday he was taken by the Armstrongs to lunch with the exiled Queen Marie José of Italy, at Merlingue where she had a villa. It was in open country with an indifferent view. In front of it was a huge lawn composed entirely of dandelions, and edged with cannas.

She is, it seems, short of money. She has a rich Swiss lady as her *dame de compagnie*, and a Geneva *bonne*. The latter is round and gay and raucous, dressed in a blue *tricot* out of which emerge red forearms and little purple hands. We sat there on the terrace and had a glass of port. Then the *bonne* waddled out and said (with some pomp, I admit), '*Sa Majesté est servie.*' So we all went into the dining-room. We were given a few mushrooms on toast with custard over them, and then the bits of a chicken. The latter must have been very old when it died and must have enjoyed ill health for years. But it was served on magnificent plates bearing the arms and crown of the House of Savoy. Then we went back on the terrace and had coffee. The Queen is a thin, tall, spotty, sulky wench – discontented with life – not given to conversation. She only perked up when the *bonne* waddled out again and set down upon the table a bottle of Chartreuse. '*Voilà, Majesté!*' she said in a fat, comfortable voice, knowing that the exiled Queen would be pleased thereby. As indeed she was. She explained that the Chartreuse had got into her luggage by mistake and came from the Quirinal cellars. Then the telephone rang and the *Dame de Compagnie* went into the house and returned radiant. '*Les bagages sont arrivés, Madame.*' Sudden animation on the part of the Queen. It seems that all her luggage at the time of her escape from Italy was sent to Portugal by mistake. A pardonable mistake since her husband is at Estoril. But for months she has had only two dresses. So in the end she sent her car and her chauffeur all the way to Lisbon to collect the togs. And there it was arrived at Merlingue. We saw that she was itching to unpack her belongings, so we took our departure. In the drive outside the villa was the car from Lisbon. Never at its best a very handsome car, it was travel-stained. They had already un-strapped some of the suitcases and dumped them on the gravel. If I were Queen of Italy I should have luggage like that of Lorenzo the Magnificent. But no – they were just such suitcases as one might buy at a jumble sale at Empoli. And inside the car, crushed against the windows, was a bundle consisting of a flowered counterpane in which royal possessions had been jumbled and tied with string. As we drove back I thought of that muzzy and unhappy woman unpack-ing the dresses which she had worn in the Palace at Naples or in the colonnade of Racconigi.[36]

Not a very sympathetic picture of the poor sad Queen of Italy who had been forced to leave her adopted country with the minimum of possessions, without the husband who had left her, and without, so it seemed, her children to console her.

At Sissinghurst Vita was correcting proofs of her guide book to Knole which she had undertaken to write for the National Trust. It enveloped her in a deluge of unhappiness. She was bewildered that the revived memory of mere stones, and courtyards and rooms, should be so poignant. Harold was able to sympathise because he understood how her whole identity was merged in the house of her ancestors. Knole for her was more than a house. It was a person. It was as if Vita had had only one deep love in her life, and that love had been stolen away by another who did not properly understand its meaning.

Back at Sissinghurst Harold busied himself with weekly articles, reviews, broadcasts, lectures, committees and boards. They were his livelihood; and he had to forgo serious writing in order to exist. He was out of the swim. He was depressed. His depression evidently had an adverse effect on a series of World Affairs broadcasts he was giving that autumn. An internal note from a director of talks to the Director-General of the B.B.C. severely criticised one broadcast on the mechanics of conferences, not admittedly a very inspiring subject. It was, the man wrote, an 'obtuse, vague, slipshod and perfunctory piece, written in cliché for which he gropes like a man in a dream. Does he do so for the guineas? This is not the hand that wrote the sketch of Curzon.' The truth is that Harold was doing far too much pot-boiling. He was bored, and feeling unwanted. Was his sense of neglect made worse by the award to Vita of the Companionship of Honour? Harold would never have admitted such an unworthy thought, even to himself. Of course he was genuinely delighted in Attlee's – for it was his – honour to Vita; and he was amazed that she took the whole thing so phlegmatically, without excitement and without, it appeared, much appreciation. She was even irritated by the publicity and in her curious individualist way resented her name being associated with his. Nevertheless the bestowal of an honour upon her was in marked contrast to the official disregard of himself. And it was not made more palatable when he believed that his name had been on the list of New Year peerages and taken off because Vita's was included for the Companionship.

Suddenly Harold received an invitation from Transport House to take on a bye-election at North Croydon caused by the resignation of the sitting Conservative member. He was appalled. It was not what he wanted at all. He wanted to be handed a safe parliamentary seat for which he need not fight. The prospect of contesting at his age a by-election in the full glare of publicity was abhorrent to him. But, such was the position into which he had got himself by joining the Labour Party, that he could not honourably refuse. If the local committee would adopt him, he must accept. Thus it was that he found himself addressing the divisional committee, candidly outlining all his shortcomings: the New Party, National Labour, his loyalty to Churchill, his election address of 1945, his inability to be violent or denunciatory, his belonging to the upper class, Sissinghurst, Vita, Nigel a Conservative candidate, Ben, an ex-royal servant, the lot. The catalogue of self-denigration was to no avail. True, he gained the impression that his auditors listened to these admissions as grave disadvantages, but were too embarrassed to say so. One elderly woman and one young man dared to express the opinion that he was too right-wing. A vote was taken. He was adopted by eight votes to two. The die was once again cast. There was no way out. He must go through the whole beastly charade once again.

He promised Vita that this time he was not going to impose Croydon upon the family. It was his own sorrow, his own cross which he would bear alone. Vita did not disapprove, and she did not take part. She merely dreaded the escapade on his behalf.

For the next three months Harold endured what he called his North Croydon crucifixion. Everything associated with it was distasteful to him. To begin with Ben was lukewarm; Nigel by virtue of his nursing a Conservative seat could not help him; and Vita was indifferent. Furthermore throughout the campaign she was lecturing in North Africa. When he went to tea with his mother she clenched her teeth and said, 'I pray that you may be defeated'. Harold replied, 'But that is not very encouraging, Mummy'. She said, 'I always put my country above my family'.[37]

Before plunging into the campaign he had time for a visit to Paris. He lectured on the Commonwealth and the British Empire to the Ecole de Guerre, and did some more Constant research. In this he was accompanied by Pierre de Lacretelle. Pierre was by now in a bad way, much addicted to morphia, jobless and penniless. But having written a book on Madame de Staël, he was an admirable dragoman. He directed Harold to various Constant sites which Harold would not have found on his own. He took him to Luzarches just outside Paris on the Creil Line where Constant had a small country house. Thirty years ago the environs of Paris, unlike those of London, were still practically unchanged since the eighteenth century. They found the l'Abbaye d'Hérivaux where Benjamin and Germaine lived for six years. Hidden in a forest of venerable plane trees, the place, although a little dolled up by a rich industrialist, was still charming.

In February the date for the North Croydon by-election was fixed and the campaign opened. It evoked much public interest. At the General Election the Conservative candidate had won the seat by a slender majority of just over 600 votes. At the bye-election the new Conservative candidate was a local businessman and the Liberal a war hero in the person of Air Vice-Marshal 'Pathfinder' Donald Bennett. It was felt that a good candidate ought to be able to win over the seat to Labour.

Harold was transported from the smiling suburbs of Paris to the snow and slush of North Croydon. He had an attic room under the roof of a dreary hotel in Upper Norwood, and was intensely lonely. It was a repetition of the dismal election at West Leicester in 1945. At the end of long tiring days he brewed on a bedroom gas-ring little meals of Ovaltine or chocolate sent him by Sibyl Colefax. 'It is like having a father on Devil's Island,' Nigel wrote to his mother. 'One does what one can through the Red Cross.' Harold distributed his election address in which he made himself out to be the strong champion of social democracy. He advocated removing the main means of production from private competition and placing them under state control. His wish was to see an England in which nobody was either enormously rich or intolerably poor, 'an England in which every boy and girl was given an equal opportunity of education and success'. James Pope-Hennessy, who spent part of a day with him, was shocked by Harold's class-consciousness. In spite of the appalling cold he would not wear his fur-lined coat lest the electorate might think him 'posh'; and he discouraged a visit from Ben because of his rather drawling, patrician voice. James was amazed that he could not be himself amongst people whose background was different from his own. It was a fact that, try as he might – and he did not always try enough – he could not be natural with uneducated people. For instance, although he was always thoughtful and kind to his own servants, he was not friendly with other people's, even when he had known them for years. Consequently his door-to-door canvassing was sometimes interpreted as patronising. Harold was quite unaware that he made any such impression. 'I have no hesitation about penetrating into working class houses,' he wrote to Vita,[38] 'and they are so grateful and loyal. It really moves me. I am so glad I belong to the Party now.'

He conducted his campaign with irreproachable fairness. He refused to attack old Tory friends who came down to speak against him. He would not pander to extreme views when he thought them silly. A typical reply to a heckler was, 'No, I do not think it is quite fair to say that the British businessman has trampled on the faces of the poor. But he has sometimes not been very careful where he put his feet.' The campaign was not without its comical episodes. Harold was the first to appreciate them, when they were at his expense.

> The B.B.C. wanted me to do a feature on the election for the Overseas Service. So their van accompanied me while I went canvassing. We had to make sure at the first house that the occupant was in. She was not very bright and did not understand what it was all about. But I was firm with her. I pushed her inside again and told her to open the front-door when I knocked. Then the B.B.C. man advanced with the microphone and telephoned to his colleague in the van. 'We shall start recording in ten seconds from . . . NOW.' On the tenth second I knocked on the door. He put the mike quite close to my knock so that it would be heard. Mrs. Briggs opened the door, giggling sheepishly. I assumed a voice of delighted surprise: 'Mrs. Briggs, I believe? I am Harold Nicolson, Labour candidate for the division. Now, Mrs. Briggs, I want you to tell me all your troubles.' 'No,' said Mrs. Briggs, still giggling. 'No, I won't vote Labour. I won't. Me 'usband's a builder, 'e is.' (How terrible, I thought, that all this will reach the listening millions in Australia, the United States, the Union of South Africa and Singapore.) 'Now, surely, Mrs. Briggs . . .' and I began to expound the benefits which had accrued to her from a Labour Government. To my surprise, she was quite genuinely shaken. 'Yes, I admit that, Mr. Nicholls, I do truly.' In the end she said, 'Well, if you wish it, I will vote Labour, and get my man to do the same.' Now nobody, not even the B.B.C. young man, will believe that this was not a put-up job. But it wasn't. It was a marvellous recording. The B.B.C. man was delighted. 'What it is,' he said, 'to have a practised broadcaster!'[39]

The middle-class wives he called on were even stupider than the working-class ones. The dumb idiots, he told Vita, had no knowledge and no interests at all. They were just sheep. One woman thought she was intelligent and could see further and higher than her neighbours. She put on a dreamy, visionary expression. 'I want a MAN who can lead me!' she said, gazing out towards the Surrey hills which were still shrouded in fog. 'You mean Hitler?' he said. 'Oh no, not him,' she said. 'I never could like his moustache. I shall vote for the Air Marshal. He seems to be a MAN.'

He did not enjoy one moment of this election. And he was beaten by the Conservative candidate by twelve thousand votes. He had not really wanted to win; but this might be called a Pyrrhic defeat. It did not bring him the reward for his pains which he had secretly expected. His supporters had sensed all along that he would have been content to lose the fight creditably. His typist, when he asked her if she thought a more dynamic candidate would have done better, replied, 'Well, Mr. Nicolson, there *have* been moments when we thought you had not got your heart in it.'[40] Vita wrote from Tunisia that she was delighted with the result. Her only worry was lest his new bosses would let him down over the peerage. They did indeed.

It was all right for Harold to tell Vita privately that he did not in the least want to represent Croydon, which he thought a bloody place.[41] But it was quite another matter to say so in less than oblique terms in the press. His *Marginal Comment* of the 19th March on the North Croydon by-election caused an uproar. The constituents were affronted. The leaders of the Labour Party were infuriated. Herbert Morrison told him later that it fairly scotched any chances he might still have had of getting the coveted peerage. The article was certainly tactless. It was certainly mocking and flippant. But it was certainly entertaining and true. He wrote:

All elections have about them an atmosphere of unreality, but the attention aroused by a by-election renders even the most sedate candidate a motley to the view. The muscles of the cheek which operate the smile of comradeship, the smile of delighted recognition, the smile of glad benevolence, become strained and aching; one comes to realise what is meant as tennis elbow or writer's cramp . . . Nor can any man accustomed to self-analysis and self-criticism feel happy when he observes himself flinging friendliness like confetti in the air, selling cheap what is most dear, and making public display of something so intimate and cherished. I have always disliked amateur theatricals; my songs become sadly out of tune once I sing them in another key; I was certainly not intended by nature or by training for one of the central figures in a harliquinade.

To Transport House this paragraph was an audacious admission that the Labour candidate had not taken either himself or the election seriously.

> At North Croydon . . . the division is a locality rather than a place. It possesses for the stranger no identity, no pulse even, of its own; It is a line drawn round an arbitrary number of streets and houses; there is but little local patriotism or character; there is no village pump.

This from the occupant of a castle in Kent, isolated from the common herd, was gross impertinence to the self-respecting inhabitants of detached and semi-detached villas in a self-respecting London suburb.

> As the first week of testing merges on leaden feet into the second week of open combat, the staff acquire feelings of affection towards their horse, and feed the animal with crumpets, cake and constant cups of tea. He is not supposed to know anything or to care anything about their organization and the plans which they discuss.

This was reprehensible disloyalty to those worthy officials who had exerted themselves to the utmost to push the interests of a candidate whom they suspected from the first to be a patrician sheep in proletarian wolf's clothing.

> Preceded by a loud-speaker van, decked like some prime steer with a large rosette, the candidate is made to descend at the end of a street and to walk up the middle exuding charm –

but not for Mrs. Briggs, who was not taken in by it for one instant, she wasn't, and merely pretended she was going to vote for him in order to make him go away.

> The worst of being old is that one is so apt to see the other person's point of view. A good candidate should be convinced that he is more intelligent, far more honourable, and infinitely more valuable to his country than any of his opponents. I have never been adept at that sort of thing.

No, that was Harold's trouble. And it is the trouble of most very clever men that they often see the other person's point of view. The officials of Transport House were not endowed with acute perceptions, wide horizons, or much sense of fun. What they were convinced of was that the Honorable Harold Nicolson should never be elevated to the House of Lords so long as they retained any influence over Mr. Attlee.

8

ROYAL BIOGRAPHER 1948–1952

HAROLD was back where he was before the by-election. At least he now knew one thing. He would never be in the House of Commons again. But in spite of his outspokenness in *Marginal Comment*, he still entertained hopes of the other House. He thought he had done well at North Croydon. Had not Hugh Dalton written that his efforts had been a triumph? And did not Attlee tell him, 'Now, mind, Harold, don't you say you will abandon politics and return to your writing. We have other things we want of you?' Yet the King's Birthday Honours came and went, and there was no peerage for Harold.

Meanwhile he had a row with the *Daily Telegraph* for whom he had written a favourable review of an excellent book on Federal Union, a subject about which he knew a lot. They had dared to scrap it because their gossip-columnist disliked it. Harold was furious and threatened to sever all relations with the paper. Vita was delighted because she believed that short reviews of three books a week did not give him scope to justify himself. She was right. At all events the *Daily Telegraph* expressed suitable contrition and Harold graciously consented to continue reviewing for them; but not for long. The following February he resigned. In July of 1948 he also wrote his last article for the *Figaro*. The editor, Pierre Brisson, was flabbergasted.

Votre lettre me consterne [he wrote[1]]. *Mais je ne considère cet abandon que comme une interruption. Nul ne saurait vous remplacer, et nul ne vous remplacera pour ces lettres à la fois compréhensives, enjouées et si pleines au fond de sentiment. Que votre talent vous désigne pour l'honneur qui vous est fait, c'est trop naturel, hélas! Mais n'oubliez pas vos amis du Figaro.*

No sooner had Harold chucked the *Telegraph* than the *Observer* offered him a weekly article of 800 words on one book to be chosen by himself. He promptly clinched with them and for the next fourteen years was to be their principal reviewer.

Rather leisurely for him Harold began in June 1948 writing *Benjamin Constant*. He was in a bad mood and the book went slowly. Then something happened which restored his self-confidence, and he resumed the book with zest. On the 7th July he wrote to Vita:

> I am pleased at having done two chapters of Constant in one weekend. If I can keep up that record I shall have done one third of the book by the time I have my holiday in August. I am sure it is a good thing to do the notes slowly and very carefully, and then to rush the writing.

He made a lightning visit to Paris in great heat in order to look at five more houses in which Constant had lived. Again Pierre de Lacretelle was his guide. Pierre took him to an autograph shop where the owner made Harold a present of one of Constant's letters of 1828. Harold dined with Roland de Margerie who was also extremely helpful and whose knowledge of the period was amazing. Harold thought him one of the most sympathetic and intelligent men he knew. De Margerie was going through a bad patch in his diplomatic career, and yet was being philosophical and un-self pitying about it. When Harold returned to England the two friends corresponded about the virtues and failings of Madame de Staël and Madame Recamier. Margerie supplied him with much invaluable information about these two tiresome ladies who played turbulent roles in Constant's life.[2]

The 'something' which restored Harold's self-confidence and enabled him to complete *Benjamin Constant* with his customary astonishing speed coincided just at the right moment with the break in his political career. It was a merciful event. It fitted so blessedly into the neat pattern of his life. Harold like most of us had his ups and downs. But his downs never lasted as long as his ups. Always a venture presented itself – a new job, a new undertaking, a long journey – which led to a crescendo of activity to endure until the next check.

Early in June he had received a letter from his friend Sir Alan Lascelles that he had a 'proposition' to make to him. What could it be? Was it something to do with Australia which the King and Queen were scheduled to visit in the spring of 1949? Harold had been asked once before to lecture in that continent and managed to get out of it. He had no wish to visit Australia. He went, by appointment, to Buckingham Palace, and was ushered into Sir Alan's room. He was told straight away that the King had long wanted an official life of his father, George V, to be written. He, Lascelles, had consulted five distinguished persons as to who the biographer should be. Of those five, three (and one was G. M. Trevelyan) had nominated Harold. The King and the Queen agreed with them. On being told that Queen Mary had not yet been consulted Harold said he could not possibly undertake the biography unless she too consented. She might think him too Labour, or too ironical.

It was not an easy decision for him to make, and at first Harold demurred. He did not find George V a wholly sympathetic character, and he would not like having to disguise truths. Lascelles told him he would not need to descend to personalities. He would be writing a book on the subject of a myth, and would have to be mythological.[3] He would not be expected to bestow praise or eulogy. But he would have to omit incidents that might seem discreditable to the sovereign. He would be shown every scrap of paper that existed, and would have to study it in a room provided for him at Windsor Castle. The research and writing would occupy him for three years at least. The research would be very interesting; the writing very difficult. The book ought to earn him much money. The task would amount to compiling the history of his own time, with the assistance of Sir Alan, who was one of his oldest friends, and Sir Owen Morshead, the Royal Librarian, whom he liked and admired.

At once Harold consulted Vita, and laid bare to her his objection at having to be 'mythological' and not to make jokes about the monarchy. Vita's attitude was that he was being presented with 'a good solid peg on which to hang a very interesting study of the period',[4] provided King George VI allowed him a free hand. Elvira Niggeman, Harold's secretary, at once saw that the proposition was the ideal solution of Harold's present predicament. She said, 'It is just what you need – an anchor. It will keep you busy for three years and prevent you doing silly things like Croydon. People say that young men need anchors. That may be true, but people in later middle age need anchors far more.' With these words of wisdom ringing in his ears, and the agreement of Queen Mary that he was the best choice, Harold consented. Of his two sons Ben was against it, saying that his father would become the equivalent in literature of Sir Gerald Kelly in painting. Nigel was in favour, and advised his father that his readers would particularly wish to be told how far the late monarch exercised his authority.

Until Harold could get *Benjamin Constant* out of the way he would not do more about the new book beyond questioning people who had known George V well. He had a long talk with Lord Cromer[5] who had been Lord Chamberlain of the Household and an intimate of the old King. Cromer told him that George V believed princes should be brought up in fear of their fathers and that, contrary to what was

generally believed, Queen Mary went in awe of him; that he had more
than a sense of fun, he had a sense of humour; that he was a conscientious reader of parliamentary papers, and would form his own political
opinions. Harold also saw Sir George Clerk,[6] who complained that
whenever he was summoned to inform the Sovereign about a critical
situation in, say, Turkey, he was never allowed to get a word in
edgeways. The King would do all the talking, telling him what *he*
thought of Mustapha Kemal. This experience was shared by other
diplomats and hardly accorded with the King's humility. Harold had a
long talk with Sir Richard Molyneux who seemed to think that Queen
Alexandra bullied the whole royal family.[7] He talked with John Gore,
who had made such a good job of his book that there would be little
need for Harold to bother with the personal aspects of the King's life.
Mr. Gore told him that Canon Dalton, chosen as the young Prince
George's tutor, was so puritanical and disapproving of his father the
Prince of Wales's extravagant living, that he instilled into his pupil,
though Conservative at heart, some left-wing feelings which enabled
him to get on well with the Labour Government; and that the rigid,
straight-laced Princess Victoria encouraged her brother to be over-
strict with his sons.

One afternoon in August the Nicolsons entertained a young visitor
to tea at Sissinghurst who recorded the occasion vividly in his diary.[8]
Denton Welch was dying of a lingering disease. He had been obliged to
rest all morning preparatory to being motored over from his cottage
near Plaxtol where he lived. The excursion was a great effort for him.
The day was fine and clear with that crisp clutch at the throat as of the
first fingers of autumn. On the open lawns it was hot. Denton Welch
was met by Vita,

> [wearing] cord riding breeches which disappeared into tall laced
> canvas boots which were very slim. On her head she wore a large
> straw hat, floppy and flimsy, woven in pink-red checks, the sort of
> large nondescript hat that might be kept for years to wear in the
> garden and on the beach.
>
> Her manner was a little withheld, a little torpid; it was not quite
> social or bright enough to make a first meeting really easy; but on the
> other hand it would be wrong to call it boorish or neglectful. Can I
> describe it as sluggishly dignified? Her voice was slow and rather
> sleepy too – almost drawling.

They sat on the seat within the crescent-shaped wall at the west end of the Rose Garden. Conversation was a little strained – 'turgid' Denton called it. He felt ill at ease and longed for relief.

At last Harold Nicolson did approach us. I saw him out of the corner of my eye, and took in his white trousers and rather bustling walk. He did not smile at first, seemed in rather a hurry, as if we were keeping tea waiting by lolling on the seat under the nectarines. Standing up to be introduced I was able to take in the little tufts of white above each ear, the easy-going, almost chubby face. The white trousers were of some coarse silky linen. He wore a black-and-white 'fancy' belt. His jacket was dark, almost nautical. He wore canvas shoes.

Little escaped the beady eye of this frenziedly observant invalid. 'Now began the stickiest part of our visit,' he continued. They walked across the garden to the Priest's House, making half-hearted attempts at conversation.

It was strange to me that Vita and Harold Nicolson, after years of experience, should not be better at putting new guests at ease. I felt a little resentful, as if I were being forced to try to make up for their deficiency and, when my efforts failed, they were holding me responsible.

These were the querulous complaints of a very sick young man of comparatively humble background, who imagined himself being criticised, if not patronised by a couple of beings from an exalted sphere, accustomed to the great world. They should, he fancied, have known how to smooth his path among the thorns of high society. In truth, had he only known it, Harold and Vita, greatly admiring his writing and aware of his extreme fragility, were uncertain how best to entertain, without tiring him. Sibyl Colefax happened to be staying, and with her great experience of people instantly put him at ease. Denton observed the long wooden tea-table, the upright, rather uncomfortable chairs. There was tea or cider to drink. The cider had tiny flies in the keg. By the end of the meal the boy felt happier. But on his return home he was too ill to write any further about the visit. Within a matter of months he was dead.[9]

This autumn the international news was alarming. In September Count Bernadotte, the recently appointed United Nations mediator in Palestine was murdered in Jerusalem by the Stern Gang. Harold was revolted by this act of violence. 'It is not fair on our generation,' he observed, 'who possess all the susceptibilities created by the old order, to have to face the atrocities of the new.' The United Nations was becoming a farce, the Russians using it as a trumpet for their propaganda. On the 26th of the month Harold went to Berlin. He had to fly from Hamburg because the Russians had cut off every other means of getting there. It was his first visit since the war. He had interviews with various officials of the Control Commission for Germany. He also visited the British and the American Commanders-in-Chief in each headquarters.

The city was unrecognisable. He could barely find his way about. He had never believed that bombing could cause such a mess as he saw on all sides. And what bombing had not obliterated Hitler had altered by moving monuments from one place to another, so as to confuse all sense of direction. He drove to No. 24 Brücken Allee where his flat had been during his term as Counsellor at the Embassy. He was confronted by what he mistook at first for a pile of rubble. The walls still stood crazily. He was able to pass under the entrance arch and by gazing up could just discern what had been the *salon* and the *herrenzimmer*, the dining-room and the passage beyond. The rest of the street was devastated. Only the name of the little shop where Elena, his maid, used to buy butter, was identifiable. He found Berlin a nightmare fusion of the recognisable and the changed, just as if one were to come upon Knole in ruins on Salisbury Plain. Conditions were far worse than he ever imagined. He felt deep compassion for the inhabitants who seemed not sullen, but just pitiably numbed. And when the porter of the Savoy Hotel, where he called, recognised him, he was almost reduced to tears.

He got in touch with the dear German friend of his Berlin days, Lali Horstmann, now widowed. She told him that the British had no conception of the brutalities committed by the Russians on the Germans. The extent of rape by the soldiers was unbelievable. The officers made no attempt to control it. Not a single woman of no matter what age in her village was not raped some ten or twelve times by different soldiers. She herself had to jump out of her window and hide in a hay barn night after night. Daily the Russians were still kidnapping people in the region in which her country house lay. Ghastly as the experience was Harold was glad he went to Berlin to see for himself the appalling physical and moral degradation to which man was capable of reducing man.

Towards the end of October he went to Ireland, crossing the ocean from Liverpool to Dublin. He made a pious pilgrimage to Shanganagh Castle, his grandmother, Catherine Rowan Hamilton's house, where he had spent some of his school holidays. It was now a girls' school. Outside a man was digging up the lawn. He was courteous and allowed Harold to go inside. When told his name he said, 'Not the *famous* Harold Nicolson?' such being the renown accrued through broadcasting. Harold's attitude to the house was ambivalent. He both loved and feared it because of the glowing happiness and the brooding anxieties he experienced there as a highly sensitive small boy.

It is sad to find school desks in the library and drawing-room [he wrote[10]]. Odd memories stir within me like slowly shifting toads. And the sense of childhood fear returns.

He walked down to the sea. They had cut down the avenue so that only the stumps of the trees remained. The sea was angry between Bray Head on the one side and Killiney on the other. As he walked back dusk closed in on the Wicklow Mountains. A light went up in one of the Shanganagh towers, and then another. Childhood *angst* gripped him again. He was glad to escape hurriedly.[11]

Ireland was not the last of his excursions that year. In November, clad in robes, he gave a lecture to the students of Glasgow University. He went by train with Gerry Wellington to Plymouth on behalf of the National Trust. They advised how a flat might be made for the curator of Buckland Abbey, Drake's old home, without spoiling the outside walls. And Harold went to Bath in order to look at preparatory schools with Nancy Bernays for her two boys.

On accepting the royal commission to write the official biography of King George V Harold Nicolson, with his self-discipline, love of order and work to schedule, set up targets ahead. He would finish *Benjamin Constant* by the end of 1948 and would seriously start on *King George V* in the New Year of 1949. Actually he finished the text, introductory note and bibliography of *Benjamin Constant* by the end of August; and early in September despatched the finished thing to Constable's. Already, before August was over, he was beginning to read John Gore's book on King George V.[12]

For the next three years *King George V* was his primary occupation. It was to be his magnum opus in that it was the longest book he wrote, in a sense the most important, and certainly the most widely read; it should have been the most remunerative. It was in fact to become his next career, albeit of limited duration, and to take the place of politics in which he quickly lost interest, apart from the activities and tribulations of Nigel which he followed with passionate concern and anxiety. He considered it a *pis-aller* since he had failed in his previous careers. Nevertheless he would conscientiously devote himself to the task and make of it the best he could. Thus on the 6th January he took his first journey by train to Windsor Castle. But before we follow him there let us refer to his subsidiary interests.

Harold found plenty of time to fit them into his extremely full life. In addition to the National Trust, for which he was always ready to visit properties in emergencies, the National Portrait Gallery now claimed much of his leisure. He was appointed a trustee. He was eminently qualified for this duty, and found his co-trustees congenial. He calculated that his weekly *Observer* book review and his weekly *Spectator* article would provide his bread and butter until revenue from the royal biography came in. The Nicolsons were not poor at this time. Vita's unearned income after paying tax was £2,243 in addition to rents from the Sissinghurst property and her literary earnings, which alone amounted to more than Harold's. Harold, while benefiting from his wife's money to the extent that he lived free at Sissinghurst, insisted on paying for his London establishment and all personal expenses, of which entertaining his friends was probably the most onerous. Indeed the call upon his leisure and purse by his relations and friends was very considerable. It was also very enjoyable for he was the most paternal and social of men. As for relaxation he found it in gardening at Sissinghurst during the weekends and those short holidays he allowed himself in the summer.

Benjamin Constant having been disposed of in early September of 1948 lay dormant in the publisher's and printers' hands for a longer period than any of Harold's previous books; which may be taken as an indication of that torpor which began to overcome the manufacturers of books about this time, and continues to beset the trade as the years pass. The book did not appear till midsummer of 1949. Old Lady Carnock's gentle maternal carping, true to form, was her privilege which Harold took good humouredly. 'Darling,' she wrote, 'don't you use too many semicolons? I don't mind them myself, but I fear you may be criticized.' Vita was enchanted with the book. She was very proud of him. She thought it a beautifully built-up book in the way the characters emerged, and solidified, and then put on their colours. It was a work of conscious art. She was very pleased that Raymond approved of it, 'because Tray is not *commode* and has the highest standards and never says anything he doesn't mean'. For once Raymond seemed satisfied. In *The Sunday Times* he called it an exemplary book. 'The details, vividly as they are painted, never become disproportionate, the setting never encroaches upon the figures. The style is pointed, unostentatious and to an unusual degree correct.' He praised Harold's wisdom in not offering a simple explanation of Constant's involved personality. Raymond was right in this assessment, for Harold, who had been attracted by the paradoxical in Constant, saw in his character a touch of Eddy Sackville-West's egoism, a touch of Christopher Hobhouse's hauteur, and even a touch of James Pope-Hennessy's self-dramatising irresponsibility. He left this complicated intellectual, who was neither very influential nor wholly estimable, to speak for himself.

Benjamin Constant was received by the critics with reverential respect. George Painter called it 'perhaps the best creative biography since Lytton Strachey's'. The *Times Literary Supplement* reviewer was sharp enough to notice a parallel in Benjamin Constant with his biographer in that both men were aristocrat-bohemians. Both came to regard politics as their profession, whereas they were pre-eminently literary men. Neither was successful in his presumption; and neither understood that cliché-ridden nonentities often make more effective politicians than men of intellectual brilliance.

When Harold walked from the station at Windsor up to the Castle that January morning of 1949 he had already decided not to follow his usual practice in compiling a biography, which was to prepare in advance all the data about his subject from birth to death. Were he to do so in the case of George V's life, so voluminous and important, he would by the time he reached the end have forgotten the beginning. He deemed it wiser to deal first of all with the most significant events in the King's reign while some of the participants in and witnesses of them were still alive. Thus he started first with Chapters XXVI and XXVII about the 1931 crisis, and then returned to the King's early years.

He was directed straight to the Library where he was greeted by Sir Owen Morshead. Sir Owen at once introduced him to King George's diaries. There were numerous volumes of them, neatly bound in cloth and written in an adolescent, schoolboy hand. They were religiously entered from the King's earliest youth down to the last week of his life. The physical act of writing had been a torture to him. Kenneth Clark, who once watched this operation, told Harold that he had never seen any man do it so laboriously. The diaries were little more than engagement books, padded out with regular comments on the weather. They revealed nothing of the King's personality, were extremely dull and useful only for checking dates. A typical entry was, 'Played croquet with Aunt Beatrice.' But there was no comment on how well or badly Aunt Beatrice played or what she was wearing. Evidently the diaries were meant to be confidential. That for the year 1888 disclosed that he had a girl he used to sleep with at Southsea and another in St. John's Wood, whom he shared with his elder brother, Prince Eddy.[13] 'She is a ripper,' he wrote. Such pathetic indiscretions only made the utter dullness of the journals the more extraordinary. Nevertheless, Harold told Vita, it was interesting to get to know so much about so dull a man.

The mass of interesting documents consisted of memoranda by Lord Stamfordham[14] and other secretaries. They provided a great deal of original material. Harold estimated that by working at diaries and papers three days a week he would need only four months. Morshead warned him that the trickiest part of the book would be dealing with the King's relations with his children. 'The House of Hanover,' he said, 'like ducks, produce bad parents. They trample on their young.' He did not think he would have any trouble with the present King and Queen so long as he did not mock at the principle of monarchy; and he thought Queen Mary would not mind an occasional joke.

Morshead then conducted Harold to the Round Tower. At the top of the staircase of a hundred steps they were met by Miss Mary Mackenzie, Registrar of the King's Archives, a formidable lady looking as though she ought to be Principal of Girton College. Harold took a quick glance at the quantity and contents of some political files which promised to be very rewarding. He was told he would have access to all papers relating to George V that he might need except Queen Mary's letters to her husband. These were few because the couple were so seldom separated during their married life. He was shown the room he was to work in. It had a small fireplace and in severe weather was bitterly cold, with the north-east wind howling around the great tower. From the window he had an uninterrupted view of the lesser towers below him, the bend of the river, the chapel at Eton and the hills above Marlow and Henley.

Occasionally Harold stayed the night with Sir Alan and Lady Lascelles in their apartment in the Castle. Unfortunately the Round Tower shut at half past four in the afternoon, which meant there was nothing for him to do after that time. As it was, he found that more than four hours reading manuscripts without a break strained his eyes. He preferred to go to Windsor from London for the day, pause for a quick sandwich and coffee from a thermos, and resume work immediately.

He began by reading through Queen Victoria's and King Edward's correspondence on the education of the latter's sons. It was evident that the Prince of Wales, as Edward then was, resented his mother's interference, but failed to prevent it. A note from her to the Archbishop of Canterbury who was preparing the two boys for confirmation instructed him to tell them that the commandment 'Honour Thy Father and Mother' included in their case the injunction 'to honour and obey their grandmother and sovereign'. On the whole however her suggestions were sensible. Harold read all the Duke of Clarence's letters to his brother, which were downright silly, and King George's letters to Queen Alexandra whom he worshipped. They were the best of his writings because in them he let himself go, and spoke his mind. His letters to his father were so stilted and conventional as to be of no interest at all. Lord Goddard, with whom Harold discussed the Duke of Clarence, informed him that the young man had been involved in a male brothel scene, and that a solicitor had to commit perjury to clear him. The solicitor was struck off the rolls for his offence, but was thereafter reinstated. Canon Dalton in a letter to the young Duke's father wrote that his total lack of interest in anything 'must derive, I regret to confess to Y.R.H., from some affliction of the brain'. It was manifest that Dalton never cared for Prince Albert Victor from the start, whereas he was devoted to the younger brother.

In the middle of these exercises Harold received what must have been practically unique to a man of his generation – a challenge to a duel. Adrian Conan Doyle accused Harold of having insulted his father in a review. He offered Harold the choice of weapons. Harold was totally unaware of having caused the man offence, consulted his friend, Jock Murray the publisher, and on his advice wrote Conan Doyle a soothing letter. A month later he received a good-natured letter of forgiveness from the aggrieved son of Sherlock Holmes's creator, and the matter was dropped. As a regular reviewer he caused unintended offence on more than one occasion. The same year he was threatened with a libel action by a man called Alwyn Parker, whom he had never mentioned by name or even thought of when in a review he wrote that there was treachery in the Foreign Office concerning the Baghdad Railway negotiations. This threat too came to nothing.

Meanwhile Vita was making preparations for a journey to Spain where she was engaged to deliver a number of lectures. She had not been in good health. She needed a change from her public duties which had lately been onerous – she was a J.P. on the Cranbrook Bench, was a Member of the Executive Committee of the Council for the Preservation of Rural Kent, and of the National Trust's new Gardens Committee, for which she had been active in raising funds. The prospect of returning to Spain filled her with an excitement she could barely contain. She liked to regard that wild, rugged country as hers, on account of her grandmother, just as much as England was hers. Her plan was, once free of the lecture engagements, to motor to the south. Fortunately as things turned out she took with her Miss Macmillan, who since pre-war days had been her confidential secretary and friend, was a competent Scotch woman and, amongst other qualifications, a trained nurse.

Vita went to Granada where Pepita's own house was said still to stand, but it is doubtful if she saw it. Here she was billed to lecture. In a letter to Harold she pretended that the lecture had to be cancelled because the University had gone on strike. What happened was that she developed in the train a temperature of 104 and had to be put to bed on arrival. She did not want to worry Harold, whom she knew to be very depressed at Sissinghurst without her. When after her return he learned the truth he was convinced that his depression had been caused by his having sensed, without knowing, that she was ill. From now on Vita was subject to sudden rises and falls of temperature which the doctors believed were caused by a virus infection. This first attack left her with slight heart strain, and on rising in the mornings her pulse would race. She had to take things easily for several weeks. In fact her heart was permanently affected. The following year her doctor warned Harold that she had been gravely ill in Granada and might have died. It was essential that she should not overstrain it by driving her car more than one hour each day. But she refused to heed such rubbish. Harold had to point out to her severely that to oblige her he did not fly, often at great inconvenience to himself, and in return she ought to consider his feelings. Frequent recurrences of what he called her 'muzziness' worried him inordinately. Often she did not recall what had been said to her a few minutes before and at times she repeated herself over and over again.

John Gore advised Harold to see Queen Mary without delay. Her memory was still astonishingly good. On the 21st March he was granted an interview at Marlborough House.

I was first shown into a downstairs sitting-room hung with water colours. I was then summoned by a footman and taken upstairs where I was handed on to another footman. He opened a door and I found myself in a boudoir. There was a small little lady standing with her back to the light. I did not recognize Queen Mary and took her to be a lady in waiting.[15]

She asked him if he wished to put any questions to her. Harold told her that he had already taken likes and dislikes to certain individuals during his researches. For instance, he liked Queen Olga of Greece. Queen Mary told him he was quite right. She had been a second mother to the young Prince George. Similarly he had taken a dislike to Canon Dalton. The Queen was surprised. 'The King was very fond of him,' she said. Harold explained that Dalton had written letters complaining of the two Princes' fellow-officers, and had not allowed the Princes to consort with their fellow-midshipmen. The Queen admitted that this had been a fault. What she had to complain about Dr. Dalton was that he never educated the Princes. That she thought was disgraceful. She went on to say how loyal and steadfast a man the King had been. She then turned to the question of his relations with his sons. It was only with the Duke of Windsor that he did not get on well. She admitted that he was terrified lest when they were young bachelors his sons might get into the wrong company.

It was on this occasion that Queen Mary told Harold that, except for a few odd nights during the First War, she and the King were never separated. She would have liked to travel abroad, especially to Italy to look at works of art, but her husband had no such desires and did not want her to go away without him. Once when staying in Brussels on a state visit to the King and Queen of the Belgians they were given, in accordance with the etiquette of that Court, individual suites separated by long corridors. When it was time to retire to bed King George was escorted to one wing, and Queen Mary to another. She was wretched at being separated from her husband. In the middle of the night she heard the sound of her bedroom door quietly opening. She switched on the light. There, peering round the screen 'was his dear, sad little face'. He had found his way to her from a long distance, alone, and in the darkness.[16]

They were, she said, a very united couple, and if anything went wrong with the King when he was away from her, she sensed it, just as Harold had told her that he had sensed Vita's illness when she was in Granada and he at Sissinghurst. Before Harold left she begged him to come again. 'Anything you want to know,' she said, 'you can ask me. I should like to help.'

Two days later he had a long talk with Lord Carisbrooke.[17] He did not like King George, his first cousin, and said there had always been jealousy between his mother Princess Beatrice's family and King Edward's. It was caused by Queen Victoria having made far more fuss over Princess Beatrice's children than any of her other grandchildren. He denied that Queen Victoria's court was dull. It was nothing of the sort. Until he was fourteen he lunched with his grandmother every day. The legend that no one dared open his mouth at meals save to eat, was quite untrue. He said that King Edward's treatment of the Kaiser was abominable. He loathed him because he had sneaked to Queen Victoria about his liaison with Lady Warwick. He snubbed him on every possible occasion, and the latter was perfectly justified in trying to score off him when he became Emperor. Carisbrooke likewise heartily disliked his uncle for his vulgarity, selfishness and self-indulgence; also for his cruelty to anyone whom he did not care for. King Edward's affection for Prince George was due to the fact that the latter was prepared to be his complete slave. He was horrible to his daughters and Princess Louise was so frightened of him that she would faint on her way in the carriage to Buckingham Palace.[18] In other words it was a myth that he was kinder to his children than King George V was to his. Carisbrooke also told Harold that Sister Agnes had a pernicious influence over King George. She would walk with him in Buckingham Palace garden and inject him with poison and suspicion against the Prince of Wales.

In April lunching with Sibyl Colefax Harold met the Windsors again. The Duke was in England seeing the Prime Minister in the forlorn hope of being able to serve his country in a post. He looked older. His face was wizened; his teeth were yellow and crooked; and his golden hair was parched. But he was in high spirits. He talked openly about his father. He said that Sir Charles Cust was King George's greatest friend, and was the only man who dared answer him back.[19] They had tremendous rows, but always loved each other. The King's hatred of being bothered was pathological. When asked for orders he could not answer directly. The Duke said that Dalton was a perfect tyrant when Dean of Windsor and bullied the canons mercilessly, and his last words were that until Harold had seen York Cottage at Sandringham he would never understand his father.

Lord Hardinge of Penshurst, who had been Assistant Private Secretary to the King and a courtier all his life, gave Harold a great deal of private information. He said it was a mystery why George V, who was such a kind man, was such a brute to his children. He thought the reason must be deeply psychological. The Household were well aware of it and it was a question which they discussed among themselves. They hated it when the King humiliated his sons in front of the staff and the servants. On one occasion he shouted so loudly and brutally at his sons that the Duke of Gloucester (like his aunt, Princess Louise) fainted. But to a servant or an equerry he would never address an unkind word. The only one of his sons who would sometimes defy him was the Duke of Kent.

On the embarkation of his long royal biography Harold decided, rather from necessity than inclination, to renounce his custom of giving incidental lectures whenever asked, and to accept invitations only to address working-class audiences on literature. But he did not always abide by this resolution. In May he went to Switzerland. He lectured in Geneva at the headquarters of the Institut des Hautes Etudes to a packed hall. He also lectured in the large hall of the University of Lausanne. While speaking he observed out of the corner of his eye a well-dressed woman in the front row. After the lecture a woman sitting beside her, a dim little duenna with a creeping manner dressed in black, came up to him and said, '*La Reine voudrait vous parler, Monsieur.*' It was the Queen of Spain. She had preserved much of her beauty and all of her charm. They had a long chat, Harold standing in the lecturer's pulpit, she in front, while a crowd of questing people waited in a respectful half-circle. He lectured at Zürich, having visited La Chablière, Benjamin Constant's property, a pretty little house with a wonderful view, and the largest chestnut tree ever seen, planted by Benjamin's grandmother. He picked a young oak seedling from La Chablière and bought Vita a cuckoo clock, 'a gay and pertinacious little bird'. Again at the end of May he went from England to Grenoble to attend a ceremony and ball to celebrate the 600th anniversary of the incorporation of the Dauphiné in France.

In June he was obliged by the *Observer* much against his will to have a drawing of him done by Félix Topolski, an artist whose work he particularly disliked. Grumbling and inwardly fuming he went off to a little cottage-studio in St. John's Wood by the banks of the Regent's Canal.

A nice little Central European he was, and he did some six sketches of me. He would not let me see them, but from a glimpse I caught of one, it seemed a cross between a *tricoteuse* and Rembrandt's portrait of his grandmother.[20]

But then, he decided, that was doubtless just what he looked like, decayed and deaf, and really quite horribly ugly. He stayed with his old friend Gerry Wellington at Stratfield Saye after a meeting of the Wellington College trustees. There he disgraced himself by committing one of his habitual acts of clumsiness. On arrival at Stratfield Saye Gerry drove his Rolls Royce straight to the motor-house. While he got out to open the large doors Harold jumped down to pee in the bushes. Unfortunately he forgot to shut the door of the motor properly, with the result that, when Gerry drove in, the door swung wide open and was badly smashed against the entrance. Gerry was of course exceedingly angry but, as Harold admitted, not so angry as he was justified in being. Why was it, he asked himself, that he was always destroying Gerry's property – at one time a snuff box with the head of the Great Duke on it; and at another his Rolls Royce?

By midsummer Harold fell into a state of depression about the book. He had received a long letter from Sir Alan Lascelles clearly a little worried about the draft chapter on the King which he had sent him. Did he consider it too frivolous? Harold feared trouble from the Queen. Yet he was loath to cut out everything real and vivid, reducing it to a chronicle of facts. Vita ever at his elbow with sound advice exhorted him to give rein to what she called his 'Hadji-bits', and wished there were more of them. He had a touch like no other historian, and she feared he was suppressing it too much. She thought his imposed austerity a little overdone. She was to tell him later:

> I have *such* an admiration for you as a writer, that I mind when I see you shying away from yourself. You see, you have both qualities: the solid, which comes out very much in K.G.5; and the unique gift which for some odd reason has alarmed you, even when you got the proofs of *Some People* in Isfahan.[21]

He must beware, she cautioned him, of what she called his police court style getting the upper hand. She had found it too prevalent in *Benjamin Constant*.

By the beginning of July he was making headway with the pre-accession papers and would finish reading them in three more visits to Windsor. Then there would be a long interval while he wrote the pre-accession chapters; and then a further interval while he read all the memoirs and books on the reign. He would not return to Windsor until the autumn. On the 17th he started writing chapter 1: 'Prince George was born at Marlborough House, London, at 1.30 a.m. on the morning of June 3rd, 1865.' He paused to reflect, 'What a long journey I have to go before I reach his death. It is like starting in a taxi on the way to Vladivostok.' After he had progressed for a week or so his depression returned with greater vehemence than before. How was he to deal with the long blank of the King's life after the merry midshipman period and the settling down at York Cottage, and before the accession? During this time the Prince, as he then was, merely shot partridges and stuck stamps into albums. For seventeen years he made no attempt to read history or to familiarise himself with great events and the leading figures of the epoch. He did absolutely nothing worthwhile at all. Harold began to have a down on him.

In October he duly went to Sandringham. The big house, 'this most undesirable residence', reminded him of Clandeboye, not in its style which was 'Jacobethan', for his Uncle Dufferin's house was classical, but in its strong Edwardian flavour. As for York Cottage it was ghastly. How right the Duke of Windsor had been to insist upon his seeing it. 'He is no fool that man. But oh my God! what a place.' It was almost incredible that the heir to the throne could have spent so many years cooped up in the shoddiest type of suburban villa.

> The King's and Queen's baths had lids that shut down so that when not in use they could be used as tables. His study was a monstrous little cold room with a north window shrouded by shrubberies, and the walls are covered in red cloth which he had been given while on a visit to Paris . . . On the walls he had some reproductions of Royal Academy pictures. The servants' rooms are mere attics with skylights. There is no garden.[22]

By December Harold had read the diaries up to 1913. ('My word, they are dull.') Constable's had produced galley proofs of Part I of the book, with a blank sheet opposite each page for royalty to scribble notes upon. Within a few days Queen Mary had read through hers, making only minor corrections, and cutting out a few things, including a letter of Queen Alexandra's referring to Kaiser William as 'that ass William' and a letter from Dalton to George V, addressing him as 'my darling little Georgy', as too trivial and intimate. Otherwise she approved. Owen Morshead explained why the bit about the Kaiser was cut out. The English royal family had a soft spot for William II who wrote Queen Mary very affectionate letters from Doorn. The King's copy of the proofs was returned in the New Year, with only one small excision. Harold asked Morshead what would happen if he found something really damaging to George V's reputation which he felt bound to publish. The very correct and rather pompous reply was, 'The Monarchy must always come first.' 'At which,' Harold recorded,[23] 'all the contrariness in me surged up in a wave of sudden Republicanism.' He had fancied that Morshead would be an ally. He realised he was first and foremost a courtier.

He had become so immersed in the biography to the exclusion of every other interest that he was almost alarmed. 'You know what is happening to me, my dear friend?' he wrote to Sibyl Colefax. 'I am becoming a vegetable or rather a fungoid growth. Not an engaging vegetable such as an artichoke or an aubergine, but just a turnip. It all comes from King George V.'[24] The defunct monarch was a sort of honourable excuse for keeping him busy.

Harold's devotion to Sibyl did not prevent his teasing her. He went to see her one evening having come from Scotland Yard where he had been shown the museum of horror exhibits. Amongst them were two cardboard boxes, similar to those in which electric light bulbs are packed. In one box was a handful of what looked like gravel from a yard; in the other a black substance, like bitumen. 'That,' his guide told him, 'is all that remains of Mrs. Durand Deacon,' a highly respectable old lady who had been murdered in a South Kensington hotel. Harold said to Sibyl, 'I have just seen a very interesting woman, Mrs. Durand Deacon.' 'Oh?' said Sibyl, her ears alert, 'tell me all about her.' 'Well,' Harold said, 'there were only *de beaux restes*.' 'Is she a relation of Gladys Deacon's mother?' He then had to explain. Sibyl was slightly petulant, and not very amused.

In 1949 Sibyl Colefax's days were clearly numbered. And she knew it. Nevertheless she gallantly fought to live with the zest of a person half her age. On her return from Italy she had shrunk to a wraith. Her little face, formerly like a walnut, now resembled a peanut. In August 1950 she stayed at Sissinghurst where she had a bad fall in her bedroom. She returned to 19 Lord North Street to die. Vita visited her. On the eve of her death, late at night, she heard footsteps on the pavement outside. 'Run!' she said to the nurse attending her. 'Run to the door and let Sir Arthur in. He does not like to be kept waiting.' In a *Marginal Comment* article[25] Harold paid her the fervent tribute of nearly forty years friendship. 'She set no store whatsoever upon purely social eminence and cared only that her guests should be interesting, interested, and sincere . . . If sometimes she attempted to manage her friends, they accepted the discipline gladly, knowing that she gave them in return her passionate, and sometimes combative, loyalty.'

Shortly before her death Sibyl reproved the Nicolsons for not providing their sons with a suitable background where they could bring their friends to stay. She had in mind the lack of spare bedrooms and communal living-rooms at Sissinghurst. She also considered that the atmosphere of Sissinghurst was so tensely cerebral and dedicated to writing that all but a very few intellectual boys and girls would find it uncomfortable and unrelaxed. But the fact was the sons accepted Sissinghurst for what it was, their home where the family was reunited and where they could carry on undisturbed with whatever work they themselves had in hand, a place exclusive of outsiders. They did not particularly wish to bring their young friends to Sissinghurst where they would be under the critical scrutiny of their parents. For the parents had an Edwardian habit, at variance with their vaunted bohemianism, of discussing between themselves their sons' prospects of matrimony and suitable matches. They speculated about the outcome of their love affairs to an extent that was doubtless sensed, and possibly resented, by the boys, and worried themselves to distraction. 'The love affairs of our sons are not propitious,' Harold wrote to Vita in 1949,[26] 'and I feel that this is the counter-weight for many advantages.'

While on a visit to Ben's new flat, which he found bright and cheerful, Harold ruminated upon Sibyl Colefax's insinuation that he and Vita were bad parents. Had they not introduced enough gaiety into the boys' lives? Had they kept from them the society of normal, un-intellectual young people? These self-reproaches were as it happened, unfounded. In Ben's case they were largely induced by his naturally reserved manner, his head-in-the-clouds detachment, his single-track interest in paintings. Vita felt herself far more remote from him than Harold did. 'Ben is too difficult for me to cope with,' she wrote sadly, 'and I have made a failure over Ben, and I often feel unhappy about it. But Niggs is my darling and my joy, and my pride, as he is yours.'[27] Nigel indeed, more extravert than his brother, had many friends of his own of both sexes and all sorts, both high- and low-brow.

In fact it speaks well for the happy relations between the parents and their sons that Ben and Nigel, who had their own money and had experienced several years' independence on war service abroad, continued to share Harold's house during the week, and to spend most weekends at Sissinghurst over a long period after they were grown up. Ben was the first to move to rooms of his own in 1950. After all he was then thirty-five. Two years before he had wanted to set up with a friend to whom he was deeply attached. Harold had dissuaded him, not because he did not want to lose Ben but because his conventional side feared it might lead to scandal. While conceding that the friend was one of the most intelligent and well-informed young men he had ever come across, he thought he lacked a central quality and was fickle and heartless. Ben would be the sufferer in this partnership which was not calculated to endure. For four hours one night father and son had a frank, dispassionate and affectionate discussion on the subject. Harold won his point – surely an extraordinarily stuffy one – about the impropriety of two young men sharing a flat. In this particular case he was perhaps proved right because the relationship soon petered out. Vita, although she kept out of any discussion with Ben on this matter, was actually more understanding and sympathetic than Harold.

Harold Nicolson played no part whatever in the General Election of February 1950. He deliberately refused to make statements on the issues before the country for fear of embarrassing Nigel who was contesting as a Conservative his old seat now converted by boundary changes to North West Leicester. Nevertheless he and Vita followed Nigel's fortunes (he was defeated by 7,600 votes) with the keenest interest, pride and anxiety. When during the Election Nigel succumbed to a bout of influenza Harold at once assumed that his persistence in continuing the fight would permanently affect his health and rob him of his youth. Apart from Nigel's parliamentary activities, which concerned him very much indeed, Harold's interest in politics was definitely waning. His sympathy for the Labour Party, never very steadfast, had evaporated. He came more and more to feel that the Party was in the hands of the Trade Unions, and in consequence committed to a levelling down of all standards of work.

The year 1950 was devoted almost exclusively to *King George V*. In addition to the King's diaries and the mass of typed and printed documents and papers at Windsor, there were the numerous histories and memoirs covering the reign. All these Harold read with assiduity. Friends and acquaintances, strangers and the public at large knew about the work he was engaged on, and many wished to talk with him about it. Several people had information to impart. At a reception in the French Embassy he was button-holed by the King. 'Just the man I want to see,' the familiar voice said. George VI engaged him in a twenty-minute conversation. 'You must come and stay at Windsor,' he said. But Harold was spared that ordeal which he knew would have entailed being shown every one of the late King's decorations and medals. Churchill on leaving the Embassy seized his arm, saying he had much information to give him for his book. 'Clemmie, remember to ask Harold to luncheon.' He spent a day at Chatham House going through the Austrian documents. Mensdorff, the Ambassador, had always reported at great length whatever the King said to him.[28] His minutes therefore yielded far more explicit evidence of the King's views than could be gleaned from His Majesty's diaries. It made Harold angry that George V, who had been in such constant touch with interesting people and important events, could not write about them better than a railway porter. Vita advised him not to publish the book in two volumes, a mistake she thought James Pope-Hennessy had made with *Monckton Milnes*, for the enthusiasm of the average reader was apt to wane before publication of the second. Raymond on the contrary advised publication in two volumes because of the mass of material available.

Harold was fascinated by the predicament which confronted the Royal Family when they decided to change their name during the First World War. What indeed was their existing name? That was the perplexing question. Everyone knew that it must be German. It wasn't Guelph as had at first been supposed. It wasn't Wettine, which they had been told it ought to have been. It was Wipper, which distressed them very much. Wipper would not do at all, even though it had to be changed. Then it was suggested to the King that in adopting Windsor, the Earl of Plymouth, one of whose surnames it was, ought perhaps as a matter of courtesy to be consulted. The King said that double names did not count, and anyway Lord Plymouth's family ought to feel honoured. Lord Plymouth was not consulted, and presumably did feel honoured.

Harold spent most of the summer writing 40,000 words of Part II of *King George V*, which brought him to the end of the First World War. In August he took time off to make an unsuccessful expedition on board Robin Maugham's boat down the Thames from Wargrave. He was met by Robin's friend and assistant, Ken Long, who, having swathed him in oilskins, rowed him in a dinghy in pouring rain to the boat, which was stranded upstream. The next guests to arrive, a mother and child, were capsized from the dinghy by the friend and obliged to swim ashore. On the stranded boat there was nowhere to sleep, and no food to eat. Harold was landed the next morning at Windsor, where he arrived late for his work. But such was his nostalgia for his old boat the *Mar* that he enjoyed every minute of the experience. One agreeable sequel to the expedition was a first meeting with a friend of Robin Maugham's, the novelist Francis King. Harold was attracted by this reserved yet alert young novelist, who was to become a close friend and correspondent from Athens, Helsinki and Tokyo, where later he worked for the British Council. Harold much admired one of his earliest novels, *The Dark Glasses*, and was distressed by the indifferent reviews the critics gave it. His single reservation was not untypical of his fastidiousness. He deprecated Francis King's fascination with the squalors of life, and was pained by the recurrent mention of the word 'shit'. He tried unsuccessfully to get him a job on the *Listener*.

The royal biography suffered but one long interruption this year when the Nicolsons went to Italy in September. They crossed to France on the 15th staying one night in Violet Trefusis's house, St. Loup, near Provins, in her absence. In Violet's little Fiat husband and wife drove across France to Italy. They went to Florence and were greeted by Violet at the Villa l'Ombrellino. By now Violet had quite a *penchant* for Harold. Long past were the days when she wrote to Vita, 'With its Hadji this, and Hadji that, and you and he strolling about arm in arm (God, I shall go mad!) And I who love you fifty times more than life, am temporarily forgotten, set aside.'[29] Now it was, 'I like him more and more every time I see him.'[30] The appreciation was reciprocated with amusement.

The Nicolsons visited the Bargello where Harold renewed acquaintance with that work of genius, Donatello's Giovannino with the half-open mouth and hand turned sideways. They had tea with Queen Helen of Roumania at the Villa Sparta, set in a lovely garden. The walls were crammed with portraits of the Greek royal family by Laszlo. The Queen showed them her bedroom where there was a picture by Guardi and one by Caravaggio. Her beauty and sense of fun delighted them. They stayed a night at I Tatti, Bernard Berenson's villa. Nicky Mariano received them. They walked to look at the sunset, finding in the garden Berenson and Luisa Vertova, a slim, extremely intelligent art historian, who was one of the librarians. Vita, immediately taken with her, remarked to Nicky that Luisa was just the woman she would like Ben to marry. It was at I Tatti that a telegram arrived announcing Sibyl Colefax's death. They were all, the Nicolsons, Berenson and Nicky Mariano, greatly saddened.

On their return to Sissinghurst Vita began her novel *The Easter Party* while Harold resumed *King George V*. At first he had difficulty in picking up the threads. 'My mind seems encased in mud and furnished with boots of lead.' Looking over what he had written before leaving for his holiday he realised he had approached the last suspended chapter on the outbreak of the war the wrong way. It had all to be re-written.

This did not depress him. On the contrary it pleased him that his holiday had after all served to sharpen his intelligence.

An excursion was made to Bernard Shaw's house, 'a loathsome little building', at Ayot St. Lawrence, in December. Harold went on behalf of the National Trust, accompanied by Jack Rathbone, the Secretary of the Trust, and myself, to inspect the property which Shaw had left in his will. Harold's fascination with the macabre often evoked his liveliest flights of prose. He was amazed by the vanity of a man who could suppose so unprepossessing a house ought to be immortalized. And so hideous did he find it that after some misgivings he recommended its preservation by the Trust for all time as an example of the nadir of taste to which a distinguished writer could sink.

A small red brick 1880 vicarage with a sloping lawn, some conifers masking the road, and some elongated flower beds in the shape of kidneys . . . In the garden a hut in which he worked. The furniture was lodging house. Not a single good piece. The pictures all photographs of himself. The public trustee was there and then Mr. Lowenstein arrived and Mr. Horowitz representing the Shaw Society. I took against them. The trustee man told me that Shaw had left the whole of his fortune to the Spelling Bee.[31]

The 'Spelling Bee' was a crazy conviction of Shaw that the alphabet should be extended by as many extra letters as existed already, with the purpose of reducing the amount of print and effecting huge economies. He actually told me, when I visited him before his death, that the saving of money would be so great that it would enable Great Britain to pay for another war as soon as the present one was over. And if that, he observed caustically, did not appeal to the Government he did not know what would.

But darling [Harold resumed], it was thrilling. Shaw was there. In the garden there he was still, in the shape of ashes, on the rose bed and garden paths, white ashes just like the stuff Mar puts down for slugs. I could easily have picked some up and taken it home in an envelope. But I did not admire Shaw all that. Besides Jim might have thought it bad taste.[32]

What happened after Shaw's cremation was that the trustee and the doctor put the urns containing Mr. and Mrs. Shaw's ashes (she had predeceased him) on the dining table. They then emptied them both and stirred them together with a kitchen spoon. They went into the garden and dumped spoonfuls of the mixture on the flower-beds and the paths. This was a fortnight before our visit. But because it had not rained and there had been no wind in the interval, the stuff had not been washed or blown away. The housekeeper explained to us that somehow it would have seemed indecent to disperse the remains of Mr. and Mrs. Shaw with a garden fork.

'Likely, I fear, to prove a year of calamity,' is how Harold Nicolson headed his diary for 1951. Politically it was not calamitous, which is what he foresaw – but domestically it proved to be sad. His mother died and his elder brother Fred collapsed in consequence into a pathetic drunken wreck. In the ensuing horrid months Harold's deep devotion to his mother and sense of duty towards his brother took precedence over his concentration on the royal biography and his own happy life at Sissinghurst. The tasks confronting him were not such as he was naturally well equipped to fulfil, that is to say dealing with hospitals, doctors, nurses and death in his mother's case, and taking his brother to live with him in London and, worse still, rescuing him from embarrassing scenes in public. In these disagreeable duties he did not receive much support from Vita or his sons, who were busy with their own lives and work, and not entirely in sympathy with the dying Lady Carnock and the disintegrating Lord Carnock.

Harold went every day to comfort his mother. The weaker she got the more hysterical and uncontrolled his brother became. The strain on Harold was terrible, for he minded watching his mother die and retrieving his brother from the neighbouring pub nightly in a state of helpless intoxication.

> I have told Niggs and Ben that they must not go to Tedworth Square [he wrote to Vita[33]]. You see, my sweet, and you always understand – I feel *ashamed*. I do not want those whom I am fondest of to witness this atrocious situation. It would in an odd way make it worse for me if the ugliness of it all were seen by you beloved three . . . Of course if I were really unhappy I should want you immediately. But I am not unhappy. Only ashamed and hurt and disgusted. I want to hide my shame. Gwen feels the same . . . I did not tell Benzie about it because I felt he wouldn't care. He has always been beastly about my Mummy.

Vita did, however, come up to London, and Harold was pleased. On Good Friday his mother died at the age of ninety. She just floated out of

7(a) Harold canvassing a voter during the North Croydon by-election
in February 1948.

(b) He is televised at Sissinghurst in December 1959 for Ed Murrow's
Small World programme.

8(a) Feeding the ducks with his grand-daughter Juliet at Sissinghurst, Spring 1960.

(b) On S.S. *Augustus* in the South Atlantic, February 1961.

life like a bird. There would then, he imagined, have been merely a pleasant melancholy mingled with gentle memories and regrets were it not for the problem of his brother. Yet his mother's death was a deeper nervous shock to him than at first he realised. He felt untidy inside as though someone had upset a chest of drawers leaving the contents disarranged. 'I dislike,' he told Vita, 'having ceased suddenly to be anybody's son.'[34]

Indeed what was he to do with Freddy? Freddy's whole life for the past twenty years had been looking after their mother and, if left alone, he would just drink himself to death. There was only one thing to do. Harold must take him to live with him in Neville Terrace. Now that Ben had left the house there was room. Vita was very much opposed to this scheme. Her irresponsible attitude riled Harold. He told her she had no sense of family obligation.

> I suppose it is a bedint rather than an aristocratic feeling. You toffs think so much about Norman blood that you forget about the wretched Freddies and Aunt Amys of this world. Anyway I don't think Freddy will live for long. I want to feel if he dies I have done something at least to render the last stage of his life less horribly miserable than it threatens to be. But why do you get into a state about Ivy Compton-Burnett? Why are you such an angel to the Trouts [their nick-name for Christopher St. John and Tony Atwood] when you have no feeling at all about Aunt Cecilie[35] and never thought for one moment of sending flowers to my Mum? The answer to this curious enigma is that you have no sense of family obligation and that in fact you dislike it.[36]

The Aunt Amy referred to was his father's half-sister. This elderly spinster, blind, deaf and penniless, lived in a cottage at Angmering-on-Sea. Although Harold had not seen her for fifty years he felt obliged, on learning of her plight, to help. It involved visiting her bank, investigating the state of her finances, paying off her overdraft with money which he had not got, and finding a home to send her to. He was obliged to sell the Picasso painting[37] which he loved in order to raise the funds required. Whereupon Aunt Amy died three months later. Harold would not have resented his self-sacrifice had his aunt not been, in his estimation, downright dishonest in owing the bank money while refusing to sell her cottage. He liked to attribute her dishonesty to her piety. As he put it to Vita, 'People who believe profoundly in the life after death are less scrupulous than we pagans about how they comport themselves during this life on earth.'[38]

In July Harold installed Freddy on the ground floor of 10 Neville Terrace. A male nurse had to be engaged in the daytime. Harold, Nigel and Parrot, his servant, coped at night. For eleven months Lord Carnock lingered in ever worsening conditions of head and heart.

As though in relief from the sad early months of 1951 Harold and Vita visited the South Bank Exhibition in May. They were entranced from the first moment of entry by the gaiety, the spontaneity and the prettiness of the display. The Exhibition coincided with Britain's first sense of recovery from the austerities of the war. There was promise of a brighter future in the air. The public were in the mood for enjoyment and indeed it was impossible not to be carried away by the fun and glamour of the ephemeral pavilions, domes, spires, catherine wheels, the music and at dusk the infinity of lights sparkling along the south bank of the Thames by Waterloo, which were reflected joyously in the river. Harold was inspired to write a *Marginal Comment* in terms of such praise and thanksgiving that it evoked congratulations from the Exhibition's organisers. At the end of the month he went to the South of France to stay with Robin Maugham on his yacht *Clio*, anchored in Villefranche harbour. He travelled overnight in the Blue Train, waking up to see pines and red rocks, little orange houses and a lapis sea, with a rose madder light over all. There on Nice platform was Robin hopping with joy to welcome him. Although conditions weatherwise were more favourable than when Harold last went yachting with Robin on the Thames, again he was not lucky with the boat. The *Clio* developed engine trouble and was unable to leave harbour. Nevertheless for a weekend he was able to revel in the relaxation and comfort provided. But he could not endure for long the indolence and self-indulgence that went with luxury.

Harold loathed what he considered spurious people. He was inclined to be critical of actors, stage producers, scene designers, no matter how talented they might be because he associated them with the meretricious. At the same time he disliked people who moved in sophisticated society, like the jet set. Thus he could not bring himself to take Cecil Beaton seriously as a person or an artist. When brought to Cecil's house, Ashcombe in Wiltshire, he dismissed the decoration as 'just silly and rather interesting. Spangles and magenta and his bedroom designed like a merry-go-round at a country fair; Neptune in pink stucco with silver tridents.'[39] And he declined to review a book by Beaton about Ashcombe. He thought it too chi-chi to be tolerated. 'I hate the elegant bedint side of Cecil, who I believe is really a very nice man.'[40] He found him, and his set, pretentious and second-rate. It distressed him when his friend, James Pope-Hennessy, who with all his failings, was predominantly a serious writer, became bewitched by them. There was a side of Harold, hard-working, stern-thinking, puritanical, which was censorious of other people's amusements and affections that he did not share. Whether Cecil Beaton was aware of the unfavourable impression he made on Harold is uncertain. But this touchy and often vindictive man reciprocated the personal distaste. He admitted that Harold showed 'himself to be an honest, good character, sensitive to others [and] candid about himself. He is never vulgar, and always has an eye for the comic. Often he is able in the written word to move me.' But he was put off by his physical appearance; by the

> Kewpie doll mouth, the paradoxical moustache, the corpulency of hands and stomach, all these give me a 'frisson', and there is no getting over the fact that I could never get to know him well enough to become a close friend. Sad, because he could have been a help and guide and an influence for the better.[41]

On the 7th June Harold was appalled to read from the headlines of the evening papers that the two Foreign Office men, Donald Maclean and Guy Burgess had absconded to Russia. He could not believe that Guy had gone willingly because he knew him to be a coward. For a day or two people talked of nothing else. Harold minded dreadfully for a variety of reasons, of which the chief were the injury it would do to his old profession, the Diplomatic Service, and the misery it would undoubtedly entail upon Guy in the long run.

> No news or ideas about Guy Burgess . . . It means that the old easy-going confidence of the F.O. which was like the non-red-tapiness of the National Trust, will be destroyed and henceforth everybody will begin to distrust everybody else. I do hate that. It is the loss of one more element of civilization. We used to trust our colleagues absolutely. Now we cannot any more. I feel so angry with Guy in some ways – feel that he has behaved so much like a cad – but in others deeply sorry for him.[42]

He assured Vita that he was not hiding anything from her; was not involved in a spy ring, or in any of Guy's disreputable habits. He had not seen or heard from him for over two years. The more he thought about the matter the more shocked he was to see how the terrible disease of Marxism assailed even the most well-informed people. It was as if, during a cholera epidemic, those who were immune began to contract the disease. If people such as Burgess and Maclean with education and a position in the country would throw over everything in their hysterical enthusiasm for Holy Russia, then what could be expected of less well-informed people? He felt sure that Guy and Maclean *knew* that most of the Russian propaganda was lies. Why then should they have become infected? Besides, he was so desperately, persistently haunted by the fear lest the cold war might turn into a hot one. Harold was cheered that Ben too was speechless with horror and disgust – on the grounds, admittedly, that Guy had by his action betrayed his friend, Anthony Blunt. But he concluded his ruminations with, 'I do not think that Ben would be so horrified as I am by someone betraying his COUNTRY.'[43]

Harold and Vita had misgivings about several of the distinguished members of Ben's enclosed circle. Neither of them liked Anthony Blunt, who as Surveyor of the King's Pictures had not in their opinion given Ben due independence as his subordinate in the Royal Household, or credit for the work he had done. They always referred to him between themselves as the '*embusqué*' and suspected the influence of his political views upon their susceptible elder son.

In October Lord Ilchester resigned the presidency of the London Library. For the first time in its history a distinction was made between the presidency and chairmanship. The former post was filled by T. S. Eliot. Harold was nominated to the latter by the Committee, on which he had served since 1931, and the following month was formally elected by the members. Hitherto a senior member of the committee present at a meeting had been invited to take the chair. Now Harold took over his new duties with enthusiasm, for like the National Trust the London Library was an institution very close to his heart. He considered the committee more intelligent and more formative than any committee on which he sat.[44] He was to retain the chairmanship until 1957. Sir Roger Fulford who served under him avouches that he was an excellent chairman, in that he brought forward the businessmen members to keep the committee on sensible, practical lines, while 'encouraging the literary nincompoops [in which category he liked to include himself!] to speak and feel that they had made a contribution which was worth hearing'.[45] He treated the members on a friendly, personal basis which they found congenial, and never ceased to tease them without causing offence. He was a generous benefactor to the Library when it was in need of funds, as it frequently was and is.

An honour bestowed on Harold which greatly pleased him had been the Presidency of The Classical Association for the year 1951–2. It was awarded annually by the members, consisting of distinguished dons and academicians, upon a layman accounted a scholar of the classics. During his presidency Harold delivered at Liverpool University a lecture on Nature in Greek Poetry. He explained that the Ancient Greeks were not aesthetically moved by nature – seas, mountains, views, flowers, trees or birds. They regarded them as either 'fearful', inconvenient, or useful, as the case might be. They appreciated spring and youth; also shade and cool. They were extremely sensitive to light and air. A shortened version of the lecture was broadcast on The Third Programme in June, and listened to with approval by Harold and Vita, who considered it a vigorous and interesting talk.

Again Harold played no part in the General Election in the autumn of this year, beyond taking the keenest interest in Nigel's fortunes as Conservative candidate for Falmouth. Nigel's narrow defeat by Labour owing to the last moment adoption of a Liberal candidate was as great a disappointment to Harold as it was to Nigel. Harold felt sick at heart. But great was his rejoicing when, owing to Brendan Bracken's impending peerage at the end of the year, his son was adopted for Bournemouth East and Christchurch. At the by-election fought in the following February Harold's almost hysterical anxiety was uncalled for. On the eve of polling day both he and Vita went to Bournemouth. Nigel was elected by a huge majority in that stronghold of Toryism. Harold derived a vicarious fulfilment in his son's victory, in spite of his entry to Parliament as a Conservative.

By August 1951 Harold's work at Windsor Castle was nearing an end. When he finished looking through the last file of documents he climbed to the roof of the Round Tower quietly to celebrate by himself. He still had a few odd visits to make. He had never yet seen the Castle properly. One beautiful October day was spent being shown round by Sir Owen Morshead. As they moved from apartment to apartment the sun shone horizontally through the plate glass windows. A faint mist hung above the trees and river and the meadows of Eton below them. They went everywhere, including the kitchens and servants' hall. They entered the King's sitting-room, the room in which George IV,

William IV and the Prince Consort had died. A melancholy infused it for it was general knowledge that the present King's life was desperately precarious. Windsor was, Harold decided, one of the loveliest places in England.

He was greatly cheered by Raymond Mortimer's unqualified approval of what he had so far written of *King George V*. Raymond called it his best book. Harold secretly knew that *Lord Carnock* was his best book; this was his most solid book. Raymond, as well as being his greatest friend, was his most candid critic; so praise from him was praise indeed. Not that Harold always accepted his advice without protest. Raymond was able to impart what he lacked, a superior scholarship, which Harold sometimes dismissed with impatience as pedantry, and middle-class caution. Yet to others Harold would not admit that Raymond was un-creative. It was merely that his negatives were stronger than his positives. 'So water them down,' he once told him. On another occasion he wrote:

> We dovetail so well. I am hardier than you, and you are cleverer than I am: but in both cases the margin of difference, or of superiority, is just wide enough to give a sense of the supplementary and stimulating, and not so wide as to give a sense of gap.[46]

That was a quarter of a century ago; and Raymond was still the honoured and beloved mentor who in spite of their affection for one another would never pull his punches. 'It would be sad,' Harold told Vita in 1951, 'if I had devoted all those years of a declining life to something that Raymond considered affected or badly done.'[47]

Fortified by these assurances and the prospect of the end of the monumental task, he took a ten-day holiday. He and Vita went on another National Trust tour of houses and gardens in the West Country, this time by themselves. They stayed at Long Crichel House and Wilton.[48] 'What a nice holiday we had. I love getting away with you. I love it better than anything,' he wrote to Vita when it was all over.[49]

On the 19th September he wrote the last words of chapter 30. *King George V* was finished. It had taken him exactly three years to complete. He had enjoyed it from beginning to end. 'I am satisfied. It was hard, hard work, but I think the result is pretty solid. I have a Gibbon feel.'[50] In other words once again he felt at a loose end. But there was still tidying up to do. By October he received the proofs. The ailing King George VI returned his copy, and made no comments. Queen Mary, in returning hers, also wanted no alterations, and was lavish with praise.

Just before the book came out she sent for Harold, telling him to bring a copy with him. At Marlborough House he presented the book to her, bowing like the figure of a donor in a stained glass window. She looked through every page. 'What a lot of hard work!' and 'How dignified!' she murmured from time to time, as she stroked it affectionately. She looked at the picture of the King when he was a young man. 'How like he was then to my poor silly son,' she said.[51] And then: 'I think you'll be surprised at what I am going to say. Royalties are thought to be very odd people, you know, and when I die people will say that I disliked the book, so I want to inscribe it for you.' And she wrote in it, 'This is a noble work about my dear husband,' and signed her name, and said, 'If you hear any grumbles, show them that.'[52]

In August 1952 *King George V* was published at the price of 2 guineas. Harold felt like Byron when he woke up, famous. The book aroused unwonted interest and enthusiasm. It was called 'a literary event'. *The Times* devoted a leading article to it; the *Guardian* two pages; the *News Chronicle* a whole sheet. Harold should have been elated by the rave reviews it provoked. His indifference surprised himself. He supposed it was due to his age. But Vita felt sure he must be pleased by the sudden jump his literary reputation had taken, although he looked down his nose when she said so. 'Oh, yes, my sweet, you have had a success I never dreamed of.' It was not only the leading newspapers which acclaimed him, but the best-informed judges, like G. M. Trevelyan, Duff Cooper, Lord Samuel and John Connell. Within a fortnight 10,000 copies had been sold, and another 10,000 were being printed. Constable's were overjoyed.

It was indeed an historically valuable narrative. The author had been able to throw an entirely fresh light on the work of a constitutional monarch behind the scenes. Without indulging in any sycophancy he showed George V to be a man without guile, with a disinterested judgement and a remarkably retentive memory. He showed that behind his almost preposterous bluffness he was highly strung. Moreover the style in which the biography was written is extremely lucid, simple and compulsive. In these respects it makes easier reading than *The Congress of Vienna*. The 'Hadji touches' by which Vita set such store were not lacking.

Harold established George V as a good and wise king; a man against acrimony, always for conciliation and determined to act constitutionally, to the extent of subordinating his strong personal prejudices. These virtues were uppermost in his dealings with the Parliament Bill of 1911, Irish Home Rule and Britain's relations with Germany. His advice, never high falutin', was down to earth, sound. Harold revealed that his suggested amendments to Cabinet communications and despatches were often adopted. His frequent advice to Ministers was usually heeded and seldom resented. Time and time again he cautioned his Ministers not to promote provocative legislation, notably during the General Strike. He was most popular with Labour Governments, whom he befriended, guided and never patronised.

Typically, and paradoxically in view of the large sums of money which *King George V* brought Harold, he only netted 2/6d out of every £1. He had made no provision for the high tax contingency. With his customary profligacy he spent, mostly on his friends, the gross sums he received from the publishers. When the day of reckoning came he found that he owed the Inland Revenue an immense levy of over £6,000. The book broke him financially. It took him years to recover. By such means are successful English writers, artists, composers, inventors and creative men and women, who do not choose to take their well-gotten earnings and themselves abroad, by such punitive means are they treated by an indifferent and ungrateful country.

GOOD BEHAVIOUR, 1952–1954

W RITING *King George V* had since the autumn of 1948 been Harold Nicolson's principle task and interest. It was not like any of his previous books a part-time affair. It had been the God-given substitute for politics, which had been the substitute for journalism, which had filled the vacuum brought about by his resignation from the Diplomatic Service. Now, once again, he was at a loss for one absorbing preoccupation. Some years were to elapse before the publication of his next important book. The year 1952 was spent in much travel, on lecture-tours to Denmark, Italy, Greece, France and Germany, and, such was his restlessness, in motoring with Vita in Wales and Ireland.

Life was not altogether a bed of roses. There were worries. In the New Year he was wrestling with tax demands and an overdraft at the bank. It was damnable to be persecuted by the Inland Revenue just because his last book had been such a wild success. Besides he could not work harder at his age than he did. There was only one remedy open to him, and that was to cut down his expenses. But Harold was constitutionally incapable of carrying out these pious intentions. So retrenchment came to nothing. Meanwhile persecution loomed from another quarter. Roy Campbell was again on the warpath. This vindictive buccaneer had just published a second autobiographical volume, called *Light on a Dark Horse*,[1] in which he returned to his previous charges of homosexuality against the Nicolsons. 'Our brief sojourn at Sevenoaks gave us an inoculation which has lasted us beneficently for the rest of our lives,' he wrote. 'The one excuse for being a pagan is to enjoy it thoroughly. But these people [he was referring to the inhabitants of Long Barn] resembled the old Greeks as a Chelsea Eurythmic Class resembles the Pyrrhic Dance . . . There is no need to make a dreary duty of vice . . . Bloomsbury queerness [he went on] was more pompous, more solemn, touchy, respectable and self-righteous than ever Victorian prudery was.' He claimed that he and his wife preferred the hardship and poverty of Provence to the comfort, social success and literary fame as patients in the Havelock clinic. So much for the Campbell's gratitude for being given a free roof over their heads at a time when they were penniless. Harold was very upset, and not a little mystified that Vita was amused and even inclined to take Roy's side. He discussed the matter with Raymond Mortimer and Paul Hyslop. They strongly counselled him not to resort to the law. They agreed that it was a fiendish attack which was assuredly libellous. But there would be no point gained by bringing an action, which would arouse much publicity. The friends advised the Nicolsons to ignore the whole business.

However Harold went so far as to draft a letter, which he may not have sent, to Hollis & Carter, the publishers of *Light on a Dark Horse*, pointing out that the offending passages constituted obscene libel, and threatening prosecution. A few days later he accosted Christopher Hollis, one of the partners, a nice and sensitive man, at a party. Hollis assured Harold that he had not read the passages. Raymond, who was present, then joined them, and said that it was inconceivable that a reputable publishing firm could print such stuff. Hollis was much put out. He wrote Harold a deeply penitent letter, promising to withdraw the passages from the American edition and any subsequent English editions they might print.

Even so this was not the end of the matter. Roy Campbell pursued the Nicolsons after his death in 1957. In March 1958 William Plomer informed Harold that Professor W. H. Gardner of Bloemfontein was writing a biography of Campbell and wished to discuss with him the whole *Georgiad* incident. Again Raymond Mortimer was called in to tender advice. It was that Harold should write to Gardner a full and honest explanation of what had so much incensed Campbell. The advice was accepted. Harold's consequent letter was a masterpiece of candour, combining a charitable view of Campbell's odious behaviour and a defence of Vita's part in the story.

> I believe it is fair to Roy Campbell's memory to enable his biographer to realise that he was not so mean or vindictive as some people suppose.
>
> The current legend is that out of charity we lent him the gardener's cottage at our home at Long Barn, Sevenoaks. That we there introduced him to several of our literary friends who came down to dine and sleep or to stay from Saturday to Monday. That some of these friends, notably Raymond Mortimer and Edward Sackville-West (my wife's cousin) did not pay sufficient attention to the Campbells and in fact talked about people whom they did not know or books in French and German which they had not read. That Roy Campbell was incensed by this behaviour and acquired angered feelings of inferiority. That he therefore quitted the house and thereafter revenged himself on all of us in the *Georgiad*.

This legend is only partly true . . . His rage can be explained, and in some sense justified, by another reason.

Mary Campbell at that date was passing through a difficult period, and confided to my wife her resentment of Roy Campbell's ruthless selfishness. My wife was moved by her confessions and Mary Campbell (who I can well suppose had not made confidences or received sympathy before) responded with deep devotion. I do not know how far the matter went, or who of the two was most to blame. But at one stage Mary Campbell must have told her husband that her affections were becoming involved and with characteristic violence he dragged her away from the place and broke off relations. Thereafter he must have brooded and taken against Bloomsbury and us. I have never seen Roy Campbell again, and in so far as I know my wife never again saw Mary Campbell, although they sometimes wrote to each other.

These are the facts as far as I know them. I have never discussed the episode with my wife, since I know she feels ashamed at having exposed my friends and myself to an invective which was damaging and undeserved. But she has so generous and noble a nature that she bears no resentment against Roy Campbell, whom she regards as a fine poet who was slightly insane and utterly ruthless in taking vengeance.[2]

Although it was horribly distasteful for Harold to write, the letter was an ingenious exculpation of Vita's conduct in attributing to her a sense of shame whereas in fact there seems to have been only amusement.

In January Harold read and reviewed for the *Observer* the first volume of his friend James Pope-Hennessy's biography of Richard Monckton Milnes, *The Flight of Youth*. It was James's first serious book, and Harold was genuinely impressed. He considered it a triumph of construction. Although it was a compendium of newly researched material it did not give the slightest impression of effort or strain. That was what made all the difference between good and bad writing, he told James. 'The latter *seems* difficult; the former *seems* effortless.' The result was a fine literary achievement.

Your book, although discursive in form, is terribly concentrated in essence [he wrote[3]]. Very, very cunning, you are, Jamesey. But a good draftsman; good at that vital thing, *facture*; in fact a good professional writer and what more can we need in life? A little love, you may say. A little less debts, you may say. A nice holiday with an Arcadian companion at Baalbek. Yes, all these things are desirable and good; but it is best to have a job and to be good at it, to know one is good at it, and to know that the people who are also good at it know that you are good at it. That is the best.

In return James read some extracts of Harold's diary, a privilege never accorded to anyone else; and, without a moment's hesitation, told him that it was too boring for words and there was no use his going on with it.[4]

After a visit to Bournemouth to hear Nigel's final speech before polling day and a few unexpected words from Vita from the platform, which were a great success, Harold left for Rome where he stayed with the Victor Mallets at the British Embassy, then the Villa Wolkonsky. His bedroom had a splendid view of the statues crowning the tall front of the basilica of San Giovanni in Laterano. He gave at the Open Gate Club – so exclusive a society that hardly a soul was present – the same lecture which he delivered to the Danes who had received it rapturously. Here it was received in reverential silence. He strolled in the Embassy garden down the cypress avenue, called 'L'Allée des Souvenirs' in which a Princess Wolkonsky had erected tablets, urns and columns to commemorate whatever creatures, human or animal, aroused her affection or respect – a private secretary, a young cousin, Goethe, and a tame canary – very Russian, inconsequent and touching sentiments. He wandered among the crocuses, freesias and daffodils. He visited the greenhouses which were proud with cyclamen, all of the wrong colours. Sir Victor motored him wherever he wished to go – to the Villa Papa Giulia where he marvelled how at the very moment when Phidias was carving the pediments of the Parthenon, the Etruscans at Palestrina were moulding revolting little figurines, the former expressing sublimity and calm, the latter vicious fear. But the lovely Casino was bathed in sunshine and into the pretty pool streams of water were spurting from the navels of caryatides. In the Piazza di Spagna he looked at the painted rosettes on the ceiling of the bedroom at which Keats must at this month of the year have gazed during his death-bed agony. He went to the Protestant Cemetery where he was shocked by the intrusion of the tomb of 'that horrible old man Trelawny' upon Shelley's grave. And throughout his visit Rome was rinsed in that clear, crisp, golden light of February. He took an afternoon train to Brindisi, eating a delicious picnic luncheon with a flask of Chianti provided by the Mallets, in a compartment upholstered in tight, red velvet.

In Brindisi he walked to the Cathedral. There had been a wedding. The bridal pair, quite simple folk, remained chatting with their relations by the altar, but the priests had left and the smell of incense was faint on the chill air. The bride in white and the bridegroom in black linked arms and suddenly marched in procession towards the exit with a pair of children holding her train and the family following behind. At the west door much kissing went on, and photography. They were such a handsome pair and so young that Harold was reminded of his and Vita's honeymoon when they passed through Brindisi thirty-nine years previously. He was moved to kneel down before the altar, as his sister might have done, and say:

'Please God, make those two nice people happy, and rich, and healthy.' But does he care? My God, MY GOD!!! How I hate these Catholics. I mean, it was quite a nice cathedral . . . and they go and vilify the whole place by cheap oleographs. There was one of the mother of Christ dressed as a widow; looking upwards, she was actually *ogling* her son in heaven, with the corners of her mouth turned down to indicate grief. How can Gwen not see that this sort of housemaid religion is wrong?'[5]

His sister had become a Catholic, and ever afterwards Harold would make mischievous innuendos about it.

In Athens he stayed at the Embassy with the Peakes. Here a cocktail party was held in his honour and a dinner party which the Prime Minister, General Plastiras, attended. 'He looks magnificent from a distance with his white Kaiser moustache; but his wrists and hands are those of an old woman.'[6] He was taken to luncheon with Princess Nicholas of Greece.

She is the last of the Romanoffs, all the imperial family having been killed. She is an Imperial and Royal Highness and my word she looks it – in deep black with enormous rows of pearls and the *restes* of great beauty. English seems to be her native tongue. Like all royalties she is unreal, but if she were real she would be an interesting woman. I sat next to her at luncheon and she told me a lot about George V. She said that he was totally lacking in the gift of small attentions, and that he never once in his life complimented Queen Mary on her looks. *Il manquait d'amabilité* in that sort of way; but he was awfully kind to bedints, shy people and children, provided they weren't his own. She said that he was a perfect angel to the Duchess of Kent when she arrived as a shy bride. She said that Queen Mary had been deeply in love as a girl with a handsome Guards officer and that she never recovered from it.[7]

More to his taste was a visit to the Agora which was being rebuilt by the Americans, all the little old Turkish houses round it having been pulled down. Very little of the 5th century Agora remained. 'It is as if the Rajah of Mysore paid millions to get someone to pull down the Bodleian and the Radcliffe Camera and erected a huge Mysoreum on the site.'[8] Harold and the Ambassadress were conducted round by Professor Homer Thompson, the director of operations. In spite of finding much to criticise Harold was absorbed by the work in progress. He was entranced to be walking on the Sacred Way and looking up at the Parthenon above him from the place where Socrates must have raised his eyes when on trial.

The principal object of this visit was a lecture to the British Council on Constitutional Monarchy. The hall was packed.

He drove to Delphi and from the terrace of the inn looked down the gorge carpetted with olive trees, centuries old, to the splash of deep blue gulf in the distance. On either side were pink limestone rocks, and above him the snow-capped mountains. Early in the morning he strolled up the Sacred Way, past the Treasury of the Athenians to the precincts of the Delphian Apollo, making notes for Vita of the wild flowers out, anemone fulgens, the dwarf narcissus and several species of orchid. He reached the high platform where the Temple stands, and was filled with awe. He imagined the religious terror which this site must have engendered in the ancient days among those admitted to the sacred shrine when sulphur fumes used to rise from cracks in the rocks, and the priestess, a local witch, dressed in fantastic garments, would munch, slobber and scream imprecations and prognostications.

He went to Salonika where he lectured at the University on Nature in Greek History. He stayed with Francis King, who having won the Somerset Maugham Prize, was renting a tiny flat on the quay. And he returned to Athens by the slow train which took fourteen hours. At a dinner party at the Embassy the King and Queen of the Hellenes, the Queen of Roumania and Princess Nicholas, with attendant gentlemen and ladies in waiting, were present. Harold sat next to Queen Frederica. She was generally supposed to be rather bossy and managing, and to interfere too much in politics.

> I daresay that is all very true [Harold wrote to Vita[9]], but the Greeks are never contented with anyone. She is pretty for a Queen, not very well dressed for a Queen, easy to get on with for a Queen, out-spoken for a Queen. But I did not really like her. I suppose she had been told that people said she bossed the King, so she was doing the

silly but devoted little wife stunt which always makes me want to yell aloud. She told me she liked being a Queen; she told me that she would not mind being poor if she could have two hot baths a day; she told me that she has a cushion which fits on to her bath and that she lies there for half an hour listening to Bach on the gramophone; she told me that she believed in God; she told me that Queens could always tell when people were flattering them.

After dinner I had a talk with King Paul. I had known him when he was Diodach. He is an old pansy really, I suspect, but he adopts the manner of a bluff and hearty sailor. He tried on the stunt that the Americans interfered too much with Greek politics. I did my stupid stunt of not knowing anything about nothing. But I rather liked him I must say.

This time Harold lectured to the Athens University on Greek Poetry. The Rector and the heads of all the several faculties put on their chains of office in his honour as a Doctor before solemnly processing into the Aula. There was a huge crowd and the lecture went better than the Salonika one. He lectured too at Olympia. He did not care for the ruins, finding nothing particularly beautiful in that heap of stones. It made him realise that the beauty of the Parthenon and Sunium and Delphi was as much due to the site and view from these monuments as to the weathering of the Pentelic marble. Some basalt blocks in a soggy wood were nothing in comparison.

In April Harold had an unscripted wireless discussion with Simenon, the creator of Maigret, on the composition of books and another with Compton Mackenzie on growing old.

In May he was in Paris where he lectured at the Sorbonne. For once he felt nervous in confronting one of the most critical audiences in the world. But his words were received with much applause, and when the lecture was over many people, whom he failed to recognise, came up to talk to him. Among them was Violet Trefusis, who to Harold's eyes looked seventeen. He could not imagine by what devices she had achieved this rejuvenation. He dined with Philippe Jullian, the artist and writer, in whose little flat he met Roger Peyrefitte, who was older than he expected. There was a hint of rouge on his cheeks, and in his hair a hint of the barber's curling tongs. He was voluble and agreeable, and ready to laugh in a breathless manner like poor Hugh Walpole. To Harold's surprise he knew all about his books. Harold rather mischievously warned Peyrefitte that if he had his books translated into English, his French victims would be able to prosecute him, for the English laws of libel were very severe. Peyrefitte was not unnaturally alarmed by this warning. He endeared himself to Harold by his boyish distress.[10]

A few days after Harold's return from Paris his brother Freddy died. 'In my heart there is great sorrow for Freddy. I feel aching pity for him . . . It is such a wasted, lonely end,' he wrote in his diary. 'Besides, Freddy never thought an unkind thought about anyone, and, worst of all, knew himself to be a failure.'[11] Harold had to cope with the corpse, death certificate, undertaker and funeral. 'I hate death. I love life with all its energy and expansiveness. Death shakes my nerves,' he wrote to Ben,[12] after the lugubrious cremation service at Golders Green. Between these dire events he spoke at the Presidential debate at the Cambridge Union on the subject of good government being better than self-government, and was bitterly attacked by A. L. Rowse. Harold was hurt by what he considered the unnecessary scolding Rowse submitted him to, but was gratified that the undergraduates witnessed his calvary in stony, disapproving silence. He and Vita also entertained the Queen Mother to luncheon and tea at Sissinghurst. The Queen never stopped talking, seemed to be enjoying herself and enchanted everyone. Sir Alan Lascelles's report that Her Majesty was soothed by the simple and tranquil atmosphere she found at Sissinghurst provoked Harold to remark, 'SIMPLE, indeed, when I think of my Kümmel, the Moselle *wein*, and the truffles! But it was a happy occasion in spite of the cloud that hung round me.'[13]

Before his brother was even buried Harold gave notice to his couple, the Parrots, and prepared to leave Neville Terrace, which he had always disliked and had now grown to detest, for the chambers he had already taken in Albany, Piccadilly. C1 Albany on the ground floor of the west side of the Rope Walk was to be his London quarters for the rest of his active life. He shared it with Nigel and John Sparrow who made use of the servant's room in the attic. Harold rejoiced in Albany for several reasons, of which the chief was that he was divorced from Kensington which was not his spiritual home, whereas Piccadilly was. He would save money on taxis for he could now walk to the Travellers', the Beefsteak, the London Library, the National Portrait Gallery and even the National Trust in Queen Anne's Gate. He was in the centre of the London which he loved and which contained his interests. Moreover the collegiate atmosphere of this backwater with its panelled rooms, stout stair-balusters, and top-hatted doorkeeper had a strong appeal for him. It was like being in King's Bench Walk again, almost like Balliol when celibate life within cloistered walks was so full of promise. When he and Nigel moved in on the 17th July the first thing they did was to scribble their names on the top of the bathroom wall as though to establish their tenure of the place. Elvira Niggeman helped make their beds that night; and the next morning a Miss Macmillan, 'the sweetest old thing' (she turned out to be a termagant), arrived to 'do' for them.

After the publication of *King George V* in the middle of August Harold and Vita set off on their garden tour of Wales and Ireland. By now Vita was so famous because of her weekly *Observer* articles that there was no garden in Great Britain where she would not be welcomed. On the way they lunched with the Fergussons at Abbotswood, near Stow-on-the-Wold, a magnificent garden first designed by Lutyens and planted by Mark Fenwick, with glades of autumnal azaleas, shrubs, trees and heather. The present owners did not have much sense of colour and the herbaceous borders were not muted enough for the Nicolsons' taste. They stayed at Bodnant for which they had nothing but praise. Lord Aberconway devoted an entire day to showing them round the garden. They pronounced the Dell to be the most varied and successful piece of planting they had ever seen, and the whole garden to be the richest in the British Isles. Knowledge and taste combined with enormous expenditure had rendered it one of the wonders of the world.[14] They crossed to Northern Ireland and stayed at Clandeboye, of which Harold cherished tender memories. It was Vita's first visit, and Harold discovered that in describing the place to her he had conveyed the erroneous impression that it was one of the stateliest homes in the United Kingdom, packed with first-rate furniture and fine pictures. She considered it an ugly County Down house (she never cared for Georgian architecture at the best of times) with relics of Burma of the 1880s and indifferent copies of Reynoldses and Gainsboroughs. They drove to Helen's Tower which was shut, entered the Gothic chapel which Vita thought lugubrious, and the Campo Santo which she found melancholy. But she liked her hostess, Maureen Dufferin. The present Lord Dufferin, then a boy, remembers that when it was time for the Nicolsons to leave Harold could nowhere be found. Vita waited impatiently by the car, packed with their luggage. The butler hovered on the doorstep. Finally Harold appeared, looking guilty, his lounge suit covered with green stains from wet grass. He had been doing what he so often did as a child – rolling down the bank below the terrace towards the lake. The Nicolsons also stayed at Mount Stewart and Powerscourt, and Harold showed Vita Shanganagh Castle.

On their way home they motored through Yorkshire – visiting Bobby James's garden at St. Nicholas – to Norfolk. They reached Houghton where they spent a night with Lord and Lady Cholmondley. If Vita did not like this early Georgian palace built for Sir Robert Walpole by Colen Campbell and housing the most superb collection of contemporary furniture in existence, she did not say so. Harold could not fail to be impressed. 'I have never seen a house so perfect and self-contained,' he wrote in his diary . . . Certainly the loveliest 18th century house that I have ever seen.'[15]

At Houghton Harold found a letter from Sir Alan Lascelles announcing that he could not prevent his being offered the K.C.V.O. for his biography of the Queen's grandfather. In his view Harold ought to accept it. The public would think it shabby if he were fobbed off with a C.V.O., and Royalty must not be shabby. Moreover the book deserved a knighthood. If a man wrote a first-rate life of a King he must pay the penalty. Harold had in April told Lascelles that he was quite determined not to be knighted, but would accept the C.V.O., if that mediocre honour were offered. Both he and Vita felt very strongly on the subject. Their point of view is not easy to sympathise with, but not difficult to understand. To their way of thinking a knighthood was middle-class. Vita intensely disliked the idea of being addressed as Lady Nicolson, the wife of a mere knight, and when she became one, refused to allow the servants to refer to her as such. There was also in the attitude of both of them resentment that Harold had not been made a Lord. If to be made a Sir was an assessment of his work and value, then it was a low assessment which he would rather do without. It would be more dignified to remain plain Mr., or rather Honble. Harold admitted in a private letter, which he at once despatched to Sir Alan, that 'there is snobbishness, whether inverted or perverted, in our attitude of disinclination'. Nevertheless they both agreed after a long discussion of the matter that it would seem eccentric and even churlish to refuse an honour in the Queen's own gift. In these circumstances he told Sir Alan in an official letter of the 31st August that he would accept the K.C.V.O., if offered. To his diary he confided that he would rather be given a dozen bottles of champagne.

They had barely been at home a week before Vita went to stay with Violet Trefusis at the Villa l'Ombrellino in Florence. She did not enjoy the visit and longed to get home. Besides she wanted to finish her novel *The Easter Party*. But before she did get home Harold had left by night from Harwich to lecture in Germany on The Monarchy in England. She wrote to him:

> Darling, I was in love with you thirty-nine years ago today [which was the eve of their wedding] in a very young, uninformed, excited sort of way, but now 39 years later I love you more, oh yes much more, in a deep indestructible way which has survived all foolish *écarts*, and is the only thing that counts. If you died, I should take steps to die also.[16]

Harold's first lecture in Düsseldorf, a newly re-built, hard-working and prosperous town, was a huge success. His next was at Frankfurt-am-Main. As he stepped from the train he was photographed with the afternoon sun blazing in his face. He just had time to dash to the hotel, wash and change before his lecture. It was not quite so successful as the Düsseldorf one. Moreover the Landgräfin of Hesse,[17] a granddaughter of Queen Victoria, was sitting below him, looking like a sad snipe, and this chilled his style. Afterwards there was a reception. To his surprise the Grand Duchess Ludwig of Hesse, who had been the English Miss Geddes,[18] came up to him, bringing with her his old friend, Prince Philip of Hesse. He was much aged from his tribulations and sorrows since the carefree days they had spent in Rome in 1921. He had lost all touch with England and did not know that Gerry Wellesley had become a Duke. The information amused him. Harold was taken to luncheon with the Landgräfin at Schönberg. This shy, distinguished old lady lived in a tiny villa outside the gates of Kronberg, which had been her mother's home, and was then the American Officers' Club. Her villa, in size and decoration that of a lodging house, had only two rooms, of which the dining-room could seat six at a pinch. On the walls hung portraits of her husband and father, and a fine Winterhalter sketch of her mother. A few German and English books lay on a little table. The luncheon was meagre and nasty. Harold was filled with compassion for fallen royalty.[19]

It was probably at the end of his lecture at Frankfurt that a collocution took place between the chairman and the speaker which Harold repeated more or less verbatim to his friend, Patrick Leigh Fermor, as a fine illustration of the German character, so precise, so dogmatic, and often so defiantly wrong. Mr. Leigh Fermor has very kindly passed it on to me as follows:

Harold: When I sat down there was some polite applause. Then the chairman got up, a big, smiling man with steel spectacles and clipped hair. He wound up his words of thanks by saying:

'We are all feeling very grateful to Mr. Nicolson, but there is only one thing I would like to learn from him, which is always seeming strange to us in Germany. Why are the students in the Eton School always wearing straw hets while the students in Herrow College are wearing top hets?'

Harold: A very good question, Professor. But actually it's the other way about. It's at Eton College that they wear the top hats, but they do wear straw hats at Harrow School.

Chairman: No. In Herrow they are wearing the top hets. At Eton School they are always wearing the straw.

Harold: I know it's absurd and confusing, but it really *is* the way I said, Professor. I mean, straw hats at Harrow and top hats at Eton.

Chairman: No. Mr. Nicolson! In Eton the straw hets always, and the top hets in Herrow.

Harold (laughing): It's quite easy really, Professor. Straw hats, Harrow. Top hats, Eton.

At this point (Harold said), the chairman flushed a brick red to the roots of his hair. His eyes projected with hate behind their spectacles. He placed his fist on the table and hissed through clenched teeth: 'Nein! Das ist nicht so!'

In the autumn Constable's assured Harold that they had worked out a scheme whereby they could spread over the next three years what the tax collectors had left him from payments for *King George V*, and that this sum would amount to £1,000 a year. So he decided to bring to an end his *Marginal Comment* contributions to the *Spectator*. When he told the Editor that he would give up at the end of the year Wilson Harris was in despair. He begged Harold to stay on until he, Harris, resigned, and suggested that he chucked the *Observer* instead. But Harold was adamant. And he was right. He pointed out that the *Observer* reviews did not entail the same strain as having to think out a new subject each week for *Marginal Comment*. Besides the suggestion would not be fair on Wilson's successor at the *Spectator*. After all he had been writing the weekly essay, with only one year's break while he was Parliamentary Secretary at the Ministry of Information, ever since January 1939. He had admitted, not without some shame, two years ago that he enjoyed the regular task. With the passage of years it had become a companionable habit, not too irksome, not too intrusive, 'but affording the same degree of pleasurable effort as is provided by the arranging of books upon the shelves or the tidying of jumbled drawers.'[20] It had become a sedative and an agreeable occupation to weave together the pattern of memory with the pattern of words. It took him a bare two hours every Sunday to type the article straight out of his head on to the page. This very admission was a danger signal that he would soon become stale. He believed that now he was stale. And it is true that by 1952 the *Marginal Comments* became a little repetitive. To take one example, the story of Plutarch playing round the base of the statue of the lion at Chaeronea, appeared twice within a few weeks. In the last of the 670 articles which appeared on the 26th December he made it plain that the reason for bowing a way out was not a quarrel with the editor, or a bribe by another paper to leave. 'It arises from the nature of the articles themselves.' His impression was that they were losing their variety. There was a danger of his boring his readers through lack of spontaneity. 'People should refrain from dancing once their joints begin to creak,' he wrote.

Harold Nicolson's long series of *Marginal Comment* articles had become an institution. Readers of the *Spectator* looked forward to the next article as soon as they had finished the last. The articles established Harold as an outstanding essayist. Written in a brilliantly lucid style, they conveyed the unmistakeable tone of his voice already known to thousands over the air, a tone soothing, prescient, and humorous. No historian of the 1930s and 1940s can afford to ignore these dissertations on topical events, these disquisitions on past history, and forecasts of future events. On the demise of *Marginal Comment* Harold received many letters. Sir William Haley's pleased him most. Each essay, Sir William wrote, 'so invariably meant something to one's mind as well as to one's feelings. All artistic endeavour needs a living ideal as well as a dead precept. All the byeways of the past you have lightened; all the follies of the present you have pricked; and all the dreams you have set us dreaming from time to time.'

Vita's health was not improving. Harold noticed for the first time that when she walked in front of him she was becoming bent at the shoulders. This was caused by her arthritis. Besides, the rather poor reviews which *The Easter Party* was receiving coincided with an accentuation of her 'muzziness'.

Harold's qualified approval of *The Easter Party* touched but did not console her. He found the book beautifully constructed and the story very moving, in spite of the incredible theme of a man surrendering his adored dog for vivisection to an eminent surgeon on the plea that he was on the verge of a great discovery which would benefit mankind.

He knew in his heart of hearts that it was the least successful of her novels. Vita soon resumed her biography of the Grande Mademoiselle, which she had begun and postponed in order to write *The Easter Party*. It eventually appeared, after much labour and worry, in 1959 as *Daughter of France*. She also published in 1953 a second collection of her extremely popular *Observer* articles, under the title, *In Your Garden Again*.

As for Harold's health, it was not as robust as it used to be considering how he taxed it with overwork, lack of exercise beyond gardening at the weekends, and much, although never too much, alcohol. When he unexpectedly caught sight of himself in a looking-glass at the Travellers' or in a shop window he noticed that he walked more slowly than formerly, 'with a swinging movement like an elephant. It is dreadful when one notices in oneself the movements and gait of an old man.'[21] He was sixty-six. He suffered from recurring tooth trouble. He was getting deaf. He was becoming fatter and developing a paunch. His doctor warned him that he must get his weight down, for overweight enlarged his liver. He prohibited sherry, port and *vin rosé*. These drinks also contributed to that trouble to which ageing men are prone and which he called 'my secret sorrow'. It was a weakness of the bladder which assailed him with alarming lack of warning, often when he was about to make a speech or could not easily get to the lavatory. It was induced by nerves. 'Why do I dread this evening so much?' he wrote to Vita[22] as he was about to go to Oxford to address the Fellows, tutors and undergraduates of Balliol.

> It is not only secret sorrow or having to make a speech to so critical an audience. It is a decline in courage. Now what is that due to?

He had to question every motive, every impulse, every unconscious response to whatever demands were made upon him. He could take nothing for granted. His curiosity about human frailties, physical and mental, his own as well as other people's, was insatiable.

> I mean, is it physical decay? I don't think so, since the journey and the *Strappage* mean no more to me now than they would have 40 years ago. It is I think that my nerves have become more sensitive and that I fear things and mind things more than I did when I was middle-aged. It is absurd with all my experience actually funking a speech at Balliol.

As it happened, this particular speech went well enough, although the audience did not laugh at his jokes. He drew attention to the Balliol method, the Balliol tradition which, accustomed to dealing with exceptionally clever young men, knew how to cope with originality. Balliol developed an instinctive distaste for intellectual insincerity and an instinctive preference for correct methods of reflection. He could not praise too highly the superb standards that Balliol stood for. Balliol was the pattern, cradle, nurse, mentor, guardian of British intellectualism. When we recall that Harold did not particularly excel and was not even particularly happy while he was there, we may be excused for assuming that as he grew older so he invested his old college with attributes of perfection which were slightly exaggerated. Balliol became for him a dream institution, a sort of premature nirvana of beatitude and wisdom beyond compare, and almost beyond attainment, on leaving which a Balliol man's adult life must be a gradual process of falling away from grace.

Although 1952 had been, as Vita recorded on the last day of December, a fairly good year, 'Niggs getting into the House, and Ben happy at the *Burlington*; . . . the only sorrow, and it is a deep one', was not, as might have been expected, Ben's estrangement from her, but 'Nigel's appalling hair-cut!'[23]

The New Year's Honours List – the first of the young Queen Elizabeth II's reign – announced the award of the K.C.V.O. to Harold Nicolson. *The Times* leader, commenting on it, declared that the recipient was the author of the best written biography of a British monarch. But the effect on both the Nicolsons was the reverse of what most people in their position would have experienced. Harold protested that the knighthood made him look foolish, like someone who having expected to be put in the first eleven found himself in the third. He wrote to Vita from London, 'I am in a foul temper this morning.' Vita forbade Mrs. Staples the cook to call her m'lady. Nonetheless Harold was inundated with letters of congratulation, all of which came from Tories, and none from Socialists, he noted. Instead of pleasing they angered him. Yet when his friend Robin MacDouall organised a dinner party in the Travellers' Club of some choice friends, he was much moved. MacDouall took infinite pains. He had copies of the last *Marginal Comment* article pasted on the back of large sheets of drawing-paper; and on the other side he wrote the menu, which was superb.

When the time came for Harold's audience of the Queen he was strangely nervous. He found he got shyer and shyer with age; and also more anxious about his 'secret sorrow' affliction. But all went well. He was introduced to Her Majesty's presence as Mr. Nicolson. He was bowled over by the grace and dignity of her behaviour, and touched by her saying, as though she had got to know about his reluctance, 'You must understand, this is a personal present.' He admired her trim figure, her neat hair, beautiful complexion and charming voice. She lacked however the spontaneity of her mother, as she lacked her radiance. After the investiture she made him sit down. She talked to him about her home life. She confided in him that she did not share her family's passion for Sandringham. She wished to make Windsor her home because all the happiest memories of her childhood were associated with the Castle and park. She talked about her father's high spirits and chic. He used to spend hours with his tailors and had his suits tried on again and again, a habit she did not understand because, unlike her family, she did not share this interest in ceremonial dress. Harold surmised that George VI must have inherited his dress-sense from his father who regularly recorded in his diaries before undertaking a journey, 'Do my own packing.' The phrase did not mean precisely what it implied. It meant a séance with the chief valet and two assistant valets. It meant the great cupboards in King George V's dressing-room being thrown open. It meant the King pointing with one finger to indicate which of the 140 suits, 500 shirts, 6,000 pairs of socks and stockings and 50 shoes he wished to have transported to Sandringham or Balmoral.[24]

It was now the turn of King George VI to be biographised. Harold was consulted and without hesitation recommended his friend John Wheeler-Bennett, who was accepted. But from the start Wheeler-Bennett's task proved a more difficult one than Harold's. He had to compete with one of the best royal biographies ever written, and with a widowed Queen Mother who was less complaisant than Queen Mary had been. When he had finished the book Wheeler-Bennett sensed that the Queen Mother was not pleased with the dominant rôle he had assigned to her. When Harold read it he regretfully admitted that his friend's biography was dull and toadying. He was sorry because he admired Wheeler-Bennett as a good man and a serious historian.

In March Queen Mary was dying. The Duke of Windsor came to London – alone. One day he asked Harold to lunch tête-à-tête, and begged him to comment on an article the Duke was writing on constitutional monarchy. Edward was taking the composition as seriously as might the President of the United States in preparing an address to Congress. 'Do you mind, Harold,' he asked, 'if I take off my coat? I always take off my coat when I have a job of hard work to do.' In a rather touching manner he confessed he was totally self-educated, but he honestly believed that he led a very busy life. What he really did Harold could not quite make out. Harold was embarrassed by the subject of the article, and urged the Duke to drop an unflattering reference to the Labour Party, which would do him much harm if the article were to appear in this country. Finally he took the manuscript away, made certain deletions and corrections, and returned it to Lord Ednam's house where the Duke was staying.[25] The article was later published in book form under the title *The Crown and the People*. While the Duke (and indeed the Duchess) saw in Harold the model of an educated Englishman (the Duchess once wrote to Sibyl Colefax that the Duke had read the whole of *Diplomacy* aloud to her), Harold was ever more distressed by the fading charm of the Duke and the aimlessness of their life in exile. He was not sure he ever wanted to see them again, although they did in fact meet on future occasions.

Nigel's unexpected announcement over the telephone at the end of March that he was going to be married threw both his parents into a frenzy of excitement and nerves. It was what they had been hoping for for years. Harold had met Philippa Tennyson-d'Eyncourt with his son in the House of Commons in the middle of the month, and considered her 'the prettiest thing ever'.[26] But no mention of an engagement was hinted at on that occasion. Harold dashed off a letter to Ben:

> Your future sister-in-law is very pretty in a rather chocolate box way. Pink and white complexion, a ready smile over flawless teeth, saffron-coloured eyes, fair hair, good figure, about 5ft 10ins. She is 24 years of age and looks 20. She is not in the least bedint [why should she have been?] or affected . . . Obviously straight and reliable and competent and decent. Not clever I should think in the intellectual sense . . . Enormously presentable and Niggs will be proud of her . . . You will get on well with her as she is not a chatterbox and you will sit for hours speechless together while she embroiders and you think about Pollaiuolo.[27]

The Nicolsons' assessment of their daughter-in-law-to-be resembled that of a couple of horse-copers over a new mare. Their standards were extremely severe, and it speaks well for Philippa that she passed out so high on her first examination. But the ordeal of her initial visit to Sissinghurst must have been terrifying to a very young, attractive girl from a county family, whose interests were not intellectual but sporting, and whose tastes were social and conformable. The inspection took place in early April, a few days after Queen Mary's funeral which Harold and Vita attended, the latter wearing Bunny Drummond's[28] hat, Mrs. Copper the chaffeur's wife's veil, and her own 'beastly pony coat'. Philippa's visit was prefaced by an enchanting and welcoming letter to her from Harold, and a carefully thought-out drill by their nervous son. Nigel was to conduct his betrothed round the garden, while Harold and Vita were to remain out of sight in their respective rooms. Then were to come the formal introductions, first to Harold, studiedly beaming and effusive, and afterwards to Vita, reticent and awkward. Both were however at great pains to appear natural and tremendously welcoming. Vita however was so shy that she was flustered, and behaved unnaturally. 'When she gets these nerve attacks,' Harold recorded,[29] 'she gives the impression that she has been drinking heavily and her movements become confused and her words and voice muddled. It is most distressing.' Distressing it may have been to Harold, but Philippa with her cheerful and affectionate manner brushed aside all awkwardness. Besides the ice was broken by Harold saying to Nigel, 'I forget what it is the script tells me I ought to say now.' Philippa very quickly adapted herself to the cerebral atmosphere of Sissinghurst, illuminating it with vivacity and gaiety to which it was not, for all its wit and laughter, prone. She immediately won the hearts of both Harold and Vita, and the staff. Her parents-in-law came to admire her natural wisdom and her sensible treatment of her children. Harold in particular grew devoted to her, as well he might, for in his extreme old age and illness she ministered to him as though he were her own father.

In the course of the year other honours, over and above the knight-hood, accrued to Harold. He was invited to speak at the Royal Academy dinner. He was offered honorary degrees by the Universities of Newcastle, Dublin and Glasgow. They meant much to him. He was also elected an Honorary Fellow of Balliol. 'Of all the honours this earth can give, that is the one I most desire,' he wrote in his Diary.[30] In June he travelled to Glasgow to receive his doctorate. Dressed in a gown he attended a long service in the University Chapel, and then entered the huge University hall. He described how an allocution was made, and the Chancellor touched his head with a sort of black exting-uisher as he knelt before him. After an indifferent luncheon Harold had to make a long speech. He crossed to Dublin where he went through a similar ceremony, then re-crossed to Durham to receive the third honorary doctorate.

On the 30th July Nigel and Philippa were married at St. Margaret's, Westminster. There were the usual awning, a large crowd on the pavement to quiz the bride, heaped white flowers in the church, and a reception at Fishmongers' Hall. Nigel made a nice little speech referring to his parents' happy married life which drew tears from their eyes. But the wedding had been preceded by an emotional disturbance on Harold's part. He was distressed by the prospect of Nigel leaving Albany. Vita understood, and while she loved him for it, would not sympathise in the sense of being sorry for him. After all, was he not going to gain a daughter and grandchildren, and to lose nothing? She thought it was good for him to be emotionally disturbed from time to time because he found it difficult to understand such moods in other people. It is true he understood her violent feelings about Knole, but generally he was inclined to appraise emotion in others with his head rather than his heart, 'or whatever organ is involved'.[31] In this particular case Harold's depression over losing Nigel was, oddly enough, chan-nelled into remorse for the inadequacy of his love for his dead mother. It throws an interesting sidelight upon his complex character, which his breezy manner, dismissive of an undue display of affection for his friends and their display of affection for himself or others, belied. For he was fundamentally a sentimental man. His first affection, long before Vita came upon the scene, was for his mother. And it was very deep-seated. Her memory was for him a very sacred thing. It was made more sacred by the fact that neither Vita nor the boys had cared much for, or bothered about her. The resuscitation of his defiant love for his mother at the time of Nigel's marriage was brought about by a trivial incident. Vita had intended to give to Philippa as a wedding present a Persian emerald necklace which Lady Carnock had given her. The necklace had meant much to Lady Carnock, for the emeralds had been presented to her by Nasr-ed-Din Shah, and she had had them re-set as a choker. But Vita had never liked or worn the necklace. Harold resented her giving it away, even indirectly to one of the boys who had, as he thought, been *beastly* to their grandmother. This fresh betrayal of his mother's affection, as he saw it, aroused in him feelings of guilt that he himself had not been more attentive to her beyond paying her the prosaic duties of a son. 'How difficult it is to make up to people when they are dead for one's hardness to them!!!' he wrote.[32]

Harold thought up some involved ways out of the difficulty in order to mitigate his guilt. *He* (although the necklace was Vita's) would give it to Nigel, for him to give to Philippa. No, he would himself give it to Philippa. And this is what he did, with an accompanying letter:—

I want you to look at them [the emeralds] as a present from my mother . . . I know as well as I know anything that she would have *wanted* these jewels to go to you through Vita. I do hope you will regard them as coming from her and that when people say, 'What an odd ornament!' you will answer, 'Yes, it was made of jewels given by the Shah of Persia to old Lady Carnock, Nigel's grandmother.' I know you will say this, Philippa, and understand that I am rather sensitive about my dear mother and like to think that you will remember at least *about* her when you put this jewel round your lovely neck.[33]

Harold's feelings for his mother, which he could not share with his wife and sons, would he felt sure be understood by the new member of the family, this sweet, affectionate and demonstrative girl.

Vita accepted the situation calmly. She merely reproved him for his sense of guilt, lovingly.

Darling, your complex about your Mummy and the Persian jewel aroused such tender amusement in me . . . Over your Mummy you have a deep-seated feeling which probably only a psychiatrist could explain. How little, as you rightly say, does one know oneself . . . But, my darling, you must not say, as you said in your letter to me, that you 'were nice enough in the conventional way'. You were an angel to her – and I know what that meant to you – it wasn't in the conventional way at all – you poured out all your time and your sweet affection for her benefit, and of all her children you were the only one that made her happy in her old age . . . It was you who were her great comfort. I cannot imagine why you should have guilt feelings.[34]

But Vita did not know what only he knew, namely that he had not been able to adjust himself to his mother's intellectual level after he grew up and so often failed to resume the intimacies they shared during his childhood. Vita seemed to have forgotten how she suffered similar remorse about her mother after Lady Sackville's death.

Harold did of course miss Nigel when he moved out of Albany. However in September Colin Fenton, whom he had met the previous year at All Souls and described as 'a red-haired man with falcon eyes and exquisite manners,' and 'like a Persian cat, graceful, silent and purring very faintly. At least I trust he is,' and who was working at a wine merchant's in London, came to lodge in the spare room. Colin and John Sparrow, who had the upstairs room at C1, looked after him, as he explained, like two nannies. If he did not return from dining out early they telephoned his hosts to ask if he was all right.

In October, a few days after the 40th anniversary of the Nicolsons' wedding day, there came the news that Philippa was expecting a baby. Both Harold and Vita were plunged into a state of perturbation, anxiety and delight.

In November Harold delivered the first of four Chichele Lectures in the Examination Schools at Oxford on *The Evolution of Diplomatic Method*. All were extremely well received by large audiences. Constable's published them in a booklet the following year. With masterly knowledge of a subject long studied Harold began by outlining the democratic method of the Greek and the autocratic method of the Roman diplomacy, and their respective disadvantages. He went on to postulate that the post-Medieval West learned diplomacy, not from Athenian intelligence or Roman seriousness, but from the mendacious practices of the Orient. The Byzantines first taught the Venetians the art at the expense of the Greek virtues of direct negotiation. He finished his dissertations by referring to Lord Perth's[35] International Secretariat of 1919, which created the novel precept that violence could be restrained by reason. And he gave one last warning against the insidious nature of the new element in diplomacy introduced by President Wilson, namely ideology.

As Vice-Chairman of the Keats-Shelley Memorial Association Harold took a keen interest in the joint memorial to the two poets which the Dean and Chapter allowed the Association to erect in Poets' Corner of Westminster Abbey. The design by the sculptor Frank Dobson of two plaques united by a floral swag was approved by the committee of the Association in spite of Harold's misgivings. He insisted on seeing a mock-up of the memorial on the precise space of wall where it was to be affixed. I accompanied him to the site on a bitterly cold December morning to meet the Abbey architect. Harold was convinced that the swag would at the height proposed look like a sausage. He made the architect promise to urge the sculptor to deepen the cut of the swag so as to give it more light and shadow and promote the illusion of greater depth. As we walked away he emphasised how important it was for patrons always to examine the site for which a work of art was proposed, and to see for themselves where the light came from and how it would strike the object they had commissioned.

★　　★　　★　　★

HAROLD NICOLSON

'Life is becoming so precarious that I dare not predict at all.' So Harold Nicolson wrote at the beginning of his diary for 1954. It is the sort of remark which persons approaching the age of seventy are often provoked to utter. He sees the path ahead becoming narrower and stonier, and the horizon obscured. There were pitfalls at every step. January was full of catastrophes. The Assistant Librarian of the London Library was found dead in his bed. Mrs. Carey had a fatal heart attack in the Sissinghurst lane. Anne Marie Callimachi had an operation for cancer; and worst of all, Duff Cooper died suddenly on a liner on his way to the West Indies. On the 7th of the month Harold attended his memorial service at St. Margaret's, Westminster. He was distressed. He complained that the ceremony was a mixture of a society gathering and a requiem. His old friend's death was to bring him pain additional to sorrow. Harold was to be asked to write an entry on him for the 1951–60 supplement of the *Dictionary of National Biography*. He found it absurdly difficult, and more trouble than five articles would have been. It was like writing a chapter of Ezekiel on a sixpence. Then, six years after Duff's death, Harold in unveiling a memorial tablet to him in St. Paul's Cathedral, began to make a speech. But it was at the wrong stage of the proceedings and the Dean tugged at his coat, whispering, 'I come first'. When his turn did come he accorded Duff Cooper high praise. He said he had a deep passion for literature, being a writer of classic prose. As an orator he made speeches which changed the thoughts of men. With vehemence he assailed weakness and infidelity. With tenderness he loved life and love. He possessed moral and physical courage to a marked degree. He would never surrender to what he knew to be evil.

Although the extreme pressure of Harold's work had lately relaxed he was still very busy. He sat on several committees, and was chairman of some. He gave lectures. He broadcast regularly on foreign affairs for the B.B.C. overseas service. He wrote his weekly book review for the *Observer*; and he was immersed in a new book on manners, which was to be called *Good Behaviour*.

In spite of these occupations he always found time for his friends, particularly when he was in London during the week. It became the custom for them to drop in at C1 Albany after 6 o'clock most evenings for sherry. Harold referred to the occasion as his *Grande Levée* or *Débotté*. One sharp knock with the dolphin on the outside door (the dolphin which some people said became so attached to him that it wagged its tail when he arrived) and one short ring of the bell would summon John Sparrow or Colin Fenton – for Harold was becoming deaf and often did not hear – to admit old and young. There might enter his nephew Giles St. Aubyn (then a master at Eton), Sir Alan Lascelles, Bob Boothby, Richard Rumbold, Robin Maugham, Alan or Adrian Pryce-Jones, Simon Fleet, Hugh Thomas (a new friend and a budding historian), or Kenneth Rose (whose first attendance at a *Débotté* was in December of this year – he became a cherished companion of whom Harold wrote: 'I like Kenneth as he is so amused by the publicity to which, from time to time, I am exposed. I do not like being taken too seriously and I enjoy being teased.'[36] He certainly was teased by this sharp and rapid mind.). And nearly always there was a new face amongst the old familiar lot, a new face which might very well not be seen twice. The most regular attendant was undoubtedly James Pope-Hennessy. He alone was allowed to walk into C1 unannounced in the mornings and interrupt Harold's work. At this moment he was once again in serious financial straits. He was about to go bankrupt, and needed a job. 'So round he comes to this employment agency,' Harold wrote to Vita. To which she replied, 'I hope Jamesey regards C1 Albany as an employment agency only, and not as a money-lending establishment, with no interest charged and little hope of repayment'.[37]

Harold read the typescript of James's *Life of Lord Crewe*, which he found very thin, and could not understand how it was by the same hand that wrote *Monckton Milnes*. James, when told, stormed, sulked dreadfully and threatened to tear up the typescript and send back the money advanced to him by Lady Crewe who had commissioned it. 'Never mention the book to me again,' he shouted like an angry child.[38] He in his turn read chapter 2 of *Good Behaviour* on oriental manners, a subject which Harold neither liked nor understood. He made certain criticisms which Harold accepted with gratitude and humility.

It is silly to affirm [he wrote graciously[39]] opinions about a civilization, even the range of which escapes one's own experience and knowledge. My theory really is that once manners become fixed or stylised they degenerate into ceremonial and this is hateful to me. But I did not express the things tactfully or respectfully.

All his life Harold helped authors by writing prefaces to their books, and even getting them published. He once got into conversation with an elderly taxi-driver who asked him to look through the manuscript of his autobiography. Harold did so, recommended it to Constable's and offered to write an introduction if they accepted it. Anthony Powell remembers with gratitude the encouragement he received from him in 1932. Harold had written out of the blue to congratulate him on his second novel, *Venusberg*. 'I find it even better,' he wrote, 'than *After-noon Men*. Your deftness of composition makes all my own fingers feel like thumbs . . . I envy you your gifts and opportunity.'⁴⁰ Generous and welcome words for a young man of twenty-seven whom he had not even met. And in 1936 he wrote again flatteringly about Powell's *Agents and Patients*. This time he proffered some worldly advice on the different methods old men would adopt in making advances to young women and young men. In the latter case his experience told him Powell's Colonel Teape would not in real life have pressed the foot of Blore Smith in a taxi, considering that Blore Smith was unintelligent, ugly with large ears, and moreover did not appear to be acquiescent. Julian Fane remembers with gratitude the help he received in getting his first novel, *Morning*, published and was touched by Harold's modesty, and encouragement in saying he wished he could have written it himself.

He was always forward in proffering help to old and young men and women in other ways. There were his Aunt Amy and his brother Freddy. There were those German friends and acquaintances whom he got out of concentration and internment camps before and during the war. He did what he could to help a young friend of Robin Maugham who was facing a court case which ended in his being sent to prison. He helped Sandy Baird and James Pope-Hennessy by lending them money in defiance of Vita's warnings. These Samaritan acts provoked Elvira Niggeman to comment, 'It will be a great economy for us when all your friends are in prison'.

Great was the rejoicing when in June 1954 Nigel and Philippa's first child was born. The girl was known as Juliet from the start. 'I feel all different being a grandfather, and thirty years younger,' Harold wrote to Vita ecstatically. And again, 'What brains that girl inherits – all the Tennyson brains, all the Sackville brains, and all the Nicolson brains. She should make her mark on her generation. Oh dear, how right you were, my sweet, in saying it makes me miss my Mummy. Nobody but you would have realised that and what a little stab it was.'⁴¹ Before the child was two months old, just after her christening, she received a first letter from her grandfather:

I thought it noble of you to remain quiescent while your godfather and godmother promised such glum things on your behalf. But I did not think it noble of you to sneak when I gave you a silver spoon and you went and bashed your own eye and forehead with it. It is foolish, in any case, to bash oneself with spoons. But it is evil for a girl about to be blessed by a bishop to sneak about her grandfather. You did not see the look your mother gave me. You did not realise the deep suspicion with which your nurse thereafter regarded me . . .

Will you tell your mother that I really believe that you will have large eyes as lovely as she has and a character as sweet as hers, and that I really will not spoil you when you reach the age of 2, since I detest spoiled children. And even if I do spoil you, I shall do so surreptitiously in order to avoid a look from her like the spoon-look.[42]

When *Good Behaviour* was published a year later it was dedicated to Juliet.

In August Harold and Vita motored to the Dordogne in search of sites associated with the Big Miss, as they termed La Grande Mademoiselle, other places with literary associations and the Lascaux Caves. Before leaving, Vita had done a very unusual thing for her. She went to a hairdresser. It provoked Harold to applaud the unwonted action.

I am glad you have had something done to your hair as it really was getting a bit sheep-doggy, especially at the back, where Mar can't see it during those three seconds when she scowls at herself in the glass. Of course it seems strange for a bit to be tidy, but you will get used to it. I know that you hate these coiffeur things and that you long to just wear a gabardine and have your hair like a haystack. But it did NOT look right, my sweet, and I am delighted you had that 1½ hour to spare.[43]

In the course of their tour they visited Épineuil-le-Fleuriel, an unprepossessing village where Alain-Fournier[44] lived as a child, and which formed the background to *Le Grand Meaulnes*. The school-house where he was taught was exactly as he knew it, the benches and the master's desk being the very ones on which he sat and from which his father taught. There was a photograph of him with hand on chin, looking very dreamy. The Nicolsons were astonished that so meagre a site should have yielded such romance. Cocteau informed Harold that he had known Alain-Fournier well. He had been the soul of gaiety.

The tour was a great success, in spite of Harold's anxiety lest Vita might be stung by a wasp and his worry over her general frailty, her tiredness and occasional falls. On their return Harold went straight to Nottingham to open a book exhibition.

When he got back to London he found a letter from Vita which moved him so much that he marked it, 'Keep this dear letter always, HGN'. It was one of love and gratitude for their tour together:

I miss you! It is dreadful, getting so used to your daily companion-ship, whether travelling or at home. But we *were* happy, weren't we? And we can think back on that lovely country with the poplars and the green grass and the hanging woods and the quiet river and the strange caves and the patient pious oxen and the castles and the *manoirs*. But I can't tell you how happy it makes me to think that you liked and understood the Dordogne in exactly the same way as I do. It is horrid having to communicate with you by letter instead of just shouting 'Hadji!' whenever I want you. But as a result we have stored up a great cellar-full of vintage happiness and love – as we always do when we get away together alone.[45]

This letter crossed one from him to her:

What should I do without you? What should I do? I should be as lonely as a mouse in St. Sophia. Just vastness and emptiness all around me . . . Do you think when the wound had healed [he was always speculating what he would do if she died before him] I should be able to go to Conques? I mean would one like to revisit places where we had been happy together, or would it be intolerable agony? I simply do not know.[46]

It was the last time Harold and Vita went away together on a tour that was absolutely carefree. There were to be several more jaunts and voyages but all were fraught with anxiety about the health of one or the other of them. In November Harold's heart showed signs of weaken-ing. A cardiograph test disclosed some irregularity, but nothing serious.[47] Vita was beside herself with worry. Harold took it calmly. He did not feel inordinately tired, his ankles were not swelling, and he did not palpitate. But he re-made his will. He wrote to his solicitor on his 68th birthday, explaining that he had no invested capital at all and his only assets were royalties from his books. These he left to his two sons. To Ben he bequeathed his furniture and pictures; to Nigel his books and papers, appointing him his executor. He left directions in a separate letter to both his sons that his ashes were to be mingled in the same urn as Vita's when the last of them should die, to be buried together at Withyham ('The undertaker will do all this and you need have no squalid business.')[48] He enclosed a list of friends to whom he wished some small token to be given. In telling Vita about the direc-tions concerning his ashes he asked her if she thought them too conjugal and bedint.

But nobody need know anything about it and I don't like the idea of being separated. It is silly I know. But you understand, my dearest, and after all my bone meal will not take up much room or crowd the Sackvilles out or even be resented by them. I have not got on their nerves . . . I don't want to be *alone*, although I know in my brain that all these things are air and nonsense.[49]

Vita agreed. She too liked the idea of a joint urn, although admitting that the idea was only worthy of a South Sea Islander and not of two civilised Europeans.

By no stretch of the imagination could anyone say that Vita was a well dressed woman. She was totally indifferent to her clothes and appearance in a way that few women and most men are. Yet she always looked immensely distinguished. She could never be overlooked in a crowd, this tall, upright woman, with the oval face, straight nose, melancholy mouth, and deep, sad, brown eyes. Her usual dress was a plain blouse with open V neck, adorned by a single string of pearls. She wore drop ear-rings. Seldom to be seen in a skirt she preferred in the winter breeches laced below the knees, and long, laced boots, into the left one of which a pair of secateurs was stuck. In the summer she favoured loose linen trousers. These alternatives became her unvarying Sissinghurst uniform; and when she had to put on a skirt to go to meetings or sit on the Bench she felt uncomfortable. Her Sissinghurst uniform did not strike strangers as eccentric; and the masculinity of the breeches and boots was mitigated by the femininity of the upper garments. When she had to wear a hat it was of the wide-brimmed, turned down brown felt sort, weather-beaten and worn, which she crammed upon her grey hair without even conceding to the operation those three seconds of scowling which Harold observed when she brushed her hair.

Anticipation of those rare evening occasions when she had to dine at Buckingham Palace or attend a reception were unmitigated torture to her. George Dix vividly recalls seeing her at Hertford House during a reception given at the Wallace Collection in 1950. The King and Queen were present, and guests were resplendent in orders, medals and tiaras. Vita wore a long black satin dress, covered with lace, but not long enough to conceal a pair of very stalwart outdoor shoes. Round her neck a string of emeralds reached to her knees. The Order of the Companionship of Honour nestled obscurely in the flounces of the lace. Her unadorned grey hair straggled down each side of her purple face. Shy and with perfect ease she glided about the rooms, a cynosure of dignity and distinction.

HAROLD NICOLSON

On the 16th December 1954 Vita read a selection of her poems to a full audience of the Royal Society of Literature. I sat next to Harold in the front row. On this occasion a tweed skirt had taken the place of breeches and boots. Vita's wispy hair was covered with the familiar brown felt hat. With diffidence she stepped on to the platform, and in deep, clear and carefully articulated tones, began to read. Virginia Woolf had referred to her voice as 'dim' like a bird's piping through a hawthorn hedge. But to me it conjured up autumnal visions of the warm south, of Keatsian fruitfulness. It had a cello-like resonance and was probably the most beautiful voice I have ever listened to. The audience was spellbound, for she put great feeling into her words without over-stress, yet with confidence, and with occasional breaks and changes of key. When she came to that passage in *The Land* where 'the shepherd on the ridge Like his Boeotian forebear kept his flocks,' she could not remember whether the thick-headed forebear was pronounced Boetian or Beotian, and gave a desperate look of appeal to Harold, who shouted 'Boeotian' just in time. The audience was amused, and Vita laughed. It was difficult in looking at this apparently mild and sweet English lady from the country, to imagine the co-existence of that other Vita, who could in a flash be whipped into paroxysms of rage against the evil of myxomatosis, the mindless cruelty of men to animals, or the abominations committed by the Germans in two world wars.

On the 28th December Harold, true to his long habit of setting a term to his work and abiding by it, finished *Good Behaviour*. This was one of his books about which he was to feel sensitive. He considered it to be among his best, and it annoyed him that, whereas *Journey to Java* was to receive popular acclaim, it was largely ignored.[50] If the merits of a book are to be judged by the amount of time spent on its preparation then *Good Behaviour* should almost reach the excellence of *King George V* or *Lord Carnock*. As long ago as the autumn of 1952 Harold was spending hours of research in the London Library on manners, and taking notes. Fourteen months later he woke up one morning at 6 o'clock, an unusually early hour for him, to find that the plan of the book had suddenly clarified itself in his mind during the night. He called it a case of 'unconscious cerebration'. But for a long time *Good Behaviour* did not go well. He was very depressed by it and wished he had never embarked on the subject. In June of 1954 he still felt that he was too old, stupid and devoid of ideas to continue with it. What he had so far written was mere senile chatter. The truth was that the subject did not have a strong appeal for him. As he admitted to James Pope-Hennessy he found the civilization of the East unfamiliar and unsympathetic. As for *l'honnête homme*, the court of Louis XIV was profoundly distasteful to him. He loathed the ridiculous ceremonial and observance of precedence which the Sun King demanded. And what he could not treat with sympathy he could not treat with understanding. On the other hand Vita, who was far and away his most discerning critic, when given the chapter entitled *L'honnête Homme*, was fascinated. She saw at a glance that the book was going to be what she called 'a Hadji book', that is to say both serious and entertaining. In it she recognized his inimitable and individual style, which derived from his singular powers of observation. 'You are,' she wrote, 'a great stylist in the sense that it is completely peculiar to yourself, i.e. like nobody else.'[51] When she read the completed thing she pronounced it the best written of all his books.

> The texture of your prose is now so tight, so economical, and yet at moments so lyrical. Where I think you have been so skilful is in putting all your facts and information into a chapter, or even into sections of a chapter, so that one feels convinced, and then ending up the chapter or section of a chapter with a few lines which are pure Hadji, and sum up all that you have said before.[52]

Good Behaviour was published in September 1955. In this book Harold assumed that manners were dictated by the upper classes and eventually adopted by the middle and lower; whereupon the upper dropped them, and assumed others. He did not live long enough to see the reversal of this time-honoured custom, in the adoption of lower class manners, and even speech and accents, by the upper. He even professed to deplore the distinction of accents which created class hatred. He looked forward to the day when all would speak as uniformly and faultlessly as they did on the B.B.C. What however we have seen transpire is the classless accent, which emanating indeed from the B.B.C. is, on the contrary, incorrect and usually ugly.

Harold Nicolson's philosophy can be detected in *Good Behaviour*. He cast doubts upon an aristocracy of intellect as derived from Plato and Erasmus. He observed that Erasmus had failed to apprehend that intellectuals tend to become opinionated, arrogant and subjective in their teaching. All élites of whatever derivation devolve into hereditary castes, even under Communist regimes, thus degenerating into a governing class of no personal merit and no superior ability. Nonetheless, the optimist in Harold Nicolson found comfort in recalling that when mankind has progressed it has always done so owing to differences rather than samenesses.

Good Behaviour contains passages of as good writing as is to be found in any of Harold's books, notably in the first paragraph of chapter 9 describing life at Versailles; and of as much wit in the account in chapter 11 of Madame de Staël's unsuccessful visit to Goethe. The reviewers' enthusiasm over the author's easy and urbane style rather annoyed Harold. He told Elvira Niggeman that he had been publishing books for the past forty years and had always been careful about his style. Until this book came out nobody had even noticed that he had any style at all. Now they all noticed it, as though suddenly he had started to write well after years of writing indifferently. On the other hand the reviewers' enthusiasm over his opinions was more restrained. Several thought that he did not go deep enough into causes and effects. His opinions on civility were subjective. He failed to answer the several questions he provoked, such as how far the values which civilised men throughout the ages set upon the manners of their society affected their conduct. The *Financial Times*, for instance, criticised his failure to discuss American manners, whereas at the end of the book he complained that American manners would impose themselves upon the English-speaking world. In that case he ought to have explained what they amounted to. *Good Behaviour* is certainly an intensely personal and dogmatic book. It is also extremely readable. As the critic of the *Spectator* wrote: 'I could pick all sorts of holes in this book, but could never have written it myself.'

THE AGE OF REASON, 1955–1960

IN spite of the warning about the irregular beat of his heart Harold enjoyed, up to his 70th year, pretty good health for a man who had taxed his energies unsparingly, and drunk and smoked rather more than was good for him throughout his adult life. In fact when he got back to Albany from Sissinghurst in the New Year of 1955 he was suffused with happiness. While the weather was bitter outside he felt warm and cosy in his comfortable rooms with picked branches of balsam poplar beginning to form leaves from the heat of his radiators, with a vase of myrtle, fresh bay, and witch hazel, and another of jasmine and arums, all arranged for a party he was giving for a few friends. Throughout the year, even in dead of winter, he would bring by train on Mondays something from the garden or greenhouses at Sissinghurst which would last him until the end of the week. 'I love you very much,' he wrote to Vita,[1] 'My health is good. I have many friends. I have two sons and a granddaughter. I am going to the ballet tonight. I am interested in politics, love books, and enjoy architecture. So why should I worry?' It was true his increasing deafness was tiresome, but he bore it stoically as an inevitable, and not a mortal affliction. He complained too that he could no longer type automatically while thinking of the next sentence as he used to do. He also noticed that he had to look up words in the little dictionary in the trough beside him more often than formerly. 'It is not that I have difficulty in finding words, but that when they settle like pigeons around me I forget how to spell them.'[2] This and a certain stiffness of the muscles were all that reminded him of having passed the 'span of life'. He continued to sleep regularly and long. 'How age creeps on one, slouch, slough, slop. Not like a winged chariot but like an old pedlar in snow boots, which are too big for him.'[3]

Fate however has a mean trick of taking the savour out of hubris.

It annoyed Harold that James Pope-Hennessy, still in his late thirties, robust in health, a successful writer, and full of promise, should be so discontented. Harold took him to the Beefsteak Club where he sat between Bill Mabane and Malcolm Sargent. James was miserable. 'Never,' he said as they left the club, 'have I met such bores.' 'But they are *not* bores,' Harold protested. What would James be like at fifty? 'I do really think that selfishness punishes its victims more than any other form of vice,' he wrote to Vita. 'It is such a subtle punishment, so dark, and intricate and devious. Nor is there any escape. Think of Dottie.'[4]

Vita was at Sissinghurst, tearing her hair out over the Grande Mademoiselle. She was suffering from arthritis in back and hand. Deep X-ray treatment relieved it. But when her hand was very bad she could not pick a book out of her shelves.

On the 19th January Harold, having been invited to an after-dinner party at George Weidenfeld's, arrived half an hour later than the time specified, to find the dinner-guests still downstairs in the dining-room. He was a stickler for the proprieties. He was annoyed that, not having been invited to dine and having given his host and the other guests what he considered time enough to move to the drawing-room, he should come upon the party still eating. Unnecessarily perhaps, but suddenly, he lost his temper, and his control. He stormed. He had to be pacified. He caused embarrassment. Afterwards he described what happened as a nerve crisis, a temporary seizure of madness. 'Once I do lose control it is like a burst water pipe. And I can't think why, because I was quite happy and cheerful on the way there. Just a nerve storm. But why???'[5]

The outburst may have been a pre-sympton of his first stroke. Five days later he travelled via Harwich and the Hook of Holland to Munich and Bonn. In Germany he had to change trains at 5 o'clock in the morning. On Munich platform he was greeted by a bevy of Bavarian dignitaries, all dressed in green coats and hats with plumes. They were covered with little Catholic medals and said, '*Grüss Gott!*' This pleased him. He stayed in the Hotel Vier Jahreszeiten, which was one of the best hotels in the world. He was given a room glowing with central heating and a marble bathroom with a bidet. He had only to press a bell and instantly servants arrived bearing trays with bananas and carnations. He met innumerable old friends, including Graf Albrecht Montgelas, who called on him while he was shaving, and Kurt Wagenseil. The former, released from the Isle of Man by Harold during the war, adored him ever since with a sick and heavy devotion; the latter, now thin, cadaverous and bald, who had translated several of his books, obtained freedom from Dachau through Harold's influence with Otto Bismarck in 1936. Harold met a nice Abbot who assured him that his poor Aunt Clemmie had died in the arms of the Church, for lack of any other arms to die in. With Wagenseil he visited his publisher who lived in a palace and like Franz Josef at Schönbrunn received him in audience with all his staff assembled. He was given a banquet by the Bavarian Government. The Bavarian Prime Minister arrived, flanked by the obsequious manager of the hotel and his deputy-Prime Minister and the Minister of Education. Harold then gave audience to a posse of journalists. He could not have been treated with greater respect and deference. The attentions flattered him. Finally he lectured at the Bavarian State Bank to an assembly of 600 people (300 had to be turned away) on the subject of 'Statesmen I have known'. In Bonn he stayed at the Residence of the British High Commissioner, Sir Frederick Hoyer-Millar, and was given a big official luncheon. In Bonn he also lectured.

On his return to England Harold and Vita were confronted with an invitation to luncheon at Buckingham Palace to meet the Shah of Persia and Queen Soraya. This necessitated Vita acquiring another hat for the occasion. She sent her secretary, Betty Arnett, to Tunbridge Wells to choose one for her from a haberdasher's. When the time came to be motored to the Palace, Copper the chauffeur, in looking for Vita who was standing on the pavement outside Albany, failed to recognise her in her unusual clothes. She sat next to Winston Churchill, who was in his best mood and talked to her about history. After luncheon Churchill told Harold he had been sad when he, Harold, left the House of Commons because he had become a good debater.

In February distressing news came that Philippa had developed tuberculosis in one lung and had to go to hospital, where she would be incommunicable for four months. On the 25th Harold left for Portugal. The purpose of this visit was to inspect the British Council Institute in Lisbon and report on how it was working. He stayed one night en route with the Jebbs in the Paris Embassy, and continued by train without a break, because he still refused, out of political principles, to spend a night on Spanish soil.

In Lisbon he stayed in the Hotel Miraparque and took most of his free luncheons and dinners with a friend, Richard Ward, who had recently joined the Institute as a teacher of English. Ward was an interesting man, proud and sensitive, with high ideals. His intellect appealed to Harold who had not however read his poetry. Ward lived in a small room in a pension, giving on to a little terrace with a vine and a view over the rooftops to the Tagus gently lapping the shore. In addition to visits to the Institute Harold was subjected to far too many receptions. On the 2nd March he woke up in bed to find his nose bleeding. While lunching at the Embassy that day, it bled. At dinner with the Counsellor of the British Embassy it bled again. He was taken to a room where cotton wool and peroxide were applied. But the bleeding did not stop and the Duke of Palmella insisted on sending for his doctor. This time a styptic was applied and he was driven back to the hotel. 'A dear old lady' arrived and gave him an injection in the bottom.[6] The next day he felt very low and stayed in bed. He was given more injections and dined quietly with Richard Ward. In spite of feeling limp he insisted on going to Cintra to see the garden of Montserrat, where he noticed that *magnolia conspicua* was in flower.

When he got back to England he developed acute sciatica which he attributed to the 'dear old lady' having injected him too close to the sciatic nerve. He also had some teeth taken out. He crawled down to Sissinghurst and went to bed, suffering great pain from the sciatica. On the 11th March he got out of bed in the evening to have a hot bath, and while sitting on the edge of the bath afterwards had a blackout and momentary loss of control of the left hand, so that he could not feel his pyjama cord. Vita to her dismay noticed that his mouth was twisted and his speech so thick that she could barely understand what he said to her. The local doctor came and confirmed that he had had a stroke. It was a mild one. His mind was unaffected and for a time he went on correcting proofs of *Good Behaviour* which he had been doing all day. Vita lay awake in misery that night wondering how, if he were to die, she could 'most tidily dispose' of herself.[7]

For a few days Harold's sciatica was so bad that he was unable to rise from his bed. He was obliged to cancel all his plans for a fortnight. Nevertheless he managed to write his *Observer* review; and to do the index of his book and prepare some broadcasts. But to walk from his cottage to the dining-room was agony. By the end of the month he was better.

> My word, my dear Elvira [he wrote to Miss Niggeman[8]] how glad I am this horrible March is over. I am well enough now to stagger from armchair to armchair, to do some work, and to retain over my shattered and frayed ill-temper some measure of control.

Vita wrote a rather touching and affectionate letter to Elvira, describing the symptoms of the stroke and explaining that she was unsure how much Harold realised what had happened to him. He would refer to the stroke as 'my blackout'. To add to their troubles she had had a bad fall down the stairs of her turret. In consequence she was very lame and in considerable pain. A specialist pronounced that she had cracked her sacrum, and must rest as much as possible for three months.

In the first week of April Harold was up in London. Vita wrote imploring him to stay down at Sissinghurst longer for his health's sake as much as for her peace of mind. His doctor had told him that by now his heart was none too good, that he must take digitalis and not stoop, lift heavy weights or eat heavy meals. The worst deprivation was the prohibition on gardening. For this meant that he could no longer weed in what he always referred to as 'm.l.w.' (my life's work), that border of garden beside the nuttery, which was exclusively his responsibility, and for which he alone chose plants and flowers.

While both Nicolsons were plunged in suffering and distress Ben wrote to Vita that he was engaged to Luisa Vertova. So the wish that Vita had let fall to Nicky Mariano in the garden of I Tatti was about to be realised. There had been no hints whatever from Ben's recent letters that anything of the kind was going to happen. 'You could have knocked me down with a feather,' Harold exclaimed. The announcement was followed by a letter to his father, couched in such nonchalant terms that Harold wrote to Vita, 'I would expect him to approach such a matter in terms of reason and without any gush or false sentiment. But I must say he pushed reasonability rather far.' Hardly had this piece of news soaked in before Harold suffered a second stroke. It was even milder than the first. He recorded the incident in detail in his diary.[9]

> I had a good breakfast [at Sissinghurst], came over to my room, and got up to take a book out of the shelf. I noticed that the fingers of the right hand were too numb to type, so I started rubbing them. I then thought that I would go out for a breath of air and found that my right leg was wonky. It felt as if my foot or shoe was encased in lead. I staggered up to my bedroom and rang my bell for Mrs. Staples [the cook] and she came. She summoned Vita who arrived looking rather white, bless her, and sent for Dr. Parish. He said it was probably 'an arterial spasm', since it had passed off so quickly. But he warned me that arterial spasms, if repeated, led to clots, and clots to real apoplectic strokes. I must in future take things more easily. I realise that I shall become a semi-invalid. And I am not ready to depart at all, although both hands have been warmed [before the fire of life].

Although Harold was able to go on writing without a pause he was clearly worried about his condition. He believed he did not have long to live. Yet mentally he felt as alert as ever, noticing no diminution of his faculties or ability to write. But he allowed his uncertain state of health to prey on his mind. He informed anyone who was interested enough to listen that he had had two strokes until Vita told him he shouldn't do it. In the first place it was not strictly true, she lied, and in the second place it made people exaggerate. When his old friend Lord Esher suffered the same experience he wrote him a spirited letter of commiseration and encouragement.

I am terribly sorry to hear that you have had a stroke. I had two strokes in 1955 within eight weeks of each other, and therefore I consider myself an expert on the subject. What worried me at first was the unpredictability of the whole business. One stretches up to get a book from the shelf, or one leans down to pick up a piece of paper from the floor, and the next thing one realises is that 'Where am I?' and 'What happened?' feeling. One is always convinced that the thing will happen to one at the most awkward moments. One may, like Catherine the Great, be stricken when sitting alone in an empty house upon a lavatory seat. On the other hand, one may be knocked over when receiving from the hands of Her Majesty the Queen the insignia of a Knight of the Bath. Or one may (and this is my special terror) be assailed when on the top step of the longest escalator in the Underground, which would entail much tumbling and embarrassment.

My doctor told me that the thing to do was to rest in the afternoon and to go to bed early. I have followed this advice whenever possible, with the result that although I am conscious of a certain waning of my physical powers, in the sense that the thought of climbing to the top of Broadcasting House is distressing to me, I do not notice so far any marked decline in my mental powers. After all, since I had my two strokes in March and May of 1955, I have written two books and some hundred articles.

Some of my friends fear that I may pop off suddenly without having made my peace with God. But if God is aware when a sparrow falls to the ground, he must also be aware when an elderly writer tumbles from the top of an escalator to the bottom. He must be prepared for the event, and must be sufficiently tolerant to excuse the fact that while tumbling I had no time to confess my sins. Even if Hell exists (which I doubt), and even if Heaven is a reality (which I sincerely hope is not true), we shall surely be judged by the amount of good we have done in the world. By that standard your wings and harp are absolute certainties, whereas even I may be accorded a gold triangle, which I could beat at intervals of praising the Deity, and one rather fluffy little wing.[10]

Harold had to forego a British Council trip which had been prepared for him. Even so he wondered whether, had he undertaken it, the trip would have been more worrying than the appalling demand he had now to face from the Inland Revenue, namely for £2,279 in surtax, having already paid £3,000 that year in income tax. It simply meant that no author could save for his old age unless he lived in a garret in Soho. And he had no wish or intention to do any such thing. The demands could ultimately be met only by commitments to yet more writing of articles, and immediately by borrowing from Vita. Books, according to Harold's way of reckoning, were the form of writing which induced these iniquitous levies. Yet at once he decided to write another book. It was to be about Sainte-Beuve. His real reason was that he hated not having a book in hand, and it cheered Vita to see him have confidence in himself, or so he liked to think. In his heart of hearts he was sure he would not live to finish it. He got Ben, who was staying at Sissinghurst, to fetch down for him from the top shelf of his room all the volumes of *Les Causeries du Lundi*.[11]

In the General Election in May Nigel increased his majority for Bournemouth East by 5,000 Tory votes. Harold rejoiced in his son's success. Ben's wedding was the next event which had somehow to be tackled. It meant both Nicolsons going by train to Florence and staying with the Bernard Berensons at I Tatti. The ceremony took place in the Sala di Matrimonio of the Palazzo Vecchio. Harold wore a new blue suit with a pearl grey tie and stiff collar, and looked his old debonair self. In the Sala di Matrimonio some twenty relations and close friends were assembled. The City Councillor, who made Ben and Luisa man and wife, an old man with a long, untidy beard and dressed in evening tails, gave an oration which lasted forty-five minutes. In the end they had to pull his coat to get him to stop. He warned Ben not to behave either like Hamlet or Othello, and advised him to remember that Italian women were more uxorious than the English sort, and his wife would expect to be kissed whenever he left and returned to her, no matter how often in the same day. Vita was delighted with her new daughter-in-law and the fact that she was Italian. She could hardly have been more pleased if she were Spanish, but Hadji, with his anti-Franco prejudice would not have liked that. Hadji was relieved to have got through the ceremony without having had another stroke. Before the end of the year Luisa was pregnant. Ben was so excited that he actually hugged his mother in telling her. And she, who had vehemently declared that nothing, but nothing would induce her to make over Sissinghurst to the National Trust ('I won't. They can't make me. I *won't*'),[12] was moved to write to Harold, 'Perhaps in the end, when you and I are just two little handfuls of ash, those descendants of ours will be living in the place we have made and loved'.[13]

In October Harold and Vita were both sufficiently recovered to make another motoring tour to the Dordogne, this time continuing into Provence. Vita had been very upset by news, which she had only learnt from Harold in July, of the forthcoming publication by Hamish Hamilton of Francis Steegmuller's book on La Grande Mademoiselle. She even threatened to abandon her own biography altogether. But during the tour she thought better of this decision.

The holiday was a success, although not entirely free from anxiety. Vita dreaded lest Harold might be overtaken by a seizure while they were far from home. And he was alarmed by the new Jaguar she had just bought and which he thought she drove too fast. In the Dordogne the poplars and azaleas were bright gold and red. They stopped at their favourite hotel at Beynac where the proprietress, Madame Bonnet, now an old friend, gave them fresh pink pâté de foie gras. They went to Albi, but the sun was shining in the wrong direction for Harold fully to appreciate the pink effect of the city and cathedral and the red river below them. And Vita was disappointed. At Nîmes Harold ruminated upon the bestial cruelties which had taken place in the arena in Roman times; and found that they were staying in the same hotel where forty-three years ago he had stayed with his beloved Archie Clark Kerr. Archie was now a corpse at Inverchapel whereas he was an old, deaf man who limped.[14] They heard on the radio of their car that Hector McNeil[15] had died at the age of forty-eight. It was Hector who had got Guy Burgess into the Foreign Office as one of his private secretaries; Hector who had got rid of him because he was drunk at conferences, wishing Guy on to the China Department, and, when he was sent to Washington, made no protest. Yet Hector knew nothing of Guy's homosexuality and treachery, and forgave him his drunkenness, although he put a stop to his employment. At least death would relieve Hector of having to excuse his conduct in the forthcoming debate on the Burgess-Maclean affair for having employed drunkards in high positions, he and Herbert Morrison to the embarrassment of the Labour Party having been far more responsible than any of the Old Etonian Tories, for this lapse. So loyal was Harold to an old friend in disgrace that when an anonymous article in the *People* appeared about Guy's private life, he was sickened. He thought it so filthy that he felt the author (Goronwy Rees) must have gone mad. It stated that Guy kept all the letters of his friends in order to blackmail them.

While waiting to board the ferry at Boulogne on their return the Nicolsons visited the house where Sainte-Beuve was born. Larger than they expected, it was only a few yards from the harbour, and now converted to an inn. The landlord allowed them to see the birth room.

On their return to England Vita was awarded the Veitch Memorial Medal by the Royal Horticultural Society 'for services to horticulture'. The news was not released until December. It gratified her far more than the award of her C.H. Harold was present when the heavy gold medal was conferred upon her in the following February.

★　　★　　★　　★

Harold, who had not quite recovered from the effects of his two strokes, headed his diary for 1956 with the words, 'Probably the Year of my Death, 1886–1956. R.I.P.' In fact he had several years of hard work and enjoyment before him, with only a few physical set-backs. The sole noticeable change in his life's pattern was that he definitely accepted fewer invitations to lecture and attend large dinner-parties. But an invitation to stand as a candidate for the Professorship of Poetry at Oxford was more than he could resist. As he put it, the mere mention of Oxford, even on a pot of marmalade, sent him into ecstacies of excitement. Besides, his decision was a sort of defiance of old age and invalidism. Vita gently reproved him for entering this campaign, as though he had not enough duties as it was. And no sooner had he committed himself than he thought he had made a mistake. His two opponents were Wystan Auden and Professor Wilson Knight, the Shakespeare scholar. In opposing the latter he had no regrets. It was a straightforward, honourable contest. But Auden was another matter. He was a poet of distinction. Harold inwardly believed that he ought to be chosen. In his typically scrupulous and illogical way he thought he was doing wrong to stand against him for the very reason that he disapproved of his having bolted to America when he saw the war approaching. So Harold told his Oxford friends not to do any canvassing for him and not to start a whispering campaign against Auden for having become an American. In so doing he probably lost his own election. Nevertheless he wrote to Vita:

> I do think it pretty cool for Auden to claim all the rewards and honours this country can give him while deserting her in the hour of danger. Where he goes wrong to my mind is that the professorship is in fact in the nature of an academic honour rather than in that of an academic appointment. And he really has NOT merited an honour of this sort. Let him by all means be given an honorary degree at Oxford as an American poet. But not made a Professor.[16]

These sentiments were clearly quite right. Harold's equivocal behaviour in putting his own name forward and then allowing no canvassing on his behalf was yet another indication of that lack of self-assertiveness which had hindered him in public life.

On the whole the press did not favour Harold's candidature, unfairly calling him a reactionary traditionalist as opposed to Auden, the forward-looking Liberal. Vita of course could not understand why he minded being called a right-wing traditionalist. To her way of thinking it was something to be proud of. The result of the election was that Auden won the professorship with 216 votes to Harold's 192, and Knight's 91. Harold declared that he was delighted with the result.

If there was one thing needed to whip up Harold's enthusiasm for work and to instil him with inspiration it was the hopelessness of others. He received a letter from Vita's cousin, Eddy Sackville-West, which infuriated him. Eddy wrote to thank Harold for his congratulations on a flattering reference by Mario Praz to his, Eddy's, book on Thomas de Quincey. 'Glad as I was to have your comforting words,' the letter began, 'I do not in fact believe that I shall ever be any more famous than I am now.' The concentration on his fame was irritating enough. But the wallowing in his effeteness that followed was worse.

> If I could still write there might be some chance of this, but I have now lost all desire to write anything in particular – and it is futile to take up a subject just for the sake of writing something. I don't know quite why this had happened. Lack of *métier*, I daresay; but the journalistic grind of the past twenty years certainly has something to do with it as well . . . Now that my youth has gone I find that I have lost the power (it was partly a habit) of writing fiction . . .
> It is all rather depressing, but I try not to think of it. Like all facile amateurs, once I have mastered anything up to a point, I lose the desire to go on with it.[17]

There was Eddy, fifteen years younger than himself, who had never been poor and had recently come into a large income, who had no wife or children and no responsibilities, who was endowed with a very sharp brain and singular literary gifts, whose 'journalistic grind' had, compared to Harold's, been minimal, chucking up his writing and luxuriating in self-pity over a decision of his own choice, a decision dictated by nothing other than querulousness and indolence. The effect it had upon Harold was to make him set to with renewed energy upon *Sainte-Beuve*, which, because of his two strokes, he had been finding heavy-going. Similarly, he was always irritated by authors who complained that were it not for daily chores they would be able to write more and better books. In a letter of 6th April 1948 to a dear friend, Enid Bagnold, who had grumbled that so much of her energies were consumed in giving orders to servants and making arrangements for dinner-parties, he said he believed that 'inspiration is a bee which can buzz in kitchens and laundries just as well as in ivory towers, and that interruptions lose half their menace if one takes them for granted.' He gently rebuked her for attributing to outside circumstances what were inside disabilities.

Bored though Harold was by Sainte-Beuve's preoccupation with Port-Royal, sin and redemption, he went to Paris on a Sainte-Beuve hunt. He stayed two nights with Gladwyn Jebb and his wife Cynthia at the British Embassy, occupying the very room over the courtyard which he slept in on his first visit when his Uncle Dufferin was Ambassador in the 1890s. Never had Paris in spring been more intoxicating. Never had the white candlesticks of the chestnut trees been whiter. He wandered into the narrow streets between the Boulevard de Montparnasse and the Boulevard Raspail. No. 11 rue Montparnasse, a large, prosperous house, was where his hero Sainte-Beuve lived the last year of his life and where he died. With Cynthia, Nancy Mitford, who was living in Paris ('I like Nancy very much but I expect that she is a monster in real life') and Antonia Pakenham[18] he drove to Port Royal which had been the centre of Jansenist learning.

It surprised Harold how much knowledge Nancy Mitford had about Paris of the eighteenth and nineteenth centuries. He found her an intelligent, well-informed guide as well as a very entertaining companion. And when two years later she wrote him a fan letter about *Sainte-Beuve* he was pleased. But he did not take her own writings seriously and was irritated by what he considered the unwarranted adulation she received from her society friends and the low-brow public. 'She is essentially not an intellectual and there is a sort of Roedean hoydenishness about her which I dislike,' he wrote.[19] Her novels meant little to him. They were just farce, dandelion fluff, lacking wit, and not particularly funny. Her historical biographies were worse. They were a reprehensible encroachment by an amateur upon fields of scholarship. In a review of her *Madame de Pompadour* he took exception to the Roedean expressions, such as, 'I know this sounds dreadfully uncivilized and difficult'. When he read her *Voltaire* he remarked that, 'there is a sort of bouncy vulgarity about her writing which jars my nerves'.[20] As for her sister Jessica's *Hons and Rebels*, he hated it. He complained that Jessica was utterly without understanding. She just giggled about those who held views different from Philip Toynbee's. 'There is about [her] the same sort of sprightly giggle that I find so irritating in Nancy's historical works.'[21]

By the middle of September Harold had finished *Sainte-Beuve*. And when it was published in June 1957 it was held by the critics and his friends, including Clive Bell and Raymond Mortimer, to be as good as the best of his books. There was not a sign in it of staleness or senility. There was no sign of falling off whatever. The wonder was, considering he could not bring himself to like Sainte-Beuve – indeed, who could fail to be physically repulsed? – how he evoked a qualified sympathy for him. It was the style of the writer, not the personality of the man which he admired. The critic, John Raymond called Harold's book 'this brilliant biography'. He found it urbane, observant, feline, and just a shade unnatural. He did not believe there had ever been a biographer of whose essence the reader was so conscious as he turned the pages. 'He is the most obtrusively unobtrusive practioner of English prose in the language.' In fact in all Harold's books, whether essays about people, the history of his times, novels or biographies, his writing had a touch of the autobiographical. His personality peeped through whomsoever he was dissecting. And that was why, since he was never self-destructive, however self-depreciatory, he could not condemn any human being as wholly unmeritorious. He saw all men as near-failures, and their thwarted ambitions poignant. *The Times* considered the book worthy to rank with Sainte-Beuve's *Portraits Littéraires*. Indeed there was in Harold's writings not a little reflection of Sainte-Beuve's trenchant style, not to mention his faculty of investing with interest the widest variety of human types. Thus similarities to the famous *Lundis* could be traced in Harold's many sketches of persons and things, particularly in the *Marginal Comments*.

If Harold Nicolson's books fall roughly into the three categories of criticism, commentary and history, *Sainte-Beuve* which belongs ostensibly to the first, has almost as just a claim to the second. For Harold tackled literature like a novelist. Somerset Maugham declared that he could describe a person's exterior better than any novelist alive, and Maugham was chary of praising writers who competed with himself.[22] Those characters in *Some People* which were not direct portraits, and Sidney Culpeper in *Journey to Java*, are examples of his remarkable capacity for imaginative portraiture. Rose Macaulay actually regretted that he had turned away from fiction with distaste, for she saw in his sympathetic and humorous delineation of people the very stuff of which novelists were made.[23] But then he had a gift for most forms of literary prose. In 1935 Michael Sadleir forecast that he would survive as one of the leading writers of the age; and the *Daily Telegraph* claimed that he had one of the most attractive prose styles of any contemporary writer. He had the balance and clarity which come most easily to those who in youth were trained to compose in Latin and Greek. In 1960 John

Betjeman, speaking at a Guildhall dinner, called him the greatest living master of English prose.

Such a categorical statement is always arguable; but that he ranks among the greatest masters of prose of his generation there can be little question. Everything he wrote was stamped with his own inimitable quality. Vita was able to lay her finger on the secret of it more deftly than anyone else. Nigel remembers his mother endeavouring to explain to her two sons wherein lay the individuality and originality of his style by pointing to one short phrase in the essay on J. D. Marstock in *Some People*: 'The scrubbed boards and chipped enamel of school life.' In these nine words Harold managed to conjure up the unlovely bareness, ugliness, squalor and antiseptic rigours of a boys' preparatory school dining-room, with its smell of sweat and Jeyes' Fluid, its din of stacking crockery, and after-taste of sour milk puddings, which a page of description would not have rendered more vivid. The sad thing was that he never had sufficient inclination to shed his superfluous interests and devote his concentrated endeavours upon one Proust-like task. He certainly never made the time.

It must be remembered that the chief distraction (dictated by need for money) and one at which he excelled was book reviewing. All the time that he was writing political articles, attending committees, addressing meetings and doing the hundred and one voluntary things which prevented his concentrating upon the Proust-like task, he was also reviewing other peoples' books. He had done it with hardly a pause ever since he left the Diplomatic Service and became a journalist in 1930. In that year he embarked upon *Books This Week* for the *Daily Express*. He reviewed for Mosley's short-lived *Action*. In three years' time he was reviewing five books a week for the *Daily Telegraph*. Then came the weekly review of a single book for the *Observer*, which gave him the scope he needed. He was a scrupulously fair critic. He read the book entrusted to him from cover to cover, making notes on the end-papers as he went along. He never used the book to air his own prejudices and affections. He was impartial and tolerant of opinions he could not share. He was only intolerant of vulgarity and obscenity, which he detested. Rather than hurt the feelings of an author who was a friend he would refuse to review a book he did not like. His reviews err, if anything, on the charitable side. But such was his curiosity about other peoples' idiosyncracies, mannerisms, even their clothes and appearance, that he could make the dullest volume seem entertaining or even edifying. He picked on human foibles with a relish which often provoked more scintillating wit and humour in his reviews than are to be found in his own books. Thus he gave rein to those delicious little twists of phrase which make his prose so unlike anyone else's. They are poised on a knife-edge between the whimsical and the serious, without ever becoming either frivolous or sententious.

The Suez crisis of October and November 1956 made it impossible for Harold not to look up and take a keen interest in the international situation. Besides, Nigel was deeply involved and eventually lost his parliamentary seat over the Suez issue. His father began by thinking Eden was right not to give way to Nasser's pressure to nationalise the Canal, which he resented as a resounding slap in John Bull's face.

> The Tory party [he told Vita, who doubtless agreed with it] is saying we have lost all authority in the world, and nobody will regard us as a Great Power again. I fear we *have* ceased to be a Great Power and must cut our coat according to our very cheap cloth.[24]

Suez dated this consummation. Harold was irked by John Foster Dulles's attitude, which was that the American public would not stand any action on Britain's part calculated, in their view, to preserve British oil interests for the Empire. Dulles then switched to a grave charge that UNO was being ignored by us. Eden of course knew that the Security Council was divided and that to submit matters to UNO's hands was worse than useless. It would be courting disaster. So he threatened war and the Opposition in Parliament were incensed. Nigel ultimately abstained from the vote of confidence in the Government, of which he was ostensibly a supporter, with fatal consequences to his own political future.

In the middle of these international concerns Harold went to look at his new granddaughter, whom he thought the ugliest baby he had ever seen; and Vita was stung by a wasp. Her tongue, neck and throat swelled so that she could scarcely breathe, and she was whipped off to hospital in an ambulance. Harold was distraught, and violently sick.

In October Harold, Vita and Philippa motored to north-east Spain, Harold having given way to family pressure no longer to boycott General Franco. At Figueras they watched an immense wedding reception. When it got dark the bride arrived. Little lights flickered on. Salvador Dali, who lived nearby, came over to watch, and shocked Philippa by combing his hair with a pocket comb. The villagers danced the Dardanas. They made two wide circles with children forming a smaller circle in the middle. The drums beat, the piccolos thrilled, and a man blew a big bassoon. The men and girls held hands and with their feet made intricate movements, sometimes sliding and sometimes bobbing up and down. It was a dance which had been danced continuously for two thousand years.

Harold became more and more disillusioned with Eden, who was waffling. He called him a rotten person, vain and purposeless. Israel invaded Sinai. On the 31st October the Government issued an ultimatum to Egypt and Israel. Great Britain was at war with Egypt. The opportunity to gain an overwhelming victory within a week, which was our only hope of warding off the disapproval of UNO, America, the Dominions and half our own country, was botched. As it was the United Nations ordered an immediate cease-fire, and we were humiliated in the eyes of the world. The Russians took advantage of the distraction by invading Hungary.

Harold could not contain his indignation, although he was in no position of authority or influence. In the Beefsteak Club he deliberately went out of his way to pick a quarrel with the Tory members. Kenneth Rose recorded that when members complained to Harold that Eden was being stabbed in the back, Harold told them he ought not to present so much of it to view.[25] He considered our action one of the most disgraceful in history, and his fury with Eden knew no bounds. He considered he had lied in saying that our sole objective was to separate the Egyptians from the Israelis, when his real purpose was to seize the Canal and get rid of Nasser.[26] He compared the Suez crisis with Munich in bringing lasting discredit upon our trustworthiness. His reasons for being so passionately moved by the Suez crisis were twofold. Nigel was deeply implicated in the issue. But first and foremost Harold was shocked that Eden, whom at the time of Munich and throughout the war he had admired for his great personal courage, should, as he put it, 'have violated his principles and told his country a series of shameful lies'.[27] Certainly no political issue had caused so much bitterness and division amongst families and friends since Munich, and none has done so since.[28]

On the 21st November Harold celebrated his seventieth birthday. That morning after breakfast the door bell of C1 Albany rang and the knocker knocked. He was handed a letter signed by eleven old friends and enclosing a cheque for £1,370 with birthday greetings. A list of 253 subscribers was attached. Harold was overwhelmed with gratitude, but not wholly pleased. He did not like receiving money from his friends. And for a time he did not dare look at the list for fear it contained the names of some acquaintances whom he disliked. He acknowledged that his inhibition was a sort of disordered and diseased pride, of which he felt ashamed; but it was a deep instinct within him. The dinner given him by seven of his intimate friends – Lawrence Jones, Alan Pryce-Jones, Raymond Mortimer, Rupert Hart-Davis, John Sparrow, Colin Fenton and myself – in a private room at the Garrick that evening was on the contrary a very welcome affair. It was a delicious evening. There were no speeches, only toasts. He 'went to bed full of champagne and gratitude'.

The Nicolsons had for some time entertained the idea of a winter cruise. Neither of them had ever been to the Far East or to South America. They thought that on board ship they would get away from distractions in order to pursue their writing, and escape the worst months of the English winter. What better way of spending the large cheque which Harold had received as his seventieth birthday present than by sailing to Java? Accordingly on the 15th January they embarked at Southampton on the Dutch liner, *Willem Ruys*. They were away for just over two months, returning on the 17th March. It was to be the first of six successive sea voyages.

The trip was a greater success than any of the following ones. To begin with, they both kept well. They revelled in the novelty of being at sea for weeks at a time. They were most happy when on board, and although it was an experience to go ashore occasionally, the landings meant interruptions to their work and were rather resented. At Cape Town they were met by a lady of elegant appearance bearing a sheaf of gladioli, sent by a friend. Vita was delighted by the unexpected attention; Harold irritated by the fuss and bother. The lady took them to Kirstenbosch Gardens, where they were specially impressed by the African Silver Tree with alternating leaves of blue and silver which they had not seen before. In Cape Town they received letters from Nigel giving news of the aftermath of Suez and his own political predicament. The Nicolsons found Cape Town ghastly, not Dutch at all, but a mixture of Weston-super-Mare and the ramshackle quarters of New Orleans.[29] A week was spent in Java.[30] On the return journey they stopped at Singapore where Vita was greeted by a Chinese friend, whom Harold christened Chop-Suey, a boring lady who spoke English volubly but did not understand a word addressed to her.

'Tell me,' Vita began brightly, 'is there a canteen at the University where you teach?' 'Beautiful flowers,' replied Chop-Suey, 'beautiful flowers.' 'Do you teach your pupils English?' I enquired with malice. 'I know one shop near Raffles Place,' she answered, 'which has many of them . . . Most beautiful flowers, all green and blue and – how do you say? – ponk.' 'Pink,' said Vita, and the conversation languished.[31]

At Singapore Harold learned that his Albany flat had been broken into – it was the consequence of having been televised in his sitting-room – and two cigarette-cases and a thin gold watch stolen. He did not mind in the least, for he was not possessive and what he called trinkets meant nothing to him. While at sea the Nicolsons sat in their air-conditioned cabins, which were opposite each other on the same deck. Harold would rise at 7.45 and bathe in the swimming-pool before breakfast. Then work in his cabin till 12.30. After luncheon a short nap, then a walk round the deck eight times which amounted to one mile. He would read on deck till 7.15, merely lifting his eyes from the page if a shoal of flying-fish, a school of porpoises, a whale, an albatross, or even a lone oil tanker, was sighted. It does not seem that the couple had much commerce with the other passengers in spite of Harold's assertion in a letter to Raymond Mortimer that it was so good for them to mix with people different from those they encountered in Kent and Albany.[32]

He wrote to James Pope-Hennessy that he had read the *Confessions* of Rousseau. The man's self-pity and persecution mania were nauseating. It was:

disgraceful the way he convinced himself that all his self-induced misfortunes were due to the machinations of his enemies. I cannot tolerate a man who could blub over the sweet innocence of a child in the Luxembourg Gardens and deposit as many as five (repeat *five*) of his own babies on the steps of a foundling home. Worse than Shelley. Now you would never deposit your bastards basely. You would get me to adopt the elder girl, and Peggy [Crewe] to adopt the younger one, whereas the boy would be given over to the charge of Sir Anthony and Lady Eden.[33]

Having read Harold would take a hot bath in salt water, change into a white dinner jacket, and descend to the dining-saloon. After a rich and tasteless dinner he and Vita would sit together in the lounge and watch the young employees of the Burmah Oil Company and the tea and rubber plantations dance in ecstasy with each other's wives, who wore pretty pink frocks and giggled a great deal. This regular daily schedule suited them both.

HAROLD NICOLSON

While Vita happily wrote her book, *Daughter of France*, Harold completed a number of articles which he posted back to England, as well as 60,000 words of a diary which was to become *Journey to Java*.

Short though Harold's experiences of the Far East had been, his impressions of it were definite. They were that self-government in the former British and Dutch colonies had not increased the reliability of administration. The incompetence, the ignorance and the corruption of the Indonesians were absolutely terrifying. He was doubtful whether in Malaya, in Singapore or in Ceylon conditions would be any better within a foreseeable time.[34]

On their return to England the Nicolsons met with the usual catalogue of woes and pin-pricks which invariably confront home-coming travellers after several weeks' absence. Elvira Niggeman's cat had died and she was in tears; the Sissinghurst gardener's wife was unsettled and difficult, and the gardener announced his departure owing to rows with the neighbouring farmer's cowman. Moreover, he had suddenly become Communist and even given the clenched fist to their friend and neighbour, Bunny Drummond. Harold was worried about Nigel having to abandon Bournemouth East, for the local committee had already adopted another candidate. The committee had appealed to their voters on the lines of, 'Is it the wish of this meeting that the constituency should be represented by a traitor to his country?' a turn of phrase which Harold, not to mention Nigel, gravely resented. No wonder the Nicolsons lost no time in making enquiries about a cruise for the next winter.

At a dinner party at Buckingham Palace Harold had a talk to Gaitskell about the split in the Labour Party over the atom bomb issue. Gaitskell wisely remarked that a leader of the Opposition should always consider what action he would take if he were Prime Minister before making up his mind to dispute with the Government in power. As usual Harold enjoyed the beauty of the Palace rooms, furniture and pictures, while disliking the stiffness of their arrangement, and suffering from anxiety about 'secret sorrow'.

He lost no time in typing out his cruise diary in a revised and printable form. By the second week of June he had finished it. 'I am relieved', he wrote in his regular diary, 'since if I die, the book can be published.'[35]

At the beginning of *Journey to Java* the author announces that all the people mentioned in the book are real, with one obvious exception. This of course is Sydney Culpeper, who belongs to the category of the cagey queer. He is an interesting but not an entirely convincing character. He is made to serve as a sort of guinea-pig, a convenient contrivance, a fives-court wall against which to fling arguments and have them bounce back intact. Culpeper's slight unreality is caused by Harold's old reluctance to let himself 'go', that reluctance which Edmund Wilson once castigated as disingenuousness. It is evident in a sentence in which the author summarises Culpeper's character as though he, Harold, were a tolerant Archbishop of Canterbury: 'I have long since realised that essentially he is a serious and sensitive person, who has endured and enjoyed experiences different from my own.' – as it were, conveying concession to the popular but outdated misconception that the homosexual must be a frivolous, if not an evil deviant from the accepted standards of virtue and honour.

In recounting day-to-day events during a two months' cruise Harold made them a background to some philosophical thoughts, of which the main one was the cause of '*angst*'. His reading of Rousseau, Epicurus, Epictetus and other authors set him on this pursuit. He finally decided that melancholy could not be causeless and must be induced by some psychological reason or unhappy experience in extreme youth. The fictitious Sydney Culpeper was made to reveal this to him by ultimately disclosing that in his youth he had been sent to gaol for accosting men.

The book was written with remarkable speed. It contains some careless sentences, and occasional lapses in style, like, for example: 'As so many epicene men of my acquaintance, Culpeper walks firmly,' etc. The merriment is at times false, the jokiness strained, the family intimacy overcharged, and the teasing of Vita too consistent. Critical friends like Raymond Mortimer did not approve of the book, and when it came out in November the reviews were not very favourable. Yet as Nigel told his mother, his father's capacity to amaze was never ceasing. After the millions of words he had written, here was fresh originality. He had produced 'a new sort of travel book, a new sort of *Some People*, a new sort of literary and philosophical criticism, a new sort of self-portraiture.'[36] This is true, and considering the circumstances in which the book was thrown off in little more than two months by a man who had suffered two strokes, it is a remarkable performance. One friend who did approve was Guy Burgess. He wrote to Harold from distant Moscow:

One thing struck me as a possible cause of at least many of the cases of causeless misery you examine is that such misery is found in people who either don't seek or don't succeed in understanding the real world in which they live and in particular (as a Marxist I say this) the explanation, above all the historical explanation, of why it is what it is – and this includes, as a minor detail, why they are what they are. Without such knowledge . . . individuals create a vacuum round themselves and *angst* replaces the air they should breathe.[37]

This somewhat breathless statement, written off the cuff in haste, and without revision, is not uninteresting in summarising Burgess's complaint that his compatriots were failing to face up to the inevitable drift, as he saw it, of the new way of life which must soon envelop the western world.

The cruise to the Far East had clearly done much to benefit Harold's health. It was extraordinary how full his days had again become. One typical day's schedule in April was as follows: a meeting of the Historic Buildings Committee of the National Trust all morning; luncheon at the Beefsteak Club; an overseas broadcast in the afternoon; an address to the Press in the Blewcoat School about the work of the National Trust in the evening; an interview on television; and dinner with Ben and Luisa. On the 1st May he was one of a deputation of five, including Attlee, to the Prime Minister Macmillan, to urge that no executions should be carried out in Cyprus as a result of the recent troubles, and that NATO should mediate in the dispute. That evening he was present at the Royal Academy dinner. Winston Churchill was present, slumped in a little chair, child-like and dribbling about the lips, a sad travesty of himself, beneath a rude caricature by Ruskin Spear.

In May Archibald MacLeish was over from the States on a visit. MacLeish was one of Harold's American friends whom he most liked, and one of the contemporary poets he most admired. They lunched together at the Connaught Hotel. They did not discuss politics, but the passage of time. Some of the things MacLeish remembered as the happiest of his life were the early morning rides at Tehran, when Harold would rise at 6 o'clock and on his pony, Bay Rum, accompany him into the plains. He confirmed that *The Land* was one of the most enduring of modern poems; he had read it five or six times, and each time with renewed delight.[38]

The B.B.C. Overseas Department asked Harold to take part in a broadcast justifying the West. He agreed to do so. He claimed that the whole of modern civilisation derived from the Mediterranean basin, whereas only poetry and some art derived from the Orient.[39] His contempt for everything East of Suez had been confirmed by his recent cruise (via the Cape) to Java. The only exception to wholesale condemnation of self-government and manners in eastern countries which he would allow was the Chinese civilisation. A visit to Spinks's shop in St. James's and a mere glance at some of their Chinese carvings fortified this opinion. He called in to get his links repaired.

> I must say they are a gentleman's shop [he told Vita]. I was wafted upstairs to the oriental department where my little link that I held in my hand seemed so tiny and unimportant among all those lions and buddhas and malachite and tourmaline, and ossoline, and peryphony and lauk. But I might have been Jimmy Rothschild bringing in his wife's tiara to be re-set. It was, 'Yes, Sir Harold, certainly, Sir Harold,' all the way. Nobody has really ever felt less like a Sir than your old bumblebee, but it was a fine effect none the less.[40]

Having disposed of *Journey to Java* he must think quickly of a subject for another book. The hovering of Time's winged chariot was, in spite of his renewal of strength, a persistent reminder of the shortage of life's lease, and every minute before the next blow struck was precious. Moreover it was his duty, it was man's duty to squeeze the uttermost of his capacities to the last dregs. David Astor[41] made a generous proposition that he should travel all round the world, writing articles on every country he visited and publishing interviews with Khruschev, Mao Tse Tung, Nehru, and other world leaders. The offer was tempting, and it is easy to guess what a wonderful emissary Harold would have made for the cause of international understanding and peace. But it would be a great strain on his health, were he to accept. And so he reluctantly but sensibly declined. Instead for a while he contemplated a book on the minor poets of the nineteenth century. But very soon this idea was dispelled by another proposition.

In the meantime Harold's dynastic ambitions were fulfilled by the birth to Nigel and Philippa of a son, Adam. Both he and Vita were transported by joy. Harold's joy was moderated only by distress over Nigel's political recession. Nigel was still Bournemouth East's representative in the House of Commons, but on sufferance. He had been rejected by his constituency and there was no prospect as yet of his being adopted by another at the next General Election. Nigel's situation distressed himself, and made him, not unnaturally, sensitive. He believed that he was unpopular in the House just as he was unpopular with the unbending diehards of East Bournemouth. Harold wrote him a stern letter rebutting his younger son's unwarranted imaginings, but at the same time sensibly investigating possible reasons and suggesting means of avoiding them.

> Why do you feel that you are not liked in the House? All my friends tell me exactly the opposite. I imagine that you are not matey enough, not a good smoking-room pal, too austere, too shy, and apt when shy to put on an austere face or to utter Gladwyn Jebb snorts. Moreover, you have no gift for intimacy, being tied up like a lavender bag. Most politicians have got three or four intimates to whom they can pour out their difficulties, and who are able to tell others that 'once you get to know him, Nigel is really quite a human person'. I had Rob Bernays and to a less extent Bill Mabane – but you have always been more deterred by the failings or faults of your friends than you have been entranced by their virtues. I recommend a suspension of disbelief and a more lyrical attitude towards friendliness. Once one starts thinking one is not really liked, one becomes a lone black cat darting round corners to escape observation, tin cans, wild dogs and the jeers of schoolboys. That is a grave affliction that can easily be checked before it becomes a habit.[42]

At the beginning of October a partner, Mr. Lee Barker, of Doubleday, Harold's American publishers, lunched with him. Barker told Harold that his firm were proposing a series of world histories under the heading, *The Mainstream of the Modern World*, and wanted him to cover the eighteenth century. Harold considered that he was too old and unwell for that sort of work, and turned it down. But reflecting upon the offer the next morning in bed he decided that, after all, since it was physical and not mental exercise that was a threat to his health, and since the eighteenth century appealed to him, he might just as well say Yes.[43] A few days later he met Barker again, and came to terms. The book was to be 150,000 words long, and to be delivered on the 1st January 1960. 'I shall be dead by them,' he said to Vita,[44] 'but it will keep me happy and busy for the remainder of my life and they will pay me £3,000 in instalments to keep me going.' It was a good thing to embark upon a serious book again after *Journey to Java*, which he regarded as a light-weight.

Vita had gone off on a motoring tour to Suffolk with her neighbour and new friend, the artist Edith Lamont, upon whom she was growing more and more to rely. The main purpose of the tour was to absent herself from Sissinghurst while the turrets of her tower were being re-shingled. This operation, which had become absolutely essential owing to the roofs being in a very decayed condition, nearly drove her mad, not so much because the workmen were all over the place, but because, in that the Ministry of Works had given a grant towards the re-shingling, her strong sense of ownership was affronted. It was as if her castle had been appropriated by the Government. I stayed a night with her just after her return while the work was in progress and whenever she passed by the tower she shaded her eyes in order not to witness what was going on. As we sat in her room the smell of workmen was overpowering. Vita said that this must have been what Versailles smelled like. Mercifully, she added, the workmen at Sissinghurst, unlike Louis XIV's courtiers, did not relieve the calls of nature on the staircase.

From six o'clock until long past midnight we talked without stopping about everything under the sun and out of it. Let me interpolate here that never in my life have I known anyone, male or female, with whom, once the mutual preliminary shynesses were dispelled, I have felt more at ease or whose companionship I have found more congenial. Conversations with Vita transcended all barriers. There were no reservations of any kind. No topics were barred. Her curiosity about and understanding of human nature in all its aspects were limitless. Her sympathy with every human frailty and predicament was all-embracing. This was the Vita I knew and most dearly loved. The occasional visits I made to Sissinghurst for a night during the week while Harold was in London stand out as rare and luminous pictures in the lengthening galleries of memory. As dusk faded into night I would watch the outline of her noble head against the chequered Tudor casements of the tower; would watch the tip of her cigarette from a long holder glow fiery red as she drew upon it with constant but imperceptible inhalations so that her profile – always her profile of drooping eyelid, straight nose and soft rounded chin – would emerge from the darkness as in a momentary vision. I would smell, when I could no longer see, the cloud of Cypriot tobacco peculiarly her own; and listen to that deep, slightly quavering, gently-swelling voice, then most like the slumberous sea broken by eddies of short, sharp laughter, as against shingle, and the lapping interrogation, 'Oh, *do* tell me what happened next?' When eventually I descended the circular wooden stair, crossed the lawn by torch-light, navigated the now black-tented foliage of the White Garden, felt a way into the Priest's House and tumbled into bed, I would pardonably believe that Vita had enjoyed our exchange of confidences as much as I had, and I would rejoice in the knowledge that there was one human being in the world in whom perfect, unalloyed amity was to be found. Then I understood what this unique woman's love meant to Harold.

In November she had an operation on her jaw and suffered much pain. In removing a badly impacted wisdom tooth the dentist also removed bits of bone from the jaw. To ease the pain she was given drugs, which induced temperatures. In her weakened state she caught influenza, which necessitated penicillin. She had not recovered from these adversities when she and Harold sailed on the 5th December for the Caribbean on the Pacific steamer *Reina del Mar*.

The day after leaving Liverpool docks Vita's temperature rocketted to 102. While the ship's doctor attended to her in her cabin Harold leant against the deck rail outside her door in abject misery, waiting for him to come out. The doctor was not alarmed, and pronounced her heart to be 'tired'. She rested in bed and by the time the ship reached La Rochelle her temperature was normal. Unfortunately the *Reina del Mar* ran into a fearful hurricane off Corunna, and she was very sick. This delayed her recovery for several days. Even so her temperature fluctuated and for several weeks she could not leave her cabin or do any work. Nor would Harold go ashore at Bermuda without her. From the ship he thought it looked beastly, with its low mud banks, skimpy brown trees and pretentious little villas. Sir Philip and Lady Magnus-Allcroft who were also on board were the greatest comfort to Harold. With them he consented to go ashore at Havana.

They visited the Capitol which houses the Cuban Parliament.

It is copied from that at Washington. The central hall is as vast as the Baths of Caracalla and in the centre of it arises the enormous dome encrusted with gold. At the radial point below the dome, at the point where with us there is a little rosette in the pavement of the Central Hall, is a diamond let into the marble. I can well imagine how awed the constituents of the Cuban deputies may be, when they leave their sugar plantation in the wilds and are introduced to their Member amid all this marble and gold. It must have a profound psychological effect and make electors forget the corruption and brutality of their island politics. Havana itself is a magnificent modern city not unlike Detroit. But there is a little grey huddled church where Columbus lay buried until he was exhumed centuries later and a huddled arcade square the size of the forecourt at Albany – rather moving among all these skyscrapers.[45]

By the end of December Vita had recovered. Less worried, Harold began to enjoy the cruise enormously. He did some steady reading, took notes for his new book, bathed, and watched the passengers reading *Journey to Java* and eyeing him suspiciously.

The New Year of 1958 opened smilingly in Callao harbour, Peru. Lima, the capital, was a pretty and gay little city. Harold and Vita spent the whole day in glorious sunshine at the British Embassy with Sir William Montagu-Pollock, the Ambassador, and his wife. They visited the Archaeological Museum, full of relics of the Andean civilisation which flourished centuries before the Incas came. They admired the wonderfully preserved textiles dating from 200 B.C. In Chile they stayed at the British Embassy in Santiago, and were welcomed by their old friends Leon and Paes Subercaseaux who had been at the Chilean Embassy in London during the war. They loved Chile and the Chileans. In a letter to Elvira Niggeman Harold described them as:

> the kindest muddle-heads that ever existed, possessing no sense either of time or space, but so generous and helpful . . . The beauty of the country recalled Persia to us, and we had a very happy four days.[46]

By now Vita was as active as ever, rising at dawn and prepared to be motored in scorching heat for miles along the coast. She had resumed writing *Daughter of France* while Harold was making good progress on his notes for *The Age of Reason*. Throughout the cruise they both posted their weekly articles, his book review to the *Telegraph*, and her gardening notes to the *Observer*.

On the return journey they were unable to land at La Guaira in Venezuela because a revolution was in progress. The Navy and Air Force were demanding the resignation of Jiminez, the President. On the 9th February they were back at Sissinghurst. Harold at once took up the threads of the Cyprus Conciliation Committee. Attending its meetings for the next few months in the House of Commons made him feel that he was once again of use in public affairs.

Vita was plunged into depression about her book. She was so dispirited that she had to discuss it with him. She had taken more trouble over *Daughter of France* than any previous book, but felt she had failed to synthesise or compress it. By June she had worked herself (and Harold) into a frenzy of worry because it was not yet finished, and the publisher's date limit had expired. The delay had largely been caused by constant interruptions through the increased number of visitors to the Sissinghurst garden. Harold feared she might have a breakdown. He realised that the strain on her was more than she could take and he begged her to stop her *Observer* articles for a while, and live on the money he had raised by selling silver at Sotheby's. It was not that she was bored by her subject. Far from it. She was immersed in it. She had so soaked herself in the *grand siècle* that she allowed herself to be distracted by the most inconsiderable details. By dint of a superlative effort at selection and rejection Vita finished the book in August. 'Do you know what happened at 9.30 last night?' she wrote to him on the 13th of that month. 'La Grande Mademoiselle died, aged 63. This does not mean that I have not still got a lot to do, but the book is so to speak finished, and another month should clear it up. Ouf!'[47]

In April his contemporary and old colleague, Lord Eustace Percy, died.[48] Although they had never been intimates, they were friends, each of whom had a high respect for the qualities of the other. When Harold was in a quandary what to do with his life after leaving Mosley, Percy advised him to withdraw from the world, think, wait, and above all, preserve his integrity. It was not unlike the advice which Harold gave to Mosley when the New Party petered out in 1932.

Harold and Vita attended his funeral in Etchingham church. It was a dismal and depressing affair. The weather was Arctic. The hymns were badly sung by the villagers; the prayers were mumbled by the Vicar. In a small procession the mourners followed the coffin to the edge of the grave. Harold thought back to the days when his friend was regarded as one of the most gifted and promising of his generation. And what had he done with his honourable life? No doubt he did much good in his constituency at Newcastle. But what pleasures or adventures had he enjoyed? His life had been as cold, bare and empty as the church from which he had just been carried. Harold consoled himself with the reflection that when he died, nobody would think he had failed to extract the most out of life. That was something to be satisfied with. He and Vita decided, as they boarded the train which was to take them both to London, that when they died they would have their bodies handed over to the undertakers to burn as soon as possible. As the train drew out of the station they passed the graveyard which they had just left. Through the fugged window they saw three men in greatcoats and cloth caps shovelling clay down on Eustace's coffin. 'I feel almost sick with the gloom of it all,' Harold wrote.[49]

Death and burial were much on his mind. Grace Curzon also died. She had refused to be buried at Kedleston for she could not bear the idea of lying in the family vault with the first Lady Curzon, her predecessor, already there under a sumptuous effigy.

It makes me wonder [he wrote to Vita][50] if it would not be more tactful for me to have my bone meal put like Dottie's in a little box in Withyham graveyard and not intrude upon the Dukes of Dorset. But I have a quite irrational desire to be buried in the same box as Mar. Once we are both bone meal there is nothing macabre about that, and since I saw the remains of Mr. and Mrs. Shaw I have no wish to be scattered in the rondel.

The rondel is the circular centre of the rose garden at Sissinghurst, its circumference being a yew hedge, with breaks for the radiating paths.

Harold's diaries this summer were full of news concerning the situation in the Middle East, in which he took a lively back-woodsman interest because of Nigel's close involvement with it in Parliament.

An even worse worry than Nigel and Bournemouth was Ben and his marriage. A touching letter from Luisa came like a bolt from the blue. Until he received it Harold had not the slightest inkling that the couple were not getting on well. He immediately assumed that his son was to blame. He wrote to Vita:[51]

Weak men when they decide to behave badly are apt to be more cruel than strong men. Apart from everything else it will mean Ben relapses into the life he led before and that he may go rapidly downhill.

This was an astonishing prediction and assumption that Ben's pre-marital life had been one of licence and debauchery, which had never been the case at all. It had merely been rather bohemian. The phrase 'Apart from everything else,' relates to his chief dread lest the outcome of a separation would mean Vanessa going to Italy and being brought up there. He was gnawed by unhappiness, on Luisa's behalf, oddly enough, rather than Ben's. In fact the couple did not separate until 1961.

In June Harold read James Pope-Hennessy's Life of *Queen Mary* which he pronounced a remarkable book. 'It is,' he wrote to James:[52]

informative, amusing, vivid and admirably composed and written . . . It is a *pointilliste* portrait built up of a thousand significant details . . . the skill with which you catch the sparkle of every ripple. You had before you a large bowl of jumbled pins which most people would have re-arranged as a pincushion, but which in some manner you have fitted into a pattern as smooth as lacquer.

While passing on to James these well merited words of praise he counselled him to be discreet when showing to friends some amusing sketches he had written about members of the Royal Family, whom he had met in the course of collecting material for the book. At the same time he absolved him from any guilt in allowing an elderly friend of them both to fall headlong in love with him. James's reply was not the least untypical of that self-satisfied young man.

> The dreadful fact is that I am never surprised at anyone feeling that way about me, as I feel it so constantly about myself! There now I have thoroughly shocked you and you won't *ever* write to me again.[53]

Nothing that James said, or did, however outrageous, would prevent Harold from writing to him again and again. The trouble was that he could not bring himself to rebuke him enough. His reprimands, when he let them fall, were like the gentle dewdrops from heaven and not the heavy hail-stones of Jehovah wrath. Like other older friends of James he spoilt him.

Harold spent the second half of August and much of September at Sissinghurst working at *The Age of Reason*. The Nicolsons' old friend Clive Bell came to stay. He found them as welcoming as always, and Vita, whom he had not seen for years, 'to be wearing uncommonly well and to belie the stories put into circulation about her'.[54] This was a reference to her state of health.

On the 16th September 1958 Harold received a long letter from Guy Burgess in Moscow, giving him his address and intimating that, since he no longer had any news value in Russia and had more or less relapsed into private life, there was no reason why they should not correspond without fear of their letters being intercepted. Harold had certainly written to Guy on the 20th June, for he kept a copy of his letter. And it is clear that he had written others previously which had not been acknowledged. He had started the correspondence on learning from Tom Driberg, the Labour M.P. who had seen Guy in Moscow, that Guy would not have dared to be the first to write.

Harold had always had a weakness for Guy Burgess. He considered that he had one of the quickest and most acute minds he had ever come across. When just before his flight Guy became soaked and silly from drink Harold was sorry. He was sorry for the dreadful hash he had made of his life, all owing to his wanting to help someone, who at the time of the flight was his friend, but with whom he was then no longer on speaking terms. So out of the kindness of his heart and his natural affection for Burgess Harold wrote to him at regular intervals. He confined his letters to news of changes in the appearance of London, which Guy loved, the demolition of old buildings, the substitution of skyscrapers, the increasing number of coloured people in the streets, and gossip about Guy's old club, the Reform, and his friends, Anthony Blunt, Fred Warner and James Pope-Hennessy. He wrote about good books lately published. He even told him about his rage against the Tories of Bournemouth East for their treatment of Nigel, and against Eden over Suez. He warned Guy that he had better not return to England, although he had no idea whether the authorities had sufficient evidence against him for prosecution. Only Guy's solicitor could advise him on that score. Harold felt sure that none of Guy's intellectual friends would speak against him in the witness box (here I think Harold was being over-sanguine), although the average Tory would pursue him with malevolence. All Harold's letters were cautious and one senses that they were a trial for him to write.

None of Guy's letters to Harold gives the year in which it was written, and seldom the day of the month. No address was vouchsafed in the early letters, but the later ones were headed, Bolshaya Proyovska No. 53/55. His letters were always more affectionate than Harold's to him. He confided that with middle age he had ceased to lead a promiscuous sex life. He rejoiced that there was no dearth of servants in Russia, and that he lived a happy domestic life with a Russian boy. He had not become quite a compulsive drinker, which he admitted he was driven to be for a time while in Washington. He said that he had written three letters about Vita which he tore up as being totally inadequate, but did send her a telegram which he then regretted as being ill-advised. 'Gossip is,' he wrote, 'apart from the Reform Club, the streets of London & occasionally the English countryside, the only thing I really miss.' But Harold knew that he was consumed with home-sickness and longed to see his mother. He did not wish to increase Guy's unhappiness any more than he wished to compromise Guy's friends by his letters to him. But he did report a visit he made in 1960 to his mother, who was living with her husband, Colonel Bassett, in a luxury flat in Arlington Street. She was then dying of cancer. She knew no more about her son than Harold did. She agreed with him that his escape was a quixotic desire to help his friend, Maclean, and that at first he had no idea of going to Russia, merely intending to get Maclean safely as far as

Prague. He went on to Moscow only because it was more convenient. She said she feared that if he once left Russia they would not allow him back there, for he now evidently regarded the U.S.S.R. as his spiritual home.

Guy wrote generously about Goronwy Rees's hostile articles in the *People*,[55] and said he bore him no resentment. Perhaps he had been trapped by the press or driven to write the articles through penury. 'I was very proud that Rosamond Lehmann wrote to my mother saying she had told him that the one person who might not be too angry with him was Guy.' As for Nigel, he had little sympathy with him for having taken a right-wing seat like Bournemouth. He wrote about the young men of England, and of Russia. He could not understand why the former were not more angry with the social conditions prevailing in their country. The latter were buoyed up by a mutual spirit of Marxist optimism. There was general optimism in Russia, unlike the West. His first letters showed his own morale to be high, for he was engaged in semi-public activities, the precise nature of which he could not specify. (He was in fact working for the foreign department of the State Publishing House.) At least he was in a position to assure the authorities that Macmillan was a man of some originality and imagination, who was prepared and possibly able to promote détente. His work gave him the illusion of doing something useful in the perilous days they were living through. Later letters referred to enforced inactivity owing to angina pectoris. One was written from a sanatorium in the park of Prince Youssopoff's Archangelsk, fifteen miles from Moscow, where he was undergoing a cure for arterio-schlerosis, ulcers, and arthritis. He had seen Graham Greene and Stephen Spender, whom he had forgiven for turning against him. On learning that James Pope-Hennessy was broke he sent him a cheque, begging him to dine out on it, provided he invited no Indonesians or Fascists.

Harold's last letter of the series to Guy Burgess was written on the 30th May 1962, three days before Vita's death.

No letter would embarrass me [he assured him] or put me in an awkward position. I am out of politics and I am NOT a crypto-communist. It is merely that I think I understand your point of view, that I miss you much, that I have a deep respect for you, and that people here know enough about me to feel confident that I should not bat against my own side . . . All I care about is that you should not be exposed to unfounded suspicions and that you should be allowed to follow your Slavic bent without opposition.

Harold's 'respect' for Guy Burgess amounted to his brain and the courage of his convictions. He had no respect for those convictions. But his loyalty to his friend was unwavering. Nothing a person, who had once been a friend, could do, however offensive, erased in Harold's sentimental mind the memory of that friend when he had first known and been attracted to him. To Harold the drink-sodden, crapulous traitor which Guy Burgess had become, remained in his vision the bright-eyed, fresh-looking, brilliant and promising youth of the very early thirties.

Harold had now reached the age when academic honours fell thick and fast upon him. In October he was made an Associate of the New York Academy of Literature, and in December presented with his diploma by the American Ambassador. He was also accorded a decoration – *Das Grosse Verdienstkreuz mit Stern* – by the Republic of Germany, at the instigation of Chancellor Adenauer himself. When Konrad Adenauer had been in London in April he attended a party at Lancaster House. An official looked for Harold who was present and told him that the Chancellor wished to speak with him. Harold found a mask-like face with two piercing blue eyes and butterfly lips, in deep conversation with the French Ambassador. He could see that the ex-Mayor of Cologne had not the least idea who he was. So he reminded him of their first encounter in Cologne in 1929; whereupon they chatted amicably in German.[56] On the 15th October he was summoned to the German Embassy. He went by taxi. The taxi-driver was puzzled by his reception at the front door by a secretary bowing low. Harold was conducted to the Ambassador's study and left alone with him. He engaged His Excellency in conversation, only to be cut short. The Ambassador announced that he must make an allocution and present him with a *Verleihungsurkunde*. He then embarked upon a short, well worded speech, saying that if it had not been for men like Harold Nicolson who had taught our countrymen that good Germans existed, the visit of the Bundes President Theodor Heuss would have been impossible. He handed Harold a blue case with a star and order, and a portfolio, containing the *Verleihungsurkunde*. Harold expressed his thanks. They sat down. The Ambassador offered him champagne which he declined, and then a glass of Moselwein, which he accepted.[57] Chancellor Adenauer sent him a telegram of congratulation. Having dined at the Beefsteak Harold put on dress clothes with his new cross and ribbons and walked to a reception at Lancaster House, where he was presented to President Heuss, 'a nice man in spite of the fact that his hands were steeped in the blood of innocents'.[58]

The question whether or not Weidenfeld & Nicolson should publish Vladimir Nabokov's novel *Lolita* caused a great upheaval in the Nicolson family. Harold considered the book obscene. He told Nigel that he was all for works of true literature being published even if they contained obscene passages. But he was strongly opposed to the publication of this one, because it was definitely liable to corrupt. He consulted Raymond Mortimer, who while considering the book to be a work of literature, which told a cautionary tale, nevertheless feared the British public would regard it as corrupting. In these circumstances he, Raymond, also thought it a mistake for Weidenfeld & Nicolson to publish it at that moment. Nigel's argument was that *Lolita* had been pronounced a work of literature by numerous distinguished authors already, and had been published in France, Italy and Germany. To withdraw publication now would mean breaking a contract and antagonising all those persons who had supported his firm in its desire to publish. But, urged by both his parents, he told Weidenfeld that unless he submitted it to a test case before the Director of Public Prosecutions he would be obliged to resign from the firm. Harold weighed in by writing to Weidenfeld begging him to abandon publication of what he and Vita both considered a book whose obscenity outweighed its literary merits. He got J. B. Priestley and Jacquetta Hawkes to support his plea. Its publication would not only ruin Nigel's chances of being returned to Parliament, but would undoubtedly ruin the reputation of the firm. Harold worked himself up into such a state of worry and concern that he seriously thought of putting off his and Vita's January cruise to Japan. He could not understand why Nigel had so little judgment concerning his own future.

The Board of Weidenfeld & Nicolson however had no intention of paying heed to the warnings and threats of Harold, Vita, and their confederates. Besides, the Director of Public Prosecutions, having been sent an advance copy of *Lolita*, decided not to prosecute. The book was duly published, and the first edition of 40,000 was sold out before publication day.

In the *Lolita* case Harold was allowing the discretion of age to overcome the tolerance of youth. It is very doubtful whether twenty-five years earlier he would have adopted so cautious and recalcitrant an attitude. His true reason was patently a parental concern about Nigel's parliamentary future. He was loth for his younger son to give up politics and was terrified of any step which might lessen his chances of obtaining an alternative seat to Bournemouth East. For the same reason Harold was opposed to Nigel supporting the recommendations of the Wolfenden Report, which advocated tolerance of homosexual acts between consenting adults. It is inconceivable that he of all enlightened men would, in ordinary circumstances, not have wished to press for the Wolfenden recommendations to become law. [59]

On the 4th December Harold met Igor Stravinsky at a luncheon party. The composer told him how Rimsky-Korsakov spotted his talent when he was a young student in St. Petersburg, and advised him by no means to go to the Conservatoire there, for it was too academic. Harold 'swelled with pride' when Stravinsky praised *Some People* and *Lord Carnock*, which he pronounced his best book. The composer admired, above all things, technique, and he considered Harold's superb. He said how much he envied writers whose work was finished as soon as their books were published, whereas composers had to suffer interpretations of their compositions often entirely different from what they had written or intended. [60]

Just before Christmas Vita had a slight heart attack when she got up in the morning. The doctor was sent for. He was not alarmed, but insisted that she should regularly take digitalis. On the 5th January husband and wife set off on their third winter cruise, this time to Japan. On leaving Boulogne by train Harold waved from the dining-car. Vita asked him whom he was waving to. He explained that he was greeting Sainte-Beuve, at which the waiter who was serving them, smiled approvingly. Harold was delighted. What English waiter, he asked Vita, would understand a similar salutation made to Wordsworth. [61] At Marseilles they boarded the French ship, *Cambodge*, and sailed across the Mediterranean. While cruising off Crete Harold began writing chapter 1 of *The Age of Reason* on Saint-Simon, Louis XIV and the first stages of the War of the Spanish Succession. From Port Said, which, when Harold last visited it, was still thoroughly oriental, the men wearing turban or tarboosh (instead of the ubiquitous cloth cap), they made their way leisurely through the Suez Canal, and down the Red Sea to Aden. There the Governor's A.D.C., 'tall, slim, and golden-haired, with long fair eyelashes and wide shoulders tapering to a girdled waist,' by name Richard Head, son of Anthony Head, late Secretary of State for War, met them. Exquisitely polite and 'beautifully U', he drove them round the rock of pumice stone and into what was called The Crater, where the old city basked among dry rocks.[62] Until they reached Colombo Vita was suffering from liver which made her sleepy and unable to write. She then recovered and Harold suspected, without knowing, for she did not tell him, that she was beginning a novel. It was to be *No Signposts in the Sea*, her last. In the harbour at Colombo Philip Magnus-Allcroft, who with his wife was with them again, fell into the sea just where the town drain emerged. He was fished out unscathed.

In the company of the Magnus-Allcrofts, who were good travelling companions, and Michael Pitt-Rivers and his wife Sonia, the Nicolsons were happy. They found Michael charming, but could not for a time decide whether Sonia was a county magnate, a 1959 intellectual, or just Bal Musette. They regretted the Pitt-Riverses' departure at Saigon. Harold enjoyed the cruise more than the last (which was overshadowed by anxiety about Vita's health) in spite of his loathing for Japan. He was enchanted with Manila, Macao and Hong Kong, and the glimpse they had of China. From Manila he wrote to Nigel:

> The Philipinos have the most wonderful skin I have ever seen, torsos the colour of apricots. But the faces that surmount these wonderful busts consist of monkey features and grinning teeth encrusted with gold. *O formose puer nimium ne crede colori.*[63]

They drove to Macao, where Harold admired the contrast between the Portuguese churches with Baroque plasterwork, and the Chinese shop-signs. Hong Kong he found superb, like a string of Scotch lochs with high Chinese mountains across the bay.

When they got to Tokyo they were greeted on board by Harold's old friend, Dan Lascelles. The shy, solemn youth, who had joined the Berlin staff when Harold was Minister in 1928, had risen to being Ambassador to Japan. He drove them to the Embassy. He showed them beautiful sketches he had done of Afghanistan. They delighted in the company of this gifted, clever and lovable man.[64]. Had it not been for the Embassy, Japan would have been hell on earth. It struck Harold as the ugliest country he had ever visited, strewn with ramshackle industrial suburbs and pullulating with yellow, be-spectacled, jabbering monkeys. Kobe joined up with Osaka in a string of factories, oil-tanks, pylons, telegraph poles, electric cables, slung along a line of grey cement, and factories interspersed with shacks.[65] It was an abominable example of once beautiful scenery ruined by over-population. As for the famous temples and gardens of Kyoto they recalled those horrible temporary Japanese pavilions to be seen at exhibitions. Harold's disparaging view of Japan and its inhabitants was largely coloured by recollections of their barbarous treatment of our prisoners during the war. And he was not the least chastened when on his return Raymond Mortimer and Richard Rumbold rebuked him for making no endeavour to appreciate the mysticism of the Japanese. It was no good. His prejudice against them was irredeemable. And when he dined at the Japanese Embassy in London in November his revulsion from everything Japanese rose again within him.

The Embassy is horrible. White Victorian drawing-rooms with a few kakemonos of bad quality and little Louis XV side-tables bearing ikkibani[66] – a bronze chrysanthemum twisted all alone around a sham pink coral branch. Then we had dinner. The Embassy women were in kimonos and we were given chopsticks. I sat between the Yugoslav Ambassadress and the wife of an M.P. They used their chopsticks but Hadji knew that these bits of wood were not designed for him, and took a spoon. We were given hors d'oeuvres, thin slabs of raw ham accompanied by sharks' fins dried, desiccated seaweed, and the tonsils of penguins. This was accompanied by warm saki. I was cautious.

'La divine Saki, c'est ça qui
Me fait rêver à la lune.'
Then came soup with soya beans and scampi and minced chicken with enormous mushrooms and Japanese tea. I imagine it was Japanese cooking at its very best but I found it repulsive.[67]

He was violently sick during the night.

There were two things which disturbed the serenity of this cruise. One was Nigel's perpetuating trouble in Bournemouth East, news of which reached Harold by letter and cablegram. The Conservative candidate elected to succeed Nigel resigned. The papers were full of the news and pursued Nigel relentlessly. He felt, and was, absolutely guiltless of any indiscretion over the *Lolita* issue, whereas his father pretended to feel acute embarrassment. He wrote to Elvira Niggeman: 'I used to smile at little girls and pat them on the head as I passed, in avuncular benevolence. Now I dread to do so lest mothers suspect the worst.'[68] Comedy was introduced to the row raging by an announcement from Randolph Churchill that he would submit his name as a successor to Nigel. A brilliant cartoon by Vicky appeared in the *Evening Standard* of Randolph bursting into the Committee Room at Bournemouth East and saying to a group of blimps, 'I hear you are looking for a nice, solid, dependable candidate'. This piece of impertinence delighted Harold when it reached him in Bombay, because he knew Randolph to have been far more vehement against Eden over Suez than Nigel. To add to the discomfiture and embarrassment of the local Conservative Association Randolph declared that Nigel was an excellent M.P. whom, if still a candidate, he would not have dreamed of opposing. The Conservative Party chairman, Lord Hailsham, was called upon to resolve the dilemma. He persuaded the Association to hold a postal ballot to decide once and for all whether they wanted to keep Nigel, or not. The votes were counted on the 27th February and Harold learned by cable that his son had been defeated. In a dignified letter Nigel asked the Association whether they would like him to retire forthwith, or wait until the General Election. He was asked to remain until the General Election.

The second thing to worry Harold was an episode which he feared might further prejudice Nigel's reputation, although it happened after the ballot was closed. In Colombo on the 25th he was met on arrival by a Ceylonese newspaper reporter. The man discussed with him the information that Guy Burgess was applying to the Prime Minister for permission to visit England to see his ill mother. Burgess had quoted Harold as the only friend who had consistently corresponded with him. Could Harold confirm that this was true? He did confirm it. There was nothing else he could say. He added that he had felt sorry for Guy who had acted on impulse, and it was his policy never to desert his friends in distress. But he had never written him one word which he would be ashamed to see quoted in a newspaper. Of course Harold feared that this revelation would make other Conservative Associations hesitate to adopt Nigel. 'What gremlins dog his every step – *Lolita*, and now his father!' He was so upset when he got to his cabin that he was sick.[69] As it turned out Harold's admission caused no sensation.

Vita, who adored her dogs with a deep tenderness that did not always animate her relations with human beings, other than her immediate family and those women she happened to love, was greatly distressed to receive a letter announcing that her Alsatian 'Rollo' had had to be put down. She showed no outward emotion, but retired to her cabin and wept. Soon after their return to England she developed a high temperature of 103° with fever. She thought it was influenza, but blood tests declared it to be pneumonia virus. It was indeed the form of cancer, then undetected, from which she eventually died. For eight weeks she remained in bed, feeling rotten. Harold was perplexed and wretched. It was not until October that he began to suspect her temperatures meant something worse than recurrent bouts of fever. He resented being proffered contradictory advice by Vita's women-friends who scolded him for letting people visit her in bed. He was fully aware how incompetent a nurse he was. Nonetheless, 'I do so hate all this jealousy and crinkum crankum', he told her. 'All these women loathe each other'.[70] Vita on the other hand maintained that jealousy was the symptom and concomitant of true love. Fortunately Ursula Codrington took up residence at Sissinghurst in June, partly as secretary, partly as companion to Vita and Harold. Her tact, discretion and gentle manner endeared her to them both. She was able to act as a wardress in lamb's clothing by keeping at bay the streams of friends who came to see the garden. By now the reputation of the Sissinghurst garden was so widespread that the number of daily visitors was enormous.

Both Harold and Vita positively enjoyed the public sharing the garden with them. They liked the paying visitors, who behaved well and were little trouble. They were known as the 'shillings' because this was the sum they were asked to put into a box kept unguarded at the entrance. It was friends, acquaintances and friends of acquaintances who could be a nuisance in demanding to see them, or waylaying them as they crossed from one building to another. Strangers were seldom intrusive, and those who addressed them could always be dismissed politely and without ceremony.

A stroke of fortune additional to Ursula Codrington's installation at Sissinghurst during this period of decline in Vita's health was the arrival of two ladies to whom Vita had offered the post of gardeners. Pamela Schwerdt and Sibylle Kreutzberger (to be known affectionately as the 'Mädchen') were (and are) friends who had studied at Waterperry Horticultural School. The latter, whose father was private secretary to the Governor of Newfoundland, passed out top of her year when she got her diploma. Both were determined to become gardeners of first-class distinction. They succeeded. After two and a half years of learning Vita's ways and tastes in planting, and of understanding Harold's methods of landscape design, they have to this day continued to run the garden at Sissinghurst on the lines laid down by its creators, and miraculously to keep it up to the standard imposed by them. Moreover the friends' intelligence, enthusiasm and gift for growing plants greatly helped to keep alive Vita's flagging interest in the garden during her last years.

Harold attended a party given by the publishers George Allen & Unwin to celebrate the issue of James Pope-Hennessy's *Queen Mary*.

The Princess Royal and the Duke and Duchess of Gloucester were present. Sir Stanley Unwin made a speech, declaring that in all his years of publishing he had never produced a better book. James then read a speech which was modest and moderate. He was presented with a statuette of the Duke of Clarence with which he was delighted. The occasion was the highlight of his literary career.

On the afternoon of Boxing Day members of the Columbia Broadcasting System arrived at Sissinghurst in vans, in the shape of a producer, electricians, trunks, cameras, lamps and suitcases. They took over and established themselves in the kitchen, the dining-room and the store-cupboard. From 5 until 9 o'clock they made Harold sit upright in a chair with lights blazing in his eyes. In extreme discomfort and heat he had to give an impromptu talk on the functions of diplomacy, straining to hear his interlocutors, Edward Murrow in St. Moritz, Mrs. Luce in Los Angeles and Chip Bohlen in New York. He did not even see their faces, for the television pictures were pieced together later. The experience was a taxing one. Vita could not contain her indignation. She flew into a rage and abused all concerned for their callous treatment of Harold. She felt he had been exploited, put upon and possibly made a fool of.[71] Moreover they had disarranged the whole dining-room and dared to move her dining-table.

On the 28th December the Nicolsons departed for the Cape. They crossed to Calais and took the train for Venice. Once again Harold had the thrill of waking up the following morning, of raising the blind of his sleeper to see bright sunlight sweeping obliquely across the Lombardy plain. In Venice they were met by Freya Stark and conducted by her in the *vaporetto* to the Hotel Monaco. Venice was wrapped in fog, and the landing stage of the hotel looked like a description by Dickens of Wapping Stairs.

In spite of the favourable opinion they had formed of one another on their first meeting at the Junior Constitutional Club dinner in 1938 when he spoke against Chamberlain's policy, Harold had since then taken against Miss Stark. Meeting her at a party given at John Murray's in 1943 he had been annoyed by her desire to give back to Italy everything that country had lost beyond its borders, and by her complaints about the inconsiderate way the freed Italians were being treated. Whereas he, like her, loved Italy he had little sympathy with Italy's behaviour since the war. She was behaving as though she had been our ally, but in reality she was a defeated enemy. He, on the contrary, would like to deprive her of all her acquired territories. And now seventeen years later Miss Stark was still taking upon herself the role of Italy's aggrieved champion.

From Venice the Nicolsons sailed to Brindisi on the Lloyd-Triestino liner *Europa*. It was a lovely boat. It was air-conditioned. The food was excellent, and their cabins were admirably equipped for writing books, – Vita's *No Signposts in the Sea*[72] and Harold's *The Age of Reason*. They sailed through the Suez Canal, down the East Coast of Africa to Zanzibar, Durban and Cape Town. They both felt well, worked hard and enjoyed themselves.

In Zanzibar they took a rickshaw and were pulled by an ancient bent man, and pushed from behind by his slightly less ancient son. They were pleased with the picturesque, narrow streets, the Moorish-looking houses and the flowering shrubs and trees. In South Africa, which they both hated, they were appalled by overt signs everywhere of *apartheid*. It was far, far worse than anything they had supposed. Even the Tory Vita was roused to indignation by the seats marked, 'For Whites Only,' and the counters in the Post Office for whites and blacks respectively. 'My God'! Harold wrote to Nigel, 'I am glad I don't live in this country! A pall of non-conformist brutality hangs in the air. It is like the Massachusetts Bay Co. of 1750, when they burnt witches in the High Street. Dotty and Lady Ottoline Morrell would not have stood a chance'.[73] And when, just after they left, Macmillan made his courageous statement in the Cape Town Legislature of his disapproval of the South Africans' racial policy, he was delighted. On the other hand, when on the return journey they stopped at Mogadishu and were told by travellers coming aboard of the extreme poverty of Italian Somaliland, the corruption, cruelty and utter incapacity of the people to govern themselves, Harold was perplexed. What was the alternative to shooting natives for disobedience? Giving them independence and allowing the country to subside into successive dictatorships, revolutions and chaos.

Retracing their way home through Italy they stayed with Freya Stark in Asolo. They got back to England on the 19th, Vita to be visited by a slight attack of her virus temperature and Harold to be confronted with a demand of £1500 for super-tax.

Elvira warned Harold that he was practically penniless because of taxation and his profligate extravagance. He was worried but decided that he could not economise. How could he? He was not made that way. He could not possibly give up entertaining his friends to luncheon and dinner at expensive restaurants, which was where most of his earnings went. He did not overlook the fact that he had luxurious rooms in Albany in the heart of London and a first-rate secretary, both of which, to put it mildly, were not absolute necessities for a man no longer in Parliament or public life. He thought he would have to make money by writing a book for some rich City Company which would bring him a fee of £5,000 to enable him to live comfortably for three more years. 'It is sad to become poorer in one's old age when the energy to earn money has declined',[74] he complained. Vita as usual offered him money; and as usual he refused to accept it. So he confided his awkward predicament to the resourceful Nigel who had become, as it were, an elder brother and adviser in place of a younger son. Nigel instantly went to George Weidenfeld's office and returned with a proposition that his father should write a book about Monarchy on outstanding terms. Thus Harold's dread of having to leave Albany and lose Elvira Niggeman was averted. As though to celebrate this merciful solution of his financial stringency he promptly took to Christie's his precious copy of Moore's *Life of Byron*, which had belonged to and been annotated by John Cam Hobhouse, a book he greatly prized, to help raise funds for the London Library. In a May sale it fetched £600, a sum of money he could have done very well with himself. When Vita got to hear of the arrangement with Weidenfeld she again begged Harold not to be proud, and to accept £5,000 from her rather than be under an obligation to write a book which he could not possibly want to tackle. She knew he wanted to write about Goethe. But Harold also knew that he was no longer up to writing a book about Goethe, whereas he could without much strain or study rattle off a book on monarchy. He was beginning to feel tired and slack. He feared it was a portent of worse physical decline. Vita came upon him in the middle of one day sitting on the catalpa bench at Sissinghurst with a Penguin book in his hand, which was a very unusual thing for him to be doing. A few days later he lost his balance and tumbled into the moat. He was fished out by a passing 'shilling', and although his clothes were soaked, he came to no harm.

Yet he was restless. He had to be occupied. He attended a party in Carlyle's house, Chelsea, given for the journalists to whom he explained how the National Trust had re-arranged the house as nearly as possible in the way Thomas and Jane knew it during their long tenure. He went to Oxford with Kenneth Rose for the election of the University Chancellor and, in a cap and gown borrowed from John Sparrow, walked to the Divinity Schools to vote for Harold Macmillan. Afterwards he sat in the Garden Quad at Balliol, observing the heavily bearded undergraduates.[75] He went to see Robin Maugham who was recovering in St. Mary's Hospital, Paddington, from a ghastly experience in the Agadir earthquake. One foot was crushed, a rib was broken and he was covered with abrasions, besides suffering from shock after being buried for many hours at the bottom of a demolished hotel. Harold dined at the American Embassy with the Whitneys. The Queen Mother and the Macmillans were present. Lady Dorothy Macmillan told him that when they were staying at Rambouillet with the French President there was a superb chef and about fifty servants wearing silver chains. But there was no soap in their bedrooms which were so cold that they had to sleep in their woollies. She asked Madame de Gaulle if there was any place she would like to be taken to on her state visit to London, and was told that she only wanted to shop at Gorringe's. Making conversation with her was like digging at clay.

Again that autumn Vita was scolding Harold for making a long train journey to Manchester, speaking at a luncheon, giving a television interview, going to a film the same evening, and returning the next morning. It was too much for him. He was driving himself to death. But he could not stop – yet.

He always delighted at being asked for his advice which, on any other subject than finance, was usually sound. When Sir Michael Adeane, the Queen's Private Secretary, appealed to him to recommend the name of a writer worthy of the award of the O.M. he answered that no one in the literary world was worthy, and it would be better to give it a miss. Adeane protested that the Palace would then be criticised for neglecting literature. He put forward the name of Edith Sitwell. Harold consulted Vita who, much as she admired Edith, did not think she had the stature. Having ruled out a list of other poets and writers she gave Kenneth Clark as her nominee.[76] Harold told her that in consequence of their veto Adeane had cut out Edith Sitwell's name, which now made him feel guilty. But Raymond Mortimer agreed with them, so they were not alone in their cruelty.

On the 28th May Harold received a letter from the French Ambassador informing him that his Government wished to elevate him to the dignity of Commander of the Legion of Honour.

Cette promotion vous est accordée en récompense de votre intérêt pour les lettres françaises et de votre inportante contribution à la formation et l'orientation d'un large public dans l'immense variété de notre littérature.

In July he went to a party at the French Embassy, accompanied by Sir Anthony Blunt. On the way Blunt told him that he had been informed by M.I.5 that if Guy Burgess returned to England he would be arrested. There would be a trial at which Blunt would be chief witness, since he had lived with Guy for months. He would lose his job as Surveyor of the Queen's Pictures, and possibly his job at the Courtauld Institute. So he had conveyed to Guy that he must not return.[77] After a stiff little luncheon at the Embassy Gérard André, the Minister and a friend of Harold, handed the Ambassador a small box. The Ambassador put on what Harold described as 'un visage de circonstance' and made a short allocution. He hung over Harold's bowed neck a scarlet ribbon and cross. Harold then said a few words of gratitude, took off the ribbon and put on the button, which was the same as the one worn by the Ambassador, being of the grander sort. There followed champagne and toasts.

Towards the end of the month Vita's virus pneumonia returned in worse measure than before. Her temperature fluctuated alarmingly. The antibiotics she was obliged to take had a depressing effect. She would get up for luncheon, return to bed in the afternoon, and again after tea. She felt perpetually tired. The doctor pronounced her heart to be strained, but her lungs to be all right. He said she was much better than she thought, which infuriated her. But Harold was anxious as she became what he called increasingly muddly and muzzy.

Nothing gave Harold more pleasure than to be entertained by his young friends. It made him feel, like Dr. Johnson, a dog. One evening he was motored in a bubble-car to Christopher Gibbs's flat overlooking St. Paul's. Simon Fleet and Martin Newall were present. The room they ate in was exactly like Chatterton's garret. The occasion was all laughter, drink and fun. He had the word 'beatnik' explained to him for the first time. At least these young friends did not mock him as a superannuated apostle of gracious living, a francophile, a dilettante, an upper-class snob with no social conscience, which *The Twentieth Century* was about to point out to be the opinion of contemporary writers. He was, according to that review, linked with Cyril Connolly and Raymond Mortimer as the three literary critics who only five years ago had been the recognised arbiters of taste. 'How the tables have turned,' the editor pontificated.[78] Harold was impenitent. He no longer needed to conceal – not that he ever did it very effectually – from Labour constituents that his origins were patrician and his values élitist. When an American television crew interviewed him for a feature they were doing on Piccadilly they asked him if he did 'not feel embarrassed by the fact that the porters here [in Albany] wear tail-coats and top-hats'. His reply cannot have been what they expected.

I said that I should feel much more embarrassed if they didn't, since people might mistake me for a porter on the way out. I could see that they thought me very snobbish and old-fashioned. They asked whether Albany was not 'a privileged sanctuary'. I said, Yes, it was. I added that highly developed civilisations specialise in variety, whereas lower civilizations impose uniformity. That was not a welcome remark.[79]

Cant was never an escape-route to which Harold Nicolson would resort. Besides, he honestly believed that the artistocracy of the intellect had now become open to all men and women. It was up to their abilities and inclinations. One such member of this sacred élite was Aneurin Bevan, who to nearly all Tories was anathema because of his extreme left-wing views and his manner of expressing them in the most offensive terms he could muster. Nevertheless he was an intellectual, and this is what Harold respected in him. When his death in July was announced Harold was very sorry. 'He was a sensitive man with tender instincts in spite of his violence. He was a patriot in the best sense of the term and would have made an excellent Foreign Secretary.'[80] Patriotism redeemed almost any man, however opposed his views were to Harold's liberal convictions. What he could not stomach was the leftist intellectual who worked counter to the interests of his country, and who nurtured international ideals which were subversive and impractical. Such a person was not merely evil, but stupid. And stupidity was the unforgiveable sin.

The death of friends was sad enough; but what was sadder was the decline of those who went on living. John Hugh Smith the banker had become as deaf as a post. Ava Waverley was as blind as a bat. Clive Bell's physical infirmities were catching up on his gay spirits. When Clive received a letter from Harold who said that he did not yet walk on two sticks, he took comfort. 'So strengthened I decided to behave as though I were young and healthy, albeit I am nothing of the sort,' Clive told Frances Partridge.[81] Perhaps the worst of all the disabilities, in Harold's opinion, was that of becoming a bore, like poor Bruce Lockhart. 'I shall get like that about November 1962,' he wrote. He was nothing if not precise. 'Meanwhile I remain a bright bird.'[82]

★　　★　　★　　★

The speed with which Harold used to write his books (other than *King George V*, which was a mammoth and laborious task) and with which his publishers used to produce them was past. He began *The Age of Reason* in March 1958, and it was published in December 1960. As usual Harold, on finishing it, was dissatisfied. 'It is a rotten book and it saddens me,' he wrote; and again, 'I fear it is very dull, and so second-hand that it is second-rate. Decline and fall that's what it is.' On the other hand his American publishers on receiving the manuscript cabled to him, 'A wise and wonderful book.' And Vita, whom he asked to read the first batch of proofs, was entranced with its immense learning and lucidity.

It was not however a very profound study of eighteenth-century political, social and philosophical thought. It made no new discoveries, gave no startling insights. In the Author's Note Harold admitted that the book was 'not intended to be a work of historical research or reference, but to contain portraits of individuals and an account of changing states of mind'. And this it does admirably. It is well constructed, and nicely inductive. It is extremely readable and informative. It contains some vivid exposures of human foibles and frailties, with witty comments, so characteristic of Harold's best writing. It contains some thumb-nail sketches of individuals which are brilliant. A characteristic passage is the succinct description in three lines of Diderot's mistress, Sophie Volland:

who was no longer young, who suffered atrociously from indigestion, who wore spectacles, was something of a blue-stocking and whose ankles swelled most mornings and most afternoons.

But the book shows signs of falling off in some factual inaccuracies and repetitions. And it abounds in printing slips and careless corrections. At least 200 misprints were at once spotted by Raymond Mortimer who drew attention to them in a *Sunday Times* review. Harold thought his old friend 'a bit loony' to concentrate quite so severely on small mistakes, which the American reviewers would pick up so as to cause sales in that continent to drop. Vita was less charitable about 'that idiot Tray, [Raymond] who would himself be incapable of writing a single paragraph of it'.[83] Unfortunately the *Times* reviewer picked on the same quantity of misprints and misspellings. At least he saw method in the author's attractive casual approach to his subject in that it quickened appreciation of a complex and sometimes self-contradictory phase of history. The B.B.C. critics on the other hand saw little in the book that they did not know already. They found it shallow and written down to the author's readers. Indeed they questioned whether the author had any readers in mind at all when he wrote it.

THE END OF A PARTNERSHIP, 1961–1962

THE year 1961 was for Harold a year of waning powers. For Vita it was one of recovery. She had no ostensible illness, and her novel *No Signposts in the Sea* had a good reception from the critics and the reading public. On the 8th January the two of them embarked at Genoa on an Italian liner, *Augustus*, on their fifth successive cruise. They sailed to South America, calling at Barcelona, Lisbon, Rio de Janeiro, Buenos Aires and Montevideo. Again the Magnus-Allcrofts were on board. Harold made good-natured but teasing references to them – how Sir Philip left his and his wife's passports in their hotel bedroom, and Lady Magnus-Allcroft, on leaving Paris, got wedged in the train-corridor on the way from sleeper to dining-car.

Harold told his friend Lady Alexandra Metcalfe[1] that he and Vita both disliked stopping at harbours. Boats had a distressing habit of lingering for several hours tied up to docks. 'Who wants to see Buenos Aires, or Santos or Monte Video? I admit that Rio is worth a passing glance.' In fact he told Nigel[2] that Rio was more fantastically beautiful than anything he had supposed. Great sugar loafs covered with jungle trees soared out of the lapis water, each crowned with a megalithic statue of Christ dressed in day clothes as worn in Galilee in 20 A.D. The Botanic Gardens there had huge palms as beautiful and tall as Juliet Duff with a fountain in the centre tinkling merrily, the haunt of butterflies and birds. Buenos Aires, he told Elvira Niggeman,[3] was hell on earth. 'Ugly French houses of the 1900 period alternating the Coca Cola sky-scrapers. The Argentines are beastly and rude.' They wanted to confiscate Vita's camera. The press wanted to know what C.H. meant; and one member wrote against Vita's name, 'Maid of Honour to H.M. The Queen'.

Everywhere they landed they were entertained with kindness by British Ambassadors who had been forewarned of their arrival. They were given luncheon in cool embassies and driven in comfortable Rolls Royces to see the principal sights. 'Vita is less nervous in a Rolls Royce than in other cars.'[4] She found the long Atlantic cruise monotonous, missing the islands and creeks of the coastline. But she made progress with a little illustrated book about dogs, called *Faces*, which was to be the last she wrote.

During the voyage they were handed a marconigram announcing the death of Anne Sackville, the American-born wife of Vita's Uncle Charlie. Although sorry for Uncle Charlie they could not pretend to mind. 'She was an unloved woman. Her death simplifies many things – jointures, legacies and turning her out of Knole,'[5] had she survived her husband. It also led to Vita re-visiting Knole after a thirty-year interval. She felt as though her beloved home had returned to the Sackvilles once again after an occupation by an enemy alien. 'It is like the light beginning to appear at the end of a long black tunnel of exile. I have minded it all so much,' she wrote.[6] What excited her was a scheme that Nigel and Philippa might dispose of their present house in Hampshire and rent the Kennels at Knole. 'I should love to think of Juliet and Adam getting to know the Park and the garden, as I knew them myself as a Mar.'

In late March Vita made her first visit to Knole. It was an emotional return. She went with trepidation. She went prepared to disapprove of changes. Although she enjoyed her luncheon with Uncle Charlie, she was critical of what the National Trust had done.

> Someone has re-arranged the furniture in the Brown Gallery disastrously; also re-hung some pictures. The furniture in the Venetian Room is simply awful; the green velvet hangings and coverings much improved; but the gilding terrible and might have come straight from Waring & Gillow.[7]

Alas, I was doubtless partially the culprit for the alterations she deplored. In those days I was the National Trust's Adviser on Historic Buildings. I had been responsible for conducting on the Trust's behalf the tricky negotiations over the transfer of Knole. On the change of ownership of the great house and its precious contents, much repair-work to house and collections was necessary. Furthermore increasing numbers of visitors necessitated certain re-arrangements of furniture to allow the public to pass along the narrow galleries. And whenever repairs and changes had to be carried out Vita, who after all was not the incumbent, was kept informed and her approval sought. Lord Sackville was always the easiest and most complacent of donors. But Vita's special relationship with Knole made her extremely sensitive, and her resentment of the slightest change was understandable. Her next visit in July with Harold was a great success. She found Knole more beautiful than ever, and left it feeling deeply happy with the outcome of events, and the great house's salvation.

But Vita had reached that stage of life when women, in particular, are consumed with worries. If it was not one thing it was another. If it was not the re-gilding of the furniture in the Venetian Ambassador's Room at Knole, it was the forthcoming operation Harold had to undergo for the removal of a sebaceous cyst between the shoulders. The cyst was removed, and the wound healed satisfactorily. Next, precious Mrs. Staples had to have her gall-bladder taken out. Harold watched Vita, an image of acute anxiety, sitting in the porch waiting for the ambulance to arrive, with a little nosegay in one hand and the *Chanson de Roland*, which she was reading, in the other. And then came her sixty-ninth birthday.

> The black day will come when we are parted from each other [Harold wrote to her[8]] . . . Human love is all too mysterious for words. It IS a mystery. But I find myself thinking of you all the time and I realise that what is now a spasm of pleasure will become a stab of pain if we are separated.

On the 10th March Elvira met Harold in the Rope Walk of Albany. She told him that the press had been bothering her all the afternoon. About what? He had a premonition. 'Mr. Rumbold?' he asked. 'What had happened to him?' 'He is dead,' she said. He had always feared Richard would take his own life. His mother had done so. And his sister. And now he had thrown himself out of a hotel window in Palermo through the glass roof of a courtyard into the lounge below.

> That bloody Roman Catholic Church [Harold told Vita[9]] wouldn't let Richard go to Confession or Communion while he was in Sicily; and he went to Mass every day. The priest evidently knew of the interdict. This caused Richard to think he was being persecuted. Then he got the idea that his pscyhoanalyst had turned against him. He kept murmuring, 'Dr. Glover has ruined my life.'

Harold was more moved by the tragic end of this gifted, courageous, loveable and unbalanced man than he had been by the deaths of other younger friends who had meant more to him. For a very long time Richard had been more a worry than a pleasure. And although always devoted to him, in spite of his extraordinarily tiresome behaviour, Harold had never been infatuated with him. On the contrary Richard had all his adult life been infatuated with Harold. He regarded him as a father-figure, the one anchor in the shifting sands of his emotions. And by the maddest processes, such as publishing a juvenile novel, *Little Victims*, in 1933, in which he parodied Harold in a damaging light, he thereby sought, as he explained it, to win his affection.[10]

At the end of the month Harold, accompanied by Raleigh Trevelyan and Michael Ricketts, drove in a Daimler-hire to Watton-on-Stone, near Ware, close to Woodhall Park, the splendid house in Hertfordshire which the original nabob Rumbold built for himself and his posterity in the eighteenth century. They reached the cemetery at noon.

We do not enter the church but go straight to the sloping cemetery where there are flowers and moss round a trench. Richard is in a very smart coffin with brass studs and handles. It makes me sick to think of that mangled body and those already putrefying limbs within that brass box. . . . They sprinkle holy water on the coffin from a little bottle. I do hate it so although the sun is shining. 'We thank thee, merciful Father.' My God, how could he impose such atrocious misery on so sweet a man!!! Then we drive back . . . I go to bed early as I feel as if I had been beaten with heavy wooden clubs.[11]

For several weeks Harold had horrid nightmares about Richard Rumbold's fate. It preyed on his mind. Vita realised that it upset him more than he was aware, and thought it was affecting his health. In early May he had a further warning, in that over the weekend he was quite unable to write. And then he fainted while eating asparagus. Henceforth he went in dread of passing out or being sick at a public dinner or reception.

In 1957 Harold had met Michael Ricketts, who was a friend of Richard Rumbold, their mutual interest being Zen Buddhism and psycho-analysis. Michael was an intelligent youth who had just left King's School, Canterbury, and was about to go up to Balliol. His younger brother Howard who was brought to a *Débotté*, became a firm favourite in C1 Albany. Unlike his brother he was a cheerful extravert. Already an expert on firearms Howard was writing a book on arms and armour for Weidenfeld & Nicolson. Kind as well as charming he volunteered to become a more or less permanent invigilator when Harold was sleeping in London. His youthful presence was just what was needed in Albany.

As for Harold's grandchildren, Juliet and Adam were hot sunshine to him. They were good-mannered and affectionate. When staying at Sissinghurst they would, on Harold's return from London, run across the lawns and fling their arms around him. They would clamber on to his knee and ask for stories of his naughtiness when he was a child. 'Tell us,' they would plead, 'the story of how you poured milk into a gentleman's hat.' Vita was no less responsive to them. And as for Ben's Vanessa, Vita was confident she would grow up to be pretty with an elusive charm all her own.

Love of poetry and fascination with poets remained with Harold throughout his life. If his early interest in French verse waned as the years passed, he read more in English. And the more he read the more absorbed he became in the men who produced these magical notes. What were they like? Byron – with whom he was 'in love' – he knew from the soles of his tortured feet to the topmost gray hair of his chestnut curls. Tennyson's melancholy and unconscious fraudulence intrigued him. Swinburne's vanity and sexual inhibitions repelled him. But then he had written books about all these three poets. He had not written about Shelley, whom in his mid-seventies he began to read with appreciation: Shelley who was the sensitive schoolboy's dream hero. He told Vita that had he known him he would have admired his personality, although he would not have been his sort of friend. He would have derived pleasure from meeting him, just as he did whenever he saw Stephen Spender. 'I like people whose eyes are bright and timid like the eyes of a deer.'[12] Coleridge mystified him, but he did not really care for men who were visionaries and retreated into worlds befugged by fumes of laudanum and the smoke of opium. He preferred the clear, undimmed eyes of poets who looked, not askance, but direct upon the natural beauties of the world. Nevertheless he enjoyed accompanying Kenneth Rose to the re-interment ceremony of Coleridge's remains beneath the nave of St. Michael's church at Highgate.[13] The Bishop of London entered with a crozier, embroidered cope and mitre. Coleridge's grandson, whom he described as an oily clergyman (he could never withhold a jibe at a clergyman of no matter what faith) read the first lesson. The head of the Bluecoat School, of which Coleridge was a famous son, read the second. The top forms were called Grecians, and the head boy had an immense Adam's apple which rose and fell like the piston of an engine. Harold was shocked that he could not pronounce the words, *how*, *now*, or *power*. Then John Masefield, in an Oxford gown, delivered an excellent address on Coleridge. After which came anthems which of all forms of music in Harold's estimation were the worst, for they never knew how to stop, and having got to the end started howling all over again.[14]

Tributes to poets of the sort accorded to Coleridge delighted him. He was always among the first to hang laurel-leaves upon their tombs. Thus he was moved by an account given him by a friend, Jimmy Smith,[15] of a recent pilgrimage to Rupert Brooke's grave. Smith had been cruising off Greece in a yacht. When the yacht got to Skyros the crew were surprised to find a British destroyer lying off the cape. The Lieutenant-Commander came on board the yacht and invited the party to attend a re-dedication of Rupert Brooke's tomb, which his crew had re-painted and re-furbished. The men having slung their hammocks among the surrounding olive trees had slept there all night. In the morning at dawn they held a service with hymns. Three or four Greek goat-herds gathered to watch. The sailors of course had no idea who Rupert Brooke was, but they were very reverent in commemorating the spirit of a dead English poet.[16]

Of living English poets Siegfried Sassoon was a favourite. He was also an old friend. In July he sat between Rupert Hart-Davis and Harold at a Garrick Club dinner. They talked about Tennyson and Swinburne, Matthew Arnold and Gosse. They talked about their mutual friend, Robbie Ross, whom they had all loved and who could rarely bring himself to speak of Oscar Wilde, so painful the subject was to him. Sassoon had a down on Edith Sitwell who, he said, was too conceited to be tolerated. In December he unveiled a plaque to Walter de la Mare in St. Paul's Cathedral crypt. He and Harold both lunched beforehand with Sir Alan Lascelles who arrayed Sassoon in his best funeral great-coat. It was so heavy that the poet complained it felt like a suit of armour. About 150 people were present. Sassoon, always abstracted, had to be reminded by the verger to pull the unveiling cord. He made an appropriate speech. As they left the Cathedral Harold said to him, 'You looked magnificent while you spoke – like a Homeric bard'.[17] Sassoon in driving Harold back along Fleet Street burst into a passionate denunciation of the book-market for having at Sotheby's bid £5,000 for the manuscripts of Ronald Firbank. 'That giggling dypsomaniac,' he shouted, 'just could not write. He was of no literary value whatever.'

On the 27th June Harold in his turn had to unveil a plaque in honour of an old friend and his two brave accomplices. The scene was the German Embassy; the heroes were Albrecht Bernstorff,[18] Herbert Mumm and Eduard Brücklmeir, three members of that Embassy who were prepared to face death rather than subscribe to a doctrine which they knew to be unworthy of their nation. In a short address Harold referred to the anguish which assailed survivors in deploring that the dead were unaware their sacrifices had not been in vain. What a solace it would be to the dead, could they only know that some of their relations and friends were gathered in the Embassy of a liberated and powerful Germany to do them honour.[19]

Once again Harold was in financial trouble. In July he was faced with paying £1,400 income tax over and above what he had estimated for, and had to sell out the £500 he had in premium bonds. Thus he was left with no money in the bank until he delivered his manuscript on Monarchy to Weidenfeld's. He felt like Marshal Foch at the Battle of the Marne – his centre menaced, his right wing encircled, and his left wing about to crumble – who boldly cried, 'J'attaque!' His method of attack was defiantly to go to a travel agent and book passages for himself and Vita for yet another winter cruise, this time to the Caribbean on S.S. *Antilles*. By now these annual voyages had become more than a luxury habit. He believed they were absolutely essential to the health and peace of mind of them both. Vita was of the same opinion and felt quite reckless about money. Be damned to caution and thrift! 'Let us enjoy ourselves while we may,' she wrote, 'before Time's winged chariot catches up on us.'[20] She immediately clinched with the travel agency, and they were committed. But how to find the money? Her income was adequate enough for living expenses and maintenance of the garden at Sissinghurst, but it was not so easy to raise capital for out-of-the-way extravagances. So she resorted to selling her manuscripts to America. On the 22nd July Constance Hammel of Chicago and a friend came down to Sissinghurst. There and then they agreed to buy Vita's manuscripts for £1,100 and promised her a further £1,500 for Virginia Woolf's letters to her. Vita was beside herself with delight, partly because she never dreamed that any of the manuscripts of 'my silly novels' would be worth so much as £1,100 – in the end Miss Hammel gave her £1,500 for them – and partly because the sum would pay for the *Antilles*. She strongly advised Harold to sell some of his. Even typed ones fetched their price, and his stocks were now high. Harold however did not like the idea of Vita's manuscripts going to America, or of Virginia's intimate letters being sold. He would have preferred the money to come from some anticipated legacy or book payment rather than from acquired cash, a means of raising the wind typical of the inveterate spendthrift. But he was touched that Vita was determined to pay for the cruise, largely on his account. Certainly her attitude to the sale of Virginia's letters was unexpected. Only four years previously she had been profoundly shocked when Leonard Woolf sold seven of his wife's manuscripts to America. She had thought how annoyed he must be that she had safely got the manuscripts of *Orlando*, *Mrs. Dalloway* and quite a lot of *The Common Reader*. 'Poor though I may be I would not part with them,' she told Harold at the time.[21]

In August Harold had, as he thought, finished his book, *Monarchy*, and signed a contract for a sequel to *The Age of Reason* in *The Age of Romance*. He took reference books on the subject out of the London Library and began to read. He estimated that it would take him three years to write. The subject fascinated him and he looked forward to tackling it, although he expressed misgivings that he might not live to complete it. He did live but, alas, he did not write the book.

In September Vita received a letter from Nigel, addressed from Weidenfeld & Nicolson, beginning: 'I'm worried, and I want your help'.[22] The gist of the letter, which he detailed at greater length in a very tactful one to his father, despatched on the same date, was that *Monarchy* was an unbalanced book, lacking direction. The original intention had been that each chapter should deal with a different aspect of kingship. The opening chapter, *The Warrior King*, started off with Alexander the Great, but lacked any reference to Charles XII, Genghis Khan, Napoleon or Elizabeth I. There then followed four chapters on the Romans. The analytical approach had been abandoned and replaced by strictly narrative history. There were far too many omissions. Nigel felt sure that if he, Harold, were reviewing the book, he would make these criticisms. He also feared that his father would be annoyed by the publisher's disappointment and hurt by his. But the foreign publishers who had agreed to take the book and the *Sunday Telegraph* which was to serialise it, all having read it, reached the same conclusion, and would cancel their contracts unless it were largely re-written. Moreover if it were published as it stood it would gravely harm his reputation. 'I know', he told his father, 'you think that publishers who bother their authors are bad publishers . . . I think they are bad publishers if they don't.' He begged Vita to support him.

Harold was deeply disturbed. He confided in his diary that he felt quite giddy at the prospect of revising the book. But he was not the least self-pitying. He bore Nigel no resentment whatever. What Nigel really meant was that he was getting gaga. His sympathy was all for Nigel. 'Poor Niggs! It must have been an unpleasant letter for him to write.' To Vita he wrote pathetically from Albany about the obvious waning of his powers. And Vita, who agreed that Nigel had been quite right, at once consoled him. He still had too many commitments. She was worried about his constant tiredness, even when he was at Sissinghurst. She was glad he was resigning from the vice-chairmanship of the National Trust and exhorted him to cut down further commitments. That evening he dined with me at Brooks's to meet John Fowler. 'An agreeable evening,' he wrote in his diary, 'after a shattering day.' That night I stayed at C1 as invigilator. Not once during dinner or afterwards did he refer to the blow he had received to his pride and the curfew that was tolling the knell of his parting days.

With great courage he straightway set about re-writing and expanding *Monarchy*. By the end of the year he had done all he could. In fact he only partly met Nigel's criticisms. He told James Pope-Hennessy that the re-writing had caused him more trouble and effort than the whole book put together. 'One must have zest to write well and fluently, and whoever had zest in a *rechauffé*?'[23] When Vita read the page-proofs in the following February she tried to cheer him. She told him she enjoyed the book. 'The gift you have of suddenly startling one by the use of an unexpected though utterly *right* word, or by a little scene sharply described with the utmost economy.' Yet she was well aware of the book's falling away from his customary high standard.

Another source of sadness was the final break-up of Ben's and Luisa's marriage that autumn. It was no longer unexpected. Ben told James Pope-Hennessy that marriage was a trap and a prison, and warned him against it. There was little need. 'It is always like that,' sighed Ben. 'If one is highly sexed one goes after the housemaid, and if one isn't, the marriage breaks up from inanition.' 'I suppose you are right,' said James, thinking, not of housemaids, but of troopers in the Horse Guards.[24] The end of Ben's marriage was followed by the forty-eighth anniversary of Harold's and Vita's and provoked her to tell him what a very exceptional one theirs had been.

> Yet I swear it has turned out more happily than most. I love you more now than I did on the 1st October 1913, and I think you love me more also. I can't think why, because I haven't been what is called a good wife to you. I mean, I haven't ever been a help to you, either in diplomacy or politics. You ought to have married someone like Baba.[25]

Both of them had long been obsessed by the unorthodoxy of their marriage, and convinced that this unorthodoxy, coupled with the tolerance and understanding of both, was the main reason why their marriage had not only endured, but prospered.

I suppose [we] have been about as unfaithful to one another as one well could be from the conventional point of view [she had written twenty years before[26]], even worse than unfaithful if you add in homosexuality . . . It is queer, isn't it? It does destroy all orthodox ideas of marriage . . . I do think we have arranged things cleverly.

They certainly had in the circumstances that were theirs. But had one been homosexual and the other not, or one been understanding and the other not, the outcome might not have been so clever or the mutual love so enduring.

If Vita had occasional misgivings about her lack of co-operation with her husband's various careers Harold too went through moments when he was wretchedly aware of his inadequacy as a husband, even at the age of seventy-five. One occasion which I am about to relate may seem trivial, and to dog-dislikers ridiculous. But both Harold and Vita were dog-adorers, and those people who are not will never understand the miseries which those who are undergo when they lose a dog. Vita had decided that Dan, her collie and the successor to Rollo, the Alsatian, had to be destroyed because he had taken it upon himself to bite other dogs and children. Unaware, at least consciously, of his impending fate Dan had a heart-attack in the tower room, lying on the sofa trembling. Harold who was present, instantly left the scene, descended to the porch, a draughty place, in order to be out of the way and yet within call if wanted. His excuse was that he did not know what to do in the crisis, and he knew Vita did not like being stared at when she was distraught and in tears. It followed that he was accused of incompetence and lack of feeling. He was scolded. 'It is torture to me to see you distressed,' he wrote. 'I wish I were more competent at coping with such disasters, but I was NOT being indifferent, only muddled. I miss Dan and his funny ways more than you think . . . now that I am becoming senile I have got worse than ever.'[27] When Dan recovered from the heart attack Vita packed him into the car and took him to the vet. She returned with his lead and collar in pitiable distress, crying, 'He is dead. I have killed him.' Two new puppies, at once given her by Edie Lamont, were no consolation. 'I keep thinking of my little Dan down in the wet woods and feel a traitor.'[28]

The 21st November 1961 was Harold's seventy-fifth birthday. To celebrate the event the B.B.C. invited him to give a broadcast message to the millions of listeners to whom his voice had for two generations been a popular delight. He told them succintly that he still preserved an unquenchable curiosity about life. His birthday publicity brought him dozens of telegrams, including one from Lady Churchill which he valued, and many tiresome letters and requests from strangers, and even presents from people he did not care for. 'I like being a violet under a stone and not a prinking orchid,' he told Vita.[29]

More important still, interviews by Kenneth Harris on his life and opinions were published that month in the *Observer*. They had been recorded during the past year. Harold found Kenneth Harris an excellent interrogator because he made his subject think about himself, and by his intelligent and provocative questions demanded and got candid replies. The interviews elicited from Harold probably the most direct information about his views on life, politics, literature, manners and religion, that he ever granted.

Asked if he suffered any regrets he replied, Yes, that he had been bad at games and had never been to China. His inability to play games had ruined his schooldays at Wellington. But he had no regrets at not having become an Ambassador. Above all, he regretted not being a scientist which cut him off from half the fields of the world's knowledge. In consequence he could not claim to be an all-round man. He believed that to be cultured meant having the ability to enjoy at least one additional literature to one's own language. He was a strong upholder of the discipline imposed by the study of Greek and Latin. The art form most essential to culture was poetry. It deepened feeling in a way that prose could not do, although novels extended one's awareness. Virginia Woolf had been more responsible for extending his than any contemporary novelist. He regretted that modern poetry had become a private, secret form of communication, the correspondence of a coterie, exclusive of the vast number of intelligent readers. Mysticism and religion meant nothing to him. His philosophy of life was to help others to be happy. He thought happiness was the purpose of life, happiness in Aristotle's sense of the word, namely to be usefully active and to develop the best in one's nature. That was the great teleological principle. To be unhappy in Aristotle's sense, namely to be un-useful, was the sin. And sinners went to hell in this world. The capacity for enjoyment was curiosity.

When asked by Kenneth Harris which of the Prime Ministers or Foreign Secretaries he had known had he respected the most, he answered – Asquith. Of all the statesmen he had met Asquith brought to his mind words like Integrity, Probity and Dignity. It was untrue that he became a womaniser and drunkard. He liked pretty girls and he drank rather too much. Since all good Liberals hated war, he was not a good war leader. 'If greatness is a matter of mind and behaviour,'

Harold said, 'and not of producing effects, he is by far the greatest man I have ever known.'[30]

In the course of his political interview he was asked why he was a member of the Labour Party. He replied that he was a Liberal Socialist. He was sure that the immense boon of the National Health Service would never have been introduced except under state Socialism. But then he was not the right kind of person for politics. He did not feel at ease with the majority of his party. He felt at ease only with intellectuals. His hatred of the Tories largely accounted for his Labour side. It had sprung from his experiences as a child in St. Petersburg where he had been revolted by the pomp, grandeur and mentality of the Russian upper classes towards the rest of their countrymen. Nor could he forgive the Tories for their treatment of his son at Bournemouth. The title of the first *Observer* interview, *Why I hate the Tories*, did not convince Iain Macleod who responded that Harold Nicolson was far too nice a man to hate anyone.

In November Vita, busily planting in the garden with the *Mädchen*, was apparently well and happy. On New Year's Eve Harold rejoiced that she seemed far stronger than she had been for months.

January 1962 was bitterly cold. While Vita sat huddled over a little electric fire fetched from the dining-room and writing in her tower room at Sissinghurst, a llama skin rug over her knees, Harold in London met Oliver Esher creeping with a stick down the slippery Rope Walk of Albany, saying he knew he was destined to break his hip and become bedridden. Harold told him, 'When you were young you would have said, *leg*, not *hip*. Your grand-children will say *femur* rather than hip. Such is the progress and advance of science.' 'Yes,' Lord Esher replied, 'you and I are interested in the same things, such as changes in vocabulary.'[31]

On the 19th the Nicolsons set forth on their last, and disastrous cruise – to the West Indies. Whatever premonitions Vita may have had about her health Harold was blissfully unaware of impending trouble. On the eve of their departure he wrote a gossipy, indiscreet letter to James Pope-Hennessy in Mauritius. He was looking forward to his visit to Government House, Trinidad, which had been the scene of James's unhappy term as A.D.C. to a former Governor of Trinidad, Sir Hubert Young. 'I shall wander round the Botanic Gardens reflecting sadly and gladly on how much you have meant to me in the last twenty years,' he

wrote.[32] A mutual friend of theirs had just brought round to Albany a
friend in the Rifle Brigade. 'I expected him to look like a sergeant, but
he didn't look like a sergeant in the very least. He had a profusion of
black hair and lovely blue eyes.' The encounter led Harold to discourse
on the advantage of being seventy-five years old. With him all passion
was spent. No longer was he tempted by ungainly relationships.
Nevertheless, his interests, as distinct from his actions, were in no way
diminished. He still crossed the road to Hatchard's seeking to discover
whether the back view of someone gazing at the books displayed in the
shop-window was supplemented by a front view of equal elegance.

Once again Sir Philip and Lady Magnus-Allcroft came on the cruise.
Also Vita had persuaded her friend Mrs. Lamont to accompany them.
This turned out to be very fortunate. At Waterloo they were seen off by
Ben who unexpectedly brought with him Vanessa, hugging a large
teddy-bear. On the train to Southampton Vita suffered a serious
haemorrhage. She was naturally, and with reason, alarmed; and was
able to confide in Edie. They agreed that Harold should on no account
be told. Concealing their anxiety the two women followed the others
into the French liner, *Antilles*. On embarking Harold tripped on a step
and fell flat on his face, which he interpreted as a bad omen. The
moment Vita was ensconced in her cabin she developed a severe cold
and temperature, which turned to bronchitis. She was also laid low
with lumbago, and unable to leave the ship and go on excursions.
Harold, now sick with worry, and as always superstitious in adversity,
attributed their misfortunes to his fall.

By dint of plugging Vita with drugs the ship's doctor succeeded in
bringing her temperature down. By a great effort she managed to lunch
with Ronald Tree in his beautiful villa in Heron's Bay, Barbados. But
on her return to the ship she collapsed with exhaustion. In Trinidad
Harold called on the Governor-General, his old friend Patrick Buchan-
Hepburn, now Lord Hailes, and his wife. He described to James his
reception.

We were asked to sign our names in THE BOOK and would gladly
have done so had not the pen been coated with Guava jelly and unable
to either absorb or to communicate ink. They then telephoned up to
the house and in a trice as it were a little man of the name of Hamilton
came tripping through the Samaana Tree and said that His Excellency wished to see me immediately. He was your successor and I very
nearly implanted on his thin lips a kiss of lust but that would not have
been welcomed I could see from a mile away. We walked up to the

house and entered the high white hall with its imitation portrait of the
Queen. Lady Hailes arrived; her West Indian secretary arrived; an
orange squash arrived; and eventually clad in grey samite, mystic,
wonderful, His Excellency arrived. He was certainly pleased to see
me and took me out into the garden. On the way there I examined the
staircase and pictured you in your neat little uniform walking in front
of the Youngs about to present guests. I mentioned this picture to
Patrick and he grunted, 'No West Indians in those days invited,' and I
thought how infinitely more complicated even than it was would the
introduction ceremony have been for James had there been a row of
uniformly thick blubbered *negroes* to be introduced. Patrick took me
to your little Liberty cottage with its two nice rooms and its verandah
and I got a lump in my throat.[32]

At Trinidad Evelyn Waugh and his charming daughter Margaret
came on board, for the return journey to Southampton. Harold was
appalled by his rudeness. In the smart hotel in Caracas where they were
all bathing in the azure pool, a polite American offered them drinks. He
said, 'Now that you have drunk my drinks I insist on shaking hands
with the author whom I so much admire', and thereupon stretched out
a freckled Middle Western forearm. Evelyn Waugh recoiled sharply. 'I
am afraid not,' he said. 'I hate physical contacts with social adventurers
and vulgarians.' Acute shame reduced the party to embarrassed silence.

Yet Harold himself was not beyond snubbing those passengers on
board whose intimacies he took for officiousness. He admitted to
Kenneth Rose that he found pleasure in picking little quarrels. When
the first day on board a military-looking gentleman accosted him with
the question, 'Is that an Old Harrovian tie you are wearing?' he replied,
'No, it is an Old Wellingtonian tie'. 'Ah, Wellington, very good
school.' 'You know nothing about it,' Harold retorted, 'It is a very bad
school.' Again when a woman passenger boasted to him that before she
sailed Anthony Eden had sent her some cigarettes, he could not refrain
from saying, 'And you mean to tell me that you accepted a present from
the Prime Minister who had done more to dishonour the name of this
country than any man since Lord North?' The lady had never heard of
Lord North. Even Philip Magnus felt the lash of Harold's tongue.
When Harold dropped his spectacles at luncheon one day Philip very
kindly dived under the table to retrieve them, at which Harold exploded, 'I will not be treated like an invalid.' Immediately after this
outburst Harold was very contrite, and bought Philip a large bottle of
scent at the ship's stores, which, Kenneth Rose observed, was a peculiar
present in the circumstances.[34]

In fact he much resented being helped and being handled. He recoiled in horror if a stranger with the politest intention tried to assist him with his greatcoat. His young friends soon learned to refrain from any such intrusive zeal. To Harold it implied that old age, which he so much dreaded, was catching up on him, that he was becoming too decrepit to do things for himself. It also betokened interference. He once turned abruptly on Elvira Niggeman, to whom he was devoted and from whom he would accept almost any admonition, because she had suggested that he ought not to go out in the cold without his muffler. 'I won't be managed!' he shouted at her. Elvira was vastly amused. The phrase became a stock joke in the family and was constantly quoted by Vita in letters to Harold as a forewarning that she was about to proffer unwelcome advice. He likewise shunned the physical touch. He would wince if anyone took his arm, even avoided shaking hands if he could do so without causing offence, and was never known to embrace his most intimate women friends. Some deep-rooted inhibition prevented this warm-hearted and affectionate man from palpably demonstrating his emotions, although he could freely give rein to them in writing. He was a sort of paper lover whose carnal desires were fulfilled perfunctorily and summarily as though bodily contact were a distasteful or even a shocking necessity, and better substituted by distant satisfaction through the eyes.

Owing to Vita's indisposition the cruise was far from being a success. She was greatly relieved to be home in mid-February and for a day or two took pleasure in the Sissinghurst garden where the parrotia was in full flower, the witch-hazel out and a few crocuses were in bud. But to her diary she confided: 'I feel really ill, and try to hide it from Hadji. The sooner I see the doctor the better,'[35] while Harold wrote in his: 'I think Vita is better, but she never lets me know.'[36] Vita was not better. She was inordinately tired. The doctor having assured her that she was not anaemic, advised that she should consult a specialist. She went alone to London to see one who told her she must at once go to a hospital for a thorough examination. It was then that she admitted to Harold about the haemorrhage in the train. 'The shock has a strange effect on me,' he wrote. 'It seems to sunder my life in two – the past being radiant with sunshine, and the present and future dark as night. Familiar objects (my pipe, my sponge, the book I have been reading) all seem like voices from the past. "Last time I handled you, all was sunlit."'[37] Arrangements were made for her to go to the Royal Free Hospital in Canonbury. Edie Lamont was to accompany her.

I am so relieved that dear Edie is coming with you [Harold wrote to Vita]. Edie's tact, and discernment and reticence about the tragedy in the boat train has wiped out all trace of jealousy. It was ridiculous of me to feel jealous, and Edie knew I suspected it and was wonderfully considerate. But I *was* jealous, idiot that I am. I do not allow myself to get worried in the watches of the night. I forbid myself to brood in misery but concentrate my mind on our happiness together, on the great moment at Kermanshah, and other occasions and above all on our deep love of each other, which no catastrophe can ever take away. Thus my heart is filled with pity for you, knowing how you hate hospitals, etc . . . But I am not as brave as you are and I miss my Mummy who would comfort me. Knowing your secrecy, or more accurately your love of privacy, I shall not tell anyone and merely say that you are 'in hospital for observation'.[38]

And on the same day Vita wrote to him in London,

This is not a nice patch for us to be going through . . . I am not going to indulge in self-pity, and I am not going to be more of a bore and a worry to anybody, but more especially to you my sweet who are not a person who ought to be worried.[39]

On the 1st March they operated on her. *Dies Irae*, Harold committed to his diary. The lady surgeon who did the operation telephoned him. 'Did you find cancer?' he asked. 'Yes.' He felt like fainting, but drank some sherry. During the afternoon a knock came from the dolphin on the door of C1 Albany and a uniformed messenger handed Elvira Niggeman a letter of sympathy and encouragement from the Queen despatched to him by Sir Michael Adeane.

Harold visited the hospital and sat beside Vita's bed reading, and occasionally speaking a word. He was horribly conscious of his inability to do anything practical. He wrote to me:

So hour after hour she lies there listening to the chink of hurried footsteps of hospital life. . . She is still too weak to hold a spoon and if I tried I should spill soup all over the bed. But Mrs. Lamont is deft and competent. I am the most incompetent man since Noah.[40]

His sons and friends rallied to him. Elvira was a pillar of moral support and a fount of cheerfulness; and James accompanied him to luncheon and dinner in clubs and restaurants. Harold was being filmed in Albany by the B.B.C., which was a diversion, if an exhausting one. He was also being irritated by a few of Vita's women friends and his sister Gwen, who, he assumed, were under the impression that he failed to realise how ill Vita had been. 'How little they understand,' he said.

Vita left the hospital for Sissinghurst a week after her major operation. She picked up only a little. She was barely able to struggle into the garden. Towards the end of May both she and Harold realised that she might never recover. 'I write you such dull letters,' she told him, 'but then my life is dull. I wonder how long it will go on. If only I could see an end to it . . . but everyone is so vague. Weeks? Months?'[41]

Ursula Codrington, now back at Sissinghurst, was a bulwark of solace to husband and wife. Friends visited Vita one at a time for short periods, Edie Lamont, Vi Pym, Bunny Drummond, and my wife. Then the doctor, worried about her slow recovery, pronounced that she must undergo deep-ray treatment at Pembury Hospital every day, except weekends, for five weeks. She began this treatment, accompanied by Edie, while Ursula remained at Sissinghurst to comfort Harold. But after a couple of visits to the hospital she was too weak to continue. On the 1st June the doctor warned Harold that he 'must face the fact that there is little hope. He does not think she will suffer much. I return to my room in a haze of fear. Niggs comes down late at night.'[42] The weather being perfect and the garden divinely beautiful somehow exacerbated the misery at Sissinghurst. And then the following day Harold recorded: 'It is a lovely morning. I get up early and walk round the garden [with the dogs]. Glen dances on the lawn with his brother Brandy.' He forced himself to write a review while Ursula was with Vita in her room. By 1 o'clock it was clear to Ursula that Vita was dying. At a quarter past 1 she stopped breathing. 'Ursula comes to tell me. I pick some of her favourite flowers and lay them on the bed.'[43]

On the morning of the 5th June her funeral took place in Sissinghurst church. The lugubrious building was filled with flowers and packed with friends. On the back of the service-sheet her sons had had printed that long passage from *The Land* called *The Island*, which begins with the lines:–

> She walks among the loveliness she made,
> Between the apple-blossom and the water –
> She walks among the patterned pied brocade,
> Each flower her son, and every tree her daughter.

There was no address and the vicar when mentioning her by name omitted, on the express direction of Harold, to include his. On leaving the church Harold, with remarkable control, walked down the aisle, shaking hands with special friends and patting others on the shoulder as if to console their grief. The body was cremated and the ashes, having been put into a little pink marble sarcophagus which for years had reposed on her writing-table, were taken to the Sackville crypt at Withyham. They lie close to the remains of her Uncle Charlie, the 4th Lord Sackville who had died a month before at the age of 91.

12

EPILOGUE, 1962–1968

VOLUME III of Harold Nicolson's published diaries ends with Vita's death in June 1962. It seems that he did not keep his diary during the remainder of that year. He resumed however in January 1963, and continued it until October 1964, more out of habit than for pleasure. The entries were never as full, amusing or as edifying as they had been. Indeed they became progressively more concise until they lapsed into scrappy records of what he had done or had not done during the previous day, such as: 'Go to a huge party at Longman's where I meet very many people and try to hide in a back room', and (the last of all): 'Pick flowers for tomorrow. Otherwise do nothing but sit about. It is wonderfully fine weather.'[1]

With Vita's departure the light of his life went out. Before that event his health had gradually been declining; but her death was the final knock-out blow. He did not recover. For a time he carried on, like a man in a trance, endeavouring to enjoy himself and take an interest in what went on about him. But the savour of existence was absolutely lacking, and after 1964 he gave up entirely. Even his sons, and daughter-in-law Philippa, whose affection, so long as he was *compos mentis*, he relied upon totally, meant less and less, and then nothing to him. By August 1962 he complained that his mind had gone 'mushy'. He could write only short reviews of books that were not too serious. He even made excuses not to write and was noticed by Nigel aimlessly wandering round the garden at Sissinghurst, as though putting off the effort of taking to his typewriter, a state of affairs inconceivable before Vita's death unless he was temporarily indisposed.

The process of disintegration was gradual. Nigel, to whom Vita had left Sissinghurst, and Philippa soon established themselves with their family in the castle, Harold having been left his cottage and small garden. In the first dark days the grandchildren were a great solace and delight to him. And Philippa, who attended to him solicitously, almost became that substitute mother figure which all his adult life Vita had, amongst other roles, supplied, and in his childhood Lady Carnock had been. It was to Philippa that he addressed most of his letters for the few lucid months that were left to him. In her he confided the terrible loss that Vita meant.

What hurts me most is when I forget that Vita is dead and think, 'I must tell her in my letter tomorrow; it will amuse her,' and then the lance of memory swoops down and pierces me with the cry, 'You will never write to her again.' I keep on trying to persuade myself that man must pay a price for 50 years of unbroken love and happiness. But still the tears ooze and splash whenever I find myself alone in my room . . . I fear Ben intends to sell his share of the jewelry. I had wanted all those emerald rings to go to Juliet . . . But they will sparkle on the plump finger of Mrs. Da Soto of Caracas.[2]

In August John Sparrow and James Pope-Hennessy took him to Bergamo for a few weeks. It was the first time he had flown over the Alps and the spectacle entranced him. He looked down upon the 'great elephant flanks of precipices and glaciers and flakes of snow' of Mont Blanc. At Milan airport they hired a car which John Sparrow drove to Bergamo. Harold in a letter to Philippa described the journey by road with his customary amused detachment.

The little Fiat with its attendant was waiting for us. The attendant explained to John how the gears worked. I thought John was a trifle inattentive, but then I assumed that he was a natural mechanic who can understand gears in a trice. It was a dear little car and meant no harm at all. Off we went, keeping the right side of the road, and driving slowly. Then we came to a level crossing and John had to change gear. He did so deftly, but the car stopped suddenly and would not move again. He tried every gear, until WHOOP! the car gave a mighty spring and bounded across the railway lines. Then on we went until the city of Bergamo appeared dotting the hills opposite. We lunched in the lower town and thereafter drove on to the upper town. This means traversing a succession of zigzags and at every zig or zag the car stalled. John got angrier and angrier. So did James. 'Really, John,' said the latter, 'you are the worst driver I have ever known.' At which John turned round in his seat and delivered to James a terrific box on the ear. James gave a great gasp, started to cry, and then embarked upon one of his tirades. 'I shall go tomorrow to join my brother in Florence. I am not accustomed to being struck by my friends. I now understand, John, why you have made such a mess of your life. A failure at the Bar, a failure in the Army, and regarded, not by All Souls only, but by the whole University with contempt and dislike. I have always wondered how it came that you have deteriorated into a figure of fun. Now I know.'
I during this was making soothing gestures to soothe them both down. There was no single room in the hotel for James and he had to

share with John. He retired to bed immediately with a sedative but emerged at 6 on the terrace, placid again and ready for a vermouth . . . It was like two boys of seven and six squabbling on the beach at Eastbourne, or Bournemouth . . . Your devoted old blubberbox, Harold.[3]

A few days later he told Elvira Niggeman that John and James continued to bicker, but comparatively amicably. 'John, why ever is it that you have never accomplished anything serious in life?' James asked provocatively. 'Well, James, I am the Warden of All Souls.' 'Yes, in the old days that was a most honourable title. But you have let it down and it is now just a comic job.' 'Anyhow,' John answered, 'I am not a debauched pervert such as you are.' 'You are too old in any case to indulge in debauchery,' came the swift retort. Whereupon Harold intervened: 'Now, children, shut up and let us go to the *taverna*.'

They stayed in the delightful Albergo Pianone, which had two wide terraces, a view of the plain of Lombardy from one end and the old city with its towers and cupolas from the other. There was a fountain trickling, a poodle playing, and a boy indolently scratching gravel with a rake. Harold sat in the shade most of the day reading and taking notes in a rather desultory way – work was the only occupation he enjoyed now – feeling old and broken, and thinking of Vita achingly. 'But I am not going to be a cry-baby. In any case I have no more tears to shed.'[4]

However much they sparred amongst themselves John and James were splendid with their old friend, and refused to allow him to indulge in their presence in any 'widower nonsense'. Early in September Nigel joined them; and then Michael Ricketts, whose apparent loneliness touched Harold's understanding and sympathy. One purpose of Nigel's visit was to inspect the progress of the printing of *Monarchy*, which was being done in Bergamo. The book was being lavishly produced with coloured portraits of important sovereigns, and printed in four languages, in half a million copies. Harold was taken to watch the work which gave him a thrill of pleasure. He told Kenneth Rose:

I am humiliated by the gulf that opens between my table at Sissing-hurst and my battered typewriter and the vast clean hall of Bergamo, with those bright-eyed women, and the machine with reiterant deftness pulling and stacking sheet upon sheet of my inchoate non-sense and arranging them in tidy stacks for the binder to pinch and clasp them into the shape of books for a wide and, I earnestly trust, welcoming market.[5]

The book, which had caused Nigel so much apprehension, and Harold so much despair, was issued by Weidenfeld & Nicolson at the end of the year. It was the least successful of Harold's books. Meant to be a popular work with, as the author complained quite unfairly, pictures of corgis and Princess Margaret, it turned out to be a dissertation on the kingship theory, which is what interested Harold. And this theory which originated in primitive times and developed into a philosophy under the Romans and Carolingians, claimed an unwarrantable proportion of the text. There was too little space left over for the emperors and kings of recent centuries who, in Harold's justification, did little to extend the philosophy of kingship further. Harold was unable to reconcile the dichotomy satisfactorily owing to his failing health and powers, and the book accordingly lacked that balance and shape which distinguish all his previous ones.

In January of 1963 he went to the United States by himself. This was a mistake, for by now he was in need of constant attention and care. Philippa had wanted to accompany him, but since she was starting a new baby it was not thought advisable for her to travel. He crossed the Atlantic on the *Queen Mary*. Nigel and Howard Ricketts took him to Waterloo station, where he found himself leaving from the same platform as he had done a year ago with Vita. Kenneth Rose also came to see him off. Noel Coward and the Wheeler-Bennetts were on board the liner. They kept an eye on him, and he ate at the captain's table. In New York he stayed at the Knickerbocker Club. A *New Yorker* correspondent met him there by appointment. 'His cheeks were pink, his manner was gentle, and he looked like an elegant pussycat,' the man wrote. 'I'm very well taken care of,' he said, 'although the bar which I occasionally frequent, *does* have pictures of the British surrenders at Saratoga and Yorktown'.' Nevertheless he felt lost and bewildered, and wondered why on earth he had been so foolish as to come. Yet his many friends in New York were extremely kind. He saw Monroe Wheeler, Copley Amory of Persia days, Wystan Auden and Anne Lindbergh who was so sweet about Vita that she reduced him to tears. He met every distinguished American he wished to meet – Adlai Stevenson, Alan Dulles, Alistair Cooke, Walter Lippmann and Glenway Westcott. In particular George Dix and Stuart Preston escorted him to galleries and museums. He was invited to luncheon, cocktail parties and dinners, and never ate alone. He went to Washington and stayed with Mina Curtiss who arranged receptions for him. He was astonished by the quantities of people who had read his books and wished to see him. In Boston he lost his umbrella. He was promptly given another, as well as a stout blackthorn walking-stick by his publishers, Doubleday, who all loved him, so one of the directors, Ken McCormick told Elvira Niggeman.

He wrote many letters home, and Nigel was so worried by the amount of entertaining he was subjected to that he begged his father not to put unnecessary social strain upon himself, to refuse invitations from strangers and avoid bores. By the end of his American tour he felt more cheerful, although he confessed that he had lost all capacity for enjoyment. However the change of scenery made him consider whether he might not persevere with his book on the *Age of Romance*.

He was home again by the middle of February. He was not happy, and was full of self-pity. He suffered from gushes of melancholy when he sobbed uncontrollably, called piteously upon Vita, and longed to die. On the 10th April Nigel and Philippa's third child, Rebecca, was born. But, alas, it was too late for Harold to rejoice, as he surely would have done only twelve months before, in this new addition to the family. On the 26th he lunched alone with his old rival, Violet Trefusis, who was very affectionate and sweet. She had sent him such sympathetic letters at the time of Vita's death that he had totally forgiven her the misery she had caused him in the past, now so far away.

> Darling Violet [he wrote back], you were quite right in saying you and Vita were like twins. Vita was put in a vault yesterday, among all the Sackvilles. Her companion coffins date back to the fifteenth century, which you would like. Bless you, my dear dear friend.[6]

Then towards the end of May he had another slight stroke while reviewing a book of John Sparrow's. He could not finish it and went to bed. He wrote to Elvira in London that she would scarcely recognise him since the right side of his face had slipped below the left side; that he felt confused in mind and could not pronounce his words properly. He found it curious that his consciousness seemed perfectly alert whereas he limped over a conversation.

By August he was dreadfully forgetful of engagements and unfit to go anywhere alone. Besides he was becoming a prey to some of those thousand natural ills that flesh is heir to. He who had been so fastidious a man about personal cleanliness became surprisingly indifferent to the effect its neglect had upon others. He lost his natural dignity and would cause offence as well as embarrassment to the public visiting the garden at Sissinghurst. When checked, or reproved, he would assume the pained expression of a naughty child. '*Povero vecchio!*' he would murmur in a voice choked by tears. He needed shielding as well as cherishing. So a succession of male nurses had to be engaged, whose names, all but that of the first, he could never remember, and whom he referred to as 'my man'. Although in his diary he was apt to describe everyone whom he met as charming, this was far from what many supposed he found them. For when people out of kindness visited him he often received them with grunts and sometimes was positively rude until they went away, their tails between their legs. Yet he felt lonely and was pleased when favoured friends came to see him. It was now their turn to do all the talking, for he had reached a stage when he could not give out, and could only receive.

His engagement with the *Observer* had to come to an end for he was no longer capable of writing a weekly review. This meant that he was earning no money. All he had on which to live in Albany with a secretary and a manservant, to eat twice daily at the Travellers' or the Beefsteak, and to travel every weekend to Sissinghurst, was £7,000 left him by Vita. In September he went again to Bergamo for a fortnight accompanied by his first and favourite male nurse, Tony King, and was met there by John Sparrow. This mode of living simply could not continue without retrenchment. Nigel urged John Sparrow, who had great influence with his father, to persuade him to leave Albany; but this was not brought about until the spring of 1965. He also managed to sell the serialisation rights in his father's diaries to the *Observer* for £3,000 and the book rights to Collins, the publishers, for £5,000. He thought it might amuse Harold to prepare them for the press. But the idea did not work out. The references to Vita made his father so sad he could not bear to read them. So Nigel undertook the editorship of the first volume himself on the understanding that his father should approve the typescript. By the time it was ready Harold was incapable of taking it in. He twice read the typescript without recollecting a single entry.

1964 was the last year in which Harold led anything like a normal life. In January he met Jeremy Thorpe at the Beefsteak Club and was charmed by him, largely because he spoke appreciatively of Nigel, expressing the hope that he might stand for Parliament again as a Liberal. In March he went on a cruise to Greece with Tony King, who became devoted to Harold, although he had to brace himself to respond to his emotional demands. They took the train to Marseilles and there embarked on an Israeli transport to Haifa. They reached Itea and drove up to Delphi. Tony drank at the Castalian spring and Harold derived vicarious pleasure from his enthusiasm and enjoyment. They sailed for

Rhodes where Harold did not go ashore because the island brought back painful memories. At Ephesus too he remained on board; and at Delos likewise. One beautiful April day was spent on the Acropolis. While Tony was exploring every column and fragment of marble, Harold sat in the sun, and shutting his eyes felt the whole of Greece suffuse his being. On the way back the boat called at Salerno. Tony visited the temples at Paestum and Harold sat in the car, quite happy to be alone with his memories.

In June he and Tony went to Paris, staying at the Hotel Crillon. Tony had not been there before and Harold was amused by his excitement. Like a couple of schoolboys they went up the Eiffel Tower and down to Napoleon's tomb in the Invalides. They drove to Versailles where Harold sat on a bench and watched the children playing. It was the last jaunt and in a simple way he enjoyed it. Then Tony King decided to leave him, and was replaced by another young man. But Harold was indifferent to him and his successors, for even the charms of youth held no further attractions for him.

On leaving Albany for good in May 1965 he retired to Sissinghurst which he was never to leave again. Thenceforth his existence was a slow and steady diminuendo. It was more distressing for his family, especially Nigel and Philippa who had him to live with them, than it was for him. They had to watch him stop writing, stop reading, and then stop talking. He rose at midday, had breakfast and by one o'clock would say, 'Where's my luncheon?' He would be piloted from his cottage across the garden to the wing adjoining the south-east end of the Gatehouse, which Nigel and Philippa had converted into a comfortable house for themselves and their children. He would take his seat at the head of the oak table facing the window. If an old friend came down from London he would barely acknowledge his presence beyond saying, 'Oh, dear Raymond, or Jamesey, or John'. The best salutation the visitor could hope for was the flicker of an affectionate smile. To questions about his health there would be no rejoinder; and to the friend's attempts at bright conversation he would seldom register any interest beyond a grunt. Whether he heard or understood what was said to him it was difficult to make out. Certainly he found difficulty in framing sentences. He became extremely greedy. He would fall upon his food as soon as the plateful was put before him, and demand a second helping before anyone else had started on their first. His voracious eating would be punctuated with occasional fits of choking, followed by disconcerting shouts and groans. As soon as luncheon was over he would be anxious to return to his cottage, where he would doze in his armchair in the afternoon. On summer evenings he might sit in an upright chair at his cottage door, wearing an old trilby hat, squashed squarely on his head, and grasping a stick. Under a bundle of coats and shawls he looked like a venerable buddha gazing into space. More often he would sit for hours over the television, unaware of what programme he was watching. He was easily reduced to tears, and would sob quietly when one football team was defeated by another.

He seemed to be indifferent to the publication of his diaries, whose success was phenomenal, beyond remarking to Nigel in 1966 that it was odd to publish three books which he did not realise he had written.

Kenneth Rose attended a small dinner party given for him at Sissinghurst on his 80th birthday. The occasion evidently registered with him and he responded to the unusual extent of coming into the dining-room, 'looking very smart in a blue suit and in better form than I have seen him at any time during the past two years'. He greeted Kenneth, and then:

with a large beaker of sherry in front of him receives his birthday presents. Ben and Nigel give him a drawing of Vita by William Rothenstein, which they bought at a sale the other day . . . Nobody thinks that it is a very good likeness but it goes well with a similar drawing of Harold which Rothenstein also did. Harold is grateful but remarks with characteristic bluntness: 'Vita was a beautiful woman and that is an ugly one.'

We eat pheasant and drink champagne. Harold enjoys himself enormously. Ben asks him what is his earliest memory. He replies: 'Oh, I think I remember being in my mother's arms in Tehran. And what was the name of that meaningless place in the middle of Europe? I know, Budapest!' What he cannot recall is a reference in one of his later diaries to a very pleasant episode in a tobacconist shop in Smyrna. We all give our imaginative versions and Philippa looks rather shocked.

As he was born in Tehran, I offer him one of the Persian cigarettes I recently brought back with me. He smokes it and we persuaded him to chant a bit of Omar Khayyam in the original Farsee.

Nigel asks Harold whether he has any regrets in his life.

'Well, I regret that Vita is dead – but I don't think I have any regrets for anything I could control.'

'What about leaving the Diplomatic Service?'

'No.'

'Joining Oswald Mosley?'

'Yes, I do rather regret that, but I suppose it was useful experience.'

Ben asks his father whether he now minds not having served in either war. Harold replies, 'Yes, I suppose I do rather, as I should like to have tested my courage.' At which Nigel justly interposes, 'Yes, but you were always being bombed in London during the last world war and showed no fear.'

Harold goes off to bed about 10 o'clock, having bidden us all an affectionate goodbye. I tell him what an old fraud he is for having told us all whenever we saw him at any time during the past ten years that we should never see him alive again, and we all agree to dine again on his 90th birthday.[7]

This birthday dinner was his swan-song. He quickly lapsed into an ever deepening twilight. On May-day of 1968, while undressing for bed just after midnight, he died. He was in his eighty-second year. His ashes, according to his revised instructions, did not join Vita's in the Sackville crypt at Withyham, but were buried in Sissinghurst churchyard. It was a final gesture of his good breeding, a determination not to intrude where he did not belong, a respect for Vita's independence of the matrimonial bond, and a re-affirmation that sentiment was mischievous nonsense, for once the body stopped breathing, the spirit that it contained evaporated into eternal night. On the 16th May a Memorial Service was held in St. James's Church, Piccadilly, for him and Vita jointly.

Their old friend, John Sparrow, delivered an address. He reminded us that we were met to remember a man who had excelled as diplomatist, historian, biographer, literary critic, essayist, broadcaster and commentator on the political and social scene over half a century. He gave a synthesis of Harold's life. He touched upon the rich variety of his interests, the many worlds in which he moved with ease, the many talents he possessed, and the many friends, old and young whom he loved and by whom he was beloved. Having dwelt upon his astonishing capacity for friendship, he observed that his conversation was as amusing and scintillating as his writing, and his power of communicating to others the fruits of a shrewd and perceptive understanding was unsurpassed. He testified to the trouble he took to help young writers, refugees from foreign tyrannies and all people sent to him in trouble. He dwelt upon his complicated character which was that of a nineteenth-century Whig leading an eighteenth-century existence in the twentieth century. For his loyalties and values were fundamentally Victorian, notwithstanding his acquired tolerance which was well in advance of his generation. Moreover he was one of the happiest men who had ever lived – happy in his family, his home, his books, his work, his garden, his travels, and the world of nature and people around him. Above all he was blessed in having for nearly fifty years a wife who, perhaps because in temperament and tastes she was his complement – in some respects indeed his counterpart – because she shared most of his interests and sympathised with them all, and because she maintained her own independence and respected his, was the sole possessor of his heart.

Appendix
NOTES TO TEXT

In the notes relating to Harold Nicolson's diaries and the letters between him and Vita Sackville-West and to his sons on active service *during* the 1939–45 war I have put in brackets (publ) or (unpubl). These parentheses mean that the quotations I have used either were or were not published in Nigel Nicolson's *Harold Nicolson: Diaries and Letters*, vols. I–III, 1966–68. I wrote my text before the publication in 1980 of Stanley Olson's re-issue of *Harold Nicolson: Diaries and Letters 1930–1964*, in which, as well as condensing, he has included a few extracts not in the previous three volume version. In any event all the extracts from Harold Nicolson's and Vita Sackville-West's diaries and letters to each other quoted in this book are the sole copyright of Nigel Nicolson. All other letters from or to HN quoted in the text have hitherto remained unpublished.

The abbreviations used in the Appendix are:

HN	Harold Nicolson
VSW	Vita Sackville-West
BN	Benedict Nicolson
NN	Nigel Nicolson
PN	Philippa Nicolson
JPH	James Pope-Hennessy
RM	Raymond Mortimer

Spectator refers to HN's regular 'Marginal Comment' articles in that weekly journal.

CHAPTER 1   JOURNALISM AND THE NEW PARTY, 1930–1932

1. HN Diary (unpubl), 1.1.1930. 'I shall try at least to keep a fuller diary, and type it on single sheets and then get it bound. See how that works.'
2. *Spectator*, 28.1.1941.
3. HN to VSW (unpubl), 25.5.1960.
4. Moreover the Foreign Office, in the person of Sir Robert Vansittart, was often annoyed with HN for what they believed to be leakages in the Londoner's Diary.
5. HN Diary (unpubl), 11.10.1930.
6. *People and Things*, 1931.
7. *Time and Tide: Notes on the Way*, 7.3.1931.
8. About this time HN was very much alive to the deliberate misinterpretation by his countrymen of Germany's actions before 1914, and to the cruel continuation of the blockade against German non-combatants when the war was over. 'We do not, in these later years, like to reflect upon the ruthlessness of that period. We do not allow our memory or our imagination to dwell upon the millions of children and old people whom we wantonly starved: and, being at heart a kindly race, we endeavour to escape from these reflections by hoping that it did not happen; by hoping that it was all exaggerated; by hoping that it was mainly the fault of the French.' (From HN's Preface to Geoffrey Moss's *Defeat*, 1932).

9. HN to VSW (unpubl), 26.8.1930.
10. HN Diary (publ), 10.7.1930.
11. HN Diary (unpubl), 8.4.1930.
12. HN Diary (Unpubl), 21.2.1930.
13. Rt. Hon Oliver Stanley, 1896–1940, M.P. Second son of the 17th Earl of Derby. Minister for War, 1940.
14. HN Diary (publ), 6.11.1930.
15. The Memoirs of Israel Sieff (1970).
16. 'The Garden at Sissinghurst Castle': article by VSW in Journal of Royal Horticultural Society, Nov. 1953.
17. Ibid.
18. Sissinghurst; The Making of a Garden, 1974.
19. HN to VSW (publ), 8.6.1937.
20. HN to Lady Sackville, 2.5.1931.
21. HN to BN, 19.3.1930.
22. HN Diary (unpubl), 19.10.1930.
23. Bruce Lockhart was not beyond giving his own paragraphs a Nicolson twist. One day while typing he looked up and said, 'Harold, how would you describe a slightly bogus Scotsman?' HN replied without thinking, 'Say that there's a suspicion of Jaegar pants under his kilt.' 'Bully!' said Lockhart, and put it in. The Highlander sued the Evening Standard, but the case was settled out of court.
24. HN Diary (unpubl), 20.7.1931.
25. VW to VSW, 28.4.1931.
26. HN Diary (publ), 27.4.1931.
27. Oswald Mosley – My Life, 1968.
28. HN to VSW (unpubl), 5.6.1931.
29. HN Diary (part unpubl), 22.8.1931.
30. Broken Record, 1934, and Light on a Dark Horse, 1951.
31. J. A. Gotch, 1852–1942, well-known architectural historian.
32. HN to VSW (unpubl), 27.9.1931.
33. Ibid.
34. This declaration appeared in the first issue of Action, on sale for two pence on the 1st October, 1931.
35. HN Diary (publ), 28.10.1931.
36. Raymond Mortimer to Edward Sackville-West, 1.11.1931 and 26.11.1931.
37. HN to VSW (unpubl), 3.1.1932.
38. HN to VSW (unpubl), 4.1.1932.
39. HN to VSW, (unpubl), 26.1.1932.
40. Lieut-Commander J. M. Kenworthy, R. N., Labour M.P. for Kingston-upon-Hull 1919–31. Succeeded as 10th Lord Strabolgi 1934.
41. HN Diary (unpubl), 19.4.1932.
42. Hilda Matheson, Head of the Talks Department, B.B.C. 1928. See Vol. I, pp. 343–4.
43. In a letter to Sibyl Colefax, 7.10.1932, HN told her that she was 'the onlie begetter' of Peacemaking.
44. HN to Michael Sadleir, 11.10.1932.

CHAPTER 2   AMERICA AND IN BETWEEN, 1933–1935

1. Harold Nicolson: Diaries and Letters, 1930–39 Vol. I p. 129.
2. HN Diary (publ), 5.1.1933.
3. HN to VSW (publ), 16.2.1933.

4. HN Diary (publ), 8.1.1933.
5. HN to BN, 28.1.1933.
6. Ibid.
7. HN to Raymond Mortimer, 5.3.1933.
8. HN to VSW from Baltimore (unpubl), 28.1.1933.
9. HN to BN, 13.1.1933.
10. *Daily Telegraph*, 4-15.5.1933 and HN to Lady Colefax, 12.8.1943.
11. *Peacemaking* was re-issued in 1943 with a new introduction by the author.
12. VW to Ethel Smyth, 28.12.1932. (See *The Sickle Side of the Moon: The Letters of Virginia Woolf Volume V: 1932-35*. Edited by Nigel Nicolson and Joanne Trautmann, 1979).
13. This was in 1973. See *Portrait of a Marriage*, pp. 180-81.
14. In fairness to Lady Sackville it must be stated that in 1934 she made up her quarrel with Vita. She bought Long Barn from her for £8,000 and bequeathed it back to her daughter in her will. This was in compensation for cancelling her marriage settlement.
15. HN Diary (unpubl), 24.12.1933.
16. HN Diary (publ), 24.12.1933.
17. Francis Cecil St. Aubyn, succeeded as 3rd Lord St. Levan in 1940 and died in 1978.
18. Of Paris he wrote: 'Owing to the very majesty of her alignment [she] stands superior to her own detail; she has about her an almost Apollonian quality, not, it is true, the assured and commanding calm of the Apollo of Olympia, but the gorgeous symmetry of the Epiphany of Callimachus. . . . The shapeliness of the design is so compelling that one fails to notice the frequent unseemliness of ornament. A magnificent surety has created those wide vistas, an opulent certainty has cut those calm straight lines. Compared to those of Paris, our own architectural treasures appear as fine pieces of furniture jumbled together in the recesses of some art-dealer's shop.' *Spectator*, 13.2.1948.
19. From the original version of HN's Diary, 4.2.1934.
20. HN to JLM, 11.2.1934.
21. Ibid.
22. HN Diary (publ), 11.2.1934.
23. Paul Morand to HN, 24.4.1934.
24. Sir Donald Busk in *The Craft of Diplomacy*, 1967, wrote that the Terminal Essay in *Curzon, The Last Phase*, entitled 'Some Remarks on the Practice of Diplomacy' should be required reading for every new entrant to the Service, and once a year for every Ambassador.
25. HN to VSW (unpubl), 14.5.1934.
26. HN to VSW (unpubl), 15.3.1934.
27. HN Diary (unpubl), 31.5.1934.
28. Review of *Germany Unmasked*, by Robert Dell, 6.7.1934.
29. HN to VSW (unpubl), 23.9.1934.
30. Morrow virtually saved the London Naval Treaty of 1930 from breaking down.
32. HN to VSW (unpubl), 27.9.1934.
32. HN to Raymond Mortimer, 16.10.1934.
33. HN to VSW (unpubl), 9.11.1934.
34. According to Bruce Lockhart HN asked J. P. Morgan whether Dwight Morrow was a selfish man. 'Selfish?' said Morgan, 'Why! He'd have murdered his own children if they had stood in his way.' (Bruce Lockhart Diary, 14.12.1934.)
35. HN to Lady Colefax, 11.11.1934.
36. VW to VSW, 23.9.1934. *The Letters of Virginia Woolf, Volume V* 1979.
37. Copley Amory of the American Legation in Tehran, had been a friend of HN since 1926.
38. HN to VSW (unpubl), 9.11.1934.
39. HN to VSW (unpubl), 21.11.1934.

40. *Diaries and Letters, 1930–1939*, Vol. I, pp. 195–96, Editorial Note.
41. HN to VSW (publ), 26.2.1935.
42. HN to VSW (publ), 11.3.1935.
43. HN Diary (unpubl), 1.5.1935.
44. HN to VSW (unpubl), 27.9.1932.
45. HN to VSW (unpubl), 5.7.1935.
46. HN to VSW (unpubl), 10.7.1935.
47. *Daily Telegraph*, 23.8.1935.
48. Ezra Pound's seven letters to HN, 27 Aug. 1935 to 21 Feb. 1936, were sold at Christie's on 8.3.1978. They are on yellow writing-paper, with a woodcut profile of Pound by Gaudier-Brzeska as a heading.
49. Victor Cunard's palace. HN to VSW, 3.9.1935.
50. HN to BN, 3.9.1935.
51. HN to VSW (unpubl), 5.9.1935.

CHAPTER 3   THE THREAD OF PEACE, 1935–1937

1. HN to VSW (unpubl), 27.11.35.
2. HN Diary (unpubl), 9.10.1935.
3. HN to VSW (unpubl), 13.11.1935.
4. C. G. Tuthill to JLM, 26.11.1980.
5. HN Diary (publ), 17.6.1942.
6. HN to VSW (unpubl), 23.10.1935.
7. HN Diary (unpubl), 27.10.1935.
8. VSW to HN (publ), 28.10.1935.
9. VSW to Clive Bell (undated, but probably 1925).
10. HN to VSW (unpubl), 3.5.1935.
11. VSW to HN (unpubl), 11.11.1935.
12. HN to VSW (publ), 4.12.1935.
13. *Vide* his House of Commons speech in defence of Duff Cooper, 29.6.1936, and 'Marginal Comment', *Spectator*, 20.7.1945.
14. *Chips, The Diaries of Sir Henry Channon*, 1967.
15. Derek Drinkwater, *Professional Amateur: Sir Harold Nicolson's Writings on Diplomacy* (Unpublished thesis. University of Queensland, 1977.)
16. Anne Morrow Lindbergh, *The Flower and the Nettle: Diaries and Letters, 1936–39* (20 Feb. 1936).
17. On the 18th and 20th respectively.
18. HN Diary (publ), 23.1.1936.
19. Duke of Windsor – *A King's Story*, p. 19.
20. Bernstorff refused to submit to the Nazi heresy. He was dismissed from the German Foreign Office and became a partner in a banking firm. He had the courage to shelter a Jewish family in his flat. At the outbreak of the war he was thrown into a concentration camp. After years of torture and heroic resistance he was shot in the courtyard of a Berlin prison in March 1945. He was a great Anglophile and a great German patriot.
21. *Chips, The Diaries of Sir Henry Channon*, 27.2.1936.
22. HN to VSW (publ), 10.3.1936.
23. VSW to HN (unpubl), 16.3.1936.
24. Roland de Margerie had been at the French Embassy in London.
25. HN to Roland de Margerie, 6.4.1936.
26. HN to VSW (publ), 11.6.1936.
27. HN Diary (unpubl), 13.7.1936.

28. HN to VSW (unpubl), 6.10.1936.
29. HN to VSW (publ), 7.4.1936.
30. HN to VSW (unpubl), 1.7.1936.
31. VSW to HN (unpubl), 2.7.1936.
32. HN to JPH, 12.10.1936.
33. HN to JPH, 27.10.1940., quoting a line from D.G. Rosseth's sonnet, *Lovesight*.
34. HN to VSW (unpubl), 31.8.1936.
35. *Chips, The Diaries of Sir Henry Channon*, 20.9.1936.
36. HN to VSW (unpubl), 22.9.1936.
37. HN to VSW (unpubl), 27.9.1936. Winaretta Princesse de Polignac was a daughter of the American millionaire I. M. Singer, who made a fortune out of sewing machines.
38. HN Diary (publ), 7.11.1936.
39. Lord Duncan-Sandys in conversation with JLM. Nevertheless it read well, and received praise from the press (see page 100).
40. Sir Alfred Beit in conversation with JLM.
41. HN Diary (publ), 31.5.1939.
42. Mr. Harold Macmillan in conversation with JLM, 22.2.1978.
43. HN Diary (unpubl), 10.12.1936.
44. HN to VSW (unpubl), 15.12.1936.
45. *Spectator*, 9.4.1943.
46. See *Higher Education in East Africa. Report on the Commission appointed by the Secretary of State for the Colonies*, September 1937 (afterwards called the *De La Warr Commission's Report*). Not all the Commission's recommendations were carried out.
47. For a full account of the Evreux mission, see HN *Diaries*, 10.7.37.
48. Mary Borden, novelist, wife of Sir Edward Spears.
49. HN to VSW (unpubl), 21.7.1937.
50. HN to VSW (unpubl), 13.10.1937.
51. HN to VSW (unpubl), 28.10.1937.
52. HN to VSW (unpubl), 23.11.1937.
53. HN Diary (unpubl), 8.12.1937.
54. HN to VSW (unpubl), 21.12.1937.
55. HN to BN, 8.9.1937.
56. Review of *Helen's Tower* in *Night and Day*, 9.12.1937.

CHAPTER 4   THE BRINK OF CATASTROPHE, 1938–1939

1. HN to VSW (unpubl), 25.1.1938.
2. HN to BN, 27.1.1938.
3. Commander Sir Archibald Southby, 1st Bt., R.N. 1886–1969. M.P. Epsom Division, Junior Lord of the Treasury, 1935–37.
4. *Chips, The Diaries of Sir Henry Channon*, 21.2.1938.
5. HN to Roland de Margerie, 8.3.1929.
6. HN to VSW (publ), 17.4.1938.
7. Ibid. From 'and that thing is too shaming . . .' to the end of quotation hitherto unpublished.
8. HN to VSW (unpubl), 20.4.1938.
9. HN to VSW (unpubl), 26.4.1938.
10. HN to VSW (unpubl), 10.5.1938.
11. HN to VSW (unpubl), 14.5.1938.
12. HN – *Why Britain is at War*, 1939.
13. *The Flower and the Nettle* (1976), 22.5.1938.
14. HN Diary (publ), 6.6.1938.

15. Lord Boothby is wrong in calling HN 'timid as usual' at this time. *Recollections of a Rebel*, 1978.

16. *The Flower and the Nettle* (1976), 26.9.1938.

17. HN to VSW (unpubl), 7.8.1938.

18. HN to the B.B.C., 28.8.1938.

19. HN Diary (unpubl), 15.9.1938.

20. He broadcasted it on the Empire Service of the B.B.C. that night.

21. Sir Robert Vansittart was succeeded as Permanent Under-Secretary of State to the Foreign Office by Sir Alexander Cadogan on 1 January 1938, and became Chief Diplomatic Adviser to the Foreign Office, 1938–41.

22. George Mounsey wrote a Memo to Sir Alec Cadogan in the Foreign Office deprecating this statement. He believed the Government's policy to be the right one. 'It is still more deplorable to feel that the reputation so long enjoyed by the Foreign Office for loyalty, self-discipline and efficiency should be placed at the mercy of the self-advertising publicity campaign of a mischief-minded M.P. [HN].' Sir Horace Wilson, 1882–1972, Permanent head of the Civil Service 1932–42. From 1937 he was unofficially Chief Adviser to Chamberlain on foreign affairs, having a private room in No. 10 Downing Street, while Chamberlain was Prime Minister. His influence on the Prime Minister was profound and disastrous. Victor Cazalet attributed to Horace Wilson HN's not being allowed to broadcast in the spring of 1940.

23. Martin Gilbert – *The Roots of Appeasement*, 1966.

24. A summary of the work done by HN from the 1st August 1938 to 31st July 1939 amounts to: 4,000 letters written; 120 speeches (including broadcasts and television); 23 lectures delivered; 27 committees served on; 101 articles written (including 52 *Daily Telegraph* book reviews); one book written (*Diplomacy*); 77,281 miles travelled; and 25 visits made to his constituency.

25. HN Diary (publ), 9.11.1938. Winston Churchill's more extreme group included Robert Boothby, Duncan Sandys, Lord Lloyd, Duff Cooper.

26. Freya Stark – *The Coast of Incense*, 1953.

27. HN Diary (unpubl), 29.12.1938.

28. HN Diary (unpubl), 26.1.1939.

29. It will be noticed that HN always used the word *diplomatist*, and not *diplomat*. He followed the definition in the O.E.D. of the word *diplomatist* as signifying 'one engaged in official diplomacy', and *diplomat* as 'one employed or skilled in diplomacy; one characterized by diplomatic address'.

30. HN Diary (publ), 23.9.1938.

31. Sir Robert Clive had been HN's Ambassador in Teheran in 1926.

32. The Archduke Otto, eldest son of the last Emperor Karl and the Empress Zita of Austria.

33. HN Diary (unpubl), 4.3.1939.

34. R. S. Hudson, Secretary, Department of Overseas Trade 1937–1940. Created Viscount Hudson 1952.

35. They were John and Piers.

36. HN to VSW (unpubl), 16.8.1939.

37. HN to VSW (publ), 19.8.1939.

38. *Childe Harold's Pilgrimage*, Canto 1, xii, and *Childe Harold's Goodnight*.

39. *Spectator*, 23.6.1944.

40. HN Diary (publ), 1.9.1939.

41. *Spectator*, 25.8.1939.

42. HN Diary (publ), 1.9.1939.

APPENDIX: NOTES TO TEXT

CHAPTER 5   THE SECOND WORLD WAR – STRUGGLE FOR SURVIVAL,
1939–1942

1. *Spectator*, 25.9.1939.
2. HN Diary (publ), 11.9.1939.
3. For the *Nineteenth Century* he wrote two articles (October and December), called 'Causes and Purposes'. He maintained that in the First War we were fighting for King and Country. In this war we were fighting 'to prevent mankind from relapsing into a purely animal condition. We were fighting for the destiny of the human race'. No wonder Clive Bell wrote to Frances Partridge (12.9.1939): 'Harold Nicolson is saving the country – and something more'.
4. In two 'Marginal Comment' articles (*Spectator*, 25.9.1929 and 26.4.1940) HN appealed for fair treatment of those Germans who had come to this country for political asylum; and hoped that spy mania would not lead us to treat with stupid cruelty unhappy German refugees in our midst. In Munich in 1955 HN met a member of the Bavarian Government who had been given this article to read by a kindly Governor of a Liverpool prison where he was interned. He told HN it came to him 'as a beam of light'.
5. HN to Roland de Margerie, 2.10.1939.
6. Since the outbreak of war the German battleship *Graf Spee* had been a serious menace to British communications in the South Atlantic. On the 13th December she was damaged by our Fleet and scuttled by her captain.
7. HN Diary (publ), 15.12.1939.
8. Edouard Herriot, 1872–1957. French Radical Socialist; President of the Chamber of Deputies, and patriot.
9. HN to VSW (unpubl), 9.4.1940.
10. HN Diary (publ), 9.4.1940.
11. Lord Dunglass succeeded his father as 14th Earl of Home in 1951, but later renounced the title.
12. HN Diary (publ), 10.5.1940.
13. NN – *Diaries and Letters 1939–1945* Vol. II, p. 98.
14. HN to VSW (unpubl), 4.6.1940.
15. Such as the wooden effigy of St. Barbara, which meant so much to both of them. This was actually the only object he specified by name, for sentimental reasons.
16. The St. Aubyns had rented Horserace, half a mile from Sissinghurst. Mr. St. Aubyn was most of this time away on war service.
17. VSW to HN (unpubl), 11.6.1940.
18. HN Diary (publ), 15.6.1940.
19. Ultimately he changed his mind because this was a Sackville preserve and he did not want to intrude upon it, even though Vita's ashes were interred there.
20. HN Diary (unpubl), 14.7.1940.
21. HN Diary (publ), 26.8.1940.
22. Christopher Hobhouse remained something of a legend to his generation. Mr. Seymour Karminski, in whose chambers he had worked in the Temple, assured HN that he certainly would have made a great career at the Bar. Christopher himself with superb confidence always said that he would become Lord Chancellor. After the war his friends occasionally dined together in his memory.
23. HN to VSW (unpubl), 12.10.1935.
24. HN to JPH, 28.9.1940.
25. HN to VSW (unpubl), 10.7.1940.
26. HN to VSW (unpubl), 8.11.1940.
27. HN Diary (publ), 20.11.1940.
28. HN to VSW (unpubl), 31.3.1941.
29. HN to VSW (unpubl), 2.4.1941.

30. See Footnote 2, page 139, *Diaries and Letters*, 1939–1945, Vol. II.
31. HN Diary (publ), 15.5.1941.
32. HN Diary (publ), 22.6.1941.
33. HN Diary (publ), 18.7.1941.
34. HN to VSW (publ), 21.7.1941.
35. *Truth*, an article entitled 'Bracken in Bloomsbury', 25.7.1941.
36. Letter to JLM, 27.5.1978.
37. Letter to JLM, 18.10.1977. Sir Kenneth Clark was Director of the Film Division, later Controller Home Publicity, at the Ministry of Information, 1939–41.
38. Ronald Tree – *When the Moon was High*, 1975.
39. *Crypts of Power*, 1971, p. 121.
40. Ian McLaine – *Ministry of Morale*, 1979.
41. In June 1943 Lord Cranborne sent for HN and told him he thought it would, after all, be a good idea to publish the diary. He regretted that he had dissuaded him from doing so. But in spite of this reversal of advice HN decided against publication for fear of causing offence to a number of people.
42. HN to Lady Violet Bonham-Carter, 28.8.1943.
43. Sir Frederick Ogilvie, a don, died 1949.
44. *Spectator*, 5.8.1952.
45. HN Diary (unpubl), 12.9.1941.
46. HN to VSW (unpubl), 2.1.1942.
47. HN Diary (publ), 2.1.1942.
48. HN Diary (publ), 27.1.1942.
49. Daniel Binchy had been Irish Minister in Berlin when HN was there from 1927–29.
50. HN Diary (publ), 18.3.1942.
51. HN to BN, 26.3.1942.
52. *Spectator*, 18.12.1942.
53. HN Diary (publ), 30.7.1942.
54. HN to VSW (unpubl), 8.9.1942.
55. HN Diary (unpubl), 2.10.1942.
56. HN to VSW (unpubl), 12.10.1942.
57. HN to BN (publ), 25.10.1942.
58. Ibid.

CHAPTER 6 THE SECOND WORLD WAR – SURVIVAL TO VICTORY, 1942–1945

1. VSW to HN (unpubl), 3.11.1942.
2. HN did not find Beveridge an attractive man; and his vanity amounted to idiocy. It was not for nothing perhaps that at Balliol he had been known among his contemporaries as 'Buggeryfuck'.
3. VSW to HN (unpubl), 2.12.1942.
4. HN to VSW (unpubl), 28.1.1943.
5. VSW to HN (publ), 15.7.1943.
6. On the 18th March, 1943.
7. HN to VSW (unpubl), 23.10.1943.
8. A previous secretary of the Nicolsons.
9. HN to BN and NN (unpubl), 5.12.1943.
10. HN to VSW (unpubl), 2.12.1943.
11. HN's personal attitude to Sir Oswald Mosley had changed since New Party days when he admired and liked him. HN to BN and NN (unpubl), 5.12.1943: 'God knows

that the only feeling I have about him is one of deep dislike. He is a selfish and cruel man and as cold as a fish'.

12. Smuts had said: 'France has gone and will be gone in our day, and perhaps for many a day.'
13. HN to BN and NN (publ), 31.12.1943.
14. VSW to HN (publ), 15.2.1944.
15. *Spectator*, 25.2.1944.
16. HN to BN and NN (unpubl), 19.3.1944.
17. Published 1.1.1944.
18. HN to VSW (unpubl), 22.2.1944. To Raymond Mortimer HN once intimated that in writing it was distinction he lacked, not bounce.
19. VSW to HN (publ), 24.2.1944.
20. Published 1941.
21. HN to VSW (unpubl), 17.4.1944.
22. 'Coffee cup.' A Sackville-Nicolson expression, meaning an object which conveys a twinge of sadness, like a used coffee cup that a person who has gone away had drunk out of.
23. HN to VSW (unpubl), 7.3.1944.
24. HN to VSW (unpubl), 24.11.1950.
25. HN Diary (publ), 8.9.1944.
26. HN Diary (publ), 5.8.1944.
27. HN Diary (unpubl), 8.8.1945.
28. VSW to HN (unpubl), 9.1.1945.
29. HN to Constable's, the publishers, 16.1.1945.
30. HN Diary (unpubl), 26.1.1945.
31. VSW to HN (unpubl), 26.1.1945.
32. *Spectator*, 14.2.1947.
33. Hansard. *Rebuilding of the New House of Commons*, 25.1.1945.
34. VSW to HN (unpubl), 14.2.1945.
35. HN Diary (publ), 15.2.1945.
36. HN to VSW (publ), 28.2.1945.
37. VSW to HN (unpubl), 28.2.1945.
38. HN to VSW (publ), 21.1.1945.
39. The Dumbarton Oaks Conference met between 21st August and 7th October, 1944.
40. Mussolini's fate was to hang upside down on a Milan petrol pump beside his mistress, Clara Petacci. The comment of Mrs. Groves, HN's charlady, was 'Serve him right. A gentleman like that driving about in a car with a lady not his wife!'
41. HN to NN (publ), 3.5.1945.
42. HN to NN (publ), 20.5.1945.

CHAPTER 7 NOSTALGIA FOR PARLIAMENT, 1945–1948

1. HN to NN (publ), 18.5.1945.
2. HN to NN (publ), 4.6.1945.
3. VSW to HN (unpubl), 5.6.1945.
4. HN Diary (publ), 1.8.1945.
5. HN Diary (publ), 6.8.1945.
6. HN to NN (publ), 30.8.1945. Yet, incorrigible, he once again made the same mistake in changing his Party allegiance.
7. HN to VSW (publ), 28.9.1945.
8. HN to VSW (unpubl), 5.12.1945.

9. HN to VSW (part publ), 29.10.1945.
10. HN to VSW (unpubl), 2.10.1945.
11. HN Diary (unpubl), 23.11.1945.
12. Christopher St.John (neighbour, close friend, and biographer of Ethel Smyth) to VSW, 4.6.1946.
13. *Spectator*, 2.4.1948.
14. *Congress of Vienna*, p. 236.
15. HN Diary (publ), 30.4.1946.
16. ibid (unpubl),
17. HN Diary (unpubl), 1.5.1946.
18. HN to VSW (unpubl), 23.7.1946.
19. VSW to HN (unpubl), 23.7.1946.
20. HN Diary (unpubl), 28.7.1946.
21. *Spectator*, 23.8.1946.
22. Gordon Craig was the son of Ellen Terry and brother of Edy Craig, who had recently died. Edy Craig had lived at Smallhythe, Kent, with Christopher St. John and Clare Atwood. They were close friends of Vita.
23. HN Diary (unpubl), 2.9.1946.
24. Mina Curtiss – *Other People's Letters*, 1978, p. 25.
25. HN to VSW (unpubl), 6.3.1947. 'This is NOT (repeat NOT) an impulsive gesture. I have been worrying over it for months. Oh, my sweet, what weather . . .'
26. Repeated to HN by Lady Cunard.
27. HN Diary (publ), 28.5.1947.
28. HN to VSW (unpubl), 8.7.1947.
29. HN Diary (publ), 6.8.1947.
30. HN to VSW (unpubl), 2.9.1947.
31. HN to VSW (unpubl), 5.9.1947.
32. HN to VSW (publ), 6.9.1947.
33. HN to VSW (unpubl), 6.9.1947.
34. HN Diary (publ), 8.9.1947.
35. HN to VSW (unpubl), 8.9.1947.
36. HN to VSW (unpubl), 8.9.1947.
37. HN to VSW (unpubl), 13.1.1948.
38. HN to VSW (publ), 22.9.1948.
39. HN Diary (publ), 2.3.1948.
40. HN Diary (unpubl), 10.3.1948.
41. HN to VSW (publ), 12.3.1948.

CHAPTER 8   ROYAL BIOGRAPHER, 1948–1952

1. Pierre Brisson to HN, 9.7.1948.
2. HN to Roland de Margerie, 8.9.1948: 'How much I agree with you at feeling almost physical relief at never having met Madame de Staël. She would not have been interested in me since she would have regarded me as the type of English hunting squire, but she would have been very interested in you owing to your great powers of conversation, and your whole life, my poor Roland, would have been a series of violent interruptions.'
3. HN to VSW (unpubl), 8.6.1948.
4. VSW to HN (publ), 8.6.1948.
5. HN Diary (publ), 21.7.1948. The 2nd Earl of Cromer (1877–1953).
6. HN Diary (unpubl), 7.9.1948. Sir George Clark, G.C.M.G. (1874–1951).
7. HN Diary (unpubl), 10.9.1948. Hon. Sir Richard Molyneux (1893–1954).
8. *Denton Welch Journals* (ed. Jocelyn Brooke), 1952. The entry from which the

following extracts are taken is dated, 31st August, 1948, but the actual visit to Sissinghurst took place on the 27th.

9. Actually he went into a relapse and died on the 30th December 1948. HN reviewed Denton Welch's *A Voice Through a Cloud.* He lamented him as a man of unfulfilled renown, and greatly gifted. He helped to get his *Journals* published in 1952.

10. HN Diary (unpubl), 29.10.1948.
11. HN Diary (part publ), 29.10.1948.
12. John Gore – *King George V. A Personal Memoir*, 1941.
13. Prince Albert Victor, Duke of Clarence, 1864–1892.
14. Sir Arthur John Bigge, Lord Stamfordham, 1849–1931. A royal servant since 1880. Private Secretary to Queen Victoria, King Edward VII and King George V.
15. HN Diary (unpubl), 21.3.1949.
16. Told by HN to a friend of the author.
17. Prince Alexander Albert of Battenberg, Marquess of Carisbrooke (1886–1960), the only son of Princess Beatrice, Queen Victoria's favourite and youngest daughter.
18. HN Diary (unpubl), 27.7.1949.
19. Sir Charles Cust, 3rd Bart (1864–1931). Equerry to King George V 1892–1919.
20. HN Diary (unpubl), 15.6.1949.
21. VSW to HN (unpubl), 24.7.1950.
22. HN Diary (publ), 4.10.1949.
23. HN Diary (unpubl), 17.1.1950.
24. HN to Sybil Colefax, 11.10.1949.
25. *Spectator*, 13.10.1950.
26. HN to VSW (unpubl), 10.1.1949.
27. VSW to HN (unpubl), 20.2.1950.
28. Count Albert Mensdorff-Pouilly-Dietrichstein, Austrian Ambassador in London up to 1914.
29. Violet Trefusis to VSW, May 1919.
30. Violet Trefusis to VSW, 9.1.1945.
31. HN to VSW (unpubl), 12.12.1950.
32. Ibid.
33. HN to VSW (unpubl), 16.3.1951.
34. HN to VSW (publ), 28.3.1951.
35. Cecilie, wife of Sir R. C. Cunliffe, 5th Bt., and sister of Vita's father.
36. HN to VSW (unpubl), 17.4.1951.
37. The Picasso painting of a round table in front of a window was dated 1919.
38. HN to VSW (unpubl), 19.12.1950.
39. HN Diary (unpubl), 14.10.1935.
40. HN to VSW (unpubl), 7.12.1949.
41. Cecil Beaton – *The Parting Years*, 1978.
42. HN to VSW (unpubl), 11.6.1951.
43. HN to VSW (unpubl), 12.6.1951.
44. HN Diary (unpubl), 13.1.1936.
45. Roger Fulford to JLM, 5.2.1978.
46. HN to RM, 16.8.1925.
47. HN to VSW (unpubl), 8.5.1951.
48. Long Crichel House, in Dorset, was shared by Eardley Knollys, Raymond Mortimer, Eddy Sackville-West and Desmond Shawe-Taylor. At Wilton they stayed with David Herbert in his garden house.
49. HN to VSW (unpubl), 21.8.1951.
50. HN Diary (publ), 19.9.1952.
51. HN Diary (publ), 29.7.1952.
52. HN to a correspondent of the *New Yorker*, February 1963.

HAROLD NICOLSON

CHAPTER 9   GOOD BEHAVIOUR, 1952–1954

1. In 1951.
2. HN to Professor W. H. Gardner, 27.3.1958.
3. HN to James Pope-Hennessy, 13.1.1952.
4. HN Diary (publ), 3.1.1953.
5. HN to VSW (unpubl), 26.2.1952.
6. HN to VSW (unpubl), 27.2.1952.
7. HN to VSW (unpubl), 1.3.1952.
8. HN to VSW (unpubl), 27.2.1952.
9. HN to VSW (unpubl), 10.3.1952.
10. HN to VSW (unpubl), 20.5.1952.
11. HN Diary (unpubl), 31.5.1952.
12. HN to BN, 7.6.1952.
13. HN to VSW (unpubl), 11.6.1952.
14. HN Diary (unpubl), 18.8.1952.
15. HN Diary (unpubl), 28.8.1952.
16. VSW to HN (unpubl), 30.9.1952.
17. She was Princess Margarete, fourth daughter of the Empress Frederick of Germany.
18. The Hon. Margaret Geddes, daughter of Auckland 1st Lord Geddes. She married in 1937 H.R.H. Prince Ludwig Hermann Alexander Chlodwig of Hesse und bei Rhein.
19. HN Diary (unpubl), 17.9.1952.
20. *Spectator*, 12.5.1950.
21. HN Diary (unpubl), 28.5.1950.
22. HN to VSW (unpubl), 25.11.1952.
23. VSW to HN (unpubl), 31.12.1952.
24. HN Diary (unpubl), 4.1.1953.
25. The article appeared in the June issue of *The Woman's Home Companion*, 1953. It was slightly elaborated and published in book form by Funk and Wagnell in 1954 as *The Crown and the People, 1902–1953* by H.R.H. The Duke of Windsor. There was nothing in the text of the book to which anyone could take exception. The Duke wrote objectively and fairly about his father, brother and niece, paying tribute to their excellent qualities. He also acknowledged that Harold could not have been more helpful, was sparing with cuts, and constructive with suggestions; and that he, the Duke, was well satisfied with the changes made.
26. HN to VSW (unpubl), 18.3.1953.
27. HN to BN, 5.4.1953.
28. HN Diary (publ), 31.3.1953. Bunny Drummond (died 1981) wife of Lindsay Drummond the publisher was a close family friend. The Drummonds lived at Sissinghurst Place, inherited in 1947 from Lindsay's parents, General and Mrs. (Kitty) Laurence Drummond.
29. HN Diary (unpubl), 4.4.1953.
30. HN Diary (publ), 6.5.1953.
31. VSW to HN (unpubl), 22.7.1953.
32. HN to VSW (unpubl), 21.7.1953.
33. HN to PN, 22.7.1953.
34. VSW to HN (unpubl), 22.7.1953.
35. Sir Eric Drummond, Secretary-General to the League of Nations 1919–1933, succeeded as 16th Earl of Perth in 1937.
36. HN to VSW (unpubl), 24.5.1962.
37. VSW to HN (unpubl), 8.4.1954.
38. HN to VSW (unpubl), 11.8.1954.

39. HN to JPH, 18.7.1954.
40. HN to Anthony Powell, 8.10.1932.
41. HN to VSW (unpubl), 10.6.1954.
42. HN to Juliet Nicolson (publ), 31.7.1954.
43. HN to VSW (unpubl), 5.8.1954.
44. Henri Alain-Fournier (1886–1914). Born in Cologne. Killed at St. Rémy in World War I. He left a few short stories ('Miracles', 1924) and *Le Grand Meaulnes* (1913).
45. VSW to HN (publ), 31.8.1954.
46. HN to VSW (publ), 30.9.1954.
47. His heart never became dangerously weak. But there was something wrong with the muscle of the heart which missed one beat in every five. And this deficiency, apart from his strokes, caused him discomfiture and anxiety for the rest of his life.
48. These directions were later cancelled.
49. HN to VSW (unpubl), 30.11.1954.
50. HN to JLM, 23.2.1958.
51. VSW to HN (unpubl), 28.9.1954.
52. VSW to HN (publ), 30.8.1955.

CHAPTER 10   THE AGE OF REASON, 1955–1960

1. HN to VSW (unpubl), 6.1.1955.
2. HN to NN, 12.8.1957.
3. HN to VSW (publ), 12.1.1955.
4. HN to VSW (unpubl), 6.1.1955. 'Dottie' was Dorothy Wellesley, poet, Duchess of Wellington.
5. HN to VSW (unpubl), 19.1.1955.
6. HN to VSW (publ), 3.3.1955.
7. VSW Diary (publ), 11.3.1955.
8. HN to E. Niggeman, 1.4.1955.
9. HN Diary (publ), 15.5.1955.
10. HN to 3rd Viscount Esher, 25.7.1957.
11. HN Diary (publ), 22.5.1955.
12. VSW Diary (publ), 29.11.1954.
13. VSW to HN (publ), 21.8.1955.
14. HN's old friend, Archie Clark Kerr, died 1951.
15. Rt. Hon. Hector McNeil, (1907–1955). In 1945 Attlee made him Parliamentary Under-Secretary at the Foreign Office under Bevin. He was a popular speaker on radio and television.
16. HN to VSW (unpubl), 1.2.1956.
17. E. Sackville-West to HN, 30.3.1956.
18. Subsequently Lady Antonia Fraser, the well-known biographer.
19. HN Diary (unpubl), 25.2.1957.
20. HN Diary (unpubl), 19.10.1957.
21. HN to VSW (unpubl), 17.5.1950.
22. R. Bruce Lockhart – *Diary*, 19.6.1935.
23. Rose Macaulay – 'Sir Harold Nicolson' (Feature Articles Service for the British Council), June 1956.
24. HN to VSW (unpubl), 1.8.1956.
25. Kenneth Rose – Note dated 27.11.1956 (kindly put at my disposal).
26. HN Diary (unpubl), 7.11.1956.
27. HN Diary (publ), 15.12.1956.
28. It was typical of HN's compassionate nature that when Eden resigned on the 9th

January, to be succeeded by Macmillan, he felt sorry for him, although relieved at his going.

29. HN to BN, 31.1.1957.
30. Described at length in *Journey to Java*, 1957.
31. HN Diary (publ), 21.2.1957.
32. HN to RM, 31.1.1957.
33. HN to JPH, 18.2.1957.
34. HN to Hallam Tennyson, 14.6.1957.
35. HN Diary (publ), 10.6.1957.
36. NN to VSW, 19.6.1957.
37. Letter, like most of Guy Burgess's letters, undated.
38. HN to VSW (unpubl), 23.5.1957.
39. HN Diary (publ), 13.6.1957.
40. HN to VSW (unpubl), 13.6.1957.
41. Editor of the *Observer*, 1948–75.
42. HN to NN (unpubl), 26.9.1957.
43. HN to VSW (publ), 9.10.1957.
44. HN to VSW (unpubl), 22.10.1957.
45. HN Diary (unpubl), 21.12.1957.
46. HN to E. Niggeman, 11.1.1958.
47. VSW to HN (publ), 13.8.1958.
48. Lord Eustace Percy, 7th son of the 7th Duke of Northumberland, held several Government posts as Conservative M.P., created Lord Percy of Newcastle 1953.
49. HN Diary (unpubl), 8.4.1958.
50. HN to VSW (unpubl), 2.7.1958.
51. HN to VSW (unpubl), 29.7.1958.
52. HN to JPH 2.6.1958.
53. JPH to HN, undated.
54. Clive Bell to Frances Partridge, 7.9.1958.
55. In March 1956 HN was particularly incensed by the one in which Rees implied that Burgess kept his friends' letters in order to blackmail them.
56. HN Diary (unpubl), 17.4.1958.
57. HN Diary (unpubl), 15.10.1958.
58. HN to VSW (unpubl), 23.10.1958.
59. When the *Lady Chatterley's Lover* case came before the court in 1960 HN refused to give evidence in its favour as a work of literature.
60. HN Diary (publ and unpubl), 4.12.1958.
61. HN Diary (publ), 5.1.1959.
62. HN to NN, 16.1.1959.
63. HN to NN, 31.1.1959.
64. Sir Daniel Lascelles, K.C.M.G., was obliged to retire from the Service because of angina pectoris, and died in 1968, aged sixty-six.
65. HN to E. Niggeman, 12.2.1959.
66. *Ikkibani* – a Nicolson term for vulgar and ostentatious floral decoration.
67. HN to VSW (unpubl), 19.11.1959.
68. HN to E. Niggeman, 14.1.1959.
69. HN Diary (publ), 25.2.1959.
70. HN to VSW (unpubl), 14.4.1959.
71. HN to E. Niggeman, 27.12.1959.
72. On this cruise VSW finished *No Signposts in the Sea*. Harold found the story moving. He called it a 'decent' book, which 'will make the reviewers think it old-fashioned and upper-class. But you and I prefer the upper to the middle class, even as we prefer distinction to vulgarity.' HN to VSW (publ), 1.11.1960.
73. HN to NN, 21.1.1960.

74. HN Diary (unpubl), 19.5.1960.
75. HN Diary (publ), 3.3.1960.
76. Lord Clark was awarded the O.M. in 1976.
77. HN to VSW (unpubl), 14.7.1960.
78. Bernard Wall, editor of *The Twentieth Century*, December 1960.
79. HN Diary (publ), 17.3.1960.
80. HN to VSW (unpubl), 7.7.1960.
81. Clive Bell to Frances Partridge, 7.9.1960.
82. HN to VSW (unpubl), 14.12.1960.
83. VSW to HN (unpubl), 6.12.1960. HN was hurt by the number of friends who wrote pointing out these slips. He called them *doryphores* (questing prigs), a word coined by him to describe beetles who bored away at works of literature in the endeavour to pick minute holes.

CHAPTER 11   THE END OF A PARTNERSHIP, 1961–1962

1. HN to Lady Alexandra Metcalfe, 24.1.1961.
2. HN to NN, 29.1.1961. Lady Juliet Duff (b. 1881) was the daughter of the 4th Earl of Lonsdale and the famous beauty who subsequently became Marchioness of Ripon. Lady Juliet was extremely tall and was once arrested in a Berlin night-club for masquerading as a man in drag.
3. HN to E. Niggeman, 25.1.1961.
4. HN to Lady A. Metcalfe, ibid.
5. HN Diary (unpubl), 10.1.1961.
6. VSW to HN (unpubl), 17.2.1961.
7. VSW to HN (unpubl), 23.3.1961.
8. HN to VSW (unpubl), 9.3.1961.
9. HN to VSW (unpubl), 6.4.1961.
10. HN to JLM, 14.3.1961.
11. HN Diary (unpubl), 30.3.1961.
12. HN to VSW (unpubl), 25.5.1961.
13. On the 6th June 1961. This was the result of a four-year endeavour by the novelist Ernest Raymond, to have the remains of the poet, his wife and possibly other members of his family, transferred from the crypt beneath the Highgate School chapel in what is old Highgate cemetery.
14. HN to VSW (unpubl), 7.6.1961.
15. Hon. James Smith, 1906–1980, son of 2nd Viscount Hambleden.
16. HN to VSW (unpubl), 31.5.1961.
17. Siegfried Sassoon to Dame Felicitas Corrigan, 11.1.1962.
18. See Chapter 3 note 20.
19. HN to VSW (unpubl), 18.7.1961.
20. VSW to HN (unpubl), 18.7.1961.
21. VSW to HN (unpubl), 8.7.1957.
22. NN to VSW, 20.9.1961 (quoted in full in *Diaries and Letters*, Vol. III).
23. HN to JPH, 25.12.1961.
24. HN to VSW (unpubl), 4.5.1962.
25. VSW to HN (unpubl), 4.10.1961. 'Baba' is Lady Alexandra Metcalfe, a friend to whom HN was particularly devoted.
26. VSW to HN (unpubl), 4.6.1941.
27. HN to VSW (unpubl), 10.10.1961.
28. VSW to HN (unpubl), 10.10.1961.
29. HN to VSW (unpubl), 29.11.1961.

30. *Observer* article, 12.11.1961.
31. HN to VSW (unpubl), 3.1.1962.
32. HN to JPH, 18.1.1962.
33. HN to JPH, 1.2.1962.
34. From a note recorded by Kenneth Rose on 20th February 1962, and kindly communicated to the author.
35. VSW Diary (publ), 15.2.1962.
36. HN Diary (publ), 18.2.1962.
37. HN Diary (publ), 23.2.1962.
38. HN to VSW (unpubl), 27.2.1962.
39. VSW to HN (unpubl), 27.2.1962.
40. HN to JLM, 11.3.1962.
41. VSW to HN (unpubl), 18.5.1962.
42. HN Diary (publ), 1.6.1962.
43. HN Diary (publ), 2.6.1962.

CHAPTER 12   EPILOGUE, 1962–1968

1. HN Diary (unpubl), 30.6. and 4.10.1964.
2. HN to PN, 31.7.1962.
3. HN to PN, 25.8.1962.
4. HN to E. Niggeman, 26.8.1962.
5. HN to Kenneth Rose, 10.9.1962.
6. HN to Violet Trefusis, 11.6.1962.
7. Kenneth Rose – Note dated 21.11.1966.

BIBLIOGRAPHY
TO VOLUMES I AND II
Books

Adam, Colin Forbes, *Life of Lord Lloyd*, 1948
Alastos, Doros, *Venizelos*, 1942
Alsop, Susan Mary, *Lady Sackville*, 1978
Arfa, General Hassan, *Under Five Shahs*, 1965
Bailey, Cyril, *Francis Fortescue Urquhart: A Memoir*, 1936
Barclay, Sir Thomas, *The Turco-Italian War*, 1912
Bartlett, Vernon, *And Now, Tomorrow*, 1960
Beaton, Sir Cecil, *The Parting Years*, 1978
Bell, Anne Olivier (Assisted by Andrew McNeillie), *The Diary of Virginia Woolf*, Vols. II–III, (1920–30), 1978–80
Bell, Clive, *Old Friends*, 1956
Bell, Quentin, *Virginia Woolf*, Vols. I and II, 1972
Berners, Lord, *Far From the Madding War*, 1941
Boothby, Lord, *Recollections of a Rebel*, 1978
Boyle, Andrew, *Poor Dear Brendan*, 1974
Boyle, Andrew, *The Climate of Treason*, 1979
Briggs, Asa, *The Golden Age of Wireless*, 1965
Briggs, Asa, *The History of Broadcasting in the United Kingdom, Vol IV: Sound and Vision*, 1979
Busk, Sir Douglas, *The Craft of Diplomacy*, 1967
Butler, Rohan (and E. L. Woodward), *Documents on British Foreign Policy*, Series I–III, 1919–29
Cadogan, Sir Alexander, *Diaries* (ed. David Dilkes), 1971
Campbell, Roy, *Broken Record*, 1934
Campbell, Roy, *Light on a Dark Horse*, 1951
Cartland, Barbara, *Ronald Cartland*, 1942
Channon, Sir Henry, *Chips: The Diaries of Sir Henry Channon*, 1967
Churchill, Winston, *The World Crisis: The Aftermath*, 1929
Connolly, Cyril, *The Condemned Playground*, 1945
Cooper, Duff, *Old Men Forget*, 1954
Corrigan, D. Felicitas, *Siegfried Sassoon: Poet's Pilgrimage*, 1973
Curtiss, Mina, *Other People's Letters*, 1978
Driberg, Tom, *Guy Burgess, A Portrait with Background*, 1956

Edwardes, Oliver (Sir William Haley), *Talking of Books* (see especially 'Asking for More'), 1957

Elliott, Sir Ivo (ed.), *The Balliol College Register: 1833–1933*, 1934

Furbank, P. N., *E. M. Forster: A Life*, Vols. I and II, 1977–78

Gilbert, Martin, *The Roots of Appeasement*, 1966

Gladwyn, Lord, *Memoirs*, 1972

Gooch, G. P., and Temperley, Harold (eds.), *British Documents on The Origins of the War*, 1898–1914

Gordon, Anne W., *Peter Howard's Life and Letters*, 1970

Gregory, J. D., *On the Edge of Diplomacy*, 1929

Grey of Fallodon, Viscount, *Twenty-Five Years*, Vol. III, 1928

Grubb, Sir Frederick, *Crypts of Power*, 1971

Hardinge of Penshurst, Lord, *Old Diplomacy*, 1947

Hart-Davis, Rupert, *Hugh Walpole*, 1952

Herbert, David, *Second Son*, 1972

Holroyd, Michael, *Lytton Strachey*, Vol. II, 1968

Horstmann, *Nothing for Tears* (with Introduction by HN), 1953

Hussey, Christopher, *The Life of Sir Edwin Lutyens*, 1953

House, E. M., 'The Paris Conference' (*Encyclopaedia Britannica*), 1926

Isherwood, Christopher, *Goodbye to Berlin*, 1940

James, Robert Rhodes, *Victor Cazalet*, 1976

Jones, Sir Lawrence, *An Edwardian Youth*, 1956

Jullian, Philippe (and John Phillips), *Violet Trefusis, Life and Letters*, 1976

Keynes, J. M., *Two Memoirs*, 1949

Lindbergh, Anne Morrow, *The Flower and the Nettle: Diaries and Letters, 1936–1939*, 1976

Lockhart, Sir Robert Bruce, *Diaries and Papers* (ed. K. Young), Vol. I, 1887–1938, 1973

Lockhart, Sir Robert Bruce, *Retreat from Glory*, 1934

MacCarthy, Sir Desmond, *Memories*, 1953

MacKnight, Nancy (ed.), *Dearest Andrew: Letters from V. Sackville-West to Andrew Reiber, 1951–1962*, 1980

McLaine, Ian, *Ministry of Morale*, 1979

MacPherson, Margaret, *The Built for the Future*, 1964

Marquand, David, *Ramsay MacDonald*, 1977

Maximilian, Prince Karl, *Heading for the Abyss*, 1928

Moorhouse, Geoffrey, *The Diplomats*, 1977

Mosley, Sir Oswald, *My Life*, 1968

Namier, Lewis, *Avenues of History* (see especially 'The Story of a German Diplomatist'), 1952

Newsome, David, *A History of Wellington College, 1859–1959*, 1959
Nicolson, Nigel (ed.), *Diaries and Letters of Sir Harold Nicolson 1930–1962*, 3 vols., 1966–68
Nicolson, Nigel, *Portrait of a Marriage*, 1973
Nicolson, Nigel and Trautmann, Joanne (eds.), *Letters of Virginia Woolf*, Vols. IV–V, 1978–79
Painter, George D., *Marcel Proust*, Vol. II, 1965
Pears, Sir Edwin, *Forty Years in Constantinople*, 1916
Pears, Sir Edwin, *The Life of Abdul Hamid*, 1917
Phillips, John (and Jullian, Philippe), *Violet Trefusis, Life and Letters*, 1976
Pollock, Bertram, *A Twentieth Century Bishop: Recollections and Reflections* (with a Foreword by HN), 1944
Raymond, John, *Uncle Beuve and Sir Harold (England's on the Anvil)* 1958
Rendel, Sir George, *The Sword and the Olive, 1913–1945*, 1957
Repington, Colonel C. à Court, *The First World War*, Vols. I and II, 1920
Riddell, Lord, *Intimate Diary of the Peace Conference, 1919–1922*, 1933
Rose, Norman, *Vansittart: Study of a Diplomat*, 1978
Roskill, Stephen (ed.), *Hankey, Man of Secrets, Vol. II, 1919–1936*, 1972
Rumbold, Sir Horace, *The War Crisis in Berlin, July–August 1914* (with Introduction by HN), 1944
Rumbold, Richard, *Little Victims*, 1933
St. John, Christopher, *Ethel Smyth*, 1959
Scott, Geoffrey, *Portrait of Zélide*, 1925
Scott-James, Anne, *Sissinghurst: The Making of a Garden*, 1974
Sheean, Vincent, *In Search of History*, 1935
Shone, Richard, *Bloomsbury Portraits*, 1976
Sieff, Israel, *Memoirs*, 1970
Skidelsky, Robert, *Oswald Mosley*, 1975
Stark, Freya, *The Coast of Incense*, 1953
Stevens, Michael, *V. Sackville-West*, 1973
Steiner, Zara, *The Foreign Office and Foreign Policy, 1898–1914*, 1969
Steiner, Zara, *Britain and the Origins of the First World War*, 1977
Strachey, James (and Leonard Woolf), *Virginia Woolf and Lytton Strachey: Letters*, 1956
Strachey, Lytton, *Queen Victoria*, 1918
Stuart-Wortley, Violet, *Life Without Theory: An Autobiography*, 1946
Temperley, Harold and Gooch, C. P. (eds.), *British Documents on the Origin of the War, 1898–1914*

Thompson, Neville, *The Anti-Appeasers: Conservative Opposition to Appeasement in the 1930s*, 1971

Trautmann, Joanne and Nicolson, Nigel (eds.), *Letters of Virginia Woolf*, Vols. IV–V, 1978–79

Tree, Ronald, *When the Moon was High*, 1975

Trefusis, Violet, *Don't Look Round*, 1952

Vansittart, Lord, *Autobiography*, 1958

Waterfield, Gordon, *Professional Diplomat: Sir Percy Loraine*, 1973

Weaver, J. R. H., *Henry William Carless Davis: A Memoir*, 1933

Welch, Denton, *Journals* (ed. Jocelyn Brooke), 1952

Wellesley, Dorothy, *Far Have I Travelled*, 1952

Wellington College *Register*, 7th edition, January 1859 to December 1948

Wilber, Donald N., *Iran, Past and Present*, 1948

Williams, Francis, *Nothing so Strange: An Autobiography*, 1970

Woodhouse, C. M., *The Story of Modern Greece*, 1968

Woodward, E. L. and Butler, Rohan, *Documents on British Foreign Policy*, Series I–III, 1919–39

Woolf, Leonard, and Strachey, James, *Virginia Woolf and Lytton Strachey: Letters*, 1956

Woolf, Virginia, *Orlando*, 1928

Woolf, Virginia: for *Letters* and *Diaries* see under Nicolson, Nigel, and Bell, Anne Olivier

Wright, Sir Denis, *The English Amongst the Persians*, 1977

Articles

Brogan, Sir Denis, 'The Sage of Sissinghurst', *Spectator*, 17.5.1968

Drinkwater, Derek, 'Professional Amateur: Sir Harold Nicolson's Writings on Diplomacy', Unpublished Thesis, University of Queensland, 1977

Ekstein, Michael, 'Sir Edward Grey and Imperial Germany in 1914', *Journal of Contemporary History*, Vol. 6, 1971

Ekstein, Michael, 'Some notes on Sir Edward Grey's Policy in July 1915', *Historical Journal*, Vol. 15, 1972

Hudson, Derek, 'Harold Nicolson', *Quarterly Review*, p. 305, 2.4.1967

Kronenberger, Louis, 'Diary of a U Man', *Atlantic Monthly*, p. 218, 5.11.1966

Macaulay, Rose, 'Sir Harold Nicolson', feature article service for the British Council, June 1956

Raymond, John, 'Not So Urbane', *New Statesman*, 10.5.1968

Sackville-West, Edward, 'Ethel Smyth as I Knew Her', Appendix to
  C. St. John's *Ethel Smyth*, 1959
Trevor-Roper, Hugh, 'Lord Cranfield as He Wasn't', *Spectator*,
  6.9.1968
Wilson, Edmund, 'Through the Embassy Window', *New Yorker*,
  1.1.1944

INDEX

INDEX

Nicolson, Harold – *cont.*

lations with Vita, 65, 67–8, 71, 97, 178, 210, 232–3, 250, 263, 277–8, 330, 336–7; maiden speech in House of Commons, 70; meets Lindberghs, 72; Party work, 72–3; on German threat, 74–6, 79–80; and Edward VIII, 76–8; and Maisky, 78–9; lectures and addresses, 83–4; seconds reply to Speech from Throne, 84–5, 95; aged 50, 87–8; on East African educational commission, 88–90; gives 1937 Rede Lectures, 90–91; retrieves Duchess of Windsor's papers, 91–2; in 1937 Foreign debate in Commons, 92; first filmed and televised, 93; and pre-war foreign affairs, 99–100; mission to Roumania and Bulgaria, 101–4; and Nigel's island, 108–9; opposes Chamberlain's negotiations and Munich, 110–14; and return to Foreign Office, 111; buys yawl, 113; devotion to TV, 117; sailing, 119–21; and outbreak of war, 122; early wartime activities, 123–8; visits to France, 126, 128; joins Watching Committee, 129; at Ministry of Information, 130–31, 133, 136, 140–42, 145–6; wartime suicide plans, 132; wartime optimism, 133; friendships, 134–6, 172–3, 274–5; regard for Churchill, 137, 141, 145, 149; and war aims, 141–2; dismissed from Ministry of Information, 143–5, 148–9; as Governor of BBC, 143, 146–148; indecisiveness as administrator, 144–5; proposes publication of 1939 diary, 146; in

trouble over Dublin speech, 150–51; impracticality, 151–2; wartime letters to sons, 154; and Beveridge plan, 155–6; knocked down by taxi, 156; wartime demands on, 157; on Foreign Office reform, 158–9; wartime trip to Sweden, 162–4; and release of Mosley, 164–5; fainting fit, 166; on post-war international settlements, 167; attitude to art, 168–9; shortcomings as writer, 169–70; satirised by Berners, 170–71; valued as conversationalist, 171–2; relations with mother, 172; 1944 lecture tours, 173–4; writing technique, 175; and Yalta agreement, 180–82; 1945 Paris lecture tour, 182–3; loses seat in 1945 Election, 185–9; and atom bomb, 188–9; hopes of peerage, 190–92, 196, 215, 219–20, 221; Greek lecture tour, 192–3; joins Labour Party, 196, 205; attends Nuremberg trials, 196–7; broadcasts on 1946 Paris Peace Conference, 198–202; aged 60, 203; appearance and dress, 203; awarded Legion of Honour, 208; tours National Trust properties, 208–10, 250, 261–2; visits Switzerland for Constant biography, 210–14; as Labour candidate for Croydon North, 216–20; class-consciousness, 217–18; subsidiary interests, 228; challenged to duel, 231; Topolski portrait of, 235; on sons' marriage prospects, 239; decline of political interests, 240; and mother's death, 244–5; helps Aunt Amy, 245; takes in

Sackville-West – *cont.*

HN's *Benjamin Constant*, 228–9; lecture tour in Spain, 231–2; activities, 232; and sons' marriage prospects, 239, 242; and Lady Carnock's death, 244–5; and HN's knighthood, 262, 267; stays with Violet Trefusis, 262; and Philippa, 269–71; and Lady Carnock's necklace, 271–272; in Dordogne, 277; and burial, 278–9, 308–9; appearance and dress, 279–80, 285; at royal occasions, 279, 285; on HN's *Good Behaviour*, 281; and HN's strokes, 286–7; and Ben's marriage, 289; drives Jaguar car, 290; awarded Veitch Medal, 290–91; and Oxford Poetry Professorship, 291–2; on HN's prose style, 295; sea cruises, 298–300, 306–7, 315–17, 320, 328–9, 334, 339–42; motoring holiday with Edith Lamont, 304; conversations with author, 305; operation on jaw, 306; Guy Burgess and, 311; virus pneumonia and cancer, 318–19, 324, 343; on HN's *Age of Reason*, 326; sells manuscripts, 334; and revision of HN's *Monarchy*, 335–6; and dogs, 337; operation for cancer, 342–344; death, 344–5; Rothenstein drawing of, 353

WORKS: *All Passion Spent*, 5, 27; *Another World Than This* (with HN), 194; *Collected Poems*, 48; *The Dark Island*, 53; *Daughter of France*, 204, 266, 300, 307–8; *The Easter Party*, 242, 263, 265–6; *The Edwardians*, 5, 27; *Faces*, 328; *The Garden*, 155, 178, 193; *Grand Canyon*, 155; *In Your Garden Again*, 266; *The Land*, 159, 193–194, 302; *No Signposts in the Sea*, 316, 321, 328; *Pepita*, 92, 97

Sadleir, Michael, 30, 59–60, 294
Sadler, Sir Michael, 169
St. Aubyn, Giles, 275
St. Aubyn, Gwendolen *see* St. Levan, Gwen St. Aubyn, Lady
St. Aubyn, Jessica, 79
St. Aubyn, Piers, 79
St. Aubyn, Sam *see* St. Levan, Francis Cecil St. Aubyn, 3rd Baron
St. John, Christopher, 68, 194, 245
St. Levan, Gwendolen St. Aubyn, Lady (HN's sister): relations with HN, 43, 55; travels with Vita, 44, 46, 58, 67, 83, 93; in Vita's *Dark Island*, 53; HN confides in, 55; illness, 73, 119; in war, 132; home at St. Michael's Mount, Cornwall, 152; and mother's death, 244; converted to Catholicism, 257; and Vita's illness, 344
St. Levan, Francis Cecil St. Aubyn, 3rd Baron (Sam), 43, 152
St. Michael's Mount, Cornwall, 152–3
Sainte-Beuve, Charles Augustin, 289–90, 292–4, 315
Salisbury, James Edward Hubert Gascoyne-Cecil, 4th Marquess of, 129
Salisbury, Robert Arthur James Gascoyne-Cecil, 5th Marquess of (*formerly* Viscount Cranborne), 99, 113, 146
Salter, Sir Arthur, 23
Samuel, Herbert Louis, 1st Viscount, 251
Sandringham, 237
Sargent, Sir Malcolm, 283
Sassoon, Siegfried, 333